THE WRONG MAN

THE WRONG MAN

The Final Verdict on the
Dr. Sam Sheppard Murder Case

JAMES NEFF

RANDOM HOUSE

NEW YORK

Library of Congress Cataloging-in-Publication Data

Neff, James.
The wrong man: the final verdict on the Dr. Sam Sheppard murder case / James Neff.
         p.   cm.
         Includes index.
         ISBN 0-679-45719-4
1. Sheppard, Sam—Trials, litigation, etc.   2. Trials (Murder)—Ohio—Cleveland.
3. Judicial error—Ohio—Cleveland.   4. Murder—Investigation—Ohio.   I. Title.
         KF224.S47 N44 2001
345.73′02523—dc21   2001041917

Random House website address: www.atrandom.com

2 4 6 8 9 7 5 3
First Edition

Book design by Casey Hampton

FOR CHRIS AND JAMIE

Chase after the truth like all hell and you'll free yourself,
even though you never touch its coattails.

—CLARENCE DARROW

ACKNOWLEDGMENTS

I grew up in Cleveland in the 1950s and 1960s, where I learned that Dr. Sam Sheppard, despite his 1966 acquittal, was guilty of murdering his pregnant wife. The farther I moved away from Cleveland—a student at the University of Notre Dame, working as a reporter in Chicago and Austin, Texas—the more likely it was that people, if they were familiar with the case, felt that Sam Sheppard was innocent. Journalists are drawn to conflict, and I became fascinated with the idea that this famous murder had not been solved. I began investigating this primal American drama ten years ago. Nearly everything I thought I knew about the case would turn out to be wrong.

Five years ago, I benefited from the judgment and faith of Ann Godoff at Random House, who saw a book in my early research. No author ever had a more patient editor. Whenever I thought my research was done, the Sheppard case would take another twist that delayed its conclusion: three times, important physical evidence was discovered and sent off to be DNA tested; twice, bodies were exhumed and studied for clues; when the Ohio Supreme Court ruled, in late 1998, that the estate of Dr. Sheppard would indeed be able to go to trial with a wrongful imprisonment lawsuit, the story galloped off in new directions.

I am most appreciative to my friend and research associate Joan Fechter for her tremendous contributions, both professional and personal. Over the past five years, she managed, despite her own family's demands, to meet every challenge, from tracking down long-lost jurors from the 1954 trial to getting my sons to school during family emergencies. Her critical reading of the manuscript improved it considerably.

XII   ACKNOWLEDGMENTS

I especially want to thank editor Ruth Coughlin, who joined this project at the last minute under a fierce deadline. She did an excellent job of tightening and sharpening the book, while remaining calm, funny, and available at all hours. I am lucky to have Esther Newberg of ICM as an agent, supporter, and friend. Thanks also to Margaret Wimberger, Sarajane Herman, Lauren Field, Bonnie Thompson, Chuck Antony, Sybil Pincus, Sarah D'Imperio, and Sunshine Lucas of Random House for making *The Wrong Man* a better book.

My love and appreciation go to my parents, Dorothy and Charley Neff of Cleveland, who were of great support and comfort over these years and spent hours doing records research at the Western Reserve Historical Society. My love and appreciation also to my six brothers and sisters, notably Joe for his insightful reading and comments on an early draft. Thanks also to Dr. Mark Mayer of the Cleveland Clinic for deciphering medical records and overall support; Linda and Bob House and the Lesko family for their recollections; Barb Vanarsdall for random acts of kindness; G. Boots; Dan Davis; Mark Naymik; Marian Marzynski; Peter Myers, who transferred old Dictabelts to audiocassette; and Don Ray, who tracked down vital records in California.

My gratitude goes to Investigative Reporters and Editors as well as the Society of Professional Journalists (SPJ), both of which came through with outrage and letters of protest when prosecutors tried to commandeer my research. Thanks to *Plain Dealer* executive editor Doug Clifton and editorial page director Brent Larkin for the editorial backup. I was blessed by the generous, aggressive work of First Amendment lawyer David Marburger of Baker & Hostetler, who defeated the prosecutors' efforts to obtain my work product and to compel me to testify about my methods. David and his associate Kyle Fleming put in many hours without compensation. Thanks also to the SPJ's Legal Defense Fund, which provided a small grant for legal expenses.

Members of the Sheppard and Reese families, some of whom have been hounded by journalists over the years, generously granted interviews: Sam Reese Sheppard, Stephen Sheppard, Betty Sheppard, Jan Sheppard Duval, Carol Leimbach, Dorothy Sheppard, Margaret Cellini, and Melissa Bevilacqua.

My thanks go to all who agreed to be interviewed, especially Terry Gilbert and Carmen Marino, and Jean Disbro Anderson, Harvey Aronson, F. Lee Bailey, Elizabeth Balraj, Howard Barrish, Doris O'Donnell Beaufait, Pat Bogar, Tom Brady, George Carr, Marilyn Cassidy, Jim Chapman, William Joseph Corrigan, Charles Cowan, George Cowan, Mary Cowan, Richard Dalrymple, John Davis, A. Steven Dever, Henry Dombrowski, David Doughten, Fred Drenkhan, Kathy Wagner Dyal, John Eberling, Richard Eberling, Barton Epstein, Kurt Fensel, Anne Foote, Harry Franken,

Dan Gaul, Roberta Gerber, Norm Gevitz, Andre Gibaldi, Otto and Beverly Graham, Peter Gray, Helen Hall, Leonard Harrelson, Buck Harris, Virginia Haskett, Obie Henderson, Pamela Henry, Michael Howard, Jay Hubach, Roy Huggins, Leah Jacoby, George Jindra, David Kerr, Marion Koloski, Vince Kremperger, William Lamb, Kathy Levine, William V. Levy, Jane Lowenthal, Linda Luke, Lois Mancini, William D. Mason, Timothy J. McGinty, Janet McGlothin, Doug McQuigg, Dick Moore, Phyllis Moretti, Beatrice Orenstein, Ralph Perk, John W. Reese, Faith Corrigan Refnes, Oliver Schroeder, Jessie Dill Seymour, Chester M. Southam, Leo Spellacy, Victor Strecher, Alvin Sutton, Mohammad Tahir, Emanuel Tanay, Bill Tanner, James Tompkins, Andrew Tuney Jr., Walter Vallee, Daniel Volkema, Cyril Wecht, Harold Wilbert, James Willard, William Wiltberger, Robert White, Toby Wolson, Jim Wooley, Chalmers Wylie, and Dave Zimmerman.

Many in the forensic community provided advice, services, and consultation, for which I am particularly grateful: Norah Rudin, Keith Inman, Lisa Calandro, Robin Cotton, Kathryn Colombo, Chuck Morton, John Murdock, Ed Blake, Mitchell Holland, Rebecca Reynolds, Michael Baden, Leonard Harrelson, Robert K. Ressler, and John E. Douglas, among others.

I want to thank Ohio State University's School of Journalism, where I directed the Kiplinger Reporting Program, from 1994 to 1999, and enjoyed research support, especially the hard work of Debra Baer and Ben Zeng, and also of Susan Glaser, Nan Wang, Sarah Wendell, and Angela Chundurlek.

Others who helped were Maureen Hays, Russ Mussara, John Caniglia, Tom Mudd, Carlos Davis, Darlene Brown, John O'Brien, Jim McCann, James Monroe, Dennis Kucinich, Janet Holmes, Miriam Holmes, Charles Stuart, Nick Gatz, Arthur and Shirley Cooper, Timothy M. Schaefer, and Donald G. Dutton.

Special collections, archives, and libraries held many treasures about the Sheppard case and its times. My thanks go to the following institutions and employees: Judy Lueders, Frank Baker, and Walter D. Morrill at Hanover College; Danielle Bickers at the Ohio Medical Board; Joanne Drake at the Ronald Reagan Presidential Library; Angie M. Burton at the Osteopathic Medical Board of California; Dorothy "Duffy" Knaus and Linda Long at the University of Oregon's Knight Library (Margaret Parton papers); Bill Bowers at Northeastern University (Samuel H. Sheppard papers); Michael McCormack and Ann Sindelar at the Western Reserve Historical Society (papers of Louis Seltzer, James Monroe, William Corrigan, Ralph Perk); Cliff Farrington and Avi Santo at the University of Texas's Harry Ransom Humanities Research Center (Erle Stanley Gardner collection); Henry York at Cleveland State University Library (Cleveland Press Archives); Kenneth

G. Hafeli at the Gerald R. Ford Presidential Library; Linda Wyler at Cleveland Public Library; Pat Anderson at the Richard M. Nixon Presidential Library; Betty Januska at Parke-Davis Research Library; the Bedford (Ohio) Historical Society; Susie Hanson at Case Western Reserve University's Frieberger Library; Kristine Marconi of Princeton University's Seeley G. Mudd Manuscript Library; Carol A. Turley at the UCLA Biomedical Library; Mike Widener at University of Texas's Tarlton Law Library (papers of U.S. Supreme Court justice Tom Clark); Jeff Flannery and Bradley Gernand of the Library of Congress's Manuscript Division (Harold Burton papers; Roy W. Howard papers); Dale Meyer of the Herbert Hoover Library; Glenn Longacre at the National Archives Regional Center, Chicago; Jennifer Kane Nieves at Case Western Reserve University's Dittrick Museum of Medical History (Lester Adelson papers); Sue Presnell at Indiana University's Lilly Library; and David Farrell at the University of California at Berkeley's Bancroft Library (Paul Leland Kirk collection).

Above all, my deepest love and affection go to my wife, Maureen, and sons Jamie and Chris. We made it.

CONTENTS

PART 1

Their father's dream from the time the boys were little was to have a hospital and to have his three sons working with him. What happened, naturally, destroyed that whole thing. Darn near destroyed a village.

—ESTHER HOUK,
BAY VILLAGE NEIGHBOR

1

EVE OF DESTRUCTION

EARLY SATURDAY MORNING, July 3, 1954, Dr. Sam Sheppard pulled his Lincoln into the parking lot of Bay View Hospital, housed in a huge, Georgian-style mansion built on the bluffs of Lake Erie. His family had bought the place several years earlier and had converted it into a 110-bed hospital. Dr. Stephen Sheppard, the middle Sheppard brother, pulled his car in just behind him. They talked for a few minutes about how they were going to celebrate the holiday weekend.

It promised to be a beautiful day, with low humidity, a slight breeze off the lake. Steve planned to go sailing on his Raven-class racing sloop. Sam reminded him that he and Marilyn were having a cookout the next day for about twenty couples, the hospital interns and their dates. After a quick cup of coffee in the hospital cafeteria, the brothers split up and headed into separate operating rooms. It was shortly before 7 A.M. Even on a holiday weekend, the Sheppards tried to squeeze in half a day of surgery. Bay View, an osteopathic teaching hospital, had all the business it could handle.

A little while later, less than a mile away, Marilyn Sheppard arose at the lakefront home where she and Dr. Sam lived. Her day was going to be just as busy as her husband's. She was still angry with Sam because he had volunteered to hold the intern party without first checking with her. This was not her idea of how to spend a family holiday. Sam would be out on their boat, water-skiing with the guests, leaving Marilyn, an expert skier, "getting the groceries and entertaining a lot of dull dry people who can't ski."[1]

She had to clean and shop and spruce up the yard and the boathouse while keeping an eye on their seven-year-old son, Sam, whom they called Chip. Also, she was four months pregnant, more tired and uncomfortable than usual. If Sam had just asked her first, she would have agreed to host the party without complaint because she truly wanted to be what her older sisters-in-law referred to as "a good doctor's wife"—an attractive, cheerful helpmate who could run the household like a quartermaster, manage the children, and make life easy for her ambitious, hardworking husband. She knew that Sam was obliged to the interns at Bay View, which relied in part on their low-paid labor for its success. In return, these doctors in training received invaluable education from senior doctors, such as Sam's father, Dr. Richard A. Sheppard, a highly regarded diagnostician who took referrals from all over Ohio.

Even worse than getting stuck with the intern party, Marilyn had an unwanted houseguest to deal with—Sam's old friend from medical school, Dr. Lester Hoversten. Acting on his own, Sam had agreed to let Hoversten live with them a few days while he interviewed for a job at Bay View. Marilyn thought he was a pig. A couple of years earlier he had made a crude pass at her and she'd shut him down fast, not worrying about hurting his feelings. Just being around him put her on edge. He left his room a mess and was an inconsiderate guest overall. She refused to make his bed or even go near that bedroom.

Hoversten thought of himself as a playboy, and made sexual passes at any woman who strayed within his gaze. Even though he was fourteen years older than Sam, they had gone through medical school together and had served as surgical residents at Los Angeles County General Hospital. The experience explained their friendship, the foxhole bonding of young doctors as they endured grueling hours at little pay under the intellectual hazing of senior surgeons, who themselves were famously condescending toward women. Hoversten was recently divorced and had been asked to leave his position at a Dayton hospital. He had written Sam asking for help. "I'm so depressed I wish my life were over. I'm too busy for much leisure time and I do so little surgery I'm bored with the drudgery of it all."[2]

Sam had invited him to Cleveland, but Hoversten wrote that he was reluctant to stay with them. "Your beloved wife's attitude of the past still fills me with an aversion to staying at your house much as I enjoy your son and wife."[3] But Sam insisted that he come and have a good time.

At Sam's suggestion, Hoversten had agreed to get up early that Saturday and assist him in surgery, a good way to check out Bay View's operation. But when Saturday morning came, Hoversten slept in. He didn't get up until 10 A.M., leaving him home alone with Marilyn. In the afternoon, he left for an overnight stay with a friend.

That night, the Sheppards and friends from the neighborhood, Don and Nancy Ahern, had plans for a casual dinner together. Although the intern party was the next day, Marilyn had volunteered to cook, and even baked a blueberry pie, Sam's favorite. Don and Nancy insisted on providing cocktails at their home first.

In the past year, the two couples had become close friends. Nancy and Marilyn bowled together on the Bay Village ladies' afternoon bowling league while their children were in school, and the two couples were active in the Junior Club, a Bay Village ballroom-dance club for younger couples.

That evening, Don Ahern mixed martinis for the men and whiskey sours for the women. The children played outside. It was about a quarter to seven, the start of the holiday-weekend ritual—drinks at one house, dinner at another, the kids staying up late, since it was summer. Sam dressed in a white T-shirt and brown corduroys. Marilyn wore short white shorts and a blouse, and beaded moccasins. She was attractive, with wide hazel eyes and thick, shoulder-length brown hair. Athletic, tanned, and slim, she could pass for a teenager.

Sam was comfortable enough with Don to tell him about the hardship of his day. A specialist in orthopedic surgery and neurosurgery, Sam also oversaw the emergency-room operations. Today had been an emergency-room surgeon's nightmare. A boy had been struck by a truck and rushed to Bay View. His heart had stopped. Sam, on emergency-call rotation, opened the child's chest and massaged the heart, a method to restart it in the days before defibrillators. The tiny heart kicked to life, then stopped. Sam massaged it until his fingers gave out, and another doctor took over. It was no use. The boy was dead. The father was terribly upset, lashing out at Sam for not saving his boy's life. Sam had nothing to say except that he had tried his best, he felt terrible, and was sorry.

They each had two drinks, and at about 8:20 Marilyn left the Aherns' to start dinner. Sam drove to Bay View to check the X rays of a boy who had been brought into the emergency room with a broken thigh, and returned quickly. Meanwhile, Don and Nancy brought their two children, ages seven and ten, over to the Sheppards' home on Lake Road. While Marilyn and Nancy put the final touches on dinner, Sam took the kids into the basement, showed them his punching bag, and let them pound away, stopping them at times to give pointers on how to throw a proper punch.

The children ate in the kitchen, while the parents enjoyed dinner out on the screened porch that faced Lake Erie; they watched the sun drop over the water, its last rays splintering into fiery reds and purples. Dinner was cottage ham, rye bread, green beans, and blueberry pie with ice cream. Marilyn, as usual, ate well.

They finished at about ten-thirty. Nancy cleared the dirty dishes and shut

the living room door to the screened porch. She remembered later that she
had locked the door. Don took their two children home, tucked them in, and
came back. This was Bay Village in the early 1950s, suburban and safe, and
many parents felt comfortable leaving sleeping children home alone for a
few hours.

Don listened to the Indians baseball game on the radio in the living
room—the team was in first place in the American League and would go on
to win the pennant. Chip came out in his pajamas, holding a balsa-wood air-
plane. It was broken. Sam brought glue in from the garage and fixed the toy,
telling Chip that he was doing this after bedtime as a special favor, because
Chip had been a man about the broken plane, not whining but calmly asking
for help. Marilyn took Chip back upstairs and tied on his chin brace, a sling
that pulled in his jaw. Sam felt his son's chin protruded too far, which might
cause problems later with his bite.

The two couples settled in the living room and found the movie *Strange
Holiday* on one of two channels. Watching television was still a new thing to
do in 1954. Marilyn sat on Sam's lap, and Nancy, envious, called over to
Don, "I need attention, too."

After a while, Sam moved to a narrow living room couch, more like a
short daybed, near one of the stairways to the second floor. He stretched out
and drifted in and out of sleep in the darkened living room. He was wearing
a corduroy sports coat because it had gotten chilly.

With the dishes done and Chip asleep, Marilyn finally had time to relax
with some adults. But Sam was asleep. "C'mon, Sam, it's going to improve,"
she said. He lifted his head, watched the movie for a few minutes, then fell
back asleep.[4]

About midnight, Marilyn fell asleep in her chair and the Aherns tried to
slip out quietly. Marilyn woke up anyway and walked her friends to the
kitchen door, which led to the driveway and Lake Road. They passed Sam on
the daybed, sleeping soundly.

"Jump in bed before you get over being sleepy," Nancy told Marilyn.

It was 12:30 A.M. Later, Nancy told the police that she could not remember locking the kitchen door. And, no, she could not remember if Marilyn
had locked it, either.

2

INDEPENDENCE DAY

AT 5:40 A.M. on July 4, 1954, the mayor of Bay Village was awakened by a telephone call. It was his neighbor Sam Sheppard, shouting, "My God, Spen, get over here quick! I think they've killed Marilyn!"[1]

"What!"

"Oh, my God, get over here quick!"

Spencer Houk jumped up and got dressed, waking his wife, Esther. She hated to get up early, but she knew something terrible had happened. She pulled on a dress and shoes. They lived only two houses away from Sam and Marilyn, but Spen, a butcher, had a bad knee, so they got in their car and drove to the Sheppards' house. They didn't stop to call the police or grab a weapon.

Sam and Spencer had become fairly good friends in the past year, even though they appeared at first glance to have little in common. Sam was a decade younger, just shy of thirty, and physically vigorous—he was always water-skiing and playing pickup basketball with the neighborhood boys. With his bad knee, exacerbated by long days on his feet cutting and selling meat to his Bay Village customers, Spen had to sit on the sidelines—except when they went fishing. Spen could outfish him any day; Sam didn't have the patience to fish for Lake Erie perch or walleye when he could be flying across the lake on skis at thirty miles an hour. Together they had bought a thirteen-foot aluminum boat and clamped on two powerful outboard engines. Sam liked to race sports cars in amateur road rallies; now he had another grown-up toy to satisfy his need for speed.

The Houks found the Sheppards' kitchen door unlocked. It faced Lake Road, a two-lane highway along the lake. Just inside the hallway and to the

right was the den. Sam was leaning back on a red leather swivel chair, holding his neck.

"Sam, Sam, what happened?" the mayor wanted to know.

Sam was bare-chested, his pants soaked, and moaning softly, his surgeon's fingers laced like a sling at the base of his skull.

"Pull yourself together, Sam!" Spen ordered. "What happened?"[2]

He mumbled that he was asleep on the couch in the living room, heard
Marilyn cry "Sam!" and ran up the stairs to help, and then "somebody clobbered me."[3]

Esther had gone right upstairs. In the northwest bedroom were twin beds.
The far bed was empty, its quilt and covers neatly turned down, as if waiting
for someone to quietly slide underneath. A spray of blood flecked the covers
and the pillow.

A few feet away, on the bed closer to the door, Marilyn's body lay faceup.
Her legs hung over the foot of the bed, bent at the knees, her feet dangling a
few inches above the rug. It was an odd position. Her legs were under a
wooden bar that ran from post to post across the foot of the bed. It looked as
if someone had pulled her legs under the bar, pinning her like a giant specimen. Her body was outlined by blood, a huge crimson aura. Her face was
turned slightly toward the door, as if she had been expecting someone to
walk in, and coated with stringy, clotting blood. She was unrecognizable.
About two dozen deep, ugly crescent-shaped gashes marked her face, forehead, and scalp.

Her three-button pajama top was pushed up to her neck, baring her
breasts. A blanket draped her middle. Underneath, her flimsy pajama bottoms had been removed from one leg and were bunched below the knee of
her other leg, exposing her pubis.

Esther Houk steeled herself and checked Marilyn for a pulse. Nothing.
She ran back downstairs and yelled to her husband, "Call the police, call the
ambulance, call everybody!"

Esther poured a glass of whiskey in a kitchen glass and carried it to Sam.
"You need this."

"No, no," he said. "I can't think, I've got to think." Then he asked about
Chip—was he okay?

Esther went upstairs to check. The boy's bedroom door was open. He
was sleeping, curled on his right side. From the distance, sirens wailed, grew
louder and louder, then abruptly shut down.

At 5:57 A.M. Bay Village policeman Fred Drenkhan took a radio call that
help was needed at 28924 Lake Road, the home of Dr. Sam Sheppard, a
friend. Within a few minutes, he was inside the house. On the hallway floor

he saw a black leather medical valise opened wide, standing on end, its vials and prescription pads spilled out on the wood floor.

Drenkhan found Sam in his den. On the shelves behind him were two shotguns, two small air rifles, Sam's beloved record player, and a row of medical textbooks. Two trophies lay on the floor, broken: one of Sam's treasured high school track trophies and Marilyn's bowling trophy.

Drenkhan wanted to know what had happened, and Sam gave him more details. He woke up, heard his wife shout his name, then ran upstairs. On the way up, he saw a large form wearing a white top in their summer bedroom. When he reached the top of the stairs or just inside the bedroom, he was struck from behind and knocked out. After he came to, he heard a noise downstairs, ran down, saw something in the dark—a large, dark figure, probably a man—outlined against the living room windows facing the lake. He chased him out of the house, thundered down the long flight of wooden steps, caught the figure on the sand, grappled with him, and was knocked out once again. When he woke up, he was facedown at the water's edge, his lower half in the water, his head toward the bluff. Dawn was breaking.

Fred Drenkhan, twenty-six, with only three years of police experience, didn't know what to think. It was a puzzling story, but if Sam had been knocked out twice, he would be disoriented and perhaps give an odd account. Mostly Drenkhan enforced traffic laws in a suburb that was essentially a long, narrow strip of beachfront and nice homes, bisected by a two-lane highway, Lake Road, that connected Cleveland and Toledo. His part-time partner this weekend had never even received training, just pulled on a blue uniform a year earlier and became one of the city's cops. Drenkhan had investigated break-ins, but never a homicide.

As the first policeman on the scene of what would rapidly metamorphose into a world-famous murder case, Drenkhan would soon find his life turned upside down.

At 6:10 A.M. Dr. Richard N. Sheppard, the oldest brother, arrived at Sam and Marilyn's house. He lived nearby in Bay Village and had been called by Houk. He stopped to check on Sam, but Drenkhan told him to forget about Sam and to see Marilyn upstairs. She was probably dead.

Richard ran upstairs. He had seen his share of broken bodies and split skulls at car crashes and in emergency rooms, but the sight of his sister-in-law shocked him. This was not an accident but deliberate brutality, blow after blow. He tried to find a pulse. Her body was slightly warm to the touch. He wondered who the hell could do such a thing.

Esther Houk volunteered to take Chip to her house, to shield him from such horror, but Richard said no, he would take him home. He felt that the boy should be with family. He asked Esther to put together a bag of the boy's clothes. In Chip's room, Richard fumbled with the chin brace, trying to slide it off, ignoring the ties. Esther thought Richard was so frazzled that he would hurt Chip, so she reached in and untied the ties. Even with all this commotion, the boy still slept. Like his father, he was a sound sleeper, difficult to waken.[4]

When Richard returned downstairs, he saw Sam stretched out on his back on the floor of the den, trying to immobilize his neck. Richard hunched down close and said, "Sam, she's gone," and he wailed, "No, no, no!"

Meanwhile, a Bay Village patrolman raced over to the small farm of police chief John Eaton to break the astounding news. Stout, gray-haired, and bespectacled, Eaton, who was also a high school science teacher, was sitting on his tractor, dressed in blue denim overalls, plowing a field. The news jolted him, and he hurried to the Sheppard home, not bothering to change into his uniform.

Eaton could not believe the bloody mauling. Such crimes were not supposed to happen in Bay Village. Families moved to his suburb to escape crime. And now this tragedy had befallen a fine family he had known for years. Except for Cleveland Browns quarterback Otto Graham, the Sheppard doctors were the most respected and best-known citizens of Bay Village. Their hospital was the town's biggest employer.

He and Mayor Houk walked the grounds and descended the fifty-two steep wooden stairs to the beach. About 150 feet to the east, a pier at the public Huntington Park jutted into the lake. Two men were fishing there. Eaton and Houk walked over to them along the narrow strip of wet sand and noticed two sets of footprints and those of a dog. They took the fishermen's names and asked what they had seen that morning, which was nothing.

At about this time Dr. Steve Sheppard and his wife, Betty, drove up in an emergency-equipped Ford station wagon. They and their two daughters lived in Rocky River, an upper-middle-class suburb just east of Bay Village. Theirs was the fifth car in the driveway, behind Richard's, a fire department ambulance, a patrol car, and the Houks'. They came in through the screened porch and into the living room just as Drenkhan, on the telephone to the Cleveland Police Department, was saying, "It's a homicide. We need help."

Sam was still lying flat on the floor in the den, his face turned away from the door. Betty spotted him first and thought he was dead, that he was the homicide victim. She nudged her husband and pointed at Sam. Steve went over, knelt, touched Sam, and Betty saw his foot move. He was alive but cold, unable to stop shivering.

He's in shock, Steve decided, probably suffering from a fractured neck;

he needs to be treated right away and to have his neck X-rayed. "Can you get up or do we need a stretcher?" Steve asked him.

Sam replied, "I think I can make it." Steve decided to transport him to Bay View, two minutes away, and not to use the firemen or the stretcher that was standing in the upstairs hallway.

Chief Eaton entered the house and helped Esther Houk put Chip, wrapped in a blanket, into Dr. Richard's car. Then Steve helped carry Dr. Sam out of the house and to the station wagon, which had an emergency flasher and siren.

The chief and the two Bay Village police officers watched them leave. No one said a word. They did not insist that Sam stay at the house or be taken to a different hospital. It all happened quickly.

At Bay View Hospital, the staff was near the end of its overnight shift. A call had alerted them that Dr. Sam was being rushed in for treatment. During the short ride, Sam slumped next to Betty, moaning, saying, "I don't understand what happened."[5]

Anna Franz, the night nurse, saw Sam at about 6:35 A.M. He wore a raincoat Steve had wrapped around him at the house. Underneath he was bare from the waist up. The right side of his face and his eye socket were swollen and bruised. A light film of blood coated his teeth, two of them slightly chipped.

Anna Franz and the staff stretched Sam out on an emergency-room examining table and undressed him. Franz pulled off a waterlogged shoe and a sock. The skin on his feet was wrinkled. She piled his wet clothes on a nearby table and dressed him in a gown. She put a thermometer in his mouth but could not register a temperature—he was hypothermic, so she put several hot-water bottles around his body to warm him. His blood pressure was 140 over 70, slightly elevated.

Is Chip all right? he kept asking. Is Chip all right? She didn't know what to say.

Dr. Steve came in and told Sam that Chip was safe. He ordered a sedative for Sam, and Franz gave him a one-hundred-milligram injection of the painkiller Demerol.

———

Cleveland Browns quarterback Otto Graham was driving past the Sheppards' home Sunday morning to get the newspaper—Bay Village had no morning home delivery—and noticed a swarm of cars at Sam's house, some of them police cruisers.

Somebody drowned water-skiing, he figured, and pulled in.

Graham was the best NFL quarterback of the day and knew the local police by first name. Police had not secured the crime scene or even the murder room; they allowed Graham to come inside and look.

"Oh my God," Graham thought. "It looks like someone stood in the middle of the room with a great big can of red paint and a brush and flicked it all around. This wasn't a couple of blows. Oh, no. Whoever did it, they had to be out of their mind."[6]

When he got home a little while later, he told his wife, "Marilyn Sheppard was murdered last night."

She asked, "Did Sam do it?"

Beverly Graham was a friend of Marilyn's, though Marilyn complained that Bev paid too much attention to Sam. They bowled on the same league, they water-skied together, had neighborhood potluck dinners with their families. But Beverly had lost some of her fondness for Sam. They had joined the Sheppards at what was then an unusual new leisure sport, waterskiing. Sam had given her a lesson, and she'd managed to get up on skis on her first attempt, making her an instant member of what Sam called his "club," all the friends he taught to ski who hadn't fallen their first time out.

Later, when Otto was away at football training camp and she was skiing with Sam, he taught her a trick move that she could do at the end of her run. He would bring the boat near the shore, then turn, propelling her toward the dock. At the right moment she was to drop the tow bar, glide a couple of feet parallel to the concrete dock, then, as a finale, just before losing momentum, turn and sit down on the dock. Beverly Graham was fit, but she had no intention of crashing into a concrete piling. She didn't tell Sam, but she was not going to attempt his trick.

She made her run, and as Sam pulled her close to the shore, she let go of the tow bar. But she sat down after a few yards, still in deep water, short of the dock. When Sam pulled the powerboat around to pick her up, she remembers that he erupted. "Why didn't you do that? I told you to do that!" She was surprised by his anger.

––––––––––

Chief Eaton and Officer Drenkhan thought a drug addict had broken into the doctor's house to steal narcotics. Only someone truly fiendish could batter a woman's face so relentlessly. Plus, the doctor's bag had been upended. Dr. Sam was a friend; they couldn't imagine he had anything to do with such a brutal crime. Drenkhan radioed surrounding police departments to look for suspicious persons. The chief telephoned Dr. Samuel Gerber, the Cuyahoga County coroner.

In Ohio, suspicious deaths were handled by coroners who were medical doctors elected by voters. Gerber, a Democrat, had held the office since 1937. His office investigated more than 150 violent deaths each year, and he was forever being quoted in Cleveland's three competing daily newspapers. He was savvy about press relations and dined regularly with reporters. He distributed news tips, quotes, and exclusives evenly so that he wouldn't appear to play favorites. With his gray hair and rimless glasses, Gerber could slip into a white lab coat and pass for the friendly family practitioner. He was a tiny man, only five feet three, but he compensated with a booming voice and a manner some described as arrogant. He felt he would be a good mayor for Cleveland and was trying to decide when to run.

Even though it was a holiday and he had a deputy who could work it, Dr. Gerber felt it best to handle the Sheppard case himself. He telephoned his investigator and told him to pick him up. He put on a summer suit and grabbed a Panama hat, and soon they were headed out to Bay Village. They arrived at the crime scene at about 7:50 A.M. Gerber could not believe the number of bystanders in and around the house. He assumed command and ordered the Bay Village police to clear the house.

Drenkhan related what Dr. Sam said had happened. The account struck Gerber as suspicious. In the living room, he noticed the drop-leaf desk had its three drawers neatly pulled out. What kind of murderer or burglar would ransack a home so delicately?

On the steps leading upstairs, Gerber noticed small drops of what looked like dried blood. He also saw blood smears on the doorjamb and knob plate of the pane-glass living room door that led to the screened porch. The door chain was off—he didn't know yet that Nancy Ahern would remember locking it the night before. Whoever opened the door had blood on at least one hand, perhaps from a flowing cut.

———

The first Cleveland detective arrived at about 8:10 A.M. Michael Grabowski, a thirty-eight-year-old technician in the Scientific Investigation Unit, had only eight years on the force, which may have explained why he was stuck with holiday duty. He brought in his boxy camera and flash, and as Gerber pointed out objects and shots he wanted, Grabowski began taking photos inside the house. Grabowski took shots of the stacked desk drawers, the murder room, and the blood-spattered walls. He ended up on the beach, where he photographed two different sets of footprints, one of them barefoot.

Next he turned to looking for fingerprints, which were more useful when you did *not* know the identity of a suspect. Gerber already believed Dr. Sam was the key suspect. On the surface, it looked like an open-and-shut case of domestic homicide. Normally, scientific-unit detectives might stay at a crime scene for several hours, sifting for forensic evidence such as fingerprints and hair, scraping and labeling blood samples. Grabowski's efforts to find the fingerprints of an outsider were less than exhaustive. He may have spent as little as thirty minutes looking for fingerprints, his trial testimony later would show.

He was unable to obtain a useful fingerprint from the doctor's bag. He detected smudged fingerprints, but at first glance none had the minimum seven or eight elements—swirls, ridges, and patterns—needed to build a print that was "identifiable." He checked the vials and supplies inside the medical bag, but they all appeared to have smudged prints, and he decided not to attempt any lifts.

In the living room he lifted a palm print on a drop leaf of the dark-hued wood desk. He shined his light at an oblique angle at the front of the desk drawers, but couldn't find any promising areas to try to get lifts.

He checked the door that led to the screened porch. It was unlocked but showed no pry marks. The doorknob and jamb were layered with fingerprints, a mess of smudges and overlays. He ignored this area.

In the den Grabowski found smudged, layered, or indistinct prints on the broken trophies and on two metal file boxes. He also noticed extremely fine scratches on the hard surfaces of these articles. The trophies and metal file boxes had survived a house fire the year before and most likely had been scoured, perhaps with a finely abrasive cleanser, to remove any soot. He could not detect fingerprints on the letters scattered on the den floor.[7]

He climbed upstairs to the guest bedroom, which had two windows facing Lake Erie. This room was more comfortable in the summer, and Sam and Marilyn slept on twin beds. The west window was screened and open. Grabowski dusted the sill and picked up smudged prints. He tested no other places in the bedroom for fingerprints, saying later that he didn't want to contaminate the blood spatter or physical evidence. He also ignored the banister along the steps between the first and second floors.

Meanwhile, Gerber called for an ambulance to move Marilyn's body to the county morgue for autopsy. After attendants shifted the stiffening corpse, Gerber and one of the detectives found two tooth fragments on the bedsheets. Gerber forced his finger inside Marilyn's mouth, set from early rigor mortis. He said he couldn't feel any broken teeth. So whose were they?

Grabowski left the scene of what would later evolve into perhaps the country's most enduring murder mystery, after spending at best two hours collecting evidence. By 10:30 A.M. he picked up another assignment, a safe-tampering case. Grabowski wrote a three-sentence report of his work at the Sheppard house, noting that he took thirteen photos of the crime scene and one photo of a palm print. He made no mention that trophies, file boxes, and desk items were finely scratched, making it hard to get identifiable prints. Nor did he write in his report that fingerprints were wiped from the Sheppard house, as he and his supervisors would claim in weeks to come, under intense pressure from the press and public to solve the murder.

Back at the crime scene, coroner Gerber told Chief Eaton to drive him to Bay View Hospital so he could interview Sam Sheppard. Gerber was annoyed that Sam had left the crime scene and was ensconced at the hospital. He felt that Dr. Sheppard murdered his wife and it would be harder to get his confession from a hospital bed.[8]

Gerber knew about the Sheppard doctors but had never met any of them in person. Like some in the Cleveland medical establishment, he did not like them. For one, they were osteopaths, a profession that he associated with inferior training and faulty medical science. Also, the Sheppards were openly ambitious, always calling the newspapers to get free publicity for Bay View, recounting emergency-room heroics and lives saved. With medical reporting in the 1950s pretty much limited to ribbon cutting at new hospital wings and new cures, newspaper reporters loved the dramatic and easily related news stories of emergency rescues, complete with heroes and happy endings. M.D.s felt that grubbing for publicity was unseemly. In fact, earlier that year Gerber had encountered a Bay View resident doctor, H. Max Don, and asked if he was part of "the Sheppard clan." Don replied that he was a resident at Bay View, and Gerber remarked, "I'm going to get them someday."[9]

At Bay View, Gerber talked to Sam for ten minutes. "He looked in my hair and there was no blood," Sam would say later. "He checked my fingernails most carefully and examined my wrist, eyes, ears, and eyebrows. He found no blood."[10] Gerber later would say he did not check Sam's hair for blood or sand, or look under his fingernails for blood or skin. (If Gerber did not, his oversight would be surprising, coming from the future coeditor of *Criminal Investigation and Interrogation*.)[11] Gerber did ask for Sam's clothes, and Chief Eaton gathered them up from Dr. Richard Sheppard. Sam's pants, boxer shorts, belt, and shoes were soaked. The wallet was waterlogged. Gerber saw grains of sand around the belt buckle and in the cuffs of Sam's pants. A large diffused bloodstain on the left knee had soaked through the pants to the bottom of Sam's boxers. Pinned to the flap of the wallet was a gold police-surgeon's badge for Westlake, a neighboring suburb. Inside the wallet were gas-station credit cards, business cards, and a one-thousand-dollar paycheck from Bay View Hospital, Sam's monthly draw. Sam was handsomely paid for a twenty-nine-year-old surgeon. In a hidden compartment were three twenty-dollar bills.

Gerber returned to the Sheppard house. There two Cleveland homicide detectives, Robert Schottke and Pat Gareau, had arrived and were already trying to untangle the slaying. Gerber and the detectives agreed that it looked as if someone had staged a burglary. A burglar usually dumped drawers and quickly scanned for valuables. These drawers were pulled out evenly. The position of the doctor's medical bag, resting on end in the hallway, seemed contrived. Could a burglar on the run drop a bag and have it land like that? "It's obvious that the doctor did it," Gerber was overheard to say. He told the detectives to go to the hospital and get Sam Sheppard's confession. When Gerber saw Chief Eaton and Mayor Houk, he repeated that Sam Sheppard should be arrested.

"Oh, no, not Sam!" Houk cried.

———

About an hour after Gerber's visit, Dr. Sam looked up from his bed to find two detectives introducing themselves. Robert Schottke, thirty-four, and Patrick A. Gareau, twenty-seven, had been partners for several years and solved dozens of murders. The year before, their unit investigated ninety-five homicides and solved all but one. When they found a dead female in her home, their first questions were: Is there a husband? A boyfriend? If so, and if he didn't have an alibi, he was assumed to be the murderer. And if the husband was home during the killing, only a dozen steps away, with no evidence of a jimmied lock or a broken window, then it was assumed the case would be closed later that day. Their experience told them that in all likelihood he was the killer.

Dr. Sam's story, as related to them by the Bay Village police, seemed implausible. How could he have been knocked out twice? Why hadn't the killer used his weapon on Sam as he had on Marilyn? They were suspicious about Sam's missing shirt—did he get rid of it because it was covered in blood?

At Bay View, Schottke and Gareau's suspicions were heightened by Dr. Steve Sheppard. During their questioning, he came into the hospital room at least twice to check Sam's vital signs. When interviewing any murder suspect, they wanted that person all to themselves, to establish an unbroken connection between hunters and prey. They had seen it many times before: killers in unplanned murders felt a suffocating, nearly irresistible need to purge themselves of the truth after committing a terrible, impulsive act. The confession usually came the same day, in the interrogation room. Schottke and Gareau expected to get a confession this time, too, but Dr. Steve was disrupting their efforts. Even so, Dr. Sam answered their questions freely, and they learned little that was new.[12]

After the interview, the detectives went to the Bay Village police station, where they examined Sam's clothes, which had been sent there by Gerber. His pants had what looked to be a blood spot on the knee, as if he had knelt in blood. There was a large, downward tear at the lower corner of his right front pocket where Sam had clipped on a ring of keys. The blood-spatter patterns on the murder-room surfaces indicated that drops and mist were flung widely during the crime. But the detectives found no blood on Dr. Sam's shoes, belt, or anywhere on his pants other than the knee. This could explain why the doctor dunked himself in Lake Erie, they reasoned. To wash off evidence.

————

At the county coroner's office, Dr. Lester Adelson, Gerber's top deputy, began an autopsy of the body of Marilyn Sheppard. A short, jaunty man, Adelson always wore a bow tie and a vest with a chain to his pocket watch and Phi Beta Kappa key. Unlike his boss, Dr. Adelson had been trained as a pathologist. A Harvard graduate, he had studied to be a gynecologist at Tufts University School of Medicine, but had fallen in love with legal medicine, wanting to do nothing else. He was highly skilled and nationally respected in his field. Adelson believed that in a murder case the body was the best witness. "Unlike a living witness, a victim's body does not shade the truth, tell lies, or plead the Fifth Amendment," he liked to say.

Marilyn's body was weighed and measured. By 12:30 P.M., when Dr. Adelson began to cut, he determined that rigor mortis was now complete.

This was a significant fact. His challenge was to determine, as accurately as possible, the time she was killed. A fairly precise time of death would eliminate any suspects who could prove they were elsewhere. To make the calculation, Adelson relied on the body's rigor mortis and its stomach contents.

If the body had been at room temperature, rigor mortis was usually complete six to eight hours after death, but it varied from body to body. Using six hours, it would put Marilyn's death at 6:30 A.M., after police were at the scene. Eight hours placed her death after 4:30 A.M. This estimate fit with Dr. Richard Sheppard's early-morning interpretation of the body's rigor mortis and clotted blood; he placed Marilyn's death between 4:15 and 4:45.

Adelson found her stomach empty, with only half an ounce of mucoid fluid. He learned that the Sheppards had started their evening meal at around 9:30 and finished before 10:30. A person needed five to seven hours to digest a large meal. By that measure, Marilyn had died sometime between 3:30 and

5:30. All three estimates overlapped from 4:30 to 4:45 A.M. In his report, Adelson put Marilyn Sheppard's time of death "at about 4:30 A.M."[13] She also could have died up to an hour later, 5:30 A.M., based on Adelson's autopsy findings.

However, Gerber, who was not a pathologist, told reporters that Marilyn had died at around 3 A.M. Despite his own deputy's report, Gerber would testify at trial to the earlier time of death. If she died at 3:00 and Dr. Sam didn't call Mayor Houk until 5:45 or so, what was he doing for nearly three hours? As Marilyn's time of death moved earlier, Sam's account of being knocked out became more suspicious. Adelson's typed report, recently discovered in the county coroner's office files, was either ignored by Gerber or simply withheld from the public and Sheppard for nearly five decades.

Working down from the body's head, Adelson found fifteen crescent-shaped lacerations on the forehead and scalp, most of them about one inch long and a half-inch wide. Some gouges had not cut all the way through the scalp tissue; others were deep and exposed skull bone.

Adelson counted all the body's wounds and came up with thirty-five. Her nose had been broken, and her eyelids were bruised blue and swollen shut. Two of her upper medial incisors were snapped off, one below the gum line. But her mouth did not appear bruised, though a small abrasion of crusted blood decorated her lips. The killer had fractured her skull plates with fifteen blows, but none of the strikes were powerful enough to push bone into the dura, which encased the cerebellum just under the skull bones. Adelson noted that her skull was cracked. Her frontal bones, which met at a seam called the frontal suture, were separated from the blows. Hemorrhages in the brain showed that her heart had been pumping when these blows were struck. Her lungs and windpipe were congested with blood, but no blood was in her stomach. She may have already been unconscious, unable to swallow, when the blows were landed. Her fingernails were pale blue—cyanosis, a sign of oxygen deprivation—which suggested she may have asphyxiated.

Marilyn suffered at least four blows to her left hand and wrist. She had a quarter-sized bruise on her left shoulder. Her right little finger looked broken. Her left hand was not marked except for the ring finger. Its fingernail had been torn off and was hanging by a strip of skin. There was no blood on the finger. A ring appeared pulled up to the first knuckle.

It was obvious that Marilyn had put up quite a fight and may have scratched her attacker, as suggested by her torn fingernail. Adelson scraped under each of Marilyn's fingernails, preserved the evidence in separate folded paper packets, and marked the specimens for the trace-evidence technician, Mary Cowan.

Before taking photographs of her face, Adelson washed blood from the wounds with water, a mistake. Perhaps he had been told by Gerber that Dr. Sam was the likely killer and as a result did not perform the exacting tests necessary to solve a mystery. He neglected to examine the blood from the various wounds under a microscope. A murder weapon can leave behind minute paint chips, splinters, soot, or fibers—all of it evidence to narrow the weapon or to reveal where it had been stored. Cleaning the wounds washed away possible evidence. On the autopsy table, pathologists sometimes put a fine filter over a drain or basin to capture the rinsed debris for closer examination. Adelson did not do this. In this seemingly open-and-shut case, authorities on the street and in the laboratory did not take the extra steps they normally would have to solve a mysterious case.

Adelson worked without benefit of having seen the murder scene. Had he seen it, he might have been struck by how much it resembled the tableau of a sex crime. Marilyn's body was nearly nude, her legs splayed, her breasts and pubis exposed. In the lab, Dr. Adelson noticed "creamy white exudate" in her vagina. Later, he swabbed the white substance on a microscope slide and examined it. He spotted "abundant" amounts of epithelial cells and bacteria but not sperm cells. He did not closely look inside the vagina for inflammation or tearing, evidence of rape.

Adelson had performed several thousand autopsies. He knew that domestic homicides and its telltale injuries often follow a pattern. A man and his wife or girlfriend argue, tempers boil, violence erupts. Slaps might turn to punches to the face and arms, then choking, and eventually beatings with a weapon at hand. Adelson did not find such bruises on the arms or neck.[14]

From Marilyn's uterus, Adelson removed a fetus he judged to be four months along. It would have been a boy. He preserved it in a large specimen jar. His verdict, typed later, said Marilyn Sheppard died of massive head injuries. Cause of death: homicide.

———

Marilyn's father, Thomas Reese, was a private, well-to-do man who was not close to his daughter. He had just seen Marilyn and Sam the week before at the Lakeside Yacht Club. He had shown them his new boat, and they'd spent a day helping him get it ready for its maiden launch. Reese had planned to surprise them on July 4 by sailing out to Bay Village and hailing them from shore. Instead he raced by auto to the hospital, and found Sam "heavily sedated, somewhat incoherent." Reese was stunned. "It just doesn't seem possible—alive a day or so ago and now gone."

Back at the crime scene, Dr. Gerber and Chief Eaton gathered together a team of neighbors and teenage boys to search the underbrush on the bluff behind the Sheppard house for a discarded weapon. They cut down weeds, tall grass, and vines. Larry Houk, the sixteen-year-old son of the mayor, spotted a green cloth bag and picked it up and spilled out its contents into his hand: a key chain holding keys, a class ring, and a fraternity charm, and a man's watch. It had stopped at 4:15 A.M. and had condensation under the crystal. It was shown to Gareau, who saw dried blood on its expandable metal band. If this was Dr. Sam's watch, this last clue clinched the case, he believed. In his retelling earlier, Sam did not say he had checked on his wife after he was knocked out, so how could blood get on his watch?

Around 2 P.M., Gareau and Schottke decided to confront Dr. Sam in his hospital room. In the era before *Miranda* warnings and court-appointed lawyers, the detectives were following standard procedure. They brought Chief Eaton along, because he would be the official who could order an arrest.

Schottke and Gareau had a reputation as good interrogators. In aiming for a confession, they knew they had to offer a suspect an understandable rationale for the crime he had committed. The excuse might be as flimsy as "So, she hit you first and you lost your temper, right? I'd do the same thing."

At Sam Sheppard's bedside, Gareau played the good cop. About Sam's age, he planned on getting a law degree, and was the more polished of the two detectives. As an excuse, he suggested to Sam that maybe Marilyn was unfaithful. In canvassing neighbors earlier, detectives were told that Dr. Hoversten, a houseguest, was infatuated with Marilyn and that she had spurned his advances. They learned Hoversten was forty miles away, in Kent, Ohio, having stayed overnight so he could play golf that morning with a former Bay View doctor.

Had Marilyn been seeing anyone else? Gareau asked. If she had, it would be understandable that Sam might lose his temper.

Sam said no, she was faithful, though he did know of several men who were interested in her. He had even questioned one of the men—he didn't tell them it was Mayor Spencer Houk—and was satisfied that nothing was going on between them.[15]

They showed him the watch and keys from the green bag and he said they were his. Schottke, the blunt, hard-nosed partner, laid out for Sam the case against him: no signs of a break-in, nothing of value taken, not even his wallet, and blood on his watchband. How could blood get on there unless he'd used that arm to batter her?

Schottke pulled in close. "I don't know about my partner, but I think you killed your wife."

He denied it. "I loved Marilyn," Sam insisted. He could do no such thing. He dedicated himself to *saving* people's lives.[16]

Sam pressed the nurse's call button at his hospital bed. When his brother Richard entered the room, Sam was crying. "They think I've killed Marilyn," he sobbed.

Oh my God, Richard told him. You need a lawyer. He asked the detectives to leave the hospital.

On their way out, Schottke and Gareau asked Chief Eaton what he thought. He replied that Sam was probably lying.[17]

Arrest him so that we can question him at the hospital jail, they urged Eaton. They could grill him at length, uninterrupted, and get a confession. They wanted to make their suspect feel helpless, like he would never get away with murder. In the comforting family hospital, he would still have resolve.

Eaton told the detectives he would think about arresting Dr. Sam.

By the end of the afternoon, it was clear that Dr. Sam Sheppard was not going to be arrested, and Schottke and Gareau were upset. They had approached the Sheppard crime scene with confidence. The battering of Marilyn Sheppard suggested to the detectives that her killer knew her, and for some reason really wanted to work over her face. It had to be Dr. Sam.

That night Otto Graham came to Bay View to see Sam; spotting the pack of reporters out front, he slipped in through a back door. As an NFL quarterback and a future member of the Football Hall of Fame, he knew how important it was to avoid the stigma of negative publicity.

At about the same time, Bill Corrigan sauntered through the crowd of reporters and photographers into Bay View Hospital, creating a stir. With his white hair and fiery oration, he was the most widely known criminal defense attorney in the city. He handled the celebrated cases, defending murderers, racketeers. His bread-and-butter client was the International Ladies Garment Workers Union.

Corrigan paused and turned on the steps, which gave the photographers a chance to take his picture. This was news! The victim's husband felt he needed an important defense attorney, and they fired away excitedly.

3

GATHERING STORM

ON MONDAY, JULY 5, it was hard to miss the news that something terrible had happened in a quiet, safe little suburb along Lake Erie. News editors at the three local daily newspapers—the *Plain Dealer,* the *Cleveland Press,* and the *Cleveland News*—bannered the murder story across the width of their front pages with huge headlines. DOCTOR'S WIFE MURDERED IN BAY VILLAGE, trumpeted the *Cleveland Press*. The subhead: "Drug Thieves Suspected in Bludgeoning."

A large, flattering portrait photograph of Marilyn filled the page. She was posed in a V-necked white blouse, arms crossed, nails painted, carefully made up, her brown eyes looking directly into the camera. The caption said, "Mrs. Sam H. Sheppard, an expectant mother, was murder victim in her Bay Village home."

Somehow a *Press* photographer had gotten into Sam's hospital room. Below Marilyn's picture was a photo of Dr. Sam in a hospital bed, eyes closed and mouth swollen, an orthopedic brace around his neck. Inside its front section, the *Press* ran a full broadsheet of photographs—thirteen in all—of Marilyn, Sam, Chip, the living room, the upturned medical valise.

Gerber had cleared the Sheppard house the morning of the murder and had barred the Sheppard brothers from entering. But the coroner, an elected official who cultivated the press, allowed photographers and reporters to tour the home and photograph whatever they wanted once the body was removed. Rummaging around, they'd quickly found the treasures they needed in the Sheppard photo albums. They had taken photos of photographs. But since the *Press,* alone, had the most revealing photos and the Sheppard family said it couldn't find those pictures later, most likely a reporter stole them that first day. As a result, readers reviewing that spread felt as though they were turning the pages of an instant, intimate family album. One soon-to-be-famous photo showed Sam in swim trunks and Marilyn in a formfitting two-piece bathing suit, water-skiing side by side, water spraying behind them, a good-looking, athletic, carefree couple.[1]

By midmorning on July 5, a Monday holiday, lines of cars were slowly driving past the house where a doctor's pregnant wife had been murdered. Passengers leaned out windows with cameras, taking snapshots. Some pulled up on lawns and parked. Gawkers gathered at the edges of the Sheppard property. A Bay Village policeman had to direct traffic and chase people away.

Reporters treated Dr. Sheppard sympathetically, as the bereaved spouse. " 'Dr. Sam,' as he was called at the hospital, is a virtual legend among his patients. Employing the most modern medical technique, time and again he has performed seeming miracles in what seemed like hopeless cases."[2] Except for a hint of suspicion in the caption under the photo of Koke—"the Sheppards' dog failed to sound an alarm"—the newspaper accounts told a familiar story: a favored son marries his high school sweetheart and with hard work achieves the American Dream in the suburbs. His true family history, however, was far more interesting and complex.

———

Samuel H. Sheppard, born on December 23, 1923, was the youngest of three sons of Dr. Richard A. and Ethel Sheppard. His father was a smart, ambitious doctor of osteopathic medicine; his mother was a schoolteacher, the daughter of a Methodist minister from Indiana. She taught Latin and English until her first son was born.

Sam shared his parents' attention with two older brothers, Richard and Stephen, and led a sheltered life in one of the Midwest's most beautiful suburbs, Cleveland Heights, where a new middle class had flocked in the prosperous 1920s. Cleveland's industrial leaders already lived in Georgian-style mansions along the suburb's North Park and Fairmount boulevards. John D. Rockefeller, the oil titan, had built a summer home there on sixty acres of ravine, creek, and greenery, which was later developed into a park that young Sam and his friends would enjoy.

Dr. Richard A. Sheppard was the picture of confidence, with his sturdy boxer's build, neatly trimmed mustache and gray hair, ever-present white shirt and bow tie. He had rejected the narrow dogma of osteopathy, which postulated that all disease stemmed from problems in the joints and spine, which could be manipulated and palpated to relieve pain and cure disease.[3]

In the era before antibiotics and specialized medicine, he built a successful medical practice by embracing the latest techniques developed by the wealthier, more respected allopathic doctors, or M.D.s. But since neither the Cleveland Clinic nor Cleveland City Hospital would hire osteopaths, Richard Sheppard had to learn on his own. Often he went to the Humane Society and quietly took animals that were scheduled to be destroyed. He anesthetized them and practiced surgical techniques that he would later apply to humans.

He dreamed of running his own hospital where he and his colleagues would not be shunned. In 1935, in a small building two miles east of downtown Cleveland, he founded the Cleveland Osteopathic Hospital. It was a time before certificates of need and government restriction, when an ambitious doctor could thrive as a medical entrepreneur. He wanted his three sons to carry on his work and his vision, expanding his clinic into a large group-practice hospital similar to the family-run Mayo Clinic in Rochester, Minnesota. But first he had to make sure his sons got into a good osteopathic medical school.

Sam was not a strong student. In first grade at Coventry Elementary, he fell noticeably behind his classmates, and his teacher kept him after school on Mondays and Thursdays for special help. In the later half of the year, he was marked down for not concentrating on his work and for completing it slowly.[4] "I feel Sam could do much better work if he would learn to concentrate," his second-grade teacher wrote on his report card. By fifth grade, he was getting mostly C's in reading and arithmetic and still had trouble concentrating. By eighth grade Sam still received C's in reading and math, but he excelled at physical education. Tall and more coordinated than his older brothers, Sam liked nothing more than to throw a ball, race his bike, and wrestle with friends, taking pleasure in motion or outperforming his pals on the sports fields. He dreamed of being a professional athlete, but his parents had other designs.

Ethel Sheppard was a proper woman who didn't worry about current styles in clothes and hair, save for a mink stole given to her by her husband. She was strict; cursing was not allowed in her house, and sex simply was not discussed, though she clearly expected her sons to marry, have children, and rear them as Christians. As a boy, Sam assumed her values without question. He didn't like risqué jokes and openly criticized friends who told them. At twelve, after a discussion with his parents, Sam chose to be baptized in the Methodist church. This pleased his maternal grandmother tremendously.

"God has some special work for you," she wrote to him. But she added a warning: "I have also seen disaster overtake those who broke their covenant and refused the way of the Lord."

———

On the day after Marilyn's murder, Schottke and Gareau put in another day on the sensational killing, talking to everybody they could. Along with the Bay Village police working the case, they hoped to pin down a motive for what they believed was a sudden crime of passion. Don Ahern told them Sam was "not of the emotional makeup to even make it possible for him to do what was done to Marilyn." But Nancy, who was close to Marilyn, shared some confidences with Chief Eaton that were relayed to Schottke and Gareau.

"[We were told that] Dr. Sam Sheppard had been seeing a nurse from Bay View Hospital and that he had been going out with her several times and in fact had given her several gifts, one of which was a wrist watch. This had happened in the past few years and when Mrs. Sheppard found out about this there were several arguments in which Dr. Sheppard would fly into a rage. . . . The Chief stated that he did not want this information to be known that it came from him as the Mayor (Houk) of Bay Village did not want this to get out or be known."[5]

Suddenly, sexual infidelity was injected into the crime. In a domestic slaying, homicide detectives almost reflexively look for adultery, sexual jealousy, or tangled love as motives behind murder, and motives in turn can lead to a suspect, and soon, at least in the 1950s, to a legal resolution of the felony. Schottke and Gareau were not surprised to hear such rumors. They had wondered at first if Marilyn Sheppard might have been unfaithful and contributed to her fate. They needed to find Sam's nurse and talk to her.

Schottke and Gareau stopped at Bay View to interview Sam for the third time. The reception area was roiling with people: reporters, photographers, and television cameramen, as well as Sheppard family friends and pesky curiosity seekers, all awaiting a shred of news from Dr. Sam or his family.

Before the two detectives could start their interrogation, Steve stopped them. They had to wait for Sam's lawyer, Bill Corrigan, who was on his way.

By 1954, age and heavy smoking had caught up to sixty-eight-year-old Bill Corrigan, diminishing his stamina and cunning. But he had worked many sensational cases, and recently had represented two top crime-syndicate figures during the nationally televised Kefauver mob hearings. The electricity of the Sheppard murder charged him up. He felt he could handle the press and outwit coroner Gerber.

Corrigan had worked the police beat at the *Cleveland News* while putting himself through law school. He not only knew many of the reporters but also understood the needs of a daily newspaper, how to play favorites, dole out an exclusive interview at the right time, provide a photo opportunity that presented a client in favorable light. Corrigan expected his clients to do what he told them—don't talk to the press and don't talk to the police.

A short man with a full head of white hair, his jawline toned from his daily oratory, he was the master of courtroom emotion—bluster, outrage, indignation, puzzlement. He lived in a 135-year-old farmhouse, where he entertained guests by reciting the poetry of Robert Frost. Part of his success was the respect he commanded from judges, police, and labor leaders, and his common touch. Labor leaders thought he would make a fine mayor. In 1937, while fighting to establish labor's right to picket, he was arrested at a picket line at the Federal Knitting Mills. At the time, Cleveland's mayor complained that Corrigan had engineered the arrest as a publicity stunt to help him in the mayoral primary, but Corrigan did not file for the race.

After Bill Corrigan arrived at Bay View, he allowed the Cleveland homicide detectives to quiz Sam as he sat by in the room.

From the tenor of their questions, Sam knew the police did not believe his account. "I couldn't kill a squirrel or a rabbit much less someone I loved," Sam said, then covered his face in his hands and tried to hold back sobs. The only new detail he provided was a better description of the man he said he battled: large, maybe as tall as six feet three, dark complexion, Caucasian, wearing a light shirt. With Corrigan's blessing, Steve asked the police to leave his brother alone for now. It was medically necessary.[6]

Schottke and Gareau were upset. They were not used to having a lawyer *and* a doctor interfere with their work. In Cleveland, they could have arrested Sam and questioned him regardless of his consent. But they were investigating in Bay Village and lacked arrest powers. They felt they had already lost their best opportunity to break their chief suspect and obtain a detailed, unrehearsed account that later could be picked over for inconsistencies and contradictions and thrown in his face at a future interrogation.

After the questioning, Schottke and Gareau spent much of July 5 canvassing the neighborhood, asking in particular about Sam's and Marilyn's personal life.

One neighbor volunteered that Marilyn, when asked if she was going to have another baby, remarked that she couldn't because Sam was sterile from so much time around X-ray machines. It may have been a joke, or perhaps not.

If Sam was sterile, the detectives realized, they had the motive behind the killing: Marilyn was pregnant by another man, Sam discovered her condition, then exploded in rage.

They shared the information with Dr. Gerber, whose morgue held the fetus in a specimen jar. Gerber quickly ordered the lab to test the fetus to determine blood type and, if possible, which of eleven blood antigens were present. If the blood work showed that Sam was not the father, the authorities might be able to explain at least one puzzling aspect of this murder to a jury—why a well-to-do doctor would murder his pregnant wife.

―

After two days of investigation, Dr. Gerber and the Cleveland homicide detectives were frustrated. They rarely dealt with a murder suspect whose family held community esteem and was wealthy enough to hire a famous defense lawyer. Further, Bay Village police officers Fred Drenkhan and Jay Hubach were not yet convinced that Sam was guilty—they had known him for years, and it seemed inconceivable. "The whole case seemed geared to tagging Sam," Drenkhan recalled years later. "I was an idealistic new policeman, and I was working under the premise that we gather facts and they would speak for themselves, rather than having a preconceived notion and then developing the case around it."[7]

On July 5, the Cleveland detectives once again told Chief Eaton that Sam Sheppard should be arrested and questioned in a jail. Eaton discussed the request with Bay Village's part-time city lawyer, received conflicting advice, and put off a decision.

By Tuesday morning, it was clear that a powerful player in the Sheppard murder mystery was moving to center stage: the press. Stories in the three dailies clearly cast doubt on Dr. Sam's account. In the *Cleveland Press* on page 1, Dr. Gerber was quoted as saying that he and police had discarded the theory that a drug addict had broken into the house to steal narcotics. Marilyn was killed between 3 A.M. and 5 A.M., he said, but noted that Sam didn't call anyone until nearly 6 A.M. Chief Eaton and county sheriff detective Carl Rossbach were quoted complaining that they had not been allowed to interview Sam. (In fact, each had interviewed him at least once, and the Cleveland detectives had done so on three occasions.) "Why did the family of Dr. Samuel Sheppard call in a criminal attorney, who advised them to halt police questioning of the husband of murdered Mrs. Marilyn Sheppard?" the *Press* asked in the first sentence of a front-page news story. Sam's lawyer, Bill Corrigan, "a prominent Cleveland criminal lawyer," had interrupted an interrogation, the article went on.

In the 1950s, reporters, like the police, were from working-class back-grounds and shared the same values: accepting the status quo, getting ahead financially, raising families, attending church. The coroner, the cops, and the press trusted one another. Reporters were inclined to accept the authorities' version of events, and rarely wrote about police brutality, ticket fixing, racism. Reporters and the police felt they were all on the same side, fighting crime and serving the public. To reporters, and the public, hiring a defense lawyer looked like a sign of guilt. Why would you need one otherwise?

Steve Sheppard wanted to combat the negative publicity about hiring Corrigan but realized he faced a tricky situation. He didn't want to antago-nize the coroner and the detectives and publicly attack them for concluding that his brother was a murderer. People trusted detectives; Gerber was a pop-ular elected official. So Steve told reporters that the Sheppards had called in a lawyer because the crime affected Bay View Hospital, and it was good business practice to seek counsel. Steve said Corrigan decided that Sam al-ready had told police everything he knew and "it would retard his progress if he were compelled constantly to relive the episode."[8]

But how seriously was Sam injured? Gerber had already heard from E. R. Hexter, a Bay Village M.D. he had asked to look at Sam on Sunday evening in the hospital. Hexter made a report that showed Sam had missing reflexes on his left side, but Hexter did not give that finding much weight. He told Gerber and the detectives "the only outward injury" he could find was "swelling around the right eye and cheek." Gerber and the detectives quickly decided that Sam was faking his neck injury, which reinforced their belief that he was the killer.

On July 6, Gerber met with one of his widely respected colleagues at the Western Reserve Medical School, Charles Elkins, M.D., an assistant profes-sor in clinical neurosurgery as well as chief neurosurgeon at Cleveland City Hospital. Dr. Elkins had examined Sam at the hospital, at the request of the Sheppards. Gerber wanted to know what Elkins thought of Sam's so-called injuries. Joining them were two assistant county prosecutors, John Mahon and Thomas Parrino, now assigned to the case.

Dr. Elkins's findings strongly challenged their theory of the case. Elkins said that Sam had a cerebral concussion, a spinal cord injury that robbed him of reflexes on one side.[9] When Elkins tested Sam on July 5, he had com-plained of numbness on his left side. "This morning when attempting to pass gas, he soiled his sheets with fecal material," Elkins noted in a written report, an indication of a nervous system disorder.[10]

When he stroked Sam's inner left thigh, Elkins failed to get a muscle-contraction reflex. He did not get a response when he stroked Sam's left abdomen, and when he pressed Sam's neck at the second cervical vertebra, the neck muscles went into spasms, which cannot be faked. "This is an objective sign of injury," Dr. Elkins noted. "There was a derangement going on some place in the nervous system. This reflex cannot be simulated, and I obtained that without the assistance of anything stated by Dr. Sheppard."[11]

Clearly, somebody had landed a powerful blow at the base of Sam Sheppard's skull.

After listening to Dr. Elkins, Gerber made a medical decision that Sam was not ready to be interrogated until July 8, two days away, a decision that infuriated the Cleveland detectives. By the time he testified at trial, Gerber had changed his mind and said Sam Sheppard had not been seriously hurt.

Marilyn's body was buried on July 7 in a private afternoon ceremony at Saxton Funeral Home in the suburb of Lakewood. She had become a celebrity in death. Cars slowly drove by the funeral home, and teenage girls stopped to peer inside. About 250 of Sam and Marilyn's friends and family, mostly young couples, including Otto Graham, other Cleveland Browns players, and politicians, attended the service. Sam arrived in a wheelchair, then walked in, wearing a suit but no tie, his eyes shaded behind dark sunglasses. His neck was wrapped in a stiff orthopedic collar, an image of him that would become engraved in the public's mind.

He did not want Chip there. Marilyn's father was said to be too upset to attend. At the copper-colored casket, Sam Sheppard started to sob. He held the pansies Chip had picked for his mother, then placed them inside the casket.

"Why does God let something like this happen?" the Sheppards' pastor, the Reverend Alfred Kreke of Bay Methodist Church, intoned at the service. The slaying was not the will of God but the act of a man, he answered. We all lose someone we love. "Some go more unexpectedly than others." He urged Sam and his family of physicians to continue their "service to humanity."

During the funeral police searched the Sheppard house again. Mayor Houk officially had turned the investigation over to coroner Gerber and the county sheriff. This time, detectives picked up some physical evidence that they had ignored or missed the days before or perhaps had been inadvertently dropped there by photographers, reporters, or police who had been in the house. Near the bed where Marilyn was beaten to death they found a small piece of leather and a chip of red paint or enamel. Outside the house, a commercial diving company started to dredge the lake with electromagnets, searching for a murder weapon.

It made the front pages of the late editions of the newspapers: SEARCH MURDER HOME AGAIN and DR. SHEPPARD WEEPS BESIDE COFFIN OF WIFE.[12]

By now it was clear to law enforcers, the press, and anyone closely following the case that Dr. Steve Sheppard was the leader of the family. He was outspoken and impatient, and though he looked soft, he "had a backbone of stainless steel."[13] He had a full head of prematurely silver hair and dressed nattily, wearing custom-made, monogrammed shirts, bow ties, tailored suits, a straw boater in the summer, two-toned shoes. Steve liked fine things—poetry, a turn of a phrase, a good book, a well-honed barb. He had no interest in sports, near treason in a city with the best team in both major-league baseball and the National Football League. If his inability to make small talk about sports made him seem aloof, he didn't care. He lived to sail his racing sloop; its creaking ropes and flapping sails were soothing music to him, so unlike the awful roar of the twin Evinrudes that Sam needed to pull waterskiers. Betty, his wife, wore tasteful, expensive, fashionable clothes. He was a smug young doctor "happy in the luxuries and the extra niceties of living" he bought to surround his wife and two girls. He and his brothers felt they were living in "a self-made paradise. We had no premonitions of trouble ahead. The world was good."[14]

It was, therefore, no surprise that the police selected Steve as the family member who might talk Sam into spilling his secrets. On consecutive nights just after the murder, Steve was summoned to Mayor Houk's home, which had become an informal satellite office for Gerber and the police. The first night, Steve encountered Schottke and Gareau. They urged Steve to use his influence on Sam and pressure him to confess. It will be in Sam's best interests, Steve was told; otherwise he'll face the "direst of consequences." The message was clear: cooperate, or the police will get him anyway and then he'll go to the electric chair.[15]

Steve firmly insisted that his brother did not kill his wife.

Just as firmly, the detectives concluded that Sam's aggressively protective brother must have helped him clean up the murder scene and stage a burglary.

The next night, at about eleven o'clock, Houk told Steve to come over because some of Sam's friends were there and wanted to help out. When Steve arrived, he found Otto Graham, former FBI agent Alex Davidson, and other friends from the neighborhood. Davidson argued that Sam should confess. He would be charged with manslaughter, not murder, and his friends would back him up, not abandon him.

Otto Graham, smooth and warm, joined in. Sam's confession would clear the air and calm the situation in Bay Village. "Everyone can understand how any man might lose his head in a fit of temper and strike out," Steve remembered the quarterback as saying.

It was a mix of soft sell and peer pressure, but Steve wasn't buying. He also left Houk's home wondering why the mayor in particular was so anxious to get Sam to admit to murder when Steve felt certain his brother had done nothing of the kind.[16]

He became suspicious of the mayor. Why hadn't Houk alerted police when Sam first called and said Marilyn had been killed? Why did Houk bring his wife to the murder scene, unarmed, not knowing whether a killer still lurked? It made no sense unless Houk was implicated.

4

DOC

ON JULY 8, as he had each morning since Marilyn Sheppard's murder, Dr. Gerber had his driver motor him out to Bay Village. It was an important day for him and for the investigation. Doc, as he was called, planned on having Sam Sheppard interrogated. He had agreed to wait because of Dr. Sam's spine injury. Now there would be no more medical excuses.

Gerber hoped for damaging admissions from his suspect, perhaps even a confession. It would be buttressed, he was certain, by work going on back in the coroner's laboratory. There the trace-evidence technician Mary Cowan was studying blood drops, Sam's stained clothes, hair strands from the murder scene, the blood-smeared watch from the green canvas bag, and other items.

At Bay View, Gerber was joined at Sam's hospital room by Cleveland detectives Schottke and Gareau, assistant county prosecutor John Mahon, Bay Village policeman Fred Drenkhan, and county detective Carl Rossbach. Already in the room with Sam was his brother Steve. As blunt and arrogant as Gerber, Steve complained that Sam had already talked to police four times. What else could he tell them?

Corrigan, who assumed that most of his clients were guilty, had warned Sam not to talk to detectives unless he was in the room to protect him. But Sam felt torn and said he had nothing to hide. He wanted to help the police. What do you think? Sam had asked Steve.

You're an adult, his brother had replied. Do what you want. But he objected to Schottke and Gareau questioning him. They already had accused him of murder.[1]

Sam decided to cooperate. He would go to police headquarters downtown and submit to interviews without a lawyer. It was a remarkable decision, either an act of supreme arrogance, if he was guilty, or a sure sign that he had nothing to hide.

Just then, Bill Corrigan arrived at the hospital, was told of Sam's agreement, and shouted, No! His client was hurt, in no shape for interrogation. Corrigan chased police from the room so he could talk sense to Sam. He had seen suspects admit or agree to damaging statements after hours of interrogation. At this point, uncertain of Sam's guilt or innocence, Corrigan gave him the safest advice he could give any client in a criminal case: stay away from the authorities, for as long as possible.

Gerber was furious. "Here is a witness surrounded and shielded by his own family," he told reporters. "It's a situation that's got to be straightened out immediately." Prosecutor Mahon later was quoted as saying, "In my twenty-three years of criminal prosecution, I have never seen such flagrant stalling as in this case by the family of Dr. Samuel Sheppard."

In his back pocket Gerber had a set of subpoenas to compel Sam, his father, and his brothers to be grilled under oath at a coroner's inquest. Gerber handed the subpoenas to Carl Rossbach and sent him back into Sam's hospital room to formally serve them. Corrigan said, "Whoa, whoa, let's work this out!"[2]

———

Bill Corrigan and the Sheppards underestimated the relentlessness and cunning of their primary opponent, Dr. Samuel A. Gerber. He was a gifted political operator as well as a forward-thinking medical scientist. In 1936 he had inherited a shabby coroner's office with a minuscule budget, a borrowed microscope, and a half-time employee. He worked hard to instill rigor and innovation into the emerging field of forensic science. In 1938, long before other public-health officials, he crusaded on the dangerous link between drinking and driving. In 1944, when giant tanks of natural gas exploded next to a tightly packed Cleveland neighborhood, Gerber and his staff used X rays of teeth and bones and infrared photography of tattoos and birthmarks to identify remains. His methods were adopted worldwide. Active in local and national Democratic politics, Gerber was a popular and trusted vote getter. In 1953 he convinced county voters to approve a tax levy to build a $700,000 state-of-the-art coroner's office, with classrooms, amphitheater, modern laboratory, and a morgue only a few steps from University Hospitals. He had even higher ambitions; he was convinced he was capable of running a big city like Cleveland, the nation's sixth-largest, and wanted to run for mayor.

Cleveland's medical economy was dominated by such teaching hospitals as the Cleveland Clinic and University Hospitals. The medical establishment was WASPish, Republican, and tied to charitable foundations and banks with old family money. Gerber, who grew up in Hagerstown, Maryland, was not a part of this world. He seemed insecure about his medical training. He had attended only a year of college, then enrolled in Cincinnati's Eclectic Medical College, a four-year program. He earned his M.D. in 1922 and a law degree in 1949. Later, he changed his résumé to say that his degree came from the University of Cincinnati's medical school, not the Eclectic Medical College, which closed its doors in 1929.

Few successful doctors wanted the job of county coroner. It paid too little, the hours were awful, and the work was gruesome. Further, a coroner did not reap the emotional payoffs of practicing medicine, basking in a family's gratitude after curing a loved one, for instance. Emotionally aloof, Gerber didn't seem to care for such involvement. He had been married and divorced twice and lived in a residential hotel, alone.

Gerber worked the Sheppard investigation more zealously and publicly than any other homicide of his eighteen-year career. Besides making a quick, firm decision that Sam Sheppard was guilty, Gerber was antagonistic to the Sheppard doctors as a group. There were at least two underlying reasons.

Like many of his colleagues, Dr. Gerber was affronted that osteopaths performed surgery, prescribed drugs, and competed with his allopathic physicians. He felt osteopaths were bone twisters, an inferior class of doctors, a position echoed by the powerful American Medical Association, which lobbied Congress and state legislatures for laws and regulations to crush osteopathic medicine. The AMA, mostly through decades of *Journal of the American Medical Association* articles, preached that osteopaths were medical "cultists." Under its bylaws, the AMA refused to let its member doctors teach at osteopathic medical schools, consult for an osteopath on a patient's care, or even share a common waiting room. The AMA branded such practices "unethical conduct." As a result, the two branches of medicine were isolated and did not trust each other.

The animosity between medical doctors and osteopaths spiked during World War II. All medical students, including those studying osteopathy, were draft-deferred until they finished medical school. Meanwhile, the AMA successfully lobbied the Pentagon and Congress and killed a move that would have allowed osteopaths to be commissioned in the armed services medical corps. Medical doctors served as commissioned medical officers, but osteopaths who wanted to enlist could serve only as corpsmen or nurses.[3]

This restriction backfired on the AMA. Osteopaths stayed at home instead and cared for the civilians. As a result, their practices swelled, and hundreds of thousands of new patients ended up staying with their new treating D.O.s after the war. Osteopathic doctors built hospitals and clinics and partook of the golden tide of postwar medical care that was transforming physi-cians and surgeons into elite earners. As a result, many in the medical estab-lishment, not just coroner Gerber, were willing to see a family of upstart osteopaths like the Sheppards, who ran a competing teaching hospital, get a comeuppance.

Particularly annoying to the M.D.s was the Sheppards' attitude. They knew they were good. They had undergone training that was superior to that of many M.D.s, studying at the Los Angeles College of Osteopathic Physi-cians and Surgeons, part of a large county hospital with extensive clinical fa-cilities. When Sam returned to Cleveland, he stepped into a lucrative family business as a surgical resident at Bay View and as an equal partner in their private practices in a nearby suburb, Fairview Park. By design, each brother specialized in a different area of medicine. As part of the business plan, the three brothers also became nonpaid police surgeons for Rocky River, Bay Village, Westlake, and other West Side suburbs. It was a clever patient feeder system for Bay View. Whoever was on call had to race to accidents and fires to take care of the injured; if an accident victim needed surgery or hospital-ization, the ambulance took them to Bay View.

Sam was the least-experienced physician and at first generated the fewest referrals, but that soon changed. He began traveling throughout the state, performing surgeries that Steve Sheppard later said "really made the money" for the hospital. By 1953 Sam was earning thirty thousand dollars a year, more than five times the income of a typical American family.[4]

Of all the Sheppard brothers, Sam seemed best suited to the challenge and thrill of emergency surgery. He was gifted with an athlete's fine-tuned hand-eye coordination, a surgeon's stock-in-trade, and devoured the journals on neurosurgery, keeping abreast of the latest advances. He was most happy working on life-threatening injuries from accidents, something that needed heroic effort instantly and produced dramatic results, rather than, say, re-moving an intracranial tumor, which usually resulted in a poor outlook for the patient.[5]

Sam was on emergency call more than a third of his evenings. He loved the action, roaring to the scene at breakneck speed, his surgeon's bag on the seat, ready to set a leg or massage a heart or resuscitate a dying passenger. Fred Drenkhan, the Bay Village patrolman, often witnessed the Sheppards' emergency work. Once, a drunk driver smashed his car and was pinned inside by crumpled metal, unconscious and in shock. Dr. Richard Sheppard arrived first. "Richard was kind of hemming and hawing, not sure what to do," said Drenkhan. They would have to order a welder to cut him out, but he might die in the meantime. Sam had heard the police call and raced to the scene minutes behind his brother. He made a quick assessment and, with Drenkhan's help, began dragging the man out through a window, shredding skin, probably damaging the victim's fractured legs. "He told me he could fix the legs, but he couldn't bring him back to life," Drenkhan said, impressed.[6]

In the fall of 1953, Sam came up with the idea of equipping a four-wheel-drive jeep with a cutting torch and hydraulic jacks to rescue the injured from car crashes. Of the six suburbs where they had emergency-treatment arrangements, none of the fire departments owned such gear. Bay View announced its roving rescue service with press releases, and the *Cleveland Press* gave the story good play under the headline "Doctor Squad to Aid in Accidents." Sam was quoted as saying it was "just an extension of our emergency room service."

Steve Sheppard recognized emergency services as a way to show the public that osteopaths performed all kinds of medicine, not just spinal manipulations. In a trade journal, Dr. Steve advised each osteopath to aggressively seeking municipal medical work because it "could open the eyes of the community in which he lives to the scope of his services as a member of a complete school of medicine."[7]

The Sheppards were less hidebound than M.D.s about being medical entrepreneurs. They used the press to promote the hospital and their clinics, blatantly marketing medicine as if it were any other customer service. Medical doctors considered this déclassé. One case in particular brightly illuminates the Sheppards' skill in using the press for business advantage. In May 1953 a five-year-old boy, Tommy Willard, stopped breathing at his home in Fairview Park, a suburb served by the Sheppard emergency service. The boy had severe bronchial pneumonia and had turned blue. His father, a fireman, called an emergency medical squad. As the boy was rushed to Bay View, Dr. Steve used an inhaler; at the hospital he put him into an oxygen tent. The boy stopped breathing. By now Sam had arrived, and he opened the boy's trachea and slipped in a breathing tube. Infected mucus from his lungs gushed up, and his heart stopped. Sam cut open his chest and massaged his heart, bringing him back to life as the other doctors cleared the boy's lungs. Tommy survived.

The story of Sam's triumph was passed to newspapers and professional journals.[8] A story in the *Cleveland Press* ran under a huge headline, BAY VIEW SURGEON SAVES LIFE OF FAIRVIEW FIREMAN'S SON, 5.

"Some superior power must have wished this youngster to live," Sam was quoted as saying. "Perhaps it was to allow him to help others as a doctor." He announced that he was so impressed with the boy's courage that he would pay Tommy's college tuition at Los Angeles's College of Osteopathic Physicians and Surgeons. Mrs. Willard was hugely grateful and told everyone who would listen about the "miracle" that Dr. Sam Sheppard had performed. "He's like a saint."

This heartwarming story—little boy saved, generous doctor, melodramatic references to a superior power—was perfect fodder in a city with three competing daily newspapers. But it irked the medical establishment.

Another reason coroner Gerber disliked the Sheppards had to do with abortion. Gerber believed that abortions had been performed routinely and illegally at the former Cleveland Osteopathic Hospital, founded by Dr. Richard A. Sheppard, on East Thirty-second Street and Euclid Avenue in Cleveland. In the 1950s most hospitals performed legal "therapeutic abortions" to save a woman if her pregnancy threatened her life. If a woman said she would kill herself if she didn't get an abortion, then by definition she fit the criteria. Usually, two physicians, one of them often a psychiatrist, had to vouch that the procedure was needed. In practice, middle- or upper-class women, with effort, could obtain a safe abortion from a doctor. There was tremendous demand; about half a million abortions were covertly performed each year in the United States. Nearly 90 percent of women who became pregnant before marriage had abortions.[9]

Gerber felt abortion was immoral, a serious crime, and expected doctors to report knowledge of abortions to police.[10] Other physicians, however, felt that such informing violated the confidentiality required between doctor and patient.

The coroner had begun focusing on the Cleveland Osteopathic Hospital on the near east side of downtown in the late 1940s, Steve Sheppard said. "He believed that there were all sort of fetuses buried under the parking lot. . . . He had the parking lot dug up, to no avail. The fact is that the medical community in the Cleveland area would have women come in and ask for pregnancy termination, and they were told, 'See Richard Sheppard.' " Mostly, Steve Sheppard said, his father and older brother performed abortions on women who already had suffered through a botched attempt and were in medical danger. "Before any woman got an abortion, it was necessary for the staff to do a consultation, there was necessary laboratory work. . . . It was logical and legal and proper and many lives were saved."[11] The practice continued at Bay View, with five to ten abortions performed monthly.

————

Back in Sam's hospital room, Gerber and Corrigan worked out an interrogation plan: Gerber would withdraw the inquest subpoenas. Sam would submit to questions immediately. Corrigan would leave the room. Drenkhan and others—but not Schottke and Gareau—would do the questioning.

It was a compromise. Knowing that Sam had been willing to talk before Corrigan arrived, Gerber hoped for a breakthrough. When he explained his new plan to Schottke and Gareau, the detectives were upset but could do nothing about it. Gerber and the county officials were in charge of the investigation, not the Cleveland Police Department.

Before he left the room, Corrigan warned Sam again about the police, including his friend Drenkhan. "You are accused of murdering your wife," he told Sam. "These men are out here to get a confession."

Sam broke into tears. "I didn't do anything to Marilyn."[12]

Detective Carl Rossbach of the county sheriff's office pressed Sam about what happened to his T-shirt that morning.

"I don't remember wearing one. Maybe the man I saw needed one. I don't know."[13]

How would your T-shirt fit a man the size you described?

"I don't know."

A prowler or burglar would need only one or two blows to silence your wife, Rossbach said. How do you explain that he used twenty-seven blows?

"I don't know," Sam replied.

Why didn't Koke, your Irish setter, bark?

"She was not the barking kind."

And on it went, for three and a half hours, the investigators throwing questions at Sheppard, hoping he would realize the incredibility of his account and admit what truly happened. They were the same questions that anybody who closely read the newspaper accounts wanted answered: How do you explain how neatly the house was ransacked? Why didn't the prowler see you on the couch? Why didn't he batter you first or else change his mind and run off? Why was your watch stopped at 4:15 A.M.? Why would a burglar put a watch and keys in a cloth bag from your den and then abandon them in the bushes?

Sam answered, time and again, "I don't know." But his account didn't vary from his earlier ones.

Rossbach asked their suspect to take a polygraph exam. Sam replied with the answer that Corrigan had prepared for him: I would, but I'm told I'm too emotionally upset to take the test now. I may submit to one later. (The polygraph, widely used by the military and increasingly by law enforcement, was famously unreliable when a subject was so distraught that he got overly emotional answering even innocuous control questions such as "Do you live in Ohio?")

Gerber and the detectives were stymied. Late that afternoon Rossbach halted the questioning, frustrated. Outside, he complained to the waiting re-

porters that Dr. Sheppard wouldn't answer their questions, and further, refused to take a polygraph examination. Years later, the U.S. Supreme Court
would forbid prosecutors from telling jurors that a suspect refused to take a
lie detector test, making it automatic grounds for a mistrial. But during the
early 1950s and the red scare, the public was more willing to assume a suspect's guilt based on accusations from authorities, especially if the accused
refused to cooperate. If Dr. Sam had nothing to hide, people asked, why was
he afraid of taking a lie detector test?

The public failure of Gerber and the sheriff's department to produce a
breakthrough with Dr. Sam goaded the Cleveland police brass to complain
publicly. Inspector James McArthur, in charge of Cleveland's detective bu-
reaus, said that *his* boys, Schottke and Gareau, not Bay Village cops and the
sheriff's office, should have had the three-hour shot at Dr. Sam. They would
have cracked him open like a walnut. Furthermore, McArthur said he would
not allow his experienced homicide detectives to be relegated to canvassing
Bay Village neighbors and chasing leads. "I am fed up with that type of treatment," he fumed to reporters.[14] He was pulling his men off the Sheppard case.

This outbreak of public finger-pointing created even more headlines, as
Cleveland homicide detectives, sheriff's investigators, and Bay Village police each insisted that they were not the reason why an arrest had not been
made in the sensational murder. The Sheppard investigation had become a
bureaucratic mess.

Back at the crime scene that day, detectives and assistant county prosecutors
Mahon and Parrino found two intimate letters among Marilyn Sheppard's
keepsakes that they quickly decided were evidence of motive in their murder
investigation. Although four years old, the letters contradicted Sam's assertion to police that he and Marilyn had had only minor disagreements during
their nine-year marriage.

One of the letters was from Richard's wife, Dorothy Sheppard, to Marilyn, postmarked August 28, 1950. Dorothy's letter made it clear that Sam
and Marilyn were having marital problems brought on by Sam's cheating
and that they were thinking about getting separated. Dorothy, in the role of
the older, wiser sister-in-law, wrote that she and Richard had weathered similar problems, and she begged Marilyn to persevere.

*Something I had to learn was that men are really little boys and hate to
grow up. We girls apparently accepted the roles of wife and mother a little more quickly. Rich admits that his experience really made him grow*

up, and as he says, it is almost a type of insanity when a man or woman becomes suddenly infatuated with someone else—it is almost impossible to reason with them, they forget the deep meaning of marriage vows, and all family responsibilities.

With all of these things in mind, Marilyn dear, it means trying to go on as best you can. Rich and I talked (both of us, never let it be one-sided) the situation out time and again, as it is absolutely necessary to talk out any problem relating to husband and wife. I did not appear to be demanding or suspicious of Rich's activities, but I made a point of going with him whenever he went out—on a house call, or what have you. Conversation was most difficult at times, but keep it going and keep it fascinating and interesting. It is needless to tell you to be most attractive at all times, and you are far above anyone in attractiveness and dress. . . .

Rich and I feel that Sam is too fine a man, with a good brain, which certainly will make him realize how foolish his actions are. Sam has the beginning of a wonderful life with you and Chip. He also has the ability of an outstanding doctor. His profession, a wonderful wife, and a fine son will help, we pray, to make him see how foolish anything else could be.

Hold on to yourself, Marilyn, and try in every possible way to remain the ideal wife. I know you'll do, and have been doing, everything you can.[15]

The second letter removed from the home was from Steve Sheppard to Marilyn, written three days after Dorothy's letter. In the letter he struck a confident, no-nonsense tone that physicians might use to reassure patients. As Dorothy did, he urged Marilyn to adapt to Sam and to stay with him at all costs. He also placed half of the blame on Marilyn.

"The real problem though is for you both to frankly admit you have made a mess of things, each having contributed an equal portion or share to the situation as it now stands. To realize that you owe it to one another and Chip to make this marriage go even if it kills you both (which it won't)."[16]

He advised her to accept Sam, work together, be the supportive wife, and to speak out when something bothered her. Steve built up her confidence, telling her he happily witnessed "a tremendous change in your personality. . . . Where previously you were a very reticent and inhibited person, you seemed to enter into activities this time and seemingly because you wanted to—this is a healthy thing. It may be that you really felt a part of our family group for the first time this year. I know we are a somewhat closely knit collection in some ways but in others we are quite outspoken and independent—we unthinkingly expect others to be somewhat this way not stopping to realize they may not be used to such things!"

Steve closed by urging her not to become "a bore or a snoop, and tell him you love him—never ask him if he loves you—make him want to tell you—show him how to express himself emotionally by doing so yourself, and don't ever give vent to your emotion on Chip—I think you both have done that on occasion. . . .

"Of course you know I am one hundred per cent with both of you as I love you both more deeply than you could suspect—I have trouble expressing myself emotionally too you see, but I do try!"

Marilyn kept the letters probably because she found the advice useful and the expressions of love heartwarming. In hindsight, it would have been better for her husband if she had thrown them away.

Authorities had to decide how to use these personal letters. The detectives could confront Dr. Sam with them in a private-interrogation setting, accusing him of lying about their happy marriage, as part of an effort to break him down and admit motive. Or authorities could reveal them to the world, isolating and besmirching Sam as a way to force an admission. Pressuring a suspect in a high-profile case by leaking negative information to the press was not standard procedure, but neither was it unheard-of. For several years previously Senator Joseph McCarthy had employed the technique with great success and little public protest. Gerber, the prime mover in the Sheppard investigation so far, was unbending in his belief that Sam was a killer and a medical impostor. Gerber had tried the soft sell—going through his brothers and Otto Graham and friends like Mayor Houk to get him to confess. The more public pressure that could be put on him and his family, the better. The two letters were leaked to reporters, and the aggressive *Cleveland Press* quoted from them in a front-page story: HUNT CLUES IN WIFE'S LETTERS.[17]

5

MARILYN AND SAM

MARILYN SHEPPARD WAS USED TO having her feelings hurt. Born on April 14, 1923, Florence Marilyn Reese was the first child of the former Dorothy Blake and Thomas S. Reese, an inventor and vice president of a Cleveland manufacturing company. Her father was aloof, tight with affection, but generous with his considerable income. Among his inventions was a process to transfer a wood-grain look to metal, later used by carmakers for the decorative side panels of station wagons. Marilyn did not remember a lot about her mother, who died when she was in first grade. Dorothy Reese had a difficult birth with Marilyn and put off getting pregnant again for nearly six years. This time she suffered an enormously complicated delivery. She and her infant son died during his birth.

Marilyn was shattered by her mother's death. Her father had his own grief to swallow, but at a time when each could have found solace in the other, he sent her to live with her aunt and uncle, Mary and Bud Brown. Marilyn grew up closer to Uncle Bud than to her father, and felt in essence abandoned by both of her parents. Thomas Reese remarried after a few years, and Marilyn moved back in with her father and young stepmother in Cleveland Heights but never felt close to either. With her insecure childhood, she held on tight when she found someone to love.

Marilyn set her sights on Sam. At a junior-high basketball practice, one of Sam's teammates told him about "a real cute girl" who wanted to meet him, then dragged him by the arm to the gym balcony to be introduced to Marilyn. "There was some kidding and embarrassed looks on both my and Marilyn's face," Sam said. "I went to the practice, spurred on by the thought that this cute little girl may be around to watch me. I had seen her in the 'older group' but had never considered her or any of those girls as within my reach."[1]

Sam thought Marilyn was beautiful. She had long, soft brown hair, clear skin, hazel eyes, and was trim and athletic at a time when school sports for girls consisted of leading cheers for the boys' teams. A year ahead of Sam in school, Marilyn seemed mature and exciting. Within a week, she "made it her business to cultivate me," Sam later wrote. She composed notes to him during just about every class, and he did the same.

In junior high and high school, girls usually didn't date boys who were a grade behind them, but Marilyn had snagged a local sports hero. Sam excelled at athletics—quarterback on the football team, starter in basketball, state record holder in track—and he made sure to keep his grades high enough to remain eligible for the teams. He dreamed of becoming a professional athlete, long before that career meant vast riches and celebrity. He craved all things physical—moving, racing, competing, anything as long as he put himself in motion. His basketball coach, Gaif Vannorsdall, said, "Sam Sheppard was one of the finest young men I ever coached." He was the first one on the practice field and the last one off; he kept his locker and equipment in perfect shape, and never brought personal problems to him as others did. "He wasn't the type who would hide anything," Vannorsdall said. "If Sam was wrong on an assignment or messed up a play he would be the first to admit it." The young athlete did have a flaw, the coach said. "Funny thing about Sam. If he had been more fiery and shown some temper, he would have made a better football player."[2]

Sam took charge off the field as well. After basketball games, many of the Cleveland Heights High School students went to the nearby Masonic Temple for dances. Sam served as the disc jockey, picking the hit songs to play or taking requests. He was elected class president his sophomore, junior, and senior years. Marilyn also had many extracurricular activities. She served on student council and was a member of the Modern Dance Club, the Riding Club, the Boosters Club, and the Friendship Club. Unlike other students, they did not have to work at after-school jobs.

As he would show throughout his life, Sam was not possessive of Marilyn. When his friend Bob Drury, a huge football player on the high school team, developed a crush on Marilyn, he told Sam about it, and Sam didn't mind. In fact, Drury often accompanied them on dates; Marilyn seemed to enjoy the extra attention. "Bob realized that Marilyn and my relationship was the only basis by which he could be constantly near her, dance with her, call her on the phone and discuss our situation, et cetera. He liked it that way. . . . If Marilyn ever needed anything and I was busy or not on tap, Bob was there."[3]

In her senior year Marilyn again took the lead in their relationship. She invited Sam to a barn dance sponsored by her high school sorority. During the festivities, Sam and Marilyn slipped off for a private walk. "That night," Sam later wrote, "Marilyn told me that she loved me and I was the only one for her. No one had ever said that to me before (other than relatives) and I had never told a girl I loved her. I did manage to sputter out 'me, too.' " By the time Marilyn dragged him back to the dance, she was wearing his high school fraternity pin, which they considered a sign of preengagement. "We were very happy in those days," Sam said.

In fall 1941, as the United States mobilized its troops for a war that seemed inevitable, Marilyn Reese left Cleveland to attend Skidmore College, a small women's liberal arts college in Upstate New York attended by upper-middle-class women like herself. She was very bright—she scored 136 on an IQ test, a few points below genius—but hated classes and referred to Skidmore as "a jail." She missed Sam and Cleveland and needed someone to lean on. She insisted that they write each other every day. Three months later, he missed a day and she wrote him a tearful letter in reply. "Yesterday I was quite worried and scared. I didn't get a letter from you. The first time since I've been here, so you can see how I felt."[4]

Whether out of rebellion at being sent away to school or as a way to ensure that she would flunk out and return to Cleveland Heights, Marilyn showed little discipline at Skidmore, other than writing to Sam. "I'm in history lecture now and instead of taking notes like all the good little girls are, I'm writing to you."[5] She filled her notes with the mundane. "Everyone here chews bubble gum and my jaws are so sore they just kill me. But it is fun to blow bubbles and mine always squash over my face."

Marilyn failed Spanish, got a D– in European history at a time when it seemed likely that friends and relatives would be dragged into battle overseas, and earned C's in her other courses, except for horseback riding and dance. She was athletic and earned A's in both. Her Spanish teacher noted on a report card, "Very mediocre student who made little effort, showed little interest, and cut too often."[6] After freshman year, she dropped out.

Meanwhile, Sam buckled down to his studies, in part because Marilyn had told him rather tartly that he might not have the grades to get into a medical school as his older brothers already had. When challenged, Sam often excelled, and his grades improved remarkably. On graduation day, it fell to Sam, the class president, to make a speech to the 540 graduates and their families. To the parents, he talked of the war in Europe, telling them that each member of the class was asking himself, "How can I best serve my country and win peace?" And to his classmates, he hinted at hardships likely to come. "We are about to leave perhaps the happiest period of our lives."[7] In his case, that forecast was particularly true.

Sam decided to attend Hanover College in rural Indiana, where his parents had met and his brothers studied before going to medical school. Marilyn, who now worked a clerical job at Time-Life's Cleveland office, sent him off with an expensive watch and made him promise that he would write every day. After Sam settled in at Hanover, he tried to make his dorm life seem like his Cleveland Heights home. He asked his mother to bring his shotgun and his dog, Mike, so he could go hunting. Mike lived at school with Sam, and Sam often took the dog to class, where he would nap under Sam's chair.

Sam also had a reputation for being straightlaced and bookish, and he clashed with the rowdy students in his dormitory who made a ruckus at night. "They think they are big college men and they have to get drunk to show everybody," he wrote to Marilyn that fall. "Somebody is going to get a thick lip if he isn't careful."[8]

Later that fall Marilyn wrote Sam that she had gone out on a date and wondered how he felt about it. She seemed to want him to tell her, no, don't date, that he would be much too jealous. But Sam wrote back that he still felt as he had when they discussed this issue before she left for Skidmore—that "you should date because you should get out and have a good time and I want you to, but I don't want you to have them all the time and I want you to be careful what you do and who you go with." Sam said he was so busy playing as a starter on Hanover's football team, which traveled throughout the Midwest for games, that he didn't have time for dating. "Thinking of you out with anyone else just rubs against my skin, but I want you to have a good time."[9]

Before each of her dates, Marilyn wrote to Sam, asking him what he thought, and each time he urged her to go out. He told her he loved and respected and trusted her, and since they were apart, if they did not date others, "people will think we don't trust each other."[10] From the context of their many letters, it was understood that dating did not include having sex.

Two months into his freshman year, Sam pressed Marilyn to join him at Hanover. He told her how much he loved and missed her and then, "Boy!! I wish we could get married right now. I'm really serious! I think of nothing but you and how I love you. It is getting worse and worse."[11] In the spring, he brought it up again. "Golly, we ought to get married too pretty soon. It seems like everyone else is doing it."[12]

Sam was swept up in the times. The country was at war with Germany and Japan, and many young couples were jumping into marriage before the men enlisted or were drafted, then shipped overseas. Sam decided to rush through his undergraduate studies. Back home in Cleveland Heights in summer 1943, Sam took science classes at nearby Case Institute. When not in school, he worked on an old Model A roadster he had bought for one hundred dollars and parked in the driveway in front of his parents' house. A girl he knew casually in high school, Rudy Bales, saw him, stopped, and showed great interest in him. He impulsively asked her for a date, and she enthusiastically agreed. He was having second thoughts about getting married so young without playing the field.

When Ethel Sheppard learned that her son had a date with another woman, she told Sam he could date others but had a duty to tell Marilyn first. Sam agreed and did so. Marilyn was devastated and broke up with him, giving him back his fraternity pin. After a few more dates with Rudy Bales, Sam asked her to wear his frat pin. In Cleveland Heights's small world of courtship rituals, word raced back to Marilyn, who fell into a terrible depression.

——"She had evidently come to feel that I was one person who would never let her down," he said years later. "She stayed in her room crying all the time and wouldn't eat. Her grandparents were beside themselves. I couldn't bear to see Marilyn so unhappy. I hadn't decided we were through by any means but thought it would be nice to date other people and see what happened." Sam got the fraternity pin back from Rudy Bales and gave it to Marilyn. They were together again, but his desire to get to know other women was unfulfilled.

After two years at Hanover and two summers at Case Institute, Sam had nearly three years of undergraduate credits. He applied to and was accepted by the College of Osteopathic Physicians and Surgeons in Los Angeles, his brothers' medical alma mater. The once struggling student was proud of himself but also conflicted. It was just after the D-day landings by U.S. troops on Normandy Beach. That summer, Sam read about General de Gaulle taking Paris, British citizens suffering the Nazis' V-2 rocket bombardments, and others World War II developments. Like so many draft-age men, he desperately wanted to be fighting overseas. It was his nature to be active, take physical risks, and help others. These were also exciting times for the medical profession in the U.S. armed services. Doctors were using penicillin, developed as a practical antibiotic in 1940, to wipe out chronic diseases, infections, and venereal disease; scientists had just synthesized quinine, which promised to protect the Pacific troops and all but eliminate the scourge of malaria. Sam wanted to see action and was particularly jealous of Marilyn's cousin Keith Weigle, a Harvard graduate and a regular medical student who sometimes lorded it over Sam. Weigle had his medical-school tuition paid for by the army and was put in uniform; osteopathic medical students and doctors were not eligible for the medical corps because of the AMA's successful opposition on Capitol Hill. Sam and his colleagues were draft-eligible but "frozen" until the Pentagon sorted out the conflict between the AMA and osteopaths. "I wanted to drop out and join one of the services with my college and high school friends, but was told the only thing that could be done was to become so deficient in my studies that I must leave school and then I'd be taken into the service," Sam explained. Dropping out was not worth considering.

"This was hard for everyone to understand, particularly Marilyn's family. . . . Marilyn had been the target for many comments and questions by her cousin and the family about why am I not in uniform? What is the deal with osteopathic medicine?" Sometimes Sam felt that even Marilyn questioned his willingness to serve.[13]

At the medical college in Los Angeles, Sam immersed himself in schoolwork, living off a monthly allowance from his father. He was lonely, and in his nearly daily letters to Marilyn he wrote again of getting married. By Christmas 1944, he felt ready to take the plunge. By then he knew that his father planned to visit Los Angeles to teach a graduate course in surgery at the college; at the same time Marilyn's father had to make a business trip to California. Sam and Marilyn decided on a small, quickly planned wedding ceremony to take advantage of their busy fathers' schedules.

On Washington's birthday in 1945, more than three years after Sam had first asked Marilyn to be his wife, they were married in a small ceremony in the chapel of the First Methodist Church of Hollywood. The dean of the graduate school held a reception for them at his home. It was hardly Marilyn's idea of a momentous, romantic event. Two years earlier, Sam had told her that "when we get hitched I want everything to be just right. I want some time for a honeymoon and a nice wedding if it is possible."[14] Instead, two days after they were married, Sam was back in medical-school classes he felt he couldn't afford to miss. They did not go on a honeymoon.

Marilyn hid her disappointment, knowing that a payoff would come later. Sam would become an osteopathic surgeon and, with his energy and family connections and charm, would be a great success. Once the war was over and Sam was a doctor, they could begin to live the good life. Meanwhile, she threw herself into Sam's work. She typed his reports, drilled him from lists of questions and answers from his classes, serving in effect as a teacher's aide. She was even a breadwinner: her father sent her fifty dollars a month, and she worked part-time as an assistant in a research laboratory. Marilyn "was wonderful in her understanding of my work," Sam said.[15]

Sam and Marilyn loved Southern California, particularly its weather, which gave them more time to play tennis, swim, and be outdoors. They lived in a small garden apartment on Sichel Street near Los Angeles County General Hospital. They drove a convertible, played tennis on weekends, and went to the beach when Sam wasn't working. Marilyn joined some of the doctors' wives at the Hollywood Tennis Club and even took lessons from tennis star Pancho Gonzalez; she became an excellent player. She and Sam, playing doubles, could beat any pair of men from the hospital.

One couple they became close to was a wealthy surgeon named Randall "Chappie" Chapman—"one of the best neurosurgeons who ever lived," according to Sam—and his wife, Jo. They had a ranch in Big Sur, about three hundred miles up the Pacific coast. The two couples went fishing, played doubles tennis, and went to matches at the Hollywood Tennis Club, where they saw sports and movie celebrities. Sam was particularly impressed with the young Elizabeth Taylor, who "looked lovely and terrific." Chappie also let Sam in on a secret: he had what he called "his L.A. wife," a lover on the side, with whom he consorted when Jo stayed by herself at the ranch on the weekends when he was on call. Sam found this arrangement exciting, a far cry from his sheltered Midwest upbringing and the conduct of doctors like his father.

Sam had been a dutiful son who followed the path marked out by his father and trod by his two older brothers. Going to medical school in Los Angeles after World War II loosened him up. When Marilyn's cousin Keith Weigle, who ran a military hospital training program, visited them, he couldn't believe the changes in his straitlaced cousin. Before moving to California, Sam did not drink, smoke, or tolerate risqué jokes. Now Sam drank socially, smoked a pipe—he felt it made him look suave—and relished telling racy jokes in mixed company. At one gathering, Weigle remembered that a woman named Dolly, a petite, attractive medical student's wife, casually sat on Sam's lap while Marilyn appeared to ignore it.[16]

Women found Sam Sheppard handsome. He had hazel eyes and plump, almost feminine lips, full eyebrows and long lashes, and a strong jaw with a hint of a cleft. His smooth skin and light beard made him look boyish, even though his hair had just started to recede at the temples. As a doctor, he was a magnet for interested women, a man with high income and social status.

Sam had been married at a young age, with little sexual experience, to the only woman he seriously dated. Now he and Marilyn were coming of age when sexual mores were loosening, an era in which penicillin had knocked out venereal disease and many women, lonely or tasting freedom while their boyfriends and husbands were overseas, had premarital and extramarital sex. By the end of the war, radio stations debated "Are We Facing a Moral Breakdown?"[17]

In the late 1940s, Los Angeles was flush with newcomers and a fast-living crowd attached to the film industry, full of temptation and opportunity for Sam, who felt he was missing out on this new sexual awakening. His tour guide into this world turned out to be Chappie, whom Sam once described as "a man who was very active in the world of extramarital sexual activity in California." Chapman, something of a swinger, encouraged Sam to cheat. "I did have tremendous respect for this man, all the way," Sam confessed later. "In the early days, I was pretty young and green, and I did perhaps think, Oh, well, he does it. What the hell, why shouldn't I when Marilyn is away."[18] Before long, Sam strayed with Dolly.

At about this time, Sam's father wrote to him and suggested that he and Marilyn start a family. Dr. Sheppard Sr., as he was called, promised that if his daughter-in-law got pregnant, he would increase their monthly allowance by whatever amount she was earning in the laboratory. To some, it might seem overbearing for a father to tell a son when to have his first child, but Sam didn't chafe. He said he discussed his father's idea with Marilyn and "this was agreeable to us both." Within a month, Marilyn was pregnant.

It was not an easy pregnancy. At this stage, Marilyn, like many women her age, smoked. She developed a chronic cough that was exacerbated by the Los Angeles smog. In the first trimester of her pregnancy she had occasional uterine spasms, which her father-in-law felt were caused in part by nicotine. Dr. Sheppard Sr. urged her to stop smoking, and Marilyn agreed to cut down. Sam hated the cigarettes.

Marilyn also was afraid she would have terrible problems during delivery, as had her mother. Her worries turned out to be well-founded, though her problems were less grave than she imagined. The baby was positioned feetfirst in the birthing canal. Marilyn struggled through sixteen hours of labor, and a cesarean section looked likely. Sam scrubbed and assisted in the birth room while Marilyn suffered from contractions and painful back spasms. The obstetrician administered a tricky anesthesia called a low spinal block, numbing her midsection. As it turned out, he needed forceps, not a C-section, to deliver Samuel Reese Sheppard on May 18, 1947.

Relatives visited to help her with her new infant while Sam, busy with his internship, worked long hours at Los Angeles General. After the relatives returned to Cleveland, Marilyn slipped into a postpartum depression. She was alone in Los Angeles, her family thousands of miles away. She was a medical student's wife living on a tight budget, and her husband was largely unavailable. She could no longer meet Sam after classes for tennis or spur-of-the-moment get-togethers with other couples. She felt overwhelmed and alone, and Sam did not seem to have the time or inclination to rescue her.

"Marilyn was thereafter seemingly harassed with the new responsibility and different job which she never had before," he said. "She always had a grandmother, aunt or uncle, or me to take over any problems that she could not handle at first glance. I would often come home to find her crying in the kitchen with a mess of sticky pie dough which she could do nothing with. I would add a little flour and roll it out and get her back on an even keel again. This was not possible with the baby as I was becoming more active with my work and would come home more tired and was home less of the time. Marilyn loved Chip, as we called him, but grew to resent this continuous responsibility, which she had never known before and which could not be transferred to anyone else."[19]

During his fourth year in medical school, with young Sam about three or four months old, Sam went through a two-week obstetrics rotation, a night-and-day ordeal. By now, from Sam's point of view, Marilyn had lost interest in having sex, and it bothered him enough that he complained about it to other medical interns. "Marilyn had grown somewhat cool sexually as a result of associating this terrific change with Chip, who was the result of sex," he later said.[20] Sam talked to Marilyn about why she felt "harassed," as she called it, and explained to her what he thought was unfolding in her mind: she associated her unhappiness with the new baby, which was the result of sex. Sam's Freudian analysis may have been accurate, but just as likely Marilyn lost interest in sex because she was an overwhelmed new mother, and beset by postpartum depression.

Unlike Victorian mothers, who were expected to tolerate sex only for reproduction, postwar wives such as Marilyn were expected to enthusiastically enjoy sex and in fact insist on conjugal satisfaction. Unfortunately, Sam's expectation of normal sexual relations was much higher than his wife's. Sam seemed to want intercourse every night, Marilyn once confided to a family member.[21]

Sam said he decided not to press Marilyn about their sexual incompatibility, and instead sublimated his frustration into his career, working exhausting hours, sleeping at the hospital, competing avidly with the other young physicians for the highest internship rankings. At the time, he was third in his graduating class, an impressive accomplishment for an average student in high school and early college.

In the summer of 1948, Sam became Dr. Sam Sheppard, D.O. Before he could catch his breath, he began two years of intense, grueling clinical training. Soon he was assigned to the City Maternity Service at Los Angeles County General Hospital, which meant long, unpredictable night hours. This assignment placed an added strain on their marriage. On his first night out on call, Marilyn panicked just before he left for work. She was afraid to be left alone, and cried and begged Sam to call in another intern. "She was shaking all over and I had to make a decision," Sam recalled. "An expectant mother was somewhere in the city depending on me as part of a team to do a job for her." He called the wife of a classmate, who came over and sat with Marilyn. When Sam returned home in the middle of the night, Marilyn awoke and apologized, but said she found it hard when he left at night, particularly to care for a woman, any woman. He said Marilyn was simply jealous of "any and all female patients that might be mentioned by me or my fellow students."[22] More likely, she suspected he was having affairs and was terrified of being abandoned, again, by someone she loved—this time with a baby to mother.

Another of Marilyn's complaints about Sam was that he focused exclusively on his work and could barely survive at home without turning to her for help. Unlike most men his age, he had not served in the armed forces. For many, the army taught them to make a bed, shine shoes, press their clothes, and perform the mundane chores of daily life. Sam had married young and never lived without a parent, roommate, or wife; like many men of his era, he could not be bothered with housekeeping, child rearing, or running a social calendar.

"He's terrific in an emergency in the hospital," Marilyn told a friend a few years later as they prepared for a vacation. "As far as taking care of himself or knowing what to pack I have to put everything down on notes for him."

To help Marilyn "gain her bearings" during his maternity rotation, Sam said they decided that she should go to Cleveland for a few weeks with the baby, hire someone to watch him, and take it easy.[23]

While she was away, one of Sam's med-school friends, Lester Hoversten, invited him for dinner with two nurses, a date for each of them. Sam later told Marilyn about the date, that there was nothing to it, the woman was only a "jolly fat girl who had been a good friend to all the senior students." But it seemed callous to put himself in the position of telling Marilyn about his "dates," knowing she would be upset. The woman later baby-sat for them, so the dinner was probably innocent. But Sam was setting a pattern: when Marilyn was gone, he felt it was permissible to date. Another time when Marilyn was out of town with Chip, one of Sam's OB-GYN patients, a "beautiful young girl, called me to meet her when she got out," he said. He was tempted but turned her down. His reasons: Marilyn was returning soon from Cleveland; he really didn't have time to socialize; and "I had no idea of what this girl might do"[24]—that is, he did not know the young woman well enough to gauge whether she was capable of a discreet affair instead of a noisy attachment.

On the other hand, he believed Marilyn stayed faithful to him. When a Cleveland Heights sorority friend of Marilyn's moved to Los Angeles and began dating a baseball player for the Los Angeles Angels, Marilyn accompanied her to many games. One of the ballplayers "fell for Marilyn," Sam said, "but she handled him all right."[25]

By now Sam had had several affairs, one with the wife of a resident doctor on staff at Los Angeles County General Hospital, another with a nursing instructor. It was purely a physical relationship, Sam later admitted. "She had a number of young interns and residents dating her and suggesting marriage. . . . But at the same time she had a certain need and knew that I was discreet and she was a person rather ideally suited for that particular situation at the time."[26]

Sam would later say that Marilyn knew about his flings, and that he reassured her that he loved her. "She remained periodically interested in sex more or less in the fashion of performing some sort of duty which she felt her husband was entitled to. This of course was very far from what she had once been."[27] Sam did not realize that her lack of interest was probably tied to her anger that he was having affairs.

Sam was repeating a pattern sometimes found among medical students: a wife stands by her student-husband as he puts in grueling hours and earns low pay during training. He is thrown into stressful situations with nurses and female colleagues, working all night and on unpredictable and unaccountable schedules, and sometimes a battlefield bonding unfolds and blossoms into an affair. Home life seems dull by comparison. He wonders if he married the wrong woman, since she does not excite him anymore.

At the time Sam wanted more children, but Marilyn was terrified of the complications. She developed a skin rash that a doctor diagnosed as a nervous reaction to her fear of another pregnancy. Sam assured Marilyn they would not have any more children until she was sure she was ready.[28] He urged her to talk to his brother Steve about her lack of interest in sex. She did, and he suggested she read *Conditioned Reflex Therapy* as a way to feel more positive about sex.

———

Sam and Marilyn discussed staying in Los Angeles and building a practice with Dr. Chapman or other friends. But his father and brothers wanted him back home to help construct the family's budding medical dynasty. As paterfamilias, Dr. Richard Sheppard was a domineering man, and by now well-to-do, though he eschewed the expensive leisure toys—boats and sports cars—favored by his sons. Like many self-made men, he was unafraid of making enemies or taking business risks. In 1946 he bought a beautiful mansion overlooking Lake Erie with the idea of converting it into an eighty-bed hospital. After winning a bitter zoning fight—Bay Village did not have taverns or industry—he began the project. The hospital was set up as a nonprofit, without public subsidy, and run by a board of fifteen, with Dr. Sheppard Sr. holding the right to dismiss board members. It was called Bay View, but in reality it was the Sheppards' hospital.

During the summer of 1950, Marilyn and Chip again made a long visit to family in Cleveland, leaving Sam footloose in Los Angeles. Les Hoversten pressed Sam to fill in as a substitute when he couldn't make a dinner dance with an attractive woman named Margaret Kauzor. Sam escorted her that night, and they quickly developed a close friendship. Hoversten, short, balding, and older, knew that he could not compete with Sam Sheppard. By the end of the summer, with Marilyn still living in Cleveland, Sam had made Margaret Kauzor fall in love with him, and was getting close to that state himself. She suggested a few times that he get divorced so that they could truly get serious about each other, and she refused to sleep with him until he decided. Sam ruled out divorce but continued to date her. He also wrote to Marilyn, telling her about this new woman he cared for deeply.

Marilyn cried and asked why he was telling her this. Did it mean he wanted a divorce? Sam said it was up to her—not a ringing endorsement of their future as a couple. She was confused and hurt, but after some soul searching, she decided to fight to save her marriage. She explained the problem to the one person who could whip her husband into shape—his father.

At the end of the summer of 1950, Sam drove back East to see his family and pick up Marilyn and Chip. When he returned to Bay Village he found that his father, brothers, and sisters-in-law all knew about his antics. They were lined up with Marilyn against him. You have the abilities to be a fine surgeon, his father said, but you need to grow up.

With the family members as referees, Sam and Marilyn felt relieved just to air their grievances with each other. On the long drive back to Los Angeles, spending days on the road with little to do but talk or listen to the radio, they reached an understanding and arrived home in a fairly happy state. They called family back in Cleveland and announced that they were not getting separated.

6

NOISY NEWSBOY

THE SHEPPARD STORY exploded after the publication of Marilyn's intimate letters. Until then, the public had subsisted on unconfirmed gossip and speculation. Finally, the missing element of the scandal—namely, sex—was prominently etched in black and white in the city's leading newspaper. Gossip about the Sheppards and their friends, much of it outrageously false, swept through the city at gale force. For instance, Cleveland homicide detectives received a tip from a local businessman who had heard from a lakefront neighbor of the Sheppards that Sam and Marilyn, Mayor Houk, and police officials took part in hedonistic beach parties.

"The neighbor through his observance from his beach saw interchange of wives at these wild parties. Informer stated that it was a known fact that the doctor in question was sterile for the past five years and his wife was four months pregnant." With the mayor and police tied up in mate swapping and one of them probably responsible for getting her pregnant, the informer alleged, the Bay Village authorities are "therefore doing all possible to stop any investigation by outside authorities."[1]

It was a wild tale, with only hearsay support, but Gerber and the police treated it seriously. Gerber had already tried to type the blood from the fetus in Marilyn's womb, hoping to show that Sam was not the father. Now authorities wondered whether the mate-swapping rumor explained why the Bay Village mayor and police chief would not arrest Sam on July 4.

On Friday, July 9, Sam Sheppard made a move that would be risky for a guilty criminal defendant. He agreed to return to his home, which had been impounded by the police, and reenact the crime for Gerber and the county detective. "This man is so innocent it is a shame to put him through this ordeal," Bill Corrigan complained. "If I had the least inkling that my client was guilty he would not be out here and he would not be talking to police."[2]

Sam arrived at his home wearing a neck brace and sunglasses—bright light bothered his eyes after his head injury, he said. There were cars parked on the front lawn, a gauntlet of reporters and photographers, and a swarm of spectators around the perimeter of his yard. "I want them off my property!" Sam yelled. "Marilyn wouldn't like it." Police herded the crowd to the property lines, and Dr. Gerber came out of the house and moved his county car off the lawn.

Detective Rossbach of the sheriff's department was the principal interrogator this time. He hoped that Sam, questioned in a different setting, would change his story or mix up details, which would suggest he was lying and provide authorities with a wedge to peel off the truth.

Sam appeared calm. He walked through the house, holding three daisies that Chip had picked for him, and re-created the early morning of July 4. Soon he stood inside their blood-spattered bedroom, then he started to sob. Later at the beach he showed how he wrestled on the narrow strip of sand with the bushy-haired intruder. A dozen yards away, a wet-suited diver was methodically searching for a murder weapon in a 200-by-250-foot section of Lake Erie.

Sam's explanations did not deviate from his previous statements, which frustrated Rossbach. The detective again asked him to take a polygraph exam. Acting on Corrigan's advice, Sam refused.

"After six days of investigation, there's one suspect so far, and that is Dr. Sheppard," Rossbach later told reporters. "Until something turns up, we will have to keep questioning him until he gives us something to go on."[3] In other words, Rossbach believed Sam was the killer and the only solution was for him to confess.

Corrigan, Sam, and his brothers had hoped for headlines that afternoon that played up his cooperation. Instead, they got REJECTS LIE TEST.

That afternoon, a powerful new player entered the case. The feisty *Cleveland Press* gave Dr. Gerber and the police a beating in an unsigned editorial. Under the headline "Too Much Time Lost," the editorial slammed officials "on both the municipal and county levels," saying they had been "slow in getting started, fumbling when they did, awkward in breaking through the protective barriers of the family, and far less aggressive than they should have been in following out clues, tracks, and evidence."

Dr. Gerber, even though he was not named in the story, was embarrassed.

He thought the attack was unfair. After all, it was he who had stepped into the void of police leadership on the day of the murder; he had spent more time on this crime than on any other in his career. He was pressured by Cleveland detectives and harassed by his nemesis, Bill Corrigan. He was doing all his office could do, even attempting to type fetal blood, and now all he had to show for it was a critical editorial from the city's most influential newspaper, which was edited by his friend Louis B. Seltzer, a powerful figure whom he had cultivated for years.

Gerber defended himself fiercely, telling reporters that even if Dr. Sheppard had been arrested and jailed, his interrogation would have commenced only fifteen to twenty hours earlier because Sam had "a nervous system injury."[4] Gerber made an honest call and quickly paid a political price for it. Later he would disavow this medical opinion altogether.

Like everyone else who mattered in Cleveland, Gerber found it impossible to ignore Louis Benson Seltzer, editor of the *Press*. The two men had many things in common: both were short, ambitious, and politically astute; both were members of a Masonic lodge and self-professed men of the people. Seltzer was only five feet six, bald, and unremarkable except for being a foppish dresser. He always draped himself in one of his five dozen crisply pressed suits, with a starched shirt, a gold stick pin securing one of two thousand ties from his closets. Billowing from his left breast pocket was his trademark, a matching handkerchief. He walked as if he were late, striding into meetings or a luncheon at once jaunty and coiled, ready to sell the virtues of the *Press* or a civic plan he backed. He was a dynamo. Some nights, unable to sleep, he got up and vacuumed the house to wear himself out.

Seltzer's background was the near opposite of Sam Sheppard's. He had grown up impoverished, the oldest of five, the son of an out-of-work carpenter who tried to make a living writing dime novels. His mother made his clothes by cutting up discarded men's suits and shirts. Louis dropped out of sixth grade to work as an office boy at the *Press* and fell in love with the thrill of big-city newspapering during the Front Page Era, when cutthroat competition and entertainment trumped the need to be a responsible civic force. As a police-beat reporter, he entered apartments and houses to "borrow" photographs from families of crime victims to splash on page 1, a routine practice. Firehouses' coded alarms sounded in the newsroom, and he literally ran from the newsroom to be first on the scene. He witnessed seven electrocutions and took part in circulation-building stunts, such as using magician Harry Houdini to obtain evidence in exposing phony spiritualists who were preying on unsuspecting immigrants. He even got himself locked into the huge, antiquated Ohio State Penitentiary to expose its brutal conditions. He shot up the ranks at the *Press,* the flagship of the nineteen-paper Scripps Howard chain, and at only thirty years old was named editor in 1929. By 1939, he was earning seventy-five thousand dollars a year, a huge salary for an editor, as well as a bonus of 5 percent of any increases in the *Press*'s operating profits. If the *Press* did well, so did he, which gave him a financial incentive to create circulation-boosting crusades.

Seltzer was an astute marketer; he preached that a newspaper had to connect with the everyday lives of its readers from womb to tomb. Among his innovations, his staff sent cards to parents of newborns and invited couples reaching their fiftieth anniversary to a free banquet. Early in his career as editor, Seltzer set aside part of each Friday to visit one of Cleveland's forty-six ethnic neighborhoods with his wife, Marion. Many days he gave two or three speeches to clubs, women's societies, or church groups, speeding from address to address, arriving at one for the first course and hitting the other by dessert. Typically, he was home for an early family dinner at around 4 P.M., just after the late stock edition hit the streets, then changed suits and hit the dinner-speech circuit. Clevelanders felt they knew him and trusted him. They believed his newspaper would tell it like it is.

Seltzer ran a loud, loose, profane newsroom. He encouraged practical jokes. Once he threw a firecracker under the chair of a reporter interviewing a woman on the telephone. "What was that!" the startled woman demanded. A firecracker, the reporter said calmly. "What would Mr. Seltzer think about that?" she wanted to know. "Ma'am, he's the one who threw it."[5]

The day he ran the first editorial attacking the handling of the Sheppard investigation, the mass-circulation weekly *Saturday Evening Post* ran a long glowing feature about Seltzer, "Noisy Newsboy of Cleveland," that likened him to William Randolph Hearst and Joseph Pulitzer. "Most experienced newspapermen regard him as one of the ablest executives in the country, although they might disagree radically as to where time will rank him among the editorial giants of the era."[6] Celebrities cultivated him. On Seltzer's fiftieth birthday he received telegrams from Bob Hope (a Cleveland native), Frank Sinatra, Jack Benny, Danny Kaye, and other famous entertainers.

By the time of the Sheppard murder, Seltzer was known as "Mr. Cleveland," the most powerful man in the region, a political kingmaker. He believed that his newspaper, with information and a loud voice, could solve the city's problems. The *Press* was a "fighting paper" that "fought like hell for the people," he liked to explain. When local government did not function, the *Press* struck with editorial might, even if it meant using a sledgehammer to crush a gnat. Overkill could be rationalized by its editors because the cause was just, for the little guy. Anyone who tried to play outside these rules or who was per-ceived as looking down on his mostly blue-collar readers, Seltzer enjoyed taking down a peg. The players in the Sheppard murder were perfect fodder for his audience. The Sheppard family was affluent, suburban nouveau riche, osteopaths with a hint of immorality, and they had quickly retained lawyers, one of Seltzer's favorite editorial targets. Seltzer decided that the Drs. Sheppard, with status and wealth, were impeding a murder investigation and thwarting justice, thereby mocking the people's will. They needed a comeuppance.

For the rest of the Sheppard murder investigation, Seltzer and Gerber worked together closely, one creating news, the other inflating it.

In the wake of the "Too Much Time Lost" editorial, each of the four investigative agencies blamed the others. Gerber was upset that the prosecutor's office had intruded into the investigation before an arrest or indictment, something he had never seen before. The Cleveland detectives were angry at Gerber and the sheriff detectives for cutting them out of the most recent interrogation of Dr. Sam. Bay Village police were not sure Sam was the killer and wanted more investigation. As a result, they found themselves shut out of the overall investigation.

Bay Village patrolman Drenkhan and Sgt. Jay Hubach, when they had time, ran down leads that the Cleveland homicide cops felt were unimportant or pursued tips that had come in directly to them. At first they hoped to clear their most famous resident. For instance, Bay Village police arrested as suspects a crew of tree trimmers, three hard-drinking, poorly educated men, and asked to see their clothes. At the home of one, they found a bloody sweatshirt. But the trimmer's wife vouched for him: she said they had had an argument, he smacked her, and she stanched her bloody nose with his shirt. The three men were released.[7]

Going through Marilyn's household checkbook ledger, Cleveland detectives located and interviewed anyone who provided a service at the house. A June 24 entry noted a payment to Dick's Window Cleaning Service, owned by Richard Eberling, a balding twenty-four-year-old who grew up in foster homes after being abandoned by his mother. He had been referred to Marilyn by Dorothy Sheppard. After his work was done, he sometimes sat and talked to Marilyn for a bit. Detective Adelbert O'Hara and prosecutor Parrino interviewed him, and a week later O'Hara felt the need to talk to him again. It is unclear from police reports whether Eberling, like the tree trimmers, was considered a suspect, then cleared.[8] Eberling told them he knew little of Marilyn's personal life and had seen Dr. Sheppard only once, briefly, in the morning, and had never spoken to him.

7

THE OTHER WOMAN

AT 9 A.M. ON Saturday, July 10, Sam again confounded Corrigan, overruled his legal advice, and made what Corrigan considered a dangerous
move. Sam agreed to come downtown to the sheriff's headquarters in the
Criminal Courts Building and let himself be grilled by Schottke and Gareau,
the two Cleveland detectives who had accused him of killing Marilyn and
caused him to run to Corrigan in the first place. Corrigan did not accompany
Sam, who instead had to rely on the hospital's corporate lawyer, Arthur
"Pete" Petersilge, for advice.

Schottke and Gareau, still smarting from being closed out of Sam's July
8 interrogation at the hospital, were determined to get a confession. With
years of experience, they planned to fluster him, convince him that his freedom was temporary, break his will, and when he was at his lowest hold out a
promise of a leniency—a manslaughter rap, one or two years in prison,
tops—if only he would make a clean breast of the murder.

Without his confession, police had a logical but only circumstantial case:
Marilyn was undeniably murdered, there were no signs of anyone else having been in the house, only Sam was in the house, so he must have done it.

Getting a confession was the most efficient, useful technique they had,
especially in domestic slayings. A decade later the U.S. Supreme Court
would narrow the range of tactics police could legally use to obtain confessions—interrogation had to stop if a suspect asked for a lawyer, for example—but in the 1950s, homicide detectives had great success extracting
confessions from suspects by using two-detective teams in relays over eight
to ten hours.

One of the widely used police-training manuals explained three truisms about interrogation that Schottke and Gareau knew from experience: first, crimes—even when investigated by the best detectives—are solved only by an admission or confession from the guilty or from questioning other suspects. Second, criminals will not admit their guilt unless questioned in private and "for a period of perhaps several hours." Third, in dealing with criminal suspects who may actually be innocent, the "interrogator must of necessity employ less refined methods than are considered appropriate for the transaction of ordinary, everyday affairs by and between law-abiding citizens."[1] Psychological manipulation—shouting, lying—was standard practice.

After Sam was told of his constitutional rights, police asked Petersilge to leave. Joining Schottke and Gareau were the Cuyahoga County prosecutor Tom Parrino and sheriff detectives Carl Rossbach and Dave Yettra. The interrogation began at about 9:15 A.M.

By now they had figured out the names of two women with whom Sam had supposedly had affairs.

Did you kill Marilyn?

No.

Why would anyone kill her?[2]

Sam suggested "individuals who are maniacal enough that when they start something, an act like that, it becomes a compulsion, a means of satisfaction like the ordinary man has from an orgasm. She has spurned lovers, potential lovers." He provided names: a sporting-goods store owner, a contractor who worked on their house after the fire, and . . . Mayor Spencer Houk.

Do you know Julee Lossman?

She was a patient, he replied.

"Now, is it true that a very close friendship resulted?"

"I would say a close friendship with both the husband and wife."

"Isn't it a fact that it developed into a love affair?"

"No, not on my part, certainly."

"Of your own knowledge, do you know whether or not there had been a discussion between Mrs. Lossman and her husband and you and your wife, Marilyn, that there had been such an affair existing between you and Mrs. Lossman?"

"This is difficult to answer. My wife and I were present at a time when Mr. Lossman and his wife discussed some of their marital problems. We at this time did mention the belief that she had shown a particular liking to me. We merely attempted to act as referees, my wife and I."

How did this affect your wife, Marilyn?

"She thereafter felt that it would be best that we not arrange frequent social affairs with the Lossmans, and I agreed."

Did Marilyn ever accuse you of having an affair?

"She may have in questioning me about my whereabouts at various times, and in the form of reassurance I often took her with me when possible on visits to nearby cities or even the hospital."

"Is it true, Doctor, that on several occasions, when you were discussing your marital troubles, that you flew into a rage?"

"Absolutely not, never."

"Did you ever have an affair with a Sue Hayes?"

"I wouldn't call it an affair, but we have been good friends for some time, which was known to my wife."

". . . While at work you had considerable contact with her, didn't you?"

"Yes."

"To what extent?"

"She did a great deal of the technical laboratory work on all of the doctors' patients in the hospital and was the only technician practically that readily answered emergency calls on accidents or emergency surgical cases. I might also add that she was considered during her stay one of the authorities when special work was necessary."

"Is it true you socialized a lot with her?"

"In the hospital, yes. I wouldn't call it socialized. We talked, we became good friends."

"Nothing more than good friends?"

The transcript does not reveal whether Sam hesitated, put his hand to his mouth, or averted his eyes, but his answer did not fool anyone.

"No."

By now an old hand at being interrogated, Sam probably realized from the vagueness of their questions that the authorities had likely not located Susan Hayes yet. They didn't seem to know much about her. He hoped it would stay that way because his affair with her had been torrid.

It had begun shortly after he moved with Marilyn and Chip back to Cleveland in May of 1951, supposedly away from the bad influences of Dr. Chapman and the permissive Southern California lifestyle. "Marilyn wanted to come home," Steve Sheppard would say years later, "and my father and Richard and I wanted him to come home. We told him, 'We need you here, come on home. And quit fooling around.' "[3]

Sam and Susan Hayes found each other almost immediately. She had large, appealing eyes, a spray of tiny freckles across her nose, and dressed well. She was outgoing, flirtatious, and possessed "the angular sex appeal of actress Katie Hepburn," a reporter wrote.[4] She lived with her parents in a four-room, third-floor apartment in suburban Rocky River, half a block away from the apartment where Sam, Marilyn, and Chip stayed their first few months back while they hunted for a house. She did not own a car.

Sam claimed that Susan Hayes pursued him, by asking for rides to work. She walked over in the morning, opened a garage door, and sat in Sam's convertible MG, waiting for him to drive her to the hospital. Marilyn thought she was rude and presumptuous. Several times she told Susan that Sam was delayed and she'd be late for work if she waited. But Susan ignored these pointed remarks and said she would wait anyway. Sam knew how Marilyn felt but did not discourage Susan because he wanted to sleep with her.

Their affair started almost instantly. Sam picked her up at night to do lab work for his emergency calls. After he repaired a crash victim or saved a life, he would drive her home, adrenaline still pumping. One time he stopped the car and reached over to Susan, and they went at it. Soon she and Sam had casual sex during stolen moments, usually in his car or the interns' apartment, if it was unoccupied.

The affair was the talk of Bay View Hospital. At an office Halloween party, Sam arrived dressed as a woman. Sue Hayes took his ever-present pipe, put it in her mouth, wore a stethoscope, and said she was in character as Dr. Sam. She flirted so outrageously, with Sam playing along, that Marilyn fled the party. Another doctor's wife quietly put Susan Hayes in her place. "She called me a bitch," Susan complained loudly to others at the party. "She called me a bitch."

Within a year or so she took a lab technician's job in downtown Cleveland, supposedly encouraged to move on by Dr. Richard A. Sheppard, who wanted to remove temptation from his youngest son. She became engaged to a Bay View intern, Dr. Robert Stevenson, and moved briefly to Minneapolis when he had a residency there. When they moved back to Cleveland in the summer of 1953, she was wearing an engagement ring. Soon she and Sam resumed their affair, having sex about every other week.

Susan Hayes was conflicted. She was pursued by a handsome, well-to-do doctor who praised her brains and her looks, told her he loved her, and gave her status and freedom at her workplace—an intoxicating mix for a striving twenty-three-year-old who still lived in a tiny apartment with her parents. But when the physical passion subsided, he was still a married man. She said she often told him, "I don't want to see you anymore. Don't call me." He would agree, then call a week or so later, and they would meet and have sex again.

Once she told Sam that she was in love with Dr. Bob Stevenson, not him. Sam responded, "How can you be in love with Bob and be here with me?"

Susan retorted, "How can you be in love with your wife and be here with me?"

"I guess you love Bob like I love my wife," he said.[5]

All along, Sam told Susan marriage was not possible. He loved Marilyn but not with the sexual passion he had for Sue.[6] "He said it would cause too much notoriety and embarrassment if he divorced her," Susan later said.[7]

Marilyn hated Sam's philandering but didn't know what to do about it. On the surface she appeared to have what society agreed was the good life— successful husband, healthy child, a nice home. In the early 1950s women who had it all and weren't happy in marriage were encouraged to think it was their fault. Marilyn seemed to blame herself because she couldn't satisfy Sam sexually, even though his expectations were quite high. Once at a gathering of doctors' wives the topic of birth control came up and Marilyn naively wondered why they all weren't using diaphragms. It was explained to her that the birth control device was worn only when you were going to have sex. Marilyn replied that Sam wanted to have sex every day, usually in the afternoon, right after her bath. Sam, only a few minutes away by car, was able to race home from the hospital in moments. Though she didn't say so, the afternoons liaisons must have been brief if Sam kept to his busy appointment book, which may have contributed to her disinterest in sex.

According to Sam, he and Marilyn had reached an understanding by the early 1950s that was in effect a one-sided open marriage: Sam was free to have extramarital sex but only if it was discreet and did not threaten their marriage. "Marilyn realized better than anyone that she was not a terrific sexual partner during this period," Sam said. "For this reason she did not get extremely upset when she was told of the girls like Sue Hayes, but she did get upset when I'd dance with other girls at a dance or talk with another girl at a party. She didn't like my attentions to other girls at any time but she recognized my need for sex [which] she had not recaptured since Chip."[8]

Dr. Steve was not surprised that his excitement-craving brother got into trouble with extramarital sex.[9] "He was young and very innocent and naive in many ways and he got gaffled up by aggressive females. He was gifted or cursed with an overdose of testosterone." Further, Steve pointed out, "there was a sexual revolution going on—*Playboy* magazine, Hefner was pushing free love,"[10] and the once sheltered Dr. Sam wanted his share.

By the fall of 1953, Susan had stopped seeing Sam and had agreed to marry Bob Stevenson. They even set a late-December date, but Dr. Stevenson broke off their engagement, saying he wasn't ready for marriage, even though he and Susan had a reception room reserved and invitations printed. "I don't know what happens in cases like that," Susan Hayes said. "He wanted to wait and I didn't. I wanted to be married."[11] It was likely that he knew of her affair. Bay Village was such a small community, and Dr. Sam, widely recognized, had little chance for long-term privacy. Further, Sam was reckless, almost as if didn't care whether Marilyn or anyone else knew of his philandering, perhaps hoping Marilyn would demand a divorce and then he could blame it on her to his parents.

Hayes decided to make a fresh start. She quit her job and left for the golden state of California, the postwar Mecca for beatniks, movie-industry hopefuls, and sun worshippers. Before she moved, Sam gave her a signet ring and a suede coat and told her he would see her in Los Angeles in a month.

In March Sam and Marilyn left for a two-week working vacation in Los Angeles. He arranged for advanced surgery training under the flamboyant Dr. Chapman to get himself closer to certification by the credentials committee of the Board of Surgery for Osteopaths. Board certification was an important career milestone; it meant that he had put in three years of full-time study in neurosurgery and two more years of specialized practice in a neurological residency, and had performed the hundreds of supervised surgeries needed for this expert designation.

While Sam studied, Marilyn stayed with Dr. Chapman's wife, Jo, at their ranch in Big Sur, a beautiful coastal region in central California, three hundred miles to the north. "Heaven on earth," Marilyn called it.

As soon as Marilyn left, Sam called Susan Hayes. The next night Sam took her to the home of Dr. Arthur Miller, his closest friend in California. Miller invited Sam to stay there, and Sam wanted Susan to join him. Only four weeks in town, she was sleeping on a girlfriend's couch and didn't have a private place to conduct an affair. For the next two nights, she and Sam stayed with Dr. Miller and his wife and child. The first night, several younger doctors and their wives came over to the Millers' for a poker game, and in the early-morning hours, while the game continued, Sam and Susan went to bed in the guest room. Most of the women there knew Marilyn and resented being put in such an uncomfortable situation by her husband.

For the rest of the week Sam worked at the hospital during the days and spent the nights with his mistress in the Millers' guest room, then later at a nearby hotel.

Soon an event unfolded that would haunt Sam at trial. Some of the osteopaths were going to a colleague's wedding in San Diego, and Sam decided to bring Susan as his date. She protested; she said she had nothing dressy to wear. Sam, normally tightfisted, gave her money for a dress.

At the wedding's champagne reception, Sam, Susan, and his friends from Los Angeles got tipsy, then decided to go to a restaurant to eat and sober up. Sam was driving. On the way he hit a poodle and stopped to see if he could somehow save the dog, but it was dead. Probably from the influence of the drinks and the accident, Susan Hayes got sick and needed to stop at a gas-station rest room. She inadvertently left behind a small evening purse, which held her everyday watch, a Bulova. When she realized later what she had done, she became upset.

The next day Sam had to leave for the Chapmans' ranch, but first he bought Susan a seventy-one-dollar Lady Elgin, a nicer watch than the one she'd lost. He kissed her good-bye and asked her to write to him at his Fairview Park office. It was clear to Susan that despite the gifts and even though they might think they were in love, her affair with Sam had little future. "He mentioned that he would like to get a divorce," she recalled later. "But it would be impossible . . . because of his family, the notoriety that it would cause his family."[12]

During the long drive to Big Sur, Chappy confessed to Sam that his marriage was beyond repair and he was pondering his options as his wife defiantly drained his cash. Maybe he would just give the ranch to Jo, move to Cleveland with Sam, and set up a practice at Bay View.

Sam responded that he, too, had marital problems. But they weren't about money; they were about sex. He wanted more of it. Susan Hayes was good for a weekend fling, but he wasn't serious about her. Sam would later say that Marilyn knew he had been out with Hayes, "but she was not mad. Marilyn was more tolerant than average. . . . I think because she knew her father had extra-marital relations with one woman or another for as long as she can remember. She never thought it was right but it produces an attitude of acceptance."[13]

Sam made a decision. At the Chapman ranch, he told Marilyn that he had come to a realization during their week apart that "we were meant for each other" and should stay married. This must have reassured Marilyn because it was during the next few days that she became pregnant.

After they returned to Bay Village, things turned sour. Sam asked Marilyn to fill out his expense report for his business trip, and she found a receipt for the watch Sam had bought Susan. Marilyn was terribly hurt. For years she had wanted a white-gold wristwatch to match her wedding and engagement rings. At Christmas she had received such impersonal or unwanted gifts from Sam as cash or an outboard motor. Then she heard gossip about a letter from Susan Hayes to Sam that had arrived at his Fairview Park office and had been opened inadvertently.

Donna Bailey, a part-time secretary and the wife of a Bay View intern, had opened Susan's letter to Sam and read enough to know it was personal. On April 15, at a birthday party for Robert Bailey, Marilyn told Donna and Robert, "Well, Sam's done it again." He had had another affair, and now she wanted the letter as evidence to get a favorable divorce, Donna Bailey recalled later. Marilyn told the Baileys she didn't care about Sam's reputation anymore. She was tired of being hurt. She would use the letter to ruin him, and she didn't care if he suffered.[14] It's unclear how serious Marilyn was about a divorce.

She and Sam quickly had a rapprochement. On June 5 they announced the news of her pregnancy to Sam's family at a dinner party at his parents' home. They both seemed happy. At the end of June, at an amateur sports-car race near Sandusky, Ohio, seventy miles west of Cleveland, Sam and Marilyn stayed at a rental cottage on the lake. Many of their friends came up on their boats and docked near the racetrack so they could watch Sam and Otto Graham compete with the other amateur drivers. Sam later wrote that he and Marilyn made love that night and again the next morning. "Marilyn and I were as happy as we have ever been."[15]

Meanwhile, Susan Hayes, deciding she had no future with Sam, had written him a final letter, telling him that their affair definitely was over. Sam didn't care. There would be other women. He had no idea the Hayes affair would soon put his freedom and his life at risk.

After more than two hours of mind games, accusation, and persuasion, the Cleveland detectives took a break from grilling Dr. Sam. Other than details about his private life, Schottke and Gareau learned nothing new. They were disappointed. Their suspect's answers to their questions about the morning of the murder matched what he told police on July 4, July 8, and July 9. They felt they were dealing with a rare species—an intelligent, unperturbable criminal.

They made Sam sign a nine-page single-spaced typewritten account of the interrogation. Then they turned to their next challenge: to find Susan and see if she, the Other Woman, provided the time-honored motive for murder.

8

MARY COWAN

WHILE THE CITY fixated on a murder case marked by overamplified news reports and public bickering among investigators, a private investigation quietly unfolded behind the steel doors of the Cuyahoga County coroner's laboratory. There an attractive fortyish woman, wearing designer-label outfits under a white lab coat, examined blood, hair, fingernail scrapings, and other traces of physical evidence from the Marilyn Sheppard murder scene. Her name was Mary Cowan, and she did not call press conferences announcing her results.

Cowan ran the coroner's office Trace Evidence Department. She, pathologist Lester Adelson, and toxicologist Louis Sunshine, M.D., made up the scientific backbone of the coroner's office. Cowan—unmarried and living in the big brick house she grew up in—worked long and hard hours without complaint because she loved her job, attacking the fresh mystery of each new unexplained death with the tools of the rapidly advancing field of forensic science.

She was a rarity for her time, a female scientist in a public position. She had studied chemistry and zoology at Denison University, graduated in 1929, then worked in hospital labs. In 1939 Dr. Gerber, going against the grain, hired her away from the Cleveland Clinic into a job a man could use to support a family at the end of the Depression. Cowan was from a well-to-do family that had farmed for two generations in Bedford, a town founded in 1815 and bordering on southeast Cleveland. Under her mother's tutelage, Mary Cowan acquired the taste and breeding of an upper-middle-class young woman, receiving a university education and an appreciation of poetry, art, and fashion. She often bought her clothes in New York or, if overseas, Paris. When going out, she always wore a hat, gloves, and heels.

Shortly after taking the job with the Cuyahoga County coroner's office, she broke off a ten-year engagement to a college sweetheart. "I'm too darn well taken care of to get married," she said.[1] She was unconventional for her time, putting self-fulfillment first. "I believe what I most want is a home and a life of my own."[2]

By 1954, her personal and professional lives were impossible to separate. She had become devoted to Dr. Gerber and his vision of the elected coroner as an activist for public health and safety. She wrote Gerber's speeches, took care of his dog, PJ, and when he needed to get away from his tiny apartment, invited him to spend weekends at her Bedford home. Her family often wondered whether they might marry.[3]

———

On the afternoon of Sunday, July 11, after attending Baptist services and teaching a Sunday-school class, Cowan accompanied Gerber on a one-hour journey to the Sheppard crime scene. It was her first of several visits. She wanted to see if she could decode the story of the blood trail at 28924 Lake Road.

It was the end of a busy, frantic week of detection. One of her first duties had been to study the scrapings from under Marilyn's fingernails, which Dr. Adelson had collected at the autopsy and preserved in ten small separate packets. Cowan mounted the scrapings on glass slides and put them under her microscope. She spotted tiny red man-made fibers.[4] This was important. As she fought for her life, Marilyn Sheppard may have scraped her attacker's clothing.

Cowan compared the red fibers to fibers in Dr. Sam's clothes that Gerber had seized on July 4. No match. She compared the red fibers to the carpet at the Sheppard home and to the clothes Marilyn took off the night she was killed. Still no match. Cowan could not say where they had come from.

She decided to test the brown-crusted stains from the watches of Sam and Marilyn. This detective work could spin the murder mystery into a startling new direction. Marilyn had type O-negative blood, with subtypes M and S. Dr. Sam's blood type hadn't been determined yet. What if the crusted stains were human blood that did not match either Sam or Marilyn? Forensic science would then implicate an outside perpetrator, destroying Dr. Gerber's theory of the case.

Her testing showed both watches were stained with human blood. But when she tried to type the blood into the O, A, B, or AB groupings, she was disappointed. The chemical reactions in her test tubes were too weak to be conclusive, but the sample appeared to be type O, found in 42 percent of the population. Rather than retest for O with the tiny samples of blood, she typed the watch blood for subgroups M and N. Both samples tested positive for type M, found in 30 percent of the population, including Marilyn Sheppard. She was the likely source of the blood on the two watches, but others could not be ruled out.

It seemed suspicious that blood similar to Marilyn's was found on her husband's watch.

Cowan examined Sam's clothes under a microscope; she found no blood on his white socks or his brown loafers or his size-34 alligator belt. Dr. Gerber had theorized that Dr. Sam washed off the blood in the lake. Even so, blood was a difficult stain to remove.

Cowan found a few tiny spots of suspected blood on the back of Sam's trousers but no blood on the front except for a six-by-eight-inch stain around his left knee. The stain had a dark center, about three inches in diameter; the rest was uniformly lighter. It seemed as if Dr. Sam had knelt in blood when his pants were wet. The blood was type O, Marilyn's type.

Dr. Gerber had wanted blood from Marilyn's fetus typed right away, to test his theory that Sam exploded into a murderous rage because his wife was pregnant by another man. This blood work was sent to the more sophisticated lab at Maternity Hospital of nearby University Hospitals. A few days later, in a letter to Cowan, the lab's director said the fetal blood typing was unsuccessful.[5] As a result, the rumor that Sam was sterile and that Marilyn had a lover could not be proven. Nor could it be put to rest.

By the time Cowan got to the crime scene that Sunday afternoon, the murder case had become a national sensation, a lead story on three major wire services and page 1 news from New York to Los Angeles. Cowan's aunt in Columbus, Georgia, wrote to her this day, offering the impression that her friends who read the local newspaper "all were of the opinion that Dr. Sheppard is the guilty one."[6]

Usually, when Mary Cowan testified about her findings at trials, she described her role as that of a scientist, neutral and unbiased, a seeker of justice. In the Sheppard case, she also realized that evidence linking Sam Sheppard to the murder would help her boss, who had locked himself into a public position about Dr. Sam's guilt. Gerber's political reputation was at stake.

At the Sheppard crime scene, Cowan began her work on the blood trail on the screened porch, testing six quarter-inch-wide brown drops, one of them just under the screen door leading into the living room. The six tested positive for blood; she cut out a wood chip with one of the drops so she could make a definitive test for human blood later at the lab.

On the door between the living room and the porch, she tested brown crusts on the dead-bolt knob and face plate, and got negative results for blood. On steps from the kitchen to the cellar, Cowan found nine drops of blood, clearly a trail. How long they had stained the steps she could not say. She removed two of the blood spots and took them back to the trace-evidence lab. There she tested the blood from the stairs and porch with an antigen test, proving it was human. But she did not try to group the blood, as she tried to do with the blood on the two wristwatches.

Dr. Gerber knew this trail was not Dr. Sam's blood, having examined him on the morning of the murder and having found no wounds. As the veteran of hundreds of crime scenes, Gerber at least by intuition had to know that the blood on the basement steps had not come from a dripping murder weapon because the victim's blood would have congealed by then. The basement trail was unlikely to be Marilyn's blood. But if lab tests confirmed it wasn't Marilyn's blood, he then had to face an unsettling question: whose blood was it?

There could be an innocent explanation for Cowan's failure to try to type the blood trail. Days earlier, she had not been able to type the blood from the surfaces of Sam and Marilyn's watches. She later said under oath that she didn't type the trail of blood because there was not enough blood to run successful tests. Even so, other serologists had had success typing week-old quarter-inch blood spots. Cowan could have at least tried.

9

MEDDLING

THE KEYS TO SOLVING the Sheppard murder, Dr. Gerber repeatedly told reporters, were three: motive, murder weapon, and the missing T-shirt. Discover any one of them, and you could unlock this baffling case.

Gerber's challenge would have been much simpler if the public hadn't become feverishly obsessed with the case. "The whole town is talking about the Sheppard murder case and every rumor, every deduction by armchair detectives floats back to Bay Village. The gossip you heard on the bus, the 'sure thing' report you got from the fellow next to you in the restaurant, the 'absolute truth' you were told by a woman who got it from a friend (nobody appears to know these things firsthand), all get back to the principals of the case."[1]

The vast press and TV coverage gave people the sense that they commanded a detailed knowledge of the case. They hashed over the puzzling specifics with neighbors and friends. Why didn't Koke bark, if it was a burglar? Why didn't Sam turn on the hall light as he ran upstairs? What happened to the doctor's T-shirt? Why didn't Chip awaken at the sound of his mother's cry?

Applying common sense to what they read in the newspapers, people simply did not believe Sam's version of events. On the other hand, they were not presented with information that contradicted the prevailing wisdom of Gerber and the police. The public did not learn, for instance, that Chip, like his father, was a fiercely sound sleeper. (When their house caught fire, Chip had the good fortune to be staying overnight at the Houks'. He slept through the sirens and people tramping in and out of the mayor's home. "I don't know how he slept through all that noise," Esther Houk said.)[2]

Shortly after noon on July 14, Gerber received some exciting news. A few yards from the Sheppard property line, snagged on a prong of reinforcing wire in a crumbling concrete pier, was a torn white man's T-shirt. It matched the size and the brand of a T-shirt a detective had taken for comparison from Sam's dresser.[3]

Gerber hoped this was his needed breakthrough. He had the T-shirt delivered to Mary Cowan for a chemical analysis of its brownish stains. If her testing showed human blood, Dr. Sam could be arrested right away.

Gerber's clashes with the prosecutor's office and the Cleveland police underscored growing tensions among law enforcers in other big cities: the new school of forensic scientists versus the old-guard gumshoes. Gerber, a prime mover in the National Academy of Forensic Sciences, enjoyed a national reputation as an innovative medical-legal scientist. But he didn't always command such respect in his own backyard. Some Cleveland detectives could not get past his arrogance, his know-it-all approach to crime solving, based on being a doctor *and* a lawyer. In the middle of the Sheppard case, Capt. Dave Kerr, head of the homicide unit, said, "I'd rather have one good tip than a skyscraper filled with test tubes."[4] And county prosecutor Frank Cullitan publicly complained, again and again, that Dr. Sam should have been interrogated immediately.

Gerber returned Cullitan's fire, arguing that Dr. Sheppard "was quizzed immediately after the murder and gave virtually the same account he now is repeating." Besides, Cullitan was a meddler, Gerber said. "This is the first time in my 19 years as coroner that the prosecutors have ever taken part in the investigation of a crime before an indictment was returned."[5]

———

Because of the pressure or out of ignorance or sheer malice, Gerber repeatedly made misleading or untrue public statements that exonerated his office for not cracking the case.

In a long question-and-answer article on the front page of the *Press,* he made it plain that Dr. Sam was the murderer.

Q: Were any fingerprints found in the house?
A: Only a palm print on a downstairs desk.
Q: Normally there should be an abundance of fingerprints around a home, particularly after an evening of entertaining friends. How do you account for their complete absence?
A: We can only speculate.

Gerber's confirmation of a complete absence of prints in the house was flat wrong and went unchallenged. Perhaps he misunderstood Detective Grabowski's hurried processing of the murder scene on July 4. Grabowski attempted to lift prints in only a few places. He did not check countertops, doorknobs, chairs, the radio or television, the kitchen, basement, the stairway banister. In the murder room, he examined only one windowsill.

Grabowski did not find the Sheppard house wiped clean of all fingerprints; in fact, he found many prints on doorknobs, desk-drawer handles, on the broken trophies, and on the half dozen other places he shined his high-intensity lamp that morning. However, the fingerprints he found were layered and smudged, one set on top of another, as you would expect on a doorknob or windowsill. Technically, they were "unidentifiable," meaning the detective could not find impressions with seven or eight fingerprint loci needed to make a conclusive identification.

Hampering his work, Grabowski later said, were minute scratches on metal file boxes, the athletic trophies, and other hard-surfaced objects that survived the Sheppard house fire in 1953. It is likely that Marilyn, maid Elnora Helms, or even their window washer, Richard Eberling, had scrubbed the objects with a cleanser and pad to remove soot and smoke, which may explain the fine scratches.

But as the public and reporters mulled over the absence of fingerprints, they decided it didn't make sense. In late July Detective Grabowski's one-paragraph July 4 report would expand to a longer report that mentioned for the first time that he saw scratches on the trophies and the file boxes, which showed they had been wiped down.

Q: What was the time of death?
A: Between 3:10 A.M. and 4 A.M.

Dr. Adelson, his colleague, had reported Marilyn's death as occurring at about 4:30 A.M. Gerber preferred an earlier time and noted that Marilyn's Lady Hamilton watch had stopped at 3:17. But his statement was misleading. The watch indicated 3:17 when Mary Cowan tested it on July 6. But Sergeant Hubach said that when he spotted the watch on the desk in the den on July 4 it said 11:30, and "I am sure the watch was running at this time."[6]

Q: What was the murder weapon?
A: We don't know. It was some kind of blunt object. It could be a piece of wood, a medical or surgical instrument, any one of a hundred things around the house.

Q: What were Dr. Sheppard's injuries when he reported the crime?

A: Immediate examination of Dr. Sheppard by a physician called by Bay Village Police Chief John Eaton showed no visible evidence of a neck injury—only a black eye and puffed up face.

The public was quick to believe Dr. Sam's leather neck brace was a fraud, an accessory worn to gain sympathy or deflect suspicion.

Coroner Gerber was accurate—Sam displayed no "visible" injury. Why Gerber chose to reject or ignore Dr. Elkins's opinion a week earlier, that Sam had suffered nervous-system damage, is unknown. Perhaps Gerber took this adversarial position and cast the evidence in the most suspicious light because he truly believed Sheppard was guilty, and every ounce of pressure justified his conduct.

———

Back in the coroner's lab later that day, Mary Cowan began examining the T-shirt. It was made by Jockey, brand line Cooper, size large 42–44. The shirt was torn from the neck to the waist along the left seam. Sand was embedded in the fabric. She could see several orange stains.

She tested four stained pieces of the T-shirt for blood. Each result was negative. There was no blood on the T-shirt.[7]

Sam and his family were happy to learn Cowan's findings the next day from a front-page *Press* headline: FAIL TO FIND BLOOD ON T-SHIRT. They felt the lack of blood was exculpatory. It supported Sam's account.

But Dr. Gerber had started with the belief that Sam battered his wife and therefore his clothes had to be as spotted as a dalmatian. The shirt Mary Cowan tested had no blood, therefore it could not be Sam's shirt. Gerber simply dismissed the T-shirt as evidence. He told reporters he had "considerable doubt" whether the shirt was Dr. Sam's from the morning of the murder. Also, Detective Rossbach took back his remark that the recovered T-shirt was the same size and brand as Sam's; instead, he told reporters it was only *about* the same size.[8]

———

Meanwhile, detectives and reporters tried to unearth a motive for the murder, which meant hunting relentlessly for details about Sam's sexual relationship with Susan Hayes. In the 1950s, before liberalized divorce laws, it was difficult to get a divorce if one spouse refused. And for most of middle America, a divorce was a stigma. Police had seen cases in which a husband murdered his wife to be free to marry another woman.

A Cleveland *Plain Dealer* reporter found Susan Hayes first. She was living in suburban Downey, near Los Angeles, with a former Bay View nurse. Hayes was a free-spirited woman, smart enough to be an excellent laboratory technician, but the reporter painted her in traditional strokes, citing a high school yearbook entry that she was "ambitious and outspoken" in pursuit of her goal—"to be a happy housewife."

As a favor to the Cleveland police, the Los Angeles County district attorney agreed to question Hayes and called her into headquarters. Her high school classmates might not have recognized her. She was model-thin, her hair sleek and shorter. She had been spending her salary on tasteful clothes and travel.

Chief deputy district attorney George W. Kemp swore her in. Two detectives helped with the interrogation.

Did she know Dr. Samuel H. Sheppard?

Yes, she knew him and his wife. She used to swim and water-ski at parties at their home when she was engaged to Dr. Robert Stevenson, an intern at Bay View Hospital.

Did you see him in Los Angeles in March? How many times?

Susan asked to look at a calendar. Kemp handed her one, she studied it, then lied, "I saw him twice."

She gave them an innocent version of the gift watch from Sam, fudged on other questions, and said they had not corresponded, talked on the phone, or exchanged telegrams since the spring. She denied going out on a date with him.

Susan told them she did not believe Sam could be a killer. Perhaps someone had a grudge against his family. After all, his house had been destroyed by fire a year earlier.

Kemp at first seemed uncomfortable asking her if she'd had sex with Dr. Sam.

"Have you ever expressed love and affection toward him?"

"No," Hayes replied.

"Did he ever say he wanted his wife out of the way?"

"Never."

"Ever hear him threaten her?"

"Never."

"Ever hear him talk about divorcing her?"

"Never."

"Were you ever pregnant?"

"No sir."

"Have you ever had intercourse with him?"

Who could say exactly what went on during their intimate moments, other than Dr. Sam, who, according to news reports, was not talking to the police? She took a chance.

"No," she replied.

Susan Hayes had no idea how much trouble she was in.[9]

"Mr. Cleveland" loped on tiny feet through the cigar haze and typewriter clackety-clack of the *Press* newsroom, his bald pate shining and pocket handkerchief fluffed like a corsage. The Sheppard case had invigorated the competition among the city's three dailies. Louis Seltzer had never seen anything like this sensational story. Readers could not get enough details. Street sales were up, and for the moment his newspaper had the lead on the story.

But the day before, the *Cleveland News,* his afternoon competitor, had cleverly conjured a news story out of nothing. It was a stunt, an "open letter" to Cuyahoga County officials, asking them to seek assistance from Alan Moritz, M.D., chief pathologist at Western Reserve's medical school and a renowned forensic scientist. When prosecutor Cullitan invited Moritz to join the investigation, and he agreed, the *News* wrote about it, taking prominent credit for the news it manufactured.

To Seltzer, it looked as though coroner Gerber and the prosecutor's office were not going to solve the Sheppard murder case. Seltzer decided that the *Press* would have to do it. His paper would bring justice to the people.

Seltzer's working-class readership resented anyone who felt he was above the law. The *Press* played to them in particular by instinct; the follies of the well-to-do were standard fare. The rich made mistakes and ruined their lives just like the rest of the world. So when Sam Sheppard announced through his lawyers that he wasn't giving any more interviews, Seltzer crafted eleven questions and sent them to Bill Corrigan for his client's answers. If Sam refused to answer them, the *Press* could ask what he was hiding. If he answered them at all, then Seltzer's newspaper had an exclusive, maybe even some news.

Sam gave answers, which the *Press* ran on page 1, noting that the questions were "submitted to him by Louis B. Seltzer, editor of the *Press.*" Seltzer did not like Sam's comments, which were identical to what he had told police.[10] One question was, "Do you feel that the newspapers, particularly the *Press,* have treated you fairly?"

Sam answered no. "There has been a great deal of misinformation published."

Seltzer decided an incendiary editorial was in order. It ran under the headline "The Finger of Suspicion." In it, Seltzer described the "tragic mishandling of the Sheppard murder investigation." He blamed the "hostility of Bay Village officials to any 'outsiders' in the case. They rebuffed the usual assistance immediately offered by Cleveland police experts." (Actually, the Bay Village police called Cleveland homicide detectives within minutes of finding Marilyn's body.)

He also blamed the Sheppard family and Sam's lawyers for "the unusual protection set up around the husband of the victim." (Seltzer disliked defense lawyers, a favorite editorial target.)

A logical step, the editorial said, would be a meeting of the five law enforcement agencies investigating the case. "Let them select a leader, a single responsible boss for this particular case."

Gerber immediately called a meeting of officials from the five investigative agencies on the case: the coroner, county prosecutor, county sheriff, Cleveland police, and Bay Village police.

They met the next day, a Saturday, in the coroner's new amphitheater. Spread across the rows of chairs for the first half of the meeting were a dozen or more photographers and reporters. Using a blackboard and a slide projector, Gerber explained the evidence that had been collected so far. It was a grisly show: color slides of Marilyn Sheppard's battered fingers, face, forehead, and deeply gouged skull. He displayed the bloody nightclothes, Sam's pants, and the bloodstained pillow. But not the T-shirt recovered on the beach.

After the press was asked to leave, the authorities discussed Seltzer's directive. Gerber wanted to keep control and police chief Frank Story did not want to take over the case, saying it was too botched up. It would be like "being handed a scalpel and told to operate just as the patient is turning blue," Story complained.[11] But he didn't want to be under Gerber's command. As a result, no "single responsible boss" emerged.

————

As pressure increased on investigators, so too did their descriptions of the killer's cunning. The killer became "the most brilliant murderer in the annals of Greater Cleveland crime." Gerber said the way the murderer mopped up evidence made him someone of "very high intelligence, familiarity with the surroundings, and thorough knowledge of police investigative techniques." Sheriff Joseph Sweeney said that in his fifty-one years of police work he "never saw a better cover-up." They needed to give the public some reassuring explanation for law enforcement's failure.

Gerber said the killer "is still in Greater Cleveland, reading every newspaper account of the investigation, and chuckling over his shrewdness—if he remembers he committed the crime."[12]

10

DO IT NOW

DAY AND NIGHT, cars streamed past Sam and Marilyn's white Cape Cod house, slowing as passengers leaned from windows, gaping, snapping photographs, some parking and walking into the yard. In death, Marilyn had become a celebrity. Looking for the famous address, two women lost control of their car, smashed into a giant maple, and were killed.

Neighbors began to pull away from the Sheppards. At first they were embarrassed, then, after digesting the news coverage, suspicious. Up close, the Sheppard house looked "far different from the picture before the crime when the house was the center of gay activities for many members of the younger Bay Village professional set," the *Plain Dealer* noted.[1] Gerber considered it a big three-bedroom crime scene and ordered Bay Village police to secure it. When Betty or Dorothy Sheppard needed to get clothes for Chip, they had to arrange for a police escort. "It was the strangest case, that they held the whole house as evidence," said Fred Drenkhan, who later became Bay Village police chief.

Sam slept at his parents' home next to the Bay View Hospital. Chip lived at first with Richard and Dorothy, then with Steve and Betty Sheppard and their two daughters.

Despite being the chief suspect in the most famous murder since the Lindbergh-baby kidnapping, Sam remained available to reporters. He and his brothers had seen how easily in the past they could plant favorable stories in the newspapers about emergency-room heroics. Bill Corrigan, the newsman-turned-lawyer, perhaps thought he could counter some of the poisonous press by showing Sam to be a dedicated physician despite losing his pregnant wife. So Dr. Sam, in his neck brace and white lab coat, allowed a reporter and a photographer briefly to follow him at Bay View as he prepared a twenty-nine-year-old woman for an operation to drain a brain cyst.

"These people need me," he said. "I've got a job to do." He posed for a photographer as he checked her retinas. Then he took her left hand, injured at birth, and told her, "This left arm of mine is pretty weak and shaky too."

How long has she been in treatment? he was asked.

He tried but could not remember, and turned to ask a nurse. "I'm still fuzzy about things," he explained.[2]

Their efforts to shape the news did little to inoculate Sam against the virulent publicity in the press and on television news. As doctors, the Sheppards were used to being respected and adored and now were stunned by the community's anger toward them. They endured abusive telephone calls and threats. Steve Sheppard remembers getting up early to hose blood drops and animal entrails from his porch. Parents kept their children from playing with the Sheppard kids. Conversation stopped when they entered a store.

Sam borrowed a pistol from Steve and carried it loaded in a holster on his hip. This infuriated Cleveland police and editor Seltzer. To them, the osteopath seemed to be saying that he was above the law. Sam claimed he was afraid and needed protection.

Ethel Sheppard was crushed by the furor. She had led a sheltered life, and had devoted herself to her family. Unlike her younger daughters-in-law, she had no hobbies. She did not bowl, golf, or boat. She had supported her husband in his dream of building a regional osteopathic hospital, even helping in the hospital laundry room. Ethel Sheppard was an extremely private person who worried about what others thought of her and her family. Decades earlier, when her husband sunbathed nude on his second-floor porch in Cleveland Heights—getting his vitamin D, he called it—she tacked canvas around the railings in case a neighbor was trying to peep at him. Unlike her son Steve or her daughter-in-law Dorothy, Ethel Sheppard was not capable of staring down someone who intruded with a rude or nosy remark. After the murder, she withdrew even more. She could not fathom that people truly believed she possessed incriminating knowledge about the murder and actively was trying to hide it. "I resent the implication that this family knows something and is keeping it covered," she said. "This family has higher standards than that. If someone in this family did something wrong, the rest of us would certainly want to see justice done."[3]

———

Steve Sheppard took over as the leader in the fight to save Sam and the family business. He pressed the Cleveland detectives and Bay Village police to investigate other suspects. If friendships were shattered and enemies created, so be it. "We're fighting for our lives in this—not just for Sam but the whole hospital," Steve explained. "The M.D.s would relish to the chance to discredit us."[4] He pointed police to two men who had displayed romantic interest in Marilyn: Lester Hoversten and Spencer Houk.

Hoversten was an "an odd duck."[5] He seemed to be obsessed with Marilyn, even though she had spurned his aggressive passes and had made it clear she disliked him. Some of the Dayton doctors refused to operate with him, feeling that he was incompetent. Another doctor labeled him a schizophrenic. Six weeks before the murder, Hoversten wrote to Sam, depressed and complaining that he was being forced out of his surgical residency. His last day at work was June 30, 1954. The next day, he packed, drove to Bay Village, and moved into Sam and Marilyn's master bedroom.

Sam had helped his med-school buddy get an internship at Bay View in 1952, but Hoversten made a poor impression. One staff doctor said Hoversten's examinations of female patients were "not that of a doctor but more like that of an oversexed man." Many nurses refused to go into a room alone with him.[6] What puzzled Marilyn and others was why Sam stuck by him.

At first glance, Hoversten seemed like a good murder suspect. He was fortunate that he had a good alibi. At the time of Marilyn's murder, he was asleep forty miles away in Kent, Ohio, staying with Dr. Robert Stevenson, the former fiancé of Susan Hayes. After Hoversten's alibi checked out, Cleveland detectives continued to interview him, mostly for dirt about Dr. Sam's temperament and extracurricular love life.

Spencer Houk was a more promising murder suspect, and he knew it. By mid-July the Bay Village mayor resembled an advertisement for stress: he smoked incessantly, slept fitfully, and had lost weight. His dark, deep-set eyes looked like manholes at the bottom of a culvert. After Dr. Gerber told reporters that footprints found in the sand on the Sheppard beach indicated someone who walked more heavily on the right side, people eyed him with suspicion. Houk limped from a childhood injury to his knee.

Hell, the mayor wanted to say, he and Chief Eaton had walked the beach that morning, looking for clues. Of course his footprints were there.

Also making Houk anxious was his uncertainty about how much the police had learned about his relationship with Marilyn.

To anyone with the slightest ability to read faces and body language, Houk had developed an enormous crush on his pretty, athletic neighbor. He took every opportunity to see her. When she ordered special cuts of meat from his butcher shop, he personally delivered them to her kitchen. When

Marilyn was busy with a bowling-league match that ran late, Spen Houk met Chip at the school bus stop and brought him home. With Sam focused more on himself and his medical practice, Marilyn found it flattering to have Spen doting on her. She often started her morning errands by stopping at his butcher shop for a purchase, then joining him in the back office for a cup of coffee. Rumors took hold and made the rounds in the small town. Sam, of course, heard them and once asked Houk if he was sleeping with his wife. Houk said no, and Sam accepted the answer.

However, on a Tuesday near Valentine's Day in 1954, a deliveryman for Spang Bakery stopped at the Sheppard home, found the door ajar, and looked into the living room. He saw Marilyn and Spen, embracing. She was wearing a nightgown and looked upset.[7] The driver later told this to detectives.

By mid-July, Mayor Houk felt pressure from the Sheppards, particularly Steve. County prosecutors pressed him and his wife, Esther, to take a lie detector exam, and finally they consented.

They soon felt it was a mistake. Assistant county prosecutor Thomas Parrino treated them like criminals, Esther Houk said. Before her husband was hooked to the machine, the police examiner pointed at him and said ominously, "Murder will out." After the exam, Houk was told he showed deception on two questions: "What happened to the shirt?" and "Are you telling the truth to all answers?" Esther was furious. "Dr. Sam was right to refuse to take the test,"[8] she told reporters.

The Cleveland police and Dr. Gerber wanted Houk or police chief Eaton to issue a warrant for Sam's arrest. Someone in law enforcement leaked to reporters that Houk failed to pass two questions on the lie test, perhaps thinking that putting more pressure on Houk would get him to approve the warrant.

Dr. Steve was thrilled. He wanted the police to interrogate Houk even further.

But Sam still remained the only suspect as far as the county authorities were concerned. Houk asked for and took a second polygraph test within a week. After the second exam, Houk gave his test results to a *Plain Dealer* reporter, applying self-serving spin. The headlines:

MAYOR HOUK REVEALS HE VOLUNTARILY
TOOK LIE TEST IN BAY PROBE
Friend of Doctor Reported to Have Come
Through with Flying Colors

Then Houk disappeared for several days, and a doctor confined him to a hospital bed for "nervous exhaustion." To avoid reporters, Houk asked to be admitted under an assumed name.

———

By now, the Sheppard case was a lead international story, running in *Stars and Stripes* and British and French newspapers across the globe. In Cleveland, newsboys hawked the latest editions on streetcars and at busy intersections. The *Press* and the *News* published several editions throughout the afternoon, and circulation climbed. Editors recognized the murder as a once-in-a-career rarity, a near-perfect running story with all the elements of drama: attractive female victim, glamorous villain, mystery, sex, possible political corruption, talkative investigators. It struck an elemental chord with readers as the country moved from urban to suburban society. Could it happen to me in my safe home?

The biggest worry for the newspapers was running out of new developments to publish. The *Press* "was trying to keep the story alive on page one," explained Leah Jacoby, the paper's suburban-beat reporter, who knew Dr. Sam and Houk through her job. "We were checking out completely off-the-wall leads that came in. We were really reaching for straws."[9]

Without a legitimate news development, resourceful editors attempted stunts that might manufacture stories. The *Press*'s silver-haired city editor, Louis Clifford, was a master. One day in the newsroom he pulled Jacoby over and said that he had heard that Mayor Houk was the father of Marilyn's unborn child.

"Why don't you go out to city hall and ask him," he instructed.

Jacoby was not thrilled with the assignment. "He's going to throw me out."

"Well, maybe he'll say yes as he's throwing you out," Clifford replied.

Jacoby met with Houk (before his "nervous exhaustion") and asked him if he had impregnated Marilyn. Without a word, he took her arm and pulled her out of his office. She telephoned Clifford with the bad news.

"Okay, c'mon back in," he told her. "It probably wasn't a good idea."[10]

———

Marilyn Sheppard was misrepresented by the authorities and the press as the ideal suburban housewife. On July 20 Dr. Gerber told reporters that a thorough background investigation into Marilyn had shown her to be a "model wife and almost ideal mother." He described her as shy, reticent, with few close friends. "A thorough investigation has failed to turn up any unkind deed by Mrs. Sheppard. We can find no enemy who might have any reason to hate or even dislike her. She apparently had no romantic interest in anyone but her husband, who was her high school sweetheart."[11] His implication was that the murder was an inside job.

But Gerber's "model wife" assertion was undercut by an attractive twenty-three-year-old woman named Jessie Dill. Only four days earlier, she had given a detailed, credible account to Bay Village police and to assistant prosecutor John Mahon that Marilyn was having an affair.

About two weeks before the murder, Dill and her two young children were at the Fairport Harbor beach, east of Cleveland, where she struck up a conversation with a young woman wearing a navy blue skirt and a white blouse, her brown hair tucked under a scarf. The woman was sitting on a blanket and looked as if she had been crying.

Dill, a waitress, got around to talking about her ex-husband, who had cheated on her, forcing her to file for a divorce. "That's just the same kind of trouble that I am in," said the woman Dill believed to be Marilyn Sheppard. According to Dill, the woman said her trouble with her husband had started four years earlier, in California, when he had an affair with a young woman who worked with him. She wanted a divorce, but her in-laws talked her out of it because she and her husband had a young son.

It wasn't until a week after the murder that Jessie Dill read a newspaper and saw photos of Marilyn Sheppard, and recognized her as the lonely woman on the beach. Dill called Richard Sheppard, whose phone number was still listed, and spoke to his wife, who passed her name on to Sam. He handed the tip to Bay Village policeman Drenkhan. Soon Dill was being interrogated.

Her statements to the police and prosecutors contained details that had not been revealed in news stories and were still unknown to the detectives. For instance, Dill knew about Sam's carousing with Dolly. Dill said Marilyn "seemed to be talking about a second woman. She said there was this Dolly."

Dill stated, "I asked her if this woman was married," and Marilyn replied yes. "She said, it burns me up that one man ain't enough for her at a time, she has to go with somebody else's husband, too."

Dill said she told the woman she believed to be Marilyn to talk to her minister and to tell her husband how she felt. But the woman on the beach replied that she didn't think her husband "was so terrible now" because "nine months ago I started going around with a fellow. . . . He says that if I loved him I would leave my husband and marry him and he is just after me all the time that I should marry him and that's what's driving me crazy. I don't know whether to marry him or not."

What's the matter with us in Cuyahoga County? Who are we afraid of? Why do we have to kow-tow to a set of circumstances where a murder has been committed?

It is time that somebody smashed into this situation and tore aside this restraining curtain of shame, politeness and hypocrisy and went at the business of solving a murder—and quit this nonsense of artificial politeness that has not been extended to any other murder case in generations.

Seltzer's brutal display of editorial power was a business success. "Front-page editorials were to sell newspapers," said John Reese, at the time the city editor of the competing *Cleveland News.* "That was the only reason it was done. To sell papers. The whole murder was pushed. That was for circulation purposes. We were glad to have that circulation." The *News* and the *Press,* afternoon papers, were seeing their circulations slip because afternoon editions couldn't get out to the new far-flung suburbs by late afternoon. Television was beginning to siphon off advertising revenue. Fortunately, Reese said, "that murder went on and on and on."[14]

The editorial stance was a political success, too. It put tremendous pressure on the authorities and Gerber. Even so, the coroner said that he was not ready to conduct an inquest, Seltzer's idea of smashing into the situation. "I don't know when I'll have to get rough," the coroner told reporters, "but I'm prepared to do so the moment it will aid the investigation in any way."[15]

The next day, Seltzer ran another front-page editorial: "Why No Inquest, Do It Now, Dr. Gerber." It was a pointed personal attack. "What restrains him?" it asked. "Is the Sheppard murder case any different from the countless other murder mysteries where the coroner has turned to this traditional method of investigation?"

The coroner had not held "countless other" inquests; in fact, he had held only two in seventeen years. But Seltzer was running a righteous crusade that flattened the nuance of fact. Hours after the presses spun off hundreds of thousands of "Do It Now, Dr. Gerber," Dr. Gerber did so. The coroner announced that he would hold an inquest the next day.

11

INQUEST

THE NIGHT BEFORE the inquest, Bill Corrigan visited Sam at his parents' new home to prepare him for Dr. Gerber's questioning. The lawyer needed to talk to his client about Susan Hayes, and he asked for privacy. Sam took him to an upstairs room.

What if you are questioned about her? Corrigan asked.

Sam said he would admit the affair or take the Fifth. "All this means is that I was eating my cake and having it at home too," he explained. "It doesn't mean anything else. It might have given Marilyn grounds to kill me, but surely not me to kill her."[1]

Corrigan knew all that. He had to decide whether Sam should stick to what he had already told detectives on July 4, that he was not unfaithful to Marilyn. Corrigan told him his adultery was none of Gerber's business and would not be admissible if there was a criminal trial. According to Sam, he advised him to stick with his original account. "Deny any sexual relations."[2]

This was a risky position because Corrigan had not talked to Dr. Arthur Miller, Susan Hayes, or anyone else who already had given statements to the Los Angeles authorities. Perhaps Corrigan did not think Sam would get whipsawed by Gerber because the Cleveland newspapers only a few days earlier had described Hayes's relationship with Sam as "casual" and quoted a Los Angeles County district attorney who said he believed her denials about having sex with Sam.

Years later, Sam would complain that Corrigan had given him "the worst piece of legal advice a man could receive."

As an elected county coroner in Ohio, Dr. Gerber held broad powers to hold a public inquest into the cause of a mysterious death. He could subpoena

Dill told prosecutor Mahon: "Well, one thing that bothered her was, if she did get married now and this fellow couldn't seem to understand this, by the time she got her divorce she would only be married a month before she had a baby, that she was four months pregnant now, and . . . if I don't marry him, she says, then her husband would be supposed to support it."

Dill asked her new friend's name, but she would not give it. But during the hour or so they talked on the beach, she did say that her husband was a doctor, and she referred to her son as Chip, Dill told police.

The woman on the beach "didn't seem to be afraid of her husband. . . . But this other man, she says, he just got so mad and got so excited, and it was him was the one she was worried about, this boyfriend."[12]

Authorities were wary of Dill, since she had surfaced after first contacting the Sheppards. Police gave her a polygraph exam, and she passed. Now they had to decide how to use her information.[13]

———

The same day Gerber canonized Marilyn Sheppard, the *Cleveland Press*'s news coverage of the murder metastasized into something rarely seen outside the tabloids. Seltzer published a devastating editorial, not in the opinion pages but across the top of page 1 under the headline SOMEBODY IS GETTING AWAY WITH MURDER. It was accompanied by an editorial cartoon of a muscular, shadowy figure, carrying a club dripping blood and towering over a vista of suburban homes.

Seltzer, writing the editorial himself, called Marilyn's murder "the worst in local crime history." Striking populist sentiment, this unusual editorial took readers to a dark place in this manufacturing city's psyche—class resentment.

What's the matter with law enforcement authorities in Cuyahoga County? Have they lost their sense of reason? . . . If ever a murder case was studded with fumbling, halting, stupid, uncooperative bumbling-politeness to people whose place in this situation completely justified vigorous, searching, prompt and effective police work—the Sheppard case has them all.

In the background of this case are friendships, relationships, hired lawyers, a husband who ought to have been subjected instantly to the same third degree to which any other person under similar circumstances is subjected, and a whole string of special and bewildering extra-privileged courtesies that should never be extended by authorities investigating murder.

witnesses, arrest them, seize evidence—all in public view—unlike grand-jury proceedings, which were held by prosecutors in secret. The inquest, rarely practiced, was an extraordinary, powerful prosecutorial weapon.

Attacked by the *Press* and the public for his handling of the Sheppard case, Gerber saw the national reputation of his office begin to tarnish. He felt it was unfair; his technicians had done careful work with the evidence. When he retraced his steps, Gerber saw only one mistake he made: not ordering Sam's arrest for questioning on July 4. But his authority to act in Bay Village that day was unclear. And once his nemesis, Bill Corrigan, had become involved, the canny lawyer kept Gerber and the investigators off balance. Gerber knew that he had to give a command performance at the inquest in order to protect the image of the coroner's office, his life's work, and to silence the complainers among the Cleveland police brass.

Like most politicians, Gerber liked crowds, and he wanted one at the inquest. Clevelanders had a right to know what was going on, he insisted, which was why he held the inquest in a new Bay Village school, Normandy, which had a large, wood-floored gymnasium that could hold a couple of hundred folding chairs, long tables for witnesses, and the press corps.

This unusual forum was less an investigative tool than a psychological one. Gerber wanted Bay Village residents to confront what he felt was the real story of Dr. Sam Sheppard and his philandering. This might remove what remained of Dr. Sam's dwindling hometown support. Gerber and detectives had seen this divide-and-conquer strategy work within families as well, with straitlaced parents urging offspring to tell the truth and cooperate with police.

On the morning of Thursday, July 22, just as Gerber called his first witness, temperatures were climbing into the mid-eighties. Only forty spectators had taken chairs, and they were nearly outnumbered by reporters, photographers, and television crews. But by midafternoon the gymnasium was packed, steaming from body heat and hot television lights. Children waited in hallways, reading comic books and playing games, while their mothers, in sundresses and hats, sat gripped by real-life drama.

Into this crucible, Gerber summoned the Houks, the Aherns, and Bay Village police. They went over ground familiar to anyone who had read the newspapers. In the late afternoon Gerber summoned Dr. Sam from the witness room. When he got before the crowd, a detective stopped him and frisked him. Sam was humiliated and angry at Gerber's staging. He could have been searched a moment earlier in the witness room and brought in.

The public and those later watching TV news were getting their first long impression of Dr. Sam. He was tall and muscular, darkly tanned, with his shirt open at the throat, movie-star handsome even behind reflective sun-glasses and a thick neck brace. His voice didn't match his rugged looks. It was high-pitched, slightly whiny. He used abstract, high-flown words when plain talk would have sounded more sincere. When Gerber asked if he walked or ran to chase "the form" on the beach, Sam replied: "I can't give you a specific recollection. I proceeded as rapidly as I could." To viewers who didn't know that he'd been asked these questions time and again by the police, he must have seemed surprisingly cool.

Gerber pursued the line of questioning about whether Sam was sterile. "Is there any reason you can give that there were not more children?"

Marilyn had had a difficult delivery, Sam explained.

Gerber was intent on making Sam look foolish. He asked about the hospital Halloween party where Susan Hayes made a scene, flirting and smoking his pipe. "Did you have a gingham dress on?" Gerber asked.

Sam, furious, had to admit that he did. "And a monkey mask," he added, trying to show he wasn't in drag.

Gerber questioned him about seeing Susan Hayes in California, buying her a watch, and going to a wedding together. Sam dug himself into a hole. At one point, he even testified that Marilyn, before leaving him in Los Angeles and driving north to Big Sur, had suggested he look up Susan Hayes. Many women in the crowd found this preposterous.

Gerber recessed for the day. Some quick police work in Los Angeles had enabled him to set a trap for the next day.

The next morning, Gerber recalled Sam as a witness.

"Did you ever attend a strip-tease party in Lorain with Susan Hayes?" Dr. Gerber asked him.

"No."

"With two other people?"

"I have never been to a strip-tease party in this state."

Then Gerber asked a series of questions that news accounts said "electri-fied" the crowd.

"While you were at the Millers' house, did you sleep with Susan Hayes?"

Sam knew that Gerber knew.

It was a case of good fortune and police follow-up that enabled Gerber to put Dr. Sam on the spot. The head of the Los Angeles Police Intelligence Unit had received a tip from "an old-time newspaper reporter" that "Dr. Sheppard shacked up with the nurse Sue Hayes" at Dr. Arthur Miller's apartment and gave her a twelve-hundred-dollar ring. It was an old reporter's gambit: dish the tip, let cops do the legwork, and, if it panned out, hope you'd be rewarded with an exclusive.

Furthermore, someone had sent the L.A. police an anonymous letter claiming that a Dr. Dorothy Marsh had information that could put Sam Sheppard "in the electric chair." Just before the inquest, Los Angeles detectives had interviewed Marsh. She knew all the Sheppard doctors and had been Marilyn and Chip's family doctor while Sam was in medical school. She had just returned from a national convention of osteopaths in Toronto, where Marilyn's murder dominated the small talk. Marsh defended Sam. "We are convinced that Sam Sheppard could not have done that unless he was insane and we have never seen any signs of insanity," she told the police. "As near as we could figure it, Sam still loved Marilyn, but he was a mixed-up kid." She did admit being at the poker party where Sam had paraded Susan Hayes, and confirmed that the couple had stayed for several nights in the Millers' two-bedroom apartment. "Sam wanted to be a playboy," Marsh said at one point.

The Los Angeles police relayed this crucial intelligence to Cleveland authorities. It gave Gerber all the ammunition he needed.

"Did you and Sue Hayes sleep in the same bed?" Gerber asked.

Sam was hard to read behind the dark glasses. "No."

"At any time?"

"Absolutely not."

"Did you have sexual relations with Susan Hayes at that time?"

"No."

Gerber persisted: "Not during the time you were in California?"

"Not at any time."

"Not during the time you were staying at the Millers'?"

"No."

The gymnasium buzzed with excitement, and reporters couldn't wait to leave.

Gerber persisted. "You did not sleep in the same bed with Susan Hayes?"

"No, we did not."

"Four nights in a row?"

"No."[3]

Gerber was pleased that he had locked Dr. Sam into a lie. He adjourned for lunch, with Sam's foolish denials hanging in the air like a shroud. Gerber knew he had him.

Bill Corrigan was distraught throughout the proceedings. Gerber would not allow him to advise Sam during the inquest. He could only sit in the crowd and watch. Corrigan had hired a court reporter to make a transcript of the hearing. When the crowd hooted and laughed at someone's testimony, Corrigan told the court reporter to note it in the record. He was protecting his client's rights for an appeal.

Gerber didn't like this tactic and told Corrigan to keep his mouth shut or he would have to leave. Gerber also told the court reporter to stop listening to Corrigan.

"Are you working for me or what?" Corrigan demanded of the court reporter.

Gerber told Corrigan to shut up.

"I'll add to the record if I feel like it," Corrigan said. At Corrigan's next instruction, Gerber ordered him to be removed. As detectives pulled him out by his arms into the corridor, the crowd roared in approval.

Corrigan, his face florid, said he could not believe the mood of the inquisition. "This is a disgraceful exhibition by American women," he shouted.[4]

It did not seem remarkable to reporters and to the public that Gerber's publicly staged investigation focused on Sam Sheppard's sex life rather than on the forensic aspects of an unsolved murder. They were used to targets being convicted through public opinion. In the early 1950s Senator Joe McCarthy's search for Communists in government sparked little widespread public outcry and helped to legitimize assaults on civil liberties. Seltzer's accusations and Gerber's methods were a Cleveland version of what was unfolding on Capitol Hill. If you did not cooperate with authorities, it was because you had something to hide. You hired a lawyer because you were guilty—of something—and needed protection. (And if you disagreed with such sentiment, you kept your mouth shut. The day after Marilyn's murder, *Life* magazine commented that Americans, even if they disagreed with McCarthy-like attacks on nonconformists, were reluctant to speak out, fearing social censure of the majority.) Shouting "civil liberties" was something a Communist might try. Gerber and Seltzer's domestic rendition of this cold war tune struck a resounding chord in Cleveland, with its large population of immigrants from Poland, Hungary, Yugoslavia, and other countries controlled by the Soviet Union.

At the inquest that afternoon, Gerber interrogated the Sheppard brothers and their wives. Some spectators jeered as Steve, the most obstreperous of the family, took the witness chair. He was upset with Sam for risking his marriage and now his freedom for momentary pleasure. What was he thinking, Steve wondered to himself, shacking up in front of their colleagues with a lover?

Steve held his sarcasm in check as Gerber asked what he saw and did on the day of the murder. The coroner pried out nothing new and failed to rile him. At the end of his testimony, Steve turned and addressed the crowd, some of them his patients. "Most of you people who are here are here not just as morbid curiosity seekers but as members of the community you are interested in. I know that you are shocked. Certainly this was a hideous crime. But this could happen to you. And you also could be completely innocent. And you also could be subjected to the hours and hours of interrogation. And you too could be brought into a gymnasium and your entire family subjected, possibly necessarily and possibly not, to this type of thing. . . .

"But I know Dr. Sam is innocent. Dr. Sam knows he is innocent. And try—it won't be too easy—but try to, every one of you, in your hearts put yourself in the position of this man and this family for a minute. This is all I ask."

The crowd wasn't buying it. The spectators seemed to view the unusual legal proceeding as more of a sporting event, with the coroner as the home team's star quarterback. At the end of the day's testimony, women pushed their way to Gerber and hugged the tiny man and tried to kiss him. He was a national celebrity now, probably the most widely recognized county official in the country.

———

Soon Dr. Gerber issued a new "coroner's verdict," in which he took the unusual step of actually naming the murderer. "The injuries that caused this death," he wrote, "were inflicted by her husband." Gerber cited three points to support his medical verdict: "It is impossible to believe the explanation" Dr. Sheppard gave of the crime; that "at no time" did he cooperate fully with police; and that he "called in two lawyers sometime on July 4th and 5th, 1954."

Besides actually naming a suspect, what made Gerber's coroner's verdict so remarkable was that it did not cite any forensic evidence tying Sam Sheppard to the crime.

———

By now, most people in Cleveland were convinced that Dr. Sam was getting away with murder and that his brothers had hidden evidence and obstructed justice. In Bay Village, residents felt stained. Sam's friends and coworkers, who two weeks earlier had loudly defended him, now admitted to others that the newspapers were painting a convincing case. As hard as it was to believe, Sam probably did kill Marilyn.

The Reverend Alfred C. Kreke, pastor of the Bay Methodist Church and a leader in the community, was stunned by the rising public outrage against Dr. Sam. Two years earlier he had baptized Marilyn, bringing her into the Sheppard family's Methodist ethos. A month earlier she and Sam confided to him that they were expecting a child. Kreke was a good litmus test of Cleveland's anti-Sheppard hysteria. He and his family had gone on a week's vacation to Canada on July 16. For more than a week, they had not read a newspaper or listened to the radio, not even to the Cleveland Indians, perched in first place, on the way to an American League pennant. Kreke had left a community in sorrow and shock, with a few unfounded rumors. He returned in the middle of Gerber's inquest and was stunned. The Normandy school audience, some of whom were members of his congregation, displayed the baseness of a medieval inquisition. "The morbid, sadistic attitude of the audience reminded one of the blood-letting arenas of the Nero days,"[5] he said. On Sunday he told his congregation about returning from vacation "refreshed in body and soul," only to find "our community the center of an open inquest with a miniature McCarthy at the head and what seemed from all appearances to be a carefully planned persecution of not only one individual but the defamation of an honored family name, a deliberate attempt by publicity seekers and little professional men, to undermine in the eyes of the public, the qualifications and efficiency of our hospital staff and personnel."[6]

He also scorched the press. "With an eye for personal gain and profit, it seemed to be seeking each day a new angle, a new picture, to add in a feeble way some semblance of newness to the old story which had been hashed and rehashed for almost a month." The minister and the congregation had no way of knowing that this was just the beginning.

12

FOLLOWING A TRAIL

ALL ACROSS THE COUNTRY, people were intoxicated by the Sheppard murder mystery. A rich, handsome doctor was either a monstrous villain or the victim of the profoundest injustice. He became "Dr. Sam," a celebrity, no last name needed, even among children. Across Cleveland, kids played make-believe versions of "the Sheppard Case." For example, in one case some boys created an "electric chair"—a kitchen chair tied to a rope. The boy playing Dr. Sam sat in the chair. When found guilty by "the coroner," he was executed by a jerk of the rope, tipping the chair and sending him to the ground. He lay as still as a corpse and was wrapped in a sheet. "It's something like the McCarthy hearings," one boy told Hearst news correspondent James Crossley. "And he"—referring to the boy playing coroner—"is McCarthy."

Adults were just as obsessed. Instead of talking about the weather or the American League's leading Cleveland Indians, people asked, "Do you think Dr. Sam did it?" The farther from Cleveland and its gale-force gossip, the less likely people were to believe Sam Sheppard was the killer. Crossley was struck by the city's frantic rumormongering. "Some of it is honest opinion based on utter ignorance," he wrote. "But unfortunately, a lot of it is nasty, malicious slander against all the figures involved and many who aren't. . . . The way most people not only solve the mystery, but have Dr. Sheppard tried, convicted, electrocuted and buried, provides a sad commentary on the average American's knowledge" of basic civil rights.

The inquest put Sam's sworn denials of extramarital affairs into the public arena. His sex life was now fair game for prosecutors' leaks and reporters' stories. His reputation was so tarred that assistant county prosecutor John

Mahon probably felt a few more brush strokes would hardly matter. He revealed to reporters that Sam was dating one of his married patients, Julee Lossman, wife of the car dealer who sold Sam a Jaguar and an MG. Sam had set her leg and performed plastic surgery on her face after she suffered a terrible car crash. Afterward, the two couples became friends and went boating together and to amateur auto races. Once at Put-in-Bay on Lake Erie's South Bass Island, Sam and Julee left on a walk that lasted an hour. "The dealer admitted he didn't like that," Mahon told reporters, "and slapped his wife when they got back."

Reporters reached Julee Lossman, and she spilled out her life story. "I owed my life and any of my looks that I have left to him. He did such wonderful work on me as a doctor." She had become infatuated with him, she said, and was "the aggressor." "I must have lost my head. I cannot explain my actions."[1]

Cleveland mayor Anthony Celebrezze joined the pile-on. He told reporters, for the record, that another West Coast woman, not Susan Hayes, would provide a big break in the murder investigation. His inflammatory remarks made the front page of the *Press*. The woman never surfaced or testified.

At the same time, daily newspapers never had a story quite as sexy as the Sheppard case. The sex lives of celebrities were exposed in scandal sheets such as *Confidential* but not in the mainstream press. (It took another three decades before reporters routinely chased down the paramours of a philandering public figure.)[2] After the inquest Seltzer and his editors ran a devastating story that would have been unthinkable earlier:

LINK 5 WOMEN TO DR. SAM
Patient Tells About Dates

The account was built on anonymous sources. Two of the five women, "Margo" and "Dottie," were mentioned by first name only because police had not learned their surnames. Accompanying the article was a flattering photograph of Julee Lossman in high heels and a smart dress, poised on the running board of a vintage convertible.

Meanwhile, the city of Bay Village solved an embarrassing political problem by turning over formal control of the case to the Cleveland Police Department. First, the Bay Village City Council had to agree to pay Cleveland at least five thousand dollars for doing the investigative work. Chief Story was not happy about taking over the case. He said it was botched and might never be solved. Even so, on his first official day in charge, a dozen Cleveland detectives canvassed Bay Village neighbors, chased down tips, and reworked the crime scene. The lead detective from the Scientific Investigation Unit was Henry Dombrowski, a college graduate who had majored in chemistry. He and his team were determined to track every speck of blood and fiber, hoping to find physical evidence that would lead to an immediate arrest.

Unfortunately, the original crime scene had been contaminated. Detectives, reporters, children, and neighbors had tramped through the house that sunny Sunday morning. An unfiltered cigarette butt in an upstairs toilet was never preserved. Days after the slaying, detectives found that chip of red enamel paint and a tiny piece of red leather in Marilyn's bedroom, but this trace evidence was unreliable because it might have been deposited after the crime.

Dombrowski and the two other Scientific Investigation Unit detectives started on the first floor of the Sheppards' old Cape Cod cottage and worked up. When they saw a dark brown spot that could possibly be dried blood, they sprayed it with the reagent benzidine, which turned blue-green on contact with blood. On the stairway between the first and second floor they discovered blood on five of ten steps and on eight of eleven risers. At the landing, they found two blood drops on a throw rug.

At the entry to Chip's bedroom detectives found five blood drops near the threshold. On the stairs from the kitchen down to the basement, they detected blood spots on five of eight steps. In Sam's study, drops showed up on the floor and on a red leather chair cushion.

The living room carpet was dark red, hiding any dried blood spots. Dombrowski knew they would have to return and use luminol, an extremely sensitive solution that reacted with blood to throw off a glow under ultraviolet light.

Meanwhile, Dombrowski noticed a freshly made pry mark on a wood cellar door in the basement that led to a crawl space. A flat blade about half an inch wide, perhaps the tip of a large screwdriver, had made the gouge. He made a cast of the impression and noted it in his report.

The detectives also found "a small portion of blood, skin and hair" on the right side of the doorjamb in the murder bedroom. It was sent back to the Scientific Investigation Unit for analysis.[3] Usually, the coroner's laboratory analyzed trace evidence; it was equipped to perform the most sensitive and advanced forensic tests. But Mary Cowan, trace-evidence chief, never had the chance to test this bit of blood, skin, and hair. Why not?

The Cleveland Police Department, on its first official day in charge, was still at odds with Dr. Gerber and probably wanted to take full credit if its detectives solved the case quickly. Also, the police knew that Sam did not have a cut or scrape on the day of the murder. Believing Sam to be the only suspect, they probably felt this new evidence was likely blood, skin, and hair stuck to the unknown murder weapon, and therefore might only match Marilyn, as expected, and not advance the probe. Even so, police should have tested the evidence to determine blood type and released the results. It might have matched someone other than Marilyn.

Outside the Sheppard home that night, reporters and neighbors knew something was afoot from the purplish light glowing from the windows. The reporters waited for Dombrowski. Most of what they found, he said, "was just repetition." Later, the chief of detectives, James McArthur, made a more positive assessment; the scientific tests established that the killer washed off a trail of blood, missing a few specks. "Our conclusion is that the blood dripped from the murder weapon," McArthur announced.[4]

While Dombrowski investigated inside the Sheppard house, homicide detectives worked the neighborhood and beyond, chasing down every tip and rumor, however far-fetched. Their detailed homicide reports clearly show that their strategy was to put pressure on the extended Sheppard family, its reputation, and its business fortunes, as a way to convince Sam to cooperate.

Detectives chased rumors that the Sheppard doctors performed abortions at Bay View Hospital. A dietitian there told a homicide detective that she knew that doctors performed uterine scrapes—dilation and curettage, or "D & Cs." "She then further added without prompting that she had discussed this with the young Dr. Richard and he had said something about having to have two doctors present to state that the operation was needed for the women."[5]

They also hoped to show that Dr. Richard A., the father, had had an affair with a hospital employee. The woman was questioned and denied it. She said that the rumor stemmed from a hospital Halloween party in 1950, at which she worked serving drinks. Later in the evening Dr. Sheppard grabbed her and danced one dance with her. The detective reported back: "A photograph was taken of this incident and everyone around the hospital got a kick out of it that he would dance with her."[6]

Police fingerprint technicians, trying to identify a palm print from the living room desk, fingerprinted several Bay View doctors, the Houks, the Sheppards' housekeeper and baby-sitter, and even Otto Graham. (As a courtesy, the police made no official report that the NFL star had been fingerprinted in a murder case.)[7] It turned out that the palm print was made by Chip Sheppard.

Detectives also sought personal details from the Sheppards' cleaning woman, their baby-sitter, and their window washer, Dick Eberling. He told them that he had met Sam only once, had known Marilyn, who was friendly to him, but that he "had no information about their personal life."[8]

Meanwhile, Schottke and Parrino traveled to California to locate Sam's lovers. It was an easy task. On July 24 they listened to a detailed account of Sam and Susan's tryst from Dr. Arthur F. Miller and his wife. She had been furious with Sam for having brought Susan to the apartment. Probably more infuriating to Mrs. Miller, Sam had simply assumed that she would be discreet rather than hurt Marilyn, which made her into an unwilling coconspirator. Dr. Miller had pulled Sam aside at one point and told him that he "should be psychoanalyzed" for displaying Susan to them.

Schottke and Parrino were pleased. Sam's own friends contradicted what he had said under oath at the coroner's inquest. Now, at the very least, prosecutors could prove that he was a liar, tainting the rest of his denials. But first they had to get Susan Hayes to repudiate her earlier, whitewashed account of her relationship with Sam.

When the detectives confronted her, accused her of lying, and threatened perjury charges, the twenty-four-year-old woman folded. Yes, she had seen Dr. Sheppard several times and they had, in fact, slept together.

The police were jubilant.

13

ARREST

ON JULY 27 at about 7 P.M. approximately a hundred people thronged a gate at the Cleveland Hopkins Airport. It was a beautiful summer evening, and they were awaiting a commercial flight from Los Angeles. The afternoon *Press* had provided the flight number and arrival time in an article under the vast front-page headline GIRL ADMITS AFFAIR, FLIES HERE TO TESTIFY.

As Susan Hayes descended the stairs and walked onto the tarmac, a scrum of a dozen or so paparazzi rushed toward her.

Cleveland police and detectives muscled her past the pack and shoved her into a black unmarked police car. One photographer tried to pull open a back door for an unobstructed shot. A detective knocked his hand away and slammed the door, nearly crushing Hayes's foot. The police car raced out of the airport and sped downtown at seventy-five miles an hour, with the press pack in quick pursuit.

Susan Hayes was treated like a visiting movie star. "A la Hepburn, the attractive brunette wore no makeup, emphasizing her deeply suntanned face and startlingly dark spray of freckles across her nose," said the *Cleveland News*. "Long-legged and slender, she is about five feet five inches and weighs about 112 pounds." No one was allowed to interview her, so reporters had to panhandle Schottke or Parrino for shreds of information: she had knitted, eaten a chicken dinner, and read Robert Penn Warren's *Short Story Masterpieces* during the long flight. Photo editors selected the most flattering shots of her. She was the Other Woman, and had to appear tempting enough to incite a man to murder. One reporter, unable to restrain himself, described her, inaccurately, as "a former model."[1]

Police stashed her at the Carter Hotel with a policewoman who kept her company while chasing off photographers. Later, at police headquarters on East Twenty-first Street, Hayes answered dozens of questions from Chief Story, Parrino, and Schottke. Outside on the sidewalk teenage girls stood on the low wrought-iron fence that surrounded the station house, trying to catch sight of her through the high first-floor windows.

Hayes made revelations that the prosecutors felt they could use at trial: Sam had given her a suede jacket for Christmas and a signet ring. A month later, he had bought her clothes. She and Sam had sex about once every two weeks, usually on the way to her parents' tiny apartment after she had gone with him on a night emergency call to perform blood typing. They copulated in his car, in the interns' apartment, and in Los Angeles.

Afterward, one of Hayes's interrogators gave details of her account to the press pack, which portrayed her sympathetically.

DOCTOR LIES, SUSAN CHARGES;
TELLS OF GIFTS, MARRIAGE TALK
Love Secrets Bared,
Sue Glad It's Over

Like Julee Lossman, Susan Hayes had found herself intoxicated by a handsome doctor from a respected family who not only said he loved her but who praised her professional work. Even more confusing to her was Sam's insistence that he would like to marry her but they both "knew it was impossible," she told the Cleveland police.

She and Sam exchanged a few letters after their Los Angeles interlude. She said he signed his letters "with love," but had offered no plans for the future. In her fourth or fifth letter to him, she broke it off. "I told him I couldn't see any need for further correspondence," she told the police.[2]

Sam was not insisting on marriage and neither was she, but this was one fact that was not leaked to the press. Prosecutor Parrino later would argue that Sam killed Marilyn so that he could run off with Susan Hayes. It was a motive that a jury might buy, but anyone who knew the footloose Dr. Sam would not be persuaded. He wanted sex but certainly not commitment.

———

Police chief Frank Story's worst fear was being realized. His department had thrown a dozen detectives at the crime, and he received copies of all the daily reports, sometimes as many as twenty-two single-spaced pages a day. So far they had failed to build a strong case. The killer's trail was cold. Police had no confession from the prime suspect. The crime scene had been contaminated. Newly gathered evidence was contradictory. The physical evidence—fibers, particles, hair, blood—refused to cohere into a single elegant theory. The Susan Hayes motive was a stretch. Every day he was hounded by questions from the local and national press. Frustrated, Story was surprisingly blunt with reporters: "Our feeling is that Sam Sheppard killed his wife even though we can't prove it. If we had a single shred of evidence against him, I'd send the janitor out to make the arrest."[3]

It was a startling admission: Not a single shred of evidence.

———

Story's position angered Louis Seltzer. He wanted Dr. Sam arrested, and he wanted the *Press* to be able to take credit for it. Anything less would be a public embarrassment for the newspaper and for him.

The very week that Seltzer used his newspaper to repeatedly batter Sam Sheppard, Bay Village officials, and the murder investigation, he happened to back away from an important, hard-hitting series on Senator Joe McCarthy that came from the Scripps Howard Washington bureau. Seltzer's judgment angered Scripps Howard president Roy Howard. Seltzer chopped the five-part anti-McCarthy series to three parts and gave it "lackadaisical colorless inside play," Roy Howard wrote to his son, Jack, who took over the chain a few years later. "I was interested and not a bit surprised to hear from you that our great Ohio liberal LBS (Louis B. Seltzer) didn't have the guts to run the McCarthy series in heavily Catholic Cleveland," Jack Howard wrote back. "After all the hogwash in *Time,* etc. . . . I wonder how all his boys on *Time* feel about it?"[4]

In the newspaper industry there is nothing so unsatisfying as a crusade that ends in a whimper. In the last week of July, Seltzer stoked the city's anti-Sheppard hysteria to a white heat with a series of page 1 editorials and cartoons. He felt the city's civic institutions had failed; therefore, the press had a duty to enforce what it knew was justice. In other words, arrest Dr. Sam.

Under the page 1 editorial "Why Don't Police Quiz No. 1 Suspect," the *Press* wrote: "You can bet your last dollar the Sheppard murder would have been cleaned up long ago if it had involved 'average people.' They'd have hauled all the suspects to Police Headquarters. They'd have grilled them in the accepted, straight out way of doing police business." Corrigan "has made monkeys of the police," and Dr. Sam was "left free to do whatever he pleases as he pleases. . . . The whole mess is making this community a national laughing stock."

Despite Seltzer's pressure, Chief Story still would not budge. "Why don't you shake him down?" a reporter asked. "I don't think you could shake that guy down in twenty-four minutes or twenty-four hours," Story replied.

On July 30 Seltzer wrote a front-page editorial that even by his standards was audacious. "Why Isn't Sam Sheppard in Jail?" it read, then in later editions: "Quit Stalling and Bring Him In!"

"Everybody's agreed that Sam Sheppard is the most unusual murder suspect ever seen around these parts. Except for some superficial questioning during Coroner Gerber's inquest, he has been scot-free of any official grilling into the circumstances of his wife's murder." This, of course, ignored hours of police interrogation.

Lest the authorities miss his ardor, Seltzer employed uppercase letters. He wrote, in part:

THIS IS MURDER. THIS IS NO PARLOR GAME. THIS IS NOT A TIME TO PERMIT ANYBODY—NO MATTER WHO HE IS—TO OUTWIT, STALL, MAKE OR IMPROVISE DEVICES TO KEEP AWAY FROM THE POLICE OR FROM THE QUESTIONING ANY-BODY IN HIS RIGHT MIND KNOWS A MURDER SUSPECT SHOULD BE SUBJECTED TO—AT A POLICE STATION.

When Mr. Cleveland said to hold a meeting of the investigating agencies, Dr. Gerber did so. When Seltzer demanded an inquest, the coroner held one. When the *Press*'s editor demanded an arrest, he expected to get one.

On the afternoon of the "Bring Him In" editorial, everybody but Dr. Sam and his family seemed to know that he was going to be arrested. By early evening, reporters had staked out Steve Sheppard's home in Rocky River. Steve told them, "You're wasting your time. There isn't going to be an arrest tonight."

By nine that night, four cars of reporters and photographers had lined up outside Steve's house and had staked out his parents' home as well. Steve, always wanting to one-up the reporters, hatched a plan. The garage door went up, and Steve backed out the station wagon, with his wife and Sam as passengers. They were going to the private Cleveland Yacht Club for a sail. Of course, the reporters and photographers pursued them by car. Steve started driving faster, timing traffic lights, then flat-out raced. It was "a chase at breathtaking speeds, sharply turned corners and side-street maneuvering as I followed the car," one photographer recalled.

The Sheppards drove into the gated yacht club. Moments later photographer Earl Rauschkolb flashed his press card, and a security guard let him in. He parked next to Dr. Steve's car and got out with his bulky cameras.

"This is private property," Steve said sharply. "You can't take pictures of us." Sam had walked to the pier, smoking his pipe, his back to the camera. Then he said, "The hell with it." He asked Steve to take him to their parents' home.

"C'mon, Sam," said Steve's wife. She led him to the car as Steve warned again, "No pictures." Rauschkolb fired away as Sam ducked under the dashboard. Betty drove him to his parents' home.

Rumors of an arrest had spread on the radio, and a mob had gathered along the property lines and sidewalk of Sam's parents' home. Bolder onlookers walked over flower beds and peered in windows. Reporters stopped any cars slowing down as they passed and shouted, "Is Sam in this car?"

Ethel Sheppard was scared; reporters and curiosity seekers had clambered up onto the porch. It was dark, and photographers used flashes to shoot pictures through the windows, afraid this might be their only shot at Dr. Sam. His father came out on the porch and told the mob to leave. He drew only laughs.

The Bay Village police drove up at about 10:30 P.M. Fred Drenkhan got out. People shouted, "Go get him!" Dr. Richard Sheppard asked the patrolman to at least clear his porch of photographers. Drenkhan came inside instead, handed an arrest warrant to his friend, said he was sorry, handcuffed Dr. Sam, and walked him out the front door. The crowd cheered lustily. The press photographers had their shot—Dr. Sam in cuffs—and their cameras popped and flashed like lightning. The crowd turned ugly. "Murderer! Murderer!"

Bay Village police drove him to the city hall, where people again mobbed the tiny building. Police blocked the entrance. Photographers tried to climb in through the windows. After a hearing before the law director, Richard Weygandt, who had signed the warrant, police took Sam to the Cuyahoga County Jail in downtown Cleveland. "I didn't think it could happen in this country," Sam said on his way out.

Meanwhile, lawyers Corrigan and Petersilge were in the dark about the arrest. Sam's parents had called them right away, but by the time they got to Bay Village's city hall, it was locked. No one inside would answer their poundings on the door. They hustled downtown to the county jail and learned that Sam was inside. But they were not allowed in to see him. Corrigan, red-faced, shouted to the reporters, "Why criticize Russia?"

14

THIRD DEGREE

WITH SAM LOCKED IN JAIL, Cleveland homicide detectives crafted an interrogation plan they hoped would work. Their first step was not what Louis Seltzer had demanded, immediately giving Sam the "third degree." Instead police held him in isolation overnight.[1]

Over the past week, the detectives and Gerber had received tips claiming that Dr. Sam was a drug addict. The information was difficult for them to evaluate. In the 1950s, before such antidrug movies as *Reefer Madness* became camp entertainment, even doctors and cops believed that addicts, in the grips of their high, could become violent maniacs. If Dr. Sam was a drug addict, perhaps that fact could explain the gore of the crime. Some detectives, perhaps without realizing why, knew that the Sheppard murder scene did not resemble a typical domestic homicide. Marilyn was killed by a lengthy, obsessive, medium-impact battering of her skull and face, as if the killer was determined to make her appear ugly. Could he have been drug-crazed? (In fact, four days earlier, a Federal Narcotics Unit agent, at Gerber's request, interviewed the Sheppard doctors and checked their narcotics registry, looking for missing morphine or opiates. Among them, the three physicians possessed two thirty-milligram bottles of liquid Demerol and fewer than a dozen narcotic tablets. Each of the three brothers had technical violations—an old address on a prescription pad, for instance—but nothing suggested that Dr. Sam was a junkie.)

Detectives hoped that Sam, after spending a night in jail, would be suffering from withdrawal and would want to confess so that he could return to a regular cell, have a visit from one of his brothers, and get a fix.

They planned to grill him in two-man teams for as long as they could. He would demand that his lawyer be present, but the police did not have to allow it. They could hold him for up to seventy-two hours. Then a prosecutor would have to charge him at a hearing before a judge or release him.

On July 31, at 5:30 A.M., Sam was roused with the others prisoners for breakfast. He slurped down soggy cornflakes and a cup of coffee and went back to sleep.

Meanwhile, reporters camped out at the police station demanded to know why detectives hadn't started grilling the suspect the night before. Chief Story took a dig at Gerber with his answer; Sheppard seemed to be sedated at the coroner's inquest and "not as quick on the trigger as usual." Police wanted to wait until any drugs had worn off. (Gerber shot back that Sheppard was not under the influence of drugs at his inquest.) "He will now be questioned in the same manner we would interrogate any other chief suspect in a murder case," Story said. "He cannot refuse to talk to us because his attorney says so."[2]

Chief Story talked to Sam that morning as the jail physician looked him over. Then, at 11 A.M., jailers brought Sam to an interrogation room, alone. Over the past month he had spent thirty-seven hours talking to detectives from Cleveland, Bay Village, and the county sheriff's office. This morning was the first time he was completely under Cleveland police control.

Detectives Schottke and Gareau went at him first. They had been on the case since July 4 and were the first to accuse him of murder. Sam and Corrigan had dodged and thwarted them for weeks. Schottke and Gareau relished this moment. The next few hours were crucial; they knew it presented their best opportunity to get him to confess. Sam did not show signs of drug withdrawal, which had to disappoint them. They started off with tame questions. Abruptly, they pushed gory color photographs at him, close-ups of Marilyn's bloody face, with deep pie-shaped gashes across her forehead.

Dr. Sam, who opened skulls for a living and dispassionately studied viscera, turned his head. It was his wife.

Look at her! Schottke demanded. Why did you do this?

Sam denied it.

They slapped down the pathologist's color photographs of Marilyn after the autopsy. The top of her head was shaved and her skullcap sawed open. Her brain glistened.

Schottke and Gareau were taking a calculated risk. They wanted to push Sam off balance. They had seen wife murderers break down and blurt out a confession when suddenly confronted by images of their bloody handiwork.

Sam shuddered and covered his eyes with his hands, refusing to look. "I would [rather] have taken physical violence," he would say later. "I would have taken a beating with a rubber hose."³ Over and over, he denied killing his wife.

Gareau and Schottke switched gears and confronted him with an embarrassing Bay Village police report. A patrolman had caught Sam at a park one night, in his car with a young woman. She was naked from the waist up, crouching, trying to hide herself.⁴

After four hours of grilling, Sam had not changed his story, cried, or confessed. He later said he resisted the police by thinking back to his college fraternity hazing and recalling how he had survived it.

Then it was time for the next team, detectives Bill Lonchar and Pete Becker. Meanwhile, at about 6:30 P.M., Corrigan, with Steve Sheppard in tow, tried to bully his way into the jail to see his client. He made threats, his face reddening, his controlled anger working its way with jailers and administrators he had dealt with for decades. It took two hours, but he got in to see Sam. Corrigan hoped to break the momentum of the interrogation and allow Sam to catch his breath and not feel so overwhelmed.

Ten minutes later a jailer ordered Corrigan to leave or be thrown out. Don't answer any questions, Corrigan instructed Sam. Just sit there.

But Sam did not follow orders. Soon he was talking freely and pleasantly to the new detectives about everything but the day of the murder. Asked who killed his wife, he said a "maniac type person" who looked at his wife as "an idol" and who, when he found out she was pregnant, lost control, crept in, and killed her.

"As suspects, he thought of carpenters, wallpaper hangers, and in general anyone," Detective Becker reported.⁵

He and Lonchar kept pressing: Why don't you take the lie detector test?

Bill Corrigan wouldn't let him, Sam explained, and threatened to quit if he disobeyed. Sam said he realized that he was casting suspicion on himself by refusing the lie test and promised to ask Corrigan, once again, if he should submit to an exam.

Why did you hire him in the first place on the very first day?

My family did this, right after your detectives accused me of murdering Marilyn, Sam replied. His brothers felt he needed a lawyer.

Becker displayed crime-scene photos again, including a picture of Marilyn's body in her bloody bed. Again, Sam covered his eyes.

Take a look at it, Becker said. It might help you remember the stuff you're so hazy about.

Sam refused.

You're a pampered baby, Becker said. Look at the problems you've caused your family all because you're covering up.

Being called a baby struck a nerve, and Sam became riled. The detectives continued along this line.

You're not man enough to face the music you started playing, Becker said.

Sam said he was a suspect to be checked out and that was all. He was not guilty.

After five hours, these two detectives left and Sam penned a note to Corrigan. "They started very friendly and with 'open minds' but because of my 'attitude' they decided I'm guilty. The short guy called me every name he could, including spoiled, woman chaser, yellow bastard, etc. Their big pitch was that in order to clear myself—TAKE LIE DETECTOR TEST."[6]

Police had not yet discarded the drug-addict theory. Becker and Lonchar noted in their report that Corrigan and Dr. Steve had gotten in to see Sam briefly and could have medicated him.[7]

Homicide detectives in fresh two-man teams continued the interrogation for most of the day, hoping to break his will. Some of the detectives didn't know the details of the case; the idea was to maintain psychological pressure on the suspect.

All your money cannot help you now, one detective told Sam. We have low salaries, but you're the one who's locked up. What good is all your money now?

Another detective fashioned a newspaper into a club and asked repeatedly, "Why did you do it, Sam? Why? Why? Why?" He slammed the paper on the table as if battering Marilyn, shouting, "Down! Down! Down!"

On another shift, a detective used the soft sell and said he, too, had extramarital affairs and understood why Sam would stray, that wives were hard to live with sometimes and could make you lose your temper. Confess, the detective argued, and you'll get manslaughter with only a one- to ten-year sentence. We'll recommend that you get out in one year. You can't take a chance otherwise. You'll go to trial and the jury will give you the death penalty. You'll be electrocuted. You'll never see your son again.[8]

The next day Bill Corrigan was permitted to meet with Sam earlier in the morning and prepared him for another day of interrogation. He was afraid that Sam, guilty or not, eventually would confess to something terrible. After indoctrinating him, Corrigan sat and read the newspapers for about an hour, making the detectives wait, trying to throw them off their game.

Interrogation began at 1 P.M. with Schottke and Gareau, and on it went on for about ten hours. The next day, Sam was questioned for about three hours. Eventually, he said, he felt like confessing just to stop the relentless questioning. "It was mental torture at its worst," he would write later. "Hour after hour, they shouted at me, accused me, insulted me and members of my family. They tried to trick me by questioning me about facts they knew were not correct. . . . A psychological breakdown was exactly what these people were looking for."[9] A decade later, the U.S. Supreme Court would rule in an unrelated case that police could not question a suspect once he had asked for a lawyer.

It is unclear whether the police were surprised that Sam Sheppard held up. He had the stamina of an athlete and was used to being awakened at odd hours, performing surgery when tired, dealing with anger and wrenching emotion as he operated on patients who sometimes died on the table. The detectives' detailed reports of the three-day interrogation do not mention whether doubts crept in about his guilt.

Even after Sam's arrest, Cleveland detectives investigated other suspects, efforts that were hidden from the Sheppard family, their lawyers, the public, and the press. One suspect was a bushy-haired man in Columbus, Ohio. Another suspect was tracked to New Orleans, where he was arrested, questioned, and eventually released.[10]

Publicly, Captain Kerr, the homicide chief, complained to reporters that Dr. Sheppard was "well-coached by his attorney."

15

GRAND JURY

DR. GERBER TOLD FRIENDS that he had not slept well for weeks. The Sheppard case was consuming him, and he was exhausted. The weekend after Sam Sheppard's arrest, he left Cleveland and stayed with Mary Cowan at her farmhouse in nearby Bedford.

Gerber was pleased, despite his exhaustion. The Sheppard inquest had been a personal triumph, especially having his nemesis, Bill Corrigan, dragged out by a deputy sheriff as the crowd roared in approval.

Mary Cowan, who also believed firmly in Sam's guilt, was relieved. She had been worried that Corrigan would humiliate her friend. She shared her feelings with a favorite aunt in Georgia, who wrote back: "I hope you folks can prove his guilt. There have been several articles in our papers lately but I didn't save them as Dr. Gerber's name wasn't mentioned. . . . I know how wearing this is. Am glad Dr. Gerber could get out to your house and get a little rest. I don't see how he stands up under all of this. I hope for the sake of you two as well as others that it can be finished up soon."[1]

———

Twice in early August Detective Dombrowski and his colleagues in the police Scientific Investigation Unit had made late-night visits to the murder scene. They were determined to find every trace of human blood in the roped-off house using a newer technology called luminol testing. Luminol was an extremely sensitive reagent that glowed in the dark when sprayed on minute traces of blood. They "dropped to their knees and sprayed the floor, the carpet, the linoleum, items of furniture"[2] with the blood-sensitive solution, using an atomizer rigged to a sterile whiskey bottle. They hoped to find evidence that the killer, as Dr. Gerber put it, "washed off the trail of blood." Luminol would reveal evidence of the cover-up.

On the first night visit, August 3, the luminol worked like magic. On the second floor, in the darkness, they found numerous iridescent spots of suspected blood: on the hall carpet, at the door of the dressing room east of the upstairs bathroom, on a rug near a dresser in the guest room, and on a rug in Chip's bedroom.[3]

On the first floor the detectives found a "trail of 18 spots across the living room rug leading to the door going to the porch on the north side of the house. Another spot was found next to the easterly end of the register along the north wall in the west end of the living room. It was at the west end of this register that the telephone is located."[4] They found suspected human blood on the brass plate behind a drawer handle of the drop-leaf desk. Whoever opened the drawer must have had blood on a finger.

In the den they found five spots of suspected human blood on the rubber chair mat behind Sam's desk.[5] They circled each spot in chalk and then, with the lights back on, used another reagent solution to see if the blood spots were human. Most of them were.

Missing from their detailed reports those nights was any mention of finding evidence that blood had been cleaned up. Luminol testing would easily have revealed the telltale smears of wiped-up blood, which is what their supervisor told newspaper reporters had happened. Evidence of such a cover-up would have strapped Sam Sheppard in Ohio's electric chair. Instead, Dombrowski and Elmer Roubal made no notes of smears, no faintly glowing incrimination. This finding, or lack of a finding, has never been made public until now. It contradicts the inflammatory remarks of Gerber and police inspector McArthur that somebody cleaned up the crime scene.

Even so, Dombrowski was puzzled by the extent of the blood drops.[6] He could understand a blood trail starting outside Marilyn's bedroom and going down the stairs. But he and Roubal found blood evidence even out to the garage and on basement stairs. Inspector McArthur said the long blood trail proved the killer was simply panicked and "running around like a chicken with its head cut off."

On August 16, 1954, Sam appeared at a preliminary hearing before Cuyahoga County Court of Common Pleas judge William K. Thomas. Corrigan argued for bail. Prosecutors opposed it but presented no witnesses to show that the presumption of guilt was strong. They were busy trying to get a grand-jury indictment for murder. Even though the judge realized that he might be committing political suicide, he set the bond at fifty thousand dollars on the murder charge. All hell broke loose. Thomas received threatening phone calls and hate mail. Typical during the McCarthy era, the legal community was deeply divided over how to treat the accused.

Parrino and Mahon had to hurry up and get an indictment because the idea of Sam out on bail infuriated the city. They also had to decide whether to ask the grand jury for a first-degree murder indictment, which carried the death penalty. On August 16 they brought in Mayor Houk, Inspector McArthur, Dr. Gerber, and others to the grand-jury hearing.[7]

Grand-jury deliberations are supposedly secret. Even so, the *Cleveland Press* ran photos, names, and addresses of the grand jurors, which made them all minor Cleveland celebrities for that week, the recipients of all manner of advice, gossip, and theories about the sensational case. In general, prosecutors like grand-jury indictments because they can conceal their earliest evidence from the defense. There is no cross-examination of witnesses. All sorts of hearsay testimony and prejudicial remarks—comments that would never make it into evidence in a trial—are allowed. At the Sheppard grand jury the panel heard allegations and testimony that were never made public until now.

Nancy Ahern, for instance, was called before the grand jury and testified about Marilyn's version of Sam's womanizing. Ahern recounted a conversation with Marilyn that took place in May 1954 that supported the prosecutors' "other woman" motive for the murder. "Marilyn spoke of Sam having a girl she thought he was quite enamored of in California and I replied, 'You are kidding.' "[8] Marilyn said it was true and in fact there had been another woman before this one. Marilyn filled her friend in about the trip to the Chapmans' ranch in Monterey and how Chappie talked Sam out of divorce.

Ahern reported, "And then I said, 'What happened the rest of the vacation?' She said, 'We had a wonderful time. I sort of think Sam fell in love with me again and we had one of the best times we have ever had.' "[9]

"She still thought he was the sweet boy she had married and maybe he was doing his growing up now and she was still in love with him and was willing to wait for him to grow up," Nancy Ahern testified. She asked Marilyn if she "ever thought of leaving Sam. But she replied, 'What would I do?' or 'I guess I just love the guy.' 'I have no one but Sam.' Her mother was dead and she wasn't close to her father."[10]

Mayor Spencer Houk used the protective secrecy of the grand jury to undercut his former friend. In early August of 1954, Houk was probably the angriest he had ever been at the Sheppards, especially Steve, who days earlier had repeated to police that Spen had had an affair with Marilyn and was a good murder suspect. Steve said he knew this because he had counseled

Marilyn about her marriage and she told him Houk had been in love with her for two years. (Years later, even Houk's wife would admit in a taped interview that Spen had had a fling with Marilyn.)[11] Just a few days earlier Chief Story had sent detectives out to ask Houk to come in voluntarily or be arrested. Houk, caught by surprise, had come downtown in baggy blue pants and a T-shirt. The *Press* ran this latest development in huge page 1 headlines:

STORY CALLS HOUK A SUSPECT,
BRINGS HIM IN FOR QUESTIONING

Detectives had talked to Houk from 11:45 A.M. to 3:45 P.M. without a break. Then they had asked Dr. Steve to come in to police headquarters. When he entered the interrogation room, Houk had jumped up and shouted, "You're a liar!" and had to be held back from punching Steve.

Dr. Steve had come without Bill Corrigan's knowledge. The lawyer would have told him to stay away. McArthur had read to Houk a detailed version of the Sheppard brother's suspicions, as the mayor shot back, "Lies, damn lies!"[12]

Steve, unflappable, had complimented McArthur on the accuracy with which he had taken down the information. At 5:10 P.M., he had pushed through a crowd of reporters in the police station hallway and made it to the elevator without a word.

If this entire exchange was a police procedure to divide Houk from the Sheppard family, it had worked. Houk had devastating new details for the grand jury. For instance, he said he stopped to see Marilyn one day and routinely asked about Sam. "She said something to the effect, 'He is pretty good now but we had quite a battle a few nights ago.' And I didn't ask her what the battle was about and she didn't volunteer the information, but I did say, 'Why, I can't imagine Sam getting mad at anybody,' and Marilyn said, 'That's just it. Nobody around here has ever seen him get mad. He never shows it around here but when he does, he is like two different people, like a Jekyll and a Hyde.' "[13]

When Dr. Lester Hoversten was called to the grand jury, the prosecutors wanted to make sure that he wasn't feeling charitable to the Sheppards. Right off the bat, he was told, "You understand now that Dr. Steve has made you a prime suspect?"

"There is no doubt in my mind about that," Hoversten said. He had no reason to protect Dr. Sam and quickly painted an ugly picture of his former friend's rumored sexual affairs. After Chip's birth, when they were all living in Los Angeles, Sam had complained that Marilyn had lost interest in having sex "because of her fear of another pregnancy," Hoversten testified.[14]

Hoversten said that sometime in 1950 he and Sam went to a party thrown by a medical-insurance company while Marilyn visited family in Cleveland. There Sam met a woman named Margaret, got to know her, and later took her on a date.

Did he show you a letter that he wrote to Marilyn when she was in Cleveland on a vacation?

Yes, Hoversten said, Sam showed him a letter that he was going to send to Marilyn in which he said that "he felt their marriage was a failure and that they should consider a divorce." Hoversten said he convinced Sam to hold back because Marilyn would be devastated by such a letter, coming with no warning. He was uncertain whether Sam followed his advice. Sam did tell his parents about his troubled marriage because they telephoned him shortly afterward.

"His father was quite indignant, and [said something] to the effect that if Sam was not mature enough to realize his responsibility as a father to Chip and a husband to his wife, Marilyn, he better pack his bags and come home. Sam was very irked and upset about it and I tried to impress upon him his father had his best interest at heart, and that calmed him down a bit."[15]

Hoversten said he knew about Sam's affair with Susan Hayes. He told the grand jurors about a telephone code he used in the evenings when he needed medical advice from Sam while he was off with Susan at the apartment above the Fairview Park practice. Hoversten called, let the phone ring twice, hung up, and called back immediately. Unless the phone rang according to the coded rings, Sam would not answer, Hoversten said, because he did not want anyone from the hospital to wonder why he happened to be in the often unoccupied apartment at night.

Despite his poor marital record, Hoversten felt qualified to counsel Marilyn on her marriage. "I offered the suggestion that probably visiting and seeing a psychologist together would help. She always felt Sam would not agree to that and I advised her I couldn't help but feel I would get a divorce. She said she couldn't do that, Sam meant everything to her, she was in love with him, and I told her I felt very sorry for her." (His testimony rings true about the Sheppard marriage; even so, it's unclear how much weight to give Hoversten's grand-jury account because three months later he told reporters that he had "no personal knowledge of any extramarital affairs" by Sam.)[16]

The prosecutors also planted doubts about Sam's story through Elnora Helms, the maid who cleaned and ironed once a week. She said Chip's dog, Koke, barked at strangers but did not bark at people she recognized. "Mrs. Sam said she didn't know what she was going to do with Koke because she was getting to be such a barker and it annoyed the neighbors."[17]

Dr. Gerber testified that the murder was an open-and-shut case. He said he made this quick decision even before he went to Bay View Hospital at 9 A.M. on July 4 to question Dr. Sheppard. "It looked to me like it was an inside job, that the murder was committed by somebody on the inside and I thought this was a setup for a burglary that didn't appear as a burglary to me."

"And how did you come to that opinion?" he was asked.

"From my experience," Gerber said. "That's all."[18] It was a remarkable admission. Gerber was a doctor, not a homicide detective, who didn't routinely visit crimes scenes. He had just built a scientific lab that would solve crimes with microscopes and test tubes; before a single test was performed, he had locked into a theory of the case.

Finally the jurors heard from Cleveland police inspector James McArthur, who summarized the work of the dozen detectives under his command. He placed enormous weight on the many refusals by Sam and his brothers to submit to polygraph exams.

"On what theory do you base your charge of first-degree murder?"

"When anyone stands at the side of a bed for the length of time it takes to swing the number of blows struck at Marilyn, it must be premeditated. And knowing of the difficulties they had in the past and of his remarks to people that Marilyn was all right as a mother or as a brother-and-sister affair but he had no love for her, and the philandering that we know of, jumping from one to another, there is no doubt in my mind but it was premeditated."

"She refused to give him a divorce, he wanted one?" a juror inquired.

"Yes," McArthur said. "There is some evidence on that."[19]

———

That night, Sam was finishing dinner with his parents in their big new home adjacent to the Bay View Hospital grounds. At about 6 P.M. county sheriff detective Carl Rossbach and two other deputies pulled up in a blue Ford and crossed the front porch on planks laid over freshly painted gray floorboards. "Good evening, Dr. Richard," said Rossbach. "We'd like to see Sam."

"Step in, gentlemen. He's just starting to eat."

By now, the pack of reporters and photographers waiting in the hospital parking lot next door were running up a grassy knoll toward the Sheppards' house.

Inside, Rossbach spoke softly. "The grand jury returned a true bill of first-degree murder against you, Sam. We've come to pick you up."

First-degree murder carried the death penalty. Ethel Sheppard's eyes teared up. Sam's face was stony. "Can I pack a few things?"

"Sure, and you can finish your dinner, too."

Sam finished with a piece of homemade cherry pie. He piled some clothes into a paper bag. His mother added underwear and handkerchiefs until Sam stopped her, saying, "I've got enough of that stuff at the jail."

He hugged his mother. He touched his father's arm. He extended his left arm to be cuffed and smiled slightly, as if to say that life is absurd. Ethel conscripted a deputy to carry a sack of peaches, bananas, and grapes for her son. Sam draped a suede jacket over the steel bracelet and stepped into the flashes of cameras firing on the front porch.

His thirty hours of freedom on a fifty-thousand-dollar bail cost his family twenty-five hundred dollars for the surety bond, about half of the average American worker's yearly salary. It was worth it, he said later. "I am very happy to have had the opportunity to visit my boy who was at Stephen's house. I appreciate the fact that I got out on bail and I have that happy reunion."[20]

Several dozen yards away, patients at Bay View Hospital, some in white gowns, stood on a long balcony and took in an unobstructed view as Dr. Sam was taken into custody once again.

This time Corrigan tried to fight back and shape press coverage with a statement from Dr. Sam. He wanted to give the newspapers something to write about other than the law enforcement line. "I am not guilty of the murder of my wife, Marilyn," Sam said. "How could I, who have been trained to help people and devoted my life to saving life, commit such a terrible and revolting crime?"

The statement listed evidence that Sam felt proved his innocence:

He was injured, a fact supported by Gerber's own doctor, who found that he was missing the cremasteric and abdominal reflexes.

He had talked to police freely and willingly for more than fifty hours. The statement listed the dates, times, and the names of his interrogators.

"I love my wife. We rejoiced that we were to have a second child. The last three months of our married life were perhaps among the happiest we enjoyed together."

He even attacked the police for having "the idea that I was addicted to dope and all that had to be done to solve the crime and get a confession from me was to hold me until the craving for dope would break me down."

The day Sam was arraigned, Captain Kerr asked Steve Sheppard to see him in the homicide-bureau office. "Your brother is guilty as hell and you know it," he told Steve.

"I know just the opposite and so do you, Captain Kerr," Steve shot back.

You're running this the wrong way, Kerr told him. "Now then, you see your brother and tell him to confess. Goddamn it, he can plead insanity or whatever he wants. He will do six months in a hospital and then come out cured." He can return to medical practice, no more police problems, Kerr insisted.

"And if he refuses to confess to a crime he didn't commit?" Steve asked.

"Don't give me that crap, Doc," Kerr snapped. "But if he is silly enough to refuse, you can tell him for me that we'll burn him."[21]

———

Since Dr. Gerber had placed most of his political capital on the line with the Sheppard investigation, he found himself in a tricky spot. He was determined that his laboratory would crack the case with forensic wizardry and imbue his office with the respect a medical examiner's office was granted in other Western countries. (He corrected reporters and police who referred to his office as "the morgue." It was "the coroner's office," which had a "crime lab.") But not everybody agreed with his methods. Gerber clashed with the homicide detectives and the prosecutors when, without warning, he had the Sheppard crime scene dismantled. His workers removed two blood-spattered doors from the murder room, the beds, and chairs and tables from the den. His reasons were unclear. No tests on the furniture were noted in memos or in the notes of Mary Cowan, who compulsively recorded each test in the Trace Evidence Department. Prosecutors were angry. They felt they were in charge of the case, especially now that Dr. Sam had been indicted. They planned to have jurors tour the house during the trial and wanted it to look exactly as it had on July 4.

When their tiff surfaced in the newspapers, Gerber explained that he "needed" the doors and furniture so that, among other plans, his office could make three-dimensional models as trial exhibits. He had already hired an artist from the Cleveland Health Museum to create a life-size model of the victim's head. Its face looked remarkably like Marilyn's, her eyes closed, her lips in a slight frown. The model had no hair. Its scalp and forehead were marked with fifteen wide ugly gashes painted crimson. Gerber also had color slides made from the Sheppard autopsy photos, making Marilyn the first murder victim in the county to be memorialized with color film.

All of these innovations may have been fine ideas, but the prosecutors, not the coroner, were in charge of courtroom strategy, and they had other plans. Gerber quietly had the doors and furniture returned to Bay Village.[22]

———

Based on his handwritten diaries, which have not been available until now, Sam believed he would win his case. Other times he was depressed by his incarceration. The food was terrible, obscenities had been scrawled everywhere, spit and garbage flowed over the floors. "I wish we could flip a coin or I could go to sleep till this thing was over, but I've got to keep my mind operating and stay sharp. I've got to treat this like a disease. So I'm eating all the fruit possible, maintaining physical and mental activity as much as possible."[23]

His only relief, other than visits from his brothers, was playing handball outside the building against the one of the walls. When the *Plain Dealer* reported he played handball every day, Mike Ucello, the jail administrator, stopped the practice. "When I asked him about it tonight, he said he'd have to wait and see what the newspapers did. Who runs the jail? I guess the newspapers do, like the police department."[24]

Sam suffered a legal setback when Bill Corrigan tried to have the house returned to him. Gawkers still drove by the roped-off house, more than a thousand cars a day, causing about one or two car crashes each week. A local entrepreneur offered to lease Sam's home for one thousand dollars a month—a huge sum at the time—and make it "a Mecca for tourists and curiosity seekers."

Corrigan turned the man down and reassured Sam that he would get his home back soon. "I'll feel better just knowing that the pack are out of our house. The way our home has been overrun would have hurt Marilyn very, very much, and so it has affected me in a similar way."[25]

In a letter to the prosecutor, Corrigan said the impounding was outrageous and unprecedented. The police had had plenty of time to run forensic tests. He demanded all sets of keys to the house.

We are keeping it for now, county prosecutor Cullitan replied. If you need to get something out, you can go inside if accompanied by a police officer. If you don't like it, get a court order.

During the months between arrest and trial, Sam received visits from his brothers, father, and a few friends, but he did not want his mother or Chip to come to the jail. Ethel Sheppard was depressed, and seeing him in such a setting would make her even worse, Sam felt. And Chip was too young; he had to be sheltered. (Actually, Chip would have been comforted to see his father. The boy wondered why his father didn't want to see him, as if somehow he had done something wrong.) Instead, each Saturday morning, Sam paid a ten-dollar bribe to a weekend jailer and telephoned Chip at Steve and Betty's home.

On August 21, the press reported that Dr. Sam was going to commit suicide. Sam quickly wrote to Corrigan to reassure him he was not giving up. "They would like nothing better than for me to commit suicide so they could claim that to be proof of my guilt," he wrote in his diary. "I truly believe they would hand me a gun to use on myself if it were possible."

The jailer, Mike Ucello, worried about the news report, and paid Sam a visit. Sam assured him that he was fine, then asked if he could sit outside with other prisoners and get some sun.

Ucello gave him permission, then searched Sam's cell block, looking for anything Sam might use to kill himself. Deputies removed a couple of tin cans the prisoners used to heat coffee, but overlooked wire, a razor blade, and a piece of rope.

Later Ucello spotted Sam sitting on a windowsill and smiled. "Sometime I'll come out to Bay Village and we'll have a beer together."

"I'd like that," Sam said.[26]

16

PRETRIAL

THE SHEPPARD TRIAL opened during a slow time for national news. The World Series was over (the underdog New York Giants had swept the Cleveland Indians). The nation was at peace. Senator McCarthy's ballyhooed hearings into subversives in the U.S. Army had fizzled, driving a stake in his career as a rabble-rousing red-baiter. Across the nation, nearly half of the big metropolitan newspapers played the Sheppard murder on page 1.

That first morning, October 18, about fifteen hundred people gathered outside the courthouse at East Twenty-first and Payne Avenue. Perhaps thirty photographers and television cameramen clustered around the entrance and took pictures of the Sheppard family, the lawyers, police, and anyone connected to the case who managed to push through the crowd and climb sixteen steps to the entrance of the four-story stone building. In the corridor outside the smallish first-floor courtroom about a hundred hopeful trial watchers had congregated. There were only a few seats available to the public. As a sheriff's deputy brought Dr. Sam from the jail down the hallway, some teenage girls in the crush spotted him and squealed, "Oooh, isn't he handsome."[1]

Approximately sixty reporters were covering the trial, about half of them from out of town. The national press had settled in at the Statler Hotel, a five-minute walk to the courthouse. Many of these reporters seemed astonished, even appalled, by the story's grip on local citizens, especially on women. "Seventy-seven days of this delicious dish, and right now you are demanding more," a columnist wrote. "You, the public, are the ones who have been circulating unending streams of jokes about this brutal killing. Some of them are parlor stories, most of them are lascivious, and we worry about juvenile

delinquency. . . . What is there about it that frenzies us into an orgy of sala-
cious sensationalism, or more to the point, what is there about us who are
frenzied."[2] An out-of-town columnist said Clevelanders discussed the case
with "leer glinted eyes" and "drooling lips."[3]

Reporters cooperated with police and defense lawyers in ways that
might seem unprofessional today. In the 1950s, journalism was more a trade
than a profession. At the large papers with the reporters' guild, reporters
typically were high-school-educated and middle-income. Reporters often
traded information with detectives and police administrators rather than develop their own exclusives. For example, the account of the bakery deliveryman who said he saw Marilyn Sheppard being cuddled by Spen Houk
was unearthed by a reporter at a daily newspaper in Lorain, a medium-size
steel town on Lake Erie just west of Bay Village. The reporter took the man,
Jack Krakan, to Corrigan, who in turn brought him to the attention of the
county sheriff. Krakan's account did not exonerate Sam; in fact, it provided
a possible motive—Sam killed his wife in a jealous rage. But the story also
complicated the prosecutor's case by bringing in another suspect and undercutting the police theory that Sam had murdered Marilyn so he could run
off with Susan Hayes.

Handing off a hot tip to someone in authority was a reporter's trick, a
way to exploit a lead too difficult to confirm or too hot to publish by itself.
You gave the lead to officials, waited until they investigated, then pegged
your news story to the *fact* of the official investigation—hiding, of course,
the newspaper's active role in creating the story. Today, legitimate newspapers frown on this manipulative practice. Prosecutors did not pursue the
Krakan lead. Bill Corrigan chose to ignore it. He said he didn't believe it and
wouldn't use it. Marilyn was "a very decent woman."[4]

The unfaithful-Marilyn account fed into the "key club" allegations that
had taken hold and were titillating the citizenry. The editorial pages of not
only the *Press* but also the *Plain Dealer* and the *Cleveland News* weighed
in judgment, bemoaning the immorality of the Sheppard family. J. F. Saunders, an editorial writer, attacked what he called the immorality of "Sam's
set." He expanded his views in a letter to a reader in September, finding
fault with Dr. Sam for having affairs and for allowing Hoversten "the roving osteopath" to make passes at his wife. With little proof, the editorial
writer noted that "the set the doctor traveled with were not simple people
who were content to play musical chairs at their parties. To me, it all seems
to add up to an aura of sexual familiarity that is not very healthy for community or nation."[5]

The New York *Daily News,* the country's largest-circulation daily, had dispatched its ace trial reporter, Theo Wilson, a skilled and classy "sob sis-ter," a newsroom specialist at wringing drama and emotion from murder tri-als, executions, and disasters, the staples of the tabloid press. She explained the lure of the Sheppard murder: "This case contains all the elements of a best-selling murder mystery—blood, violent death, mystery and sex."[6] A veteran of scores of trials, Wilson was struck by the fact that authorities had no conclusive evidence against Sam.

The public's appetite for the murder trial clearly was whetted by televi-sion, a newer, more immediate form of news that reached into twenty-nine million homes, about half the number of newspapers sold each day. There had been sensational trials in the past—Sacco and Vanzetti, the Lindbergh-baby kidnapping—but the Sheppard case was the first driven by television news and by celebrity journalists. It quickly supplanted the earlier media cir-cuses as "the Trial of the Century." Decades later, the Sheppard murder lost its superlative to the O. J. Simpson case, which also was fueled by an emerg-ing news medium, the Internet.

Many high-profile journalists were assigned to Cleveland: Robert Fabian, a famous Scotland Yard detective, now retired, who worked for Scripps Howard (at the time, Fabian's life story was being peddled in Holly-wood as a weekly TV drama, *Fabian of Scotland Yard,* a sort of upper-crust *Dragnet*); Margaret Parton, a noted foreign correspondent for the *New York Herald Tribune;* Theo Wilson; lawyer Paul Holmes of the *Chicago Tribune;* Bob Considine, Hearst Newspapers' lead correspondent; and from New York, working sources by phone, Walter Winchell, who peppered his news-paper column and radio and TV shows with unattributed items on the case. (In one of his columns, which appeared in 150 newspapers with eight mil-lion readers, he trotted out a rumor he packaged as a scoop: "When the Shep-pard case is tried—the keyword—will be sterility." It was the first in a string of inaccurate items by one of the country's most powerful columnists.)[7]

These reporters paled in celebrity power to Dorothy Kilgallen, the queen of all media. Kilgallen starred on the popular TV quiz show *What's My Line.* She wrote a syndicated newspaper column called "The Voice of Broadway." She covered the occasional big story for Hearst's International News Ser-vice, hosted a morning radio talk show in New York City, and found time to swirl through New York's social scene in ermine and pearls.

By today's standards, she was an unlikely television star, forty-one years old, average-looking, with dark brown hair, smallish mouth, weak chin. She wore fabulous clothes, but despite the classy shoes, hats, and accessories, she came off as not all put together as she rushed about her day. Kilgallen was the daughter of Jim Kilgallen, a widely known sportswriter for Hearst

Newspapers who cut his teeth during Chicago's Front Page newspaper wars in the Roaring Twenties. Dorothy learned from a master craftsman and quickly made a name for herself. As a twenty-four-year-old Hearst reporter, she worked the Lindbergh-baby kidnapping trial in 1936, competing against scores of reporters, and nailed some exclusives. (Hearst also scored some of its Lindbergh exclusives the easy way—it bought them. The newspaper chain paid for lawyers for the accused, Bruno Richard Hauptmann, in exchange for exclusive interviews.) "She could out-wit, out-write, out-ruse anyone in yellow journalism," a competitor said.[8]

In October 1954 Kilgallen checked into the Statler Hotel with her huge wardrobe, a pink electric typewriter, and a mission. Ever since she'd appeared on *What's My Line,* the number of newspapers buying her column had doubled. But her reputation as a serious reporter suffered from her TV work and from the gossip-column mentions of her hobnobbing with swells and royalty at New York society galas. Her colleagues in print, most of them with blue-collar backgrounds and high school educations, called her "a newspaperman in a five-hundred-dollar dress."

Kilgallen wanted to use the Sheppard trial to show that she was much more than a gossip columnist. Raising the stakes for her, the faltering Hearst chain hoped her copy would boost the circulation of its newspapers in Pittsburgh, St. Louis, San Francisco, and elsewhere. Kilgallen faced some daunting problems. Being a sob sister—pulling off trial coverage with style, accuracy, and exclusives—was a full-time job, and she had other beasts to feed: her morning radio show, writing her Broadway column, filming *What's My Line* in New York City. It would be impossible to attend the entire trial.

Like most of her colleagues, she came to town assuming Dr. Sam was guilty. Kilgallen, a quick study, soon fell under the spell of the Sheppard case. "The fact that at this stage it is equally possible for the rational mind to find him innocent or guilty is what may make the Sheppard trial a celebrated cause to rank with the still unsolved Hall-Mills case or the classic puzzle of Lizzie Borden," she wrote during the first week of jury selection. Furthermore, with Susan Hayes cast as the other woman, "the case gets its final element—sex guaranteed from the start."[9]

She tried to be one of the gang, going for lunch with lowly paid reporters at the Express Grill, a smoke-filled greasy spoon next to the courthouse where hamburgers were forty cents and the jukebox played polkas. Most of the reporters respected her skill and speed and work ethic, but they resented the fanfare she created simply by appearing in public. (It took another decade before the profession got used to the public treating reporters who appeared on TV as movie stars.) Soon Kilgallen's celebrity status gave her

an edge when she wasn't looking for one, and she had the chance to write a
story that could change the course of the trial.

———

On the first day of jury selection, most of the national press corps got their
first look at the trial judge, a lean, seventy-year-old Welshman named Edward Blythin. A former Cleveland mayor, Blythin was undoubtedly the most
recognizable judge on the Cuyahoga County trial bench. He looked stern,
with a long face and strong jaw and silver hair slicked back across his skull.
He wore colorful bow ties that peeked above the neck of his black robes,
softening the image. He spoke with a slight accent, not unusual in a city full
of immigrants, having been born and reared until twenty-two in Newcastle,
Wales. He kept books for a coal company before moving to Cleveland,
studying law, and working as an assistant law director for the city. In 1939 he
was named interim mayor to replace Harold Burton, whom President Roo-
sevelt had appointed to the U.S. Supreme Court. From bookkeeper to mayor
of a great city—here was proof that America truly was the land of opportunity, Blythin liked to say.

The Sheppard trial presented several vexing problems for him. First, Blythin was faced with almost overwhelming demand from the press and the
public to sit in his courtroom every day. The courtroom measured only
twenty-one by fifty-two feet and had just four rows of twelve seats. It was bisected by its bar, a polished heavy wood banister with a swinging gate that
separated the public section from the jury box, lawyers' table, and judge's
bench. Blythin assigned three of four rows to the news media. In the back
row, on opposite sides of the aisle, sat the warring relatives of Sam and Marilyn, neither side speaking to the other. Blythin also allowed a temporary row
of sixteen chairs to be placed just inside the bar for the press corps. It was a
tight fit—the row ended six inches from the jury box. He also accommo-
dated the news pack by assigning name tags so reporters could reserve their
seats for the duration. For the first time, the judge allowed a microphone to
be set on the witness stand and wired to speakers inside and outside the
courtroom; reporters and the public who could not get inside could follow
the trial from the often scratchy and erratic sound of the testimony projected
into the rotunda. Inside, Blythin was able to fiddle with volume controls
from his bench.

Typically, the halls in the courthouse were filled with cumbersome film
cameras set on sturdy tripods, stands of lights snaking power cords, and photographers with boxy cameras and flash attachments. Ten minutes before
proceedings started, a deputy walked Dr. Sam from the police jail, through

the barrage, and into court. The camera crews rushed into the courtroom and got set up while photographers climbed on chairs behind them to get unobstructed views, and grabbed their daily shots of the perpetrator on display.

Complicating the matter for Blythin was his reelection in November. He was trying for a second term. He faced a weaker opponent, and the trial was a godsend of free publicity. However, if he made an infelicitous remark or a procedural mistake, it would be magnified a thousand times in this high-stakes case. Judge Thomas had followed the rules at Sheppard's preliminary hearing and granted bail, then had had to endure public outrage. Blythin did not want a controversy two weeks before election day and needed to avoid being maneuvered by Corrigan into making unpopular rulings, however legally defensible.

Blythin should not have been handling the Sheppard case. One of his sons, Arthur, was a Cleveland homicide detective. In July, long before his father received the assignment and had to worry about appearing fair and not discussing the case, Arthur Blythin worked with assistant prosecutor Thomas Parrino, chasing leads, interviewing possible witnesses. Even if Judge Blythin had not heard details of the case from his son, many in the legal profession felt he should have recused himself and had the case reassigned to another judge.

The question arose: would Bill Corrigan exploit this apparent conflict of interest and file a motion asking for a different judge to hear the case? Even though they had been neighbors on East 115th Street and their children played together, Corrigan and Blythin had clashed when each was more politically active. In 1948, when Blythin first ran for judge, Corrigan sat on the Cleveland Bar Association committee that screened candidates for endorsements and strongly opposed giving Blythin the powerful association's endorsement. When his own committee overruled him, Corrigan quit in protest. Now, in the fall of 1954, Corrigan had to decide whether to make an issue of Blythin.

What Corrigan really wanted was to move the trial to another Ohio county, away from jurors who had been saturated in the Seltzer-driven coverage of the *Cleveland Press* and the city's "inflamed and hostile atmosphere" against his client.[10] For ammunition, he hired a public-opinion pollster, who took a survey about voters' attitudes toward Dr. Sam. If Corrigan could get the trial moved, he also would eliminate the issue of the judge's impartiality.

Corrigan faced an even greater problem when the newspapers published the names and addresses of the seventy-five potential Sheppard jurors—nearly a month before they were required to report for duty and be warned not to discuss the case. It is easy to imagine all the advice, phone calls, crank letters, and opinions shared with these newly minted minor celebrities in this unfolding drama. Even after voir dire commenced, reporters and photographers visited the jury room, interviewed potential jurors, took photos, and ran articles. The jurors became known at work and at home. Corrigan felt that even if the state came up short in proving its circumstantial case against his client, the jurors would find it nearly impossible to return to their neighborhoods or to work and defend a vote to free Dr. Sam.

Corrigan filed a motion asking for the trial to be moved or, failing that, a delay until the publicity died down. Prosecutors, of course, opposed it. They wanted a local jury. Why should Dr. Sheppard be treated differently from any other murder suspect, they argued. Judge Blythin denied Corrigan's motion. They would wait and see if twelve jurors could be seated after being questioned extensively about their biases. To do otherwise, the judge said, would "show a lack of faith in the jury system." Privately, Blythin felt Sam Sheppard would face the inflamed publicity in every city in the country. The news story had fanned into a cause célèbre. Everyone had heard something about it, so it didn't matter where it was tried. He washed his hands of the matter, saying, "This court has never yet found any way in the world of quieting down publicity if newspapers and news media care to expound."[11]

Judge Blythin seemed to be celebrity-struck. One morning during jury selection, he asked his bailiff to bring Dorothy Kilgallen into his chambers. He wanted to meet the television star and famous Hearst columnist. In chambers, Blythin told her he watched her all the time on *What's My Line* and enjoyed the show.

"What brings you to Cleveland?" he asked. "Why come all the way from New York to cover this trial?"

Blythin was part of the Cleveland establishment, which was becoming increasingly uncomfortable with the national press corps in town, making Cleveland synonymous with murder—"giving us a black name," Mayor Celebrezze complained[12]—and attaching rubelike descriptions to midwesterners in the nation's sixth-largest city.

"It has all the ingredients of what we in the newspaper business call 'a good murder,' " she told him. "It has an attractive victim, who was pregnant. And the accused is an important member of the community—a respectable and attractive man. Then, added to that, you have the fact that it is a mystery as to who did it."

"Mystery? It's an open-and-shut case."

Kilgallen, stunned, asked what the judge meant.

"He's guilty as hell," Blythin said. "There is no question about it."[13]

Kilgallen, the competitive sob sister, had just had a scoop dropped in her lap. The judge at what was being called the Trial of the Century, before hearing the facts in court, had expressed a strong opinion concerning the defendant's guilt. This was a potential blockbuster. Once the news got out, the judge would most likely be forced to recuse himself. A new trial would have to be ordered.

Kilgallen and Blythin left his chambers together and posed for a photograph. "She's a lovely lady," Blythin said.

———

It took eight days for Corrigan and the prosecutors to select twelve jurors. Corrigan tried repeatedly to question the potential jurors about their feelings regarding extramarital sex, but the judge would not allow it. Soon the routine repetitive questioning, stripped of titillation, became tedious, and reporters struggled to infuse intrigue into their news coverage of the "grim legal battle for the highest stake in the world—a man's life."

This prologue actually heightened public anticipation and enhanced the inevitable drama. With little happening in the courtroom, the New York *Daily News* and other papers filled their news holes by printing rumors swirling around the case, cloaking the remarks as newsworthy because they were "stories Clevelanders told out-of-towners about the case." Among the rumors printed were:

"Dr. Sheppard allegedly was sterile and butchered his wife in a fit of rage when she told him their unborn child was not his."

"Marilyn Sheppard allegedly was frigid and repulsed her husband until he became nearly insane with frustration."

"The Sheppards ran around with a fast and high-living crowd which took a tolerant view of extramarital affairs."

"Marilyn Sheppard had many boyfriends."

"Marilyn Sheppard had no boyfriends."

"Marilyn Sheppard was a shy, athletic girl who disapproved of the Bay Village society crowd."

"Dr. Sam was a strange man who kept decomposed heads in his garage."[14]

Residents of Bay Village did not recognize their hometown in the racy articles in the men's magazines and the national press. "It was like reading about a place on Mars or something," recalled Esther Houk. "None of us who lived there could imagine some of the incredible stories they were printing. Nor could we in any way counteract them. We were just completely snowed under daily, weekly and monthly as reporters from all over the world

kept asking questions, and all of the waves and waves of detectives asking
the most ridiculous questions."[15]

On October 28 at 1:15 P.M. both sides told the judge that they had agreed
to the composition of the twelve-member jury.[16] There was a commotion in
Courtroom 1A as most of the reporters jumped up and scrambled out to call
their editors with the breaking news.

For the third time, Corrigan made a motion to move the trial to a different county, and for the third time the judge denied it. Corrigan never did
make a motion asking Judge Blythin to remove himself because of potential
bias. Nor did he have the benefit of what Dorothy Kilgallen knew.

———

Sam Sheppard confounded the out-of-town press corps, who expected more
life from a doctor. They complained that he just sat at the trial table, three
feet from the prosecutors, his face blank. He never chuckled at a funny remark by his lawyers as they put the jurors through delicate probing, or even
at the lamest attempt to break the tension and tedium of the courtroom. At
breaks, when Sam turned around to look for his family and caught reporters
staring at him, he narrowed his eyes and set his mouth. To a clinical observer,
he appeared depressed.

Dorothy and Betty, his sisters-in-law, sat in the back row nearly every
day, poised and unflappable. Kilgallen said their demeanor was "astonish-
ing," that they had "spines of steel." She commented on their tasteful, well-
dressed style, "wearing bright pinks and red and green and gold to keep the
mood light . . . a subtle feminine psychological move to reassure Sam that
all will be well."[17] They went to Sam at breaks and chatted, she wrote, and
when the bailiff signaled proceedings were to resume, they placed a hand on
his wrist in good-bye.[18]

Newspaper publicity continued to hamstring Dr. Sam. Soon after Kilgallen's column appeared in the *Cleveland News,* Sheriff Sweeney clamped
down on the Sheppard family. On October 27, after eight days of jury selection, he ordered his deputies not to let Steve, Richard, Dorothy, or Betty
Sheppard talk to Sam, shake his hand, or visit, even though such courtesies
had taken place for days. Dorothy and Betty were no longer allowed to while
the time in court by knitting.

Louis Seltzer's anti-Sheppard crusade gave the *Press* a vested interest in
Sam's conviction. When a newspaper mounts a crusade, it commits to running many stories and editorials, and asking for a result—a reform, a new
law, the defeat of a candidate. Newspaper crusades that did not show results
were not dropped without embarrassment. The crusading *Press* clearly felt it

deserved credit for Sam's indictment. On a live radio broadcast on the first day of jury selection, top editors at the *Press* and the *Plain Dealer* debated the topic "Which Newspaper Deserved the Most Credit for the Indictment of Dr. Sheppard?" It was assumed that the Cleveland newspapers, not the prosecutors, had gotten Sheppard charged with first-degree murder. Forrest Allen of the *Press* and James Collins of the *Plain Dealer* each claimed this highly prized honor. Allen had the easier case to make: "The *Press*'s handling of the Sheppard story produced the trial that we have got over there today because I don't think the officials were going to do anything about it."[19]

Soon after jury selection started, Sam Sheppard came to the frightening realization that he faced a community, a court system, and a powerful press corps working in apparent lockstep to convict him. "The realism of what has happened has just hit me in the past week or two. I see that these people now are going to try to railroad this thing through to protect the papers and officials who have gone out on a limb. The reporters and prosecutors, who are supposed to fight for the innocent as well as against the guilty, are having a joyous time smiling and kidding one another—Big joke!!"[20]

———

Like many of the out-of-town reporters, Kilgallen came to Cleveland loosely holding a belief that Dr. Sam probably had committed murder. But she began to change her mind the minute she saw him. She was captivated by his looks and developed a romantic view of him. She described him as a "handsome young doctor loaded with sex appeal and attractive to women all his life, [who] is[,] at this crucial hour, wary of women and fearful of their judgment." Margaret Parton, her New York competitor, wrote that Dorothy fell in love with Sam from afar. Kilgallen had an unsatisfying marriage—her husband was a closeted homosexual—and seemed starved for romance. Even though Kilgallen favored him, she still played up evidence for her readers that suggested his guilt—for instance, that the crime scene's burglary appeared fake, "a mincing kind of burglary . . . out of keeping with the fiendishness of the alleged bushy-haired stranger."[21]

Despite her sympathy for Sam Sheppard, the woman who could outwrite and outruse a pack of journalists never did write a news story exposing Judge Blythin. A decade later, Kilgallen told the story of Blythin's intemperance at an Overseas Press Club event in New York, which sparked a furor. A reporter in the audience criticized her for not revealing the story immediately. Surprised and stung, Kilgallen said that her chat with the judge had been private, that she considered the judge a confidential source and she did not reveal such confidences.

Her excuse rings off-key. Her trip to Blythin's chambers was at his invitation. She was not a journalist pressing for information, and he had not asked to be treated as a confidential source. Furthermore, Kilgallen in the past had displayed an ethic straight from *The Front Page* that said journalistic rules were meant to be broken in service of a big scoop. Indeed, she and a colleague had once jimmied a funeral-home window to get inside and view a newsworthy corpse.

Perhaps she simply missed the significance of Blythin's revelation (it came before the U.S. Supreme Court under Chief Justice Earl Warren formalized and expanded the civil rights of the accused). Or she may not have wanted to jeopardize her access to the judge and prosecutors and complicate her assignment in Cleveland.

By the time Kilgallen made her revelation, Judge Blythin had been dead for several years and could not defend himself. His family said Kilgallen lied about the encounter because the judge, of the old school, never would have used *hell* in front of a woman.

But it is clear that Blythin, long before the jury reached a verdict, repeatedly and publicly exposed his belief that Sam killed Marilyn. An employee in the court clerk's office, Edward Murray, stated under oath that the judge told him so. An unassailable account comes from a criminal-law professor and Gerber friend, Oliver Schroeder, who helped authorities pursue Sam Sheppard. Schroeder, retired from the faculty of Case Western Reserve University law school, backs up Kilgallen and Murray. During the trial, Schroeder would say years later, Blythin told him and his father that Dr. Sam was guilty. Their conversation took place near the cash register of their family bookstore, Schroeder's Books. Blythin obviously felt comfortable making such remarks because he knew the professor shared his belief. "My father looked at me and said, 'That's not right. He shouldn't be saying that,' " Schroeder later revealed.[22]

17

PROSECUTION

SOME DAYS BILL CORRIGAN seemed less a courtroom bulldog than a tired sixty-seven-year-old man, sighing wearily, pushing his hand in frustration through his full white hair, an unlighted cigar stub clenched in the corner of his mouth. He was consumed by the Sheppard trial, like the rest of the city, and he had to ignore his labor-law practice. Unlike the county prosecutor, Corrigan didn't have a team of detectives and lawyers at his command. Even with the Sheppard family's fairly deep pockets, Corrigan was outgunned and knew it.

At night he rode a city bus back to his ancient farmhouse in East Cleveland, near John D. Rockefeller's old estate, and prepared for the next day. His favorite break was to take a volume of poetry from a bookstand in the wood-floored entryway, his place marked with a long-stemmed rose from the garden, and pick up where he left off. He would pull a battered metal folding chair to a side yard, smoke, and slowly read his favorites—Emerson, Robert Frost, and Stephen Vincent Benét.

In court he seemed to follow Emerson's maxim "Nothing great was ever achieved without enthusiasm." He was a master of rhetorical passion and theatrical flourishes at a time when such techniques were beginning to be trumped by forensic science.

Corrigan needed reinforcements. Pete Petersilge, the Sheppards' business lawyer, agreed to help, but he had no criminal trial experience. Corrigan's oldest son, William Joseph, thirty, had just finished law school and joined the team. "My role was to carry the briefcases," he would say years later.[1] His father needed more than neophytes at the Trial of the Century, so he hired Fred Garmone, a seasoned lawyer whose better-paying clients included members of the Cleveland mob.

Corrigan was handicapped because Sam had talked to the police twice before getting a lawyer. It almost always hurts a defendant to lock into a detailed account early on. Even if a defendant was innocent, each time he retold his story to police it would differ in minor ways, and the discrepancies, however meaningless, could be exploited by prosecutors at trial.

Even before opening statements, Bill Corrigan made some legal decisions he would come to regret. For one, he never filed a motion asking for the recusal of Judge Blythin, his neighbor for many years on East 115th Street, on the grounds that Blythin might be partial because his son, a homicide detective, had worked the case. If Corrigan had known of the judge's intemperate remarks to Dorothy Kilgallen and Oliver Schroeder, he almost certainly would have demanded a new judge.

Another poor decision by Corrigan was his not insisting upon having his own expert examine the crime scene. He did hire A. J. Kazlauckas, M.D., a pathologist who had worked for thirteen years under coroner Gerber before leaving for private practice. Kazlauckas gave Corrigan a detailed, perceptive analysis of Dr. Adelson's autopsy work, pointing out a few oversights and suggesting cross-examination questions to fire at Adelson and Gerber. Kazlauckas was particularly surprised that Adelson had not microscopically examined the clotted blood from Marilyn's wounds to see if there was residue from the murder weapon—paint, grease, rust, or fibers, anything that might suggest a particular object, which in turn could point to a suspect. Kazlauckas also said he wanted get inside the Sheppard home and study the crime scene.[2]

This presented problems. Corrigan could not get access to Sam and Marilyn's house. The county prosecutor had impounded the house and withheld the keys. Even though county authorities had gathered the physical evidence they felt they needed, they still viewed the entire house as evidence. "We want the jury to come out and examine the premises and get a clear picture of the scene and the impossibility of Dr. Sheppard's version of the crime," prosecutor Mahon explained.[3] Corrigan could visit the home, he said, but only under a police escort.

This was not acceptable to Corrigan. He did not want to tip his hand to a nosy police escort. Furthermore, he did not know for certain whether his client was innocent, so he may have felt he was better off not knowing what surprises the blood trail might reveal. Why slam the cell door even tighter with forensic evidence of his own making? If he learned of new evidence that suggested guilt, he might be less able to summon the indignation needed to sway a jury.[4] Indeed, in early November, at the conclusion of the state's case, Mahon offered to turn over the house. Asked by reporters if he would commission a scientific examination of the house, Corrigan said, "I haven't made up my mind yet."[5]

Meanwhile, from county jail, Sam Sheppard peppered Corrigan with a series of handwritten letters that contained remarkably astute suggestions for his defense. As a doctor, Sam intuitively knew that the blood trail could not have come from a dripping murder weapon, as Parrino, Gerber, and Inspector McArthur were insisting. As far back as September, Sam told Corrigan to conduct an experiment by dipping a hand or weapon in "whole non-oxalated blood" to see how far someone could walk before the blood coagulated. Sam predicted twenty feet at most, which would contradict what detectives said they found in his house. A likely explanation, Sam wrote, was that he gave the suspect a nosebleed during their struggle.[6]

He also asked his lawyers to mount an attack on the "shoddy scientific work" of the coroner's office for not making a thorough check for semen on Marilyn's body. "Mr. Corrigan, one of the men here [in jail] asked a question which should be asked of the pathologist. Did they check the rectum for evidence of semen? Sexual perversion is not uncommon as we all know and should be most surely considered in this revolting type of crime. A person who would do a thing like this would be very likely to be a sexual pervert."[7] Another time Sam wrote: "I can't get over the negligence displayed by the lack of examining the wounds, blood and wound scrapings for evidence of foreign material! This is almost as sloppy and negligent as the way the house and grounds were not isolated."[8]

———

On November 3, a jury had been selected and was ready to view the crime scene. An early snow had swept in over Lake Erie and blanketed the lawn at the Sheppard home. A neighbor had kept the grass trimmed, but the white house and the bare trees looked washed-out and desolate against the gray lake. That afternoon dozens of spectators and reporters stood waiting just outside the property lines, tramping snow and soft ground into slop. One young woman in blue jeans said excitedly, "I saw Dorothy Kilgallen." She was asked why she was waiting in the cold. "I wanted to see Sam. He's a nice-looking guy."

Then someone said, "Here it comes!"

A city bus pulled up, and twelve jurors stepped out into biting wind and were escorted to the house. They were well-dressed—the men in suits and ties, the women in dresses, hats, and gloves, and their best daytime coats. Dr. Sam climbed out of a county sheriff's car, his wrist cuffed to a deputy.

Cuyahoga County sheriff Joseph Sweeney moved the jurors slowly from room to room, giving them a tour of house, with Sam and his lawyers trailing behind. A helicopter carrying a *Cleveland Press* photographer swung low over the property, back and forth, making it hard to hear.

Prosecutors wanted the jurors to tour the Sheppard house so they could see for themselves how the desk drawers were pulled out and how Sam's black medical bag was perched in the hallway, and to observe other details that might logically undercut Sam's version of events. Sweeney pointed out the doors, the position of the locks, the light switch at the bottom of the stairs. At the sight of Chip's well-worn stuffed teddy bear on a bedroom dresser, Sam became teary-eyed, then muffled a sob.

Bill Corrigan was frustrated. Earlier at the courthouse, after the judge had ordered a break for lunch, a pack of photographers had asked the jury to stay behind and pose in the jury box. To get their shots, the photographers stood on tables and chairs and perched on the judge's bench. "Look this way, please." "Hold it a minute, please." Corrigan could not believe what he was seeing; jurors were supposed to be protected from outsiders. In a moment, Blythin returned to his courtroom to retrieve a law book from his bench. "If the court please, I object to all this!" Corrigan shouted at Blythin. The judge picked up the book and vanished without a word. Corrigan beckoned to the court reporter, then made his record in case he had to appeal a guilty verdict: "After the jury was discharged at the end of this morning session, at the request of newspapers this jury was brought back into the room and sat in the room for a matter of 15 minutes, ten minutes and were subject to photography and television cameras of at least 10 cameramen."[9]

Back in Bay Village, as he surveyed the Sheppard backyard, Corrigan muttered about bad luck. Lake Erie was choppy. Waves splashed against the rocky bluffs, covering what normally would have been a five- to fifteen-foot-wide stretch of sand—the route, Corrigan planned to argue, that a bushy-haired intruder had taken to make his escape. Instead, jurors would have to use their imaginations.

The next day in court, assistant county prosecutor John Mahon stepped forward to give his opening statement. He was tall and gray and slightly stooped. Two days earlier, county voters had elected him to the common pleas court bench after a career in which he sent more men to death row than any other active prosecutor in Ohio. This would be the last of his hundred or so murder trials.

Unlike Corrigan, Mahon was not a shouter. He used sarcasm to make points. When he did raise his voice, his face and neck turned crimson. It wasn't that long ago that Mahon and Tom Parrino had faced off against Corrigan and Fred Garmone in the Gogan murder trial, a celebrated case of an industrialist accused of poisoning his wife. They lost that one, and he and Parrino were determined not to be defeated again.

Mahon began his opening statement with a low-key recitation of what he said was Dr. Sheppard's story to the police. With a veneer of sarcasm, Mahon told of Sam hearing Marilyn cry out his name, running upstairs, getting "clobbered," coming to, then hearing a noise, running downstairs, and chasing a man to the lake, only to get knocked out again. Mahon made it clear that he felt Sheppard's injuries were minor if not self-inflicted, worthy of ridicule.

Then there was the blood trail. It came down the stairs from the second floor, through the living room, and out the back door as well as down to the basement, Mahon noted. "But in the room where the body lay, there was no sign of a struggle. The only violence exerted in that room was exerted on Marilyn Sheppard. There was nothing missing in that room. The instrument used to strike and beat Marilyn Sheppard was not found. And the T-shirt the doctor was wearing was not found. The corduroy jacket he had been wearing . . . was neatly folded and lying on the couch that morning."

The prosecutor continued to carefully select details or interpretations of the evidence that begged explanation: the lakeside door had been bolted and chain-locked, suggesting that a fleeing killer would not have time to open a double-locked door and flee. The desk drawers were neatly pulled out, not dumped, as a burglar would do. And why would a burglar take Sam's watch, ring, and key chain, stuff them in a bag, then abandon it in the brush? "The reasonable interpretation is that the watch and chain and ring were placed into the bag and tossed out in the back there, placed there to deceive that a burglar had taken that property out."[10]

Finally, Mahon began to sell the jury on a motive. Dr. Sam had slept with other women in California, he said, and recently had conducted another adulterous affair. "We expect the evidence in this case to disclose, if you please, ladies and gentlemen, that this defendant and Marilyn were quarreling about the activities of Dr. Sam Sheppard with other women. That that is the reason she was killed."[11]

After sixty-five minutes at the lectern, the prosecutor sat down. In essence, the state's case boiled down to "Who else but Dr. Sam had the opportunity and motive to murder Marilyn?"

It seemed like a skimpy presentation to some of the national reporters. Paul Holmes, a lawyer and the *Chicago Tribune*'s trial correspondent, felt that the prosecutors, for tactical reasons, must be holding back their stronger evidence. There had to be more.

Fred Garmone, not Bill Corrigan, stood to deliver the opening statement for the defense. Garmone seemed comfortable, almost graceful, in the small courtroom. A college athlete who had tried out with the legendary 1927 New York Yankees, Garmone wore thick-templed glasses and slicked his grayish black hair straight back. Sometimes he spoke ungrammatically, a vestige of his immigrant Italian neighborhood. This made him seem folksy and enabled him to warm up witnesses. He and Corrigan had worked together several times. Part of Garmone's great value to Sam was that the judge liked him. Three years earlier Blythin had publicly helped Garmone become reinstated to practice in federal court after his license was suspended, the result of a conviction, along with business partner Alfred "Big Al" Polizzi, an ex-bootlegger and mobster, for wholesale liquor violations.

Usually in criminal cases defense lawyers such as Corrigan and Garmone focused on flaws and discrepancies they could find in the state's evidence and witnesses. Later they could argue to the jury that these problems added up to reasonable doubt that their clients were guilty. But in a case where the city of Cleveland seemed assured of their client's guilt, they needed a stronger story to sell to the jurors. They decided to attack the entire police investigation itself—not a usual defense tactic—saying that Gerber, Schottke, Gareau, and others had made up their minds quickly on July 4 that Sam Sheppard was guilty, and then had assembled evidence to implicate him while ignoring evidence that supported his innocence.

Garmone started off by painting Sheppard as an unlikely killer. He described Sam and Marilyn's late candlelit dinner on July 3 in a warm glow. They were "a loving couple" who had just had "the best four months of their marriage." Marilyn had baked Sam's favorite pie, blueberry. After dinner they had "shared the same chair, and Sam and Marilyn displayed affection toward one another."

He and Corrigan felt it important to somehow explain away the blood drops in the house. Sam felt the blood could not have come from a dripping weapon and therefore put a third person at the crime scene. His lawyers chose a different tactic. Garmone told the jury that the blood in the downstairs will be shown to be that of the Sheppards' female dog, Koke, who had free run of the house and had shed blood during menstruation.

And, despite what the state just told you, Garmone told the jurors, Dr. Sheppard had cooperated fully with police. He had been interrogated twice on July 4, the second time for one hour—without lawyers or family, when he was dazed. "There will be no evidence," Garmone insisted firmly, "of any mythical wall that was thrown up around this young man."[12]

Deputy coroner Lester Adelson, M.D., took the stand as the first prosecution witness. He had a surprise in store.

Adelson was sworn in and trotted through his impressive credentials as a pathologist. Then Mahon and Parrino had the blinds drawn in the high-ceilinged courtroom and brought out a slide projector, a device so unfamiliar in the courtroom that some newspapers referred to it as a "magic lantern." This was not a day for squeamish jurors. Adelson had brought seven color slides taken of Marilyn Sheppard's head during autopsy. Corrigan quickly shouted objections to letting the jury see gruesome images as evidence. Blythin overruled.

The courtroom fell silent as Marilyn's bloody face was projected in four-foot-square images on the screen. Jurors and spectators gasped. Some shut their eyes. Other put hands over their faces and peeked like children through parted fingers at the deep, ugly, red, half-moon gashes across the victim's forehead and partially shaved scalp.

You could not help but be moved at the sickening sight of a young woman's face, brutally disfigured, an act calling out for punishment. In a page 1 editorial at the start of the trial, the *Press* asked, "Who will speak for Marilyn?" If Adelson and his slides were words, they could have filled a volume with outrage. Adelson had testified in a nondescript case the year before using projected images of the victim—a first in the county and probably first among coroners' offices nationwide. The national press corps, including trial specialists such as New York *Daily News* reporter Theo Wilson, had never seen such an unsettling display. "Unprecedented in criminal trial history," she wrote. Coroner Gerber, the lawyer-doctor, prided himself on running an innovative office.

Dorothy Kilgallen was fascinated. As a nineteen-year-old rookie, she had been assigned to cover New York City's morgue to see if she had what it took to survive at Hearst News. She had gotten used to gore and evisceration. "It was strange," she wrote.

No picture of Marilyn Sheppard, of the many taken when she was smiling and wide-eyed and alive, has shown her to be so lovely as she was in death—discolored and slashed and broken.

Her face was oval, her skin the very fair kind with fine pores. Where there were no wounds, it had a peach-like tone, faintly damp with the dewiness of the newly dead. . . . Her face was not distorted at all. It was in remarkable repose considering how she died. But the wounds of her forehead and cheeks were too numerous and too gaudy, like the wounds of St. Sebastian in cheap plaster statues seen in the churches of little Italian towns. Marilyn's slayer was an extravagant slayer, wasteful of blows. . . . She was so beautiful. So lovely and so bruised. So gentle with her eyes closed, sleeping under the vermilion gashes.[13]

Adelson calmly described each of Marilyn's wounds, tapping a wood pointer at different spots on the first six images, detailing thirty-five in all, fifteen alone on her face and skull. Meanwhile, Sam had edged his chair to the side of the courtroom, behind the screen, out of sight of Adelson's display.

The seventh slide gave even Kilgallen pause. For an instant, the courtroom was puzzled by the huge, glistening, suetlike shape surrounded by a shiny red corona. "This," Adelson said, "is the skull of Marilyn Sheppard after the scalp has been peeled away." Sam put his head to his hands. His shoulders quivered and a few tears rolled down his cheeks as reporters scribbled notes like mad.[14]

Many of the reporters resented the exhibition, this last slide in particular, and described it in news accounts as "sickening," "an ordeal," and "grisly." Prosecutors justified the display, saying the jury needed to see the spiderweb of fractures in Marilyn's skull. (Later, appeals courts stopped prosecutors in many cases from showing such raw, unsettling photographs to jurors, calling the practice more prejudicial than probative.) Ray Sprigle, a Pulitzer Prize winner from the *Pittsburgh Post-Gazette,* recovered quickly, however, and leaned over to Theo Wilson and asked, "Hey, kid, wanna go out and get some liver?" Later, in the courthouse's small, crowded pressroom, Sprigle banged out a lead that did not make it past his editors: "If Sam Sheppard doesn't burn after today's testimony, he's incombustible."[15]

When Bill Corrigan rose to cross-examine, he hoped to make three points. First, that Adelson had made mistakes and assumptions with his autopsy work that fit the defense's theme about a "rush to judgment." Second, that Marilyn's head wounds may have been inflicted by several swings of a many-pronged instrument. Corrigan wanted to paint the crime as one of passion, an explosion of a handful of blows, moving it into second-degree murder, thus sparing his client, if convicted, a death penalty. Most important, Corrigan had to bring alive the "bushy-haired" intruder, to build a case that a third person was at the crime scene.

It is easier to tear down a witness than to build one up through careful, sometimes dull direct examination. Corrigan was well prepared by Dr. Kazlauckas and scored several points. He pressed Dr. Adelson to admit that he did not use a microscope to examine the blood from Marilyn's gashes for residue that might shed light on the composition of the murder weapon.

Adelson also stated that he did not test for seminal fluid on Marilyn's body or on the sheets. The pathologist said he did make a vaginal swab and smeared it on a glass slide to examine for sperm microscopically. It's unclear whether Dr. Adelson personally looked at this slide. He used the pronoun *I* to describe making the swab during the autopsy. Moments later, under Corrigan's aggressive questioning, Adelson used *we* for the first time, to say that no sperm had been found. (Years later, trace-evidence supervisor Mary Cowan would say that it was the University Hospitals lab that had looked at the slide for sperm.) Whoever reviewed the slide saw only large "abundant epithelial cells," none of the tiny sperm cells that could survive a day or longer. Adelson also admitted that many of Marilyn's head wounds were evenly spaced, which could suggest a two-pronged weapon such as fireplace tongs.

Corrigan brought up a July meeting of all the investigating authorities at the coroner's amphitheater and linked it to questions about Marilyn's broken teeth and minor injuries inside her mouth.

"Did anybody suggest in that meeting to begin looking for a person whose finger had been bitten?" Corrigan asked.

"I don't recall that that was ever mentioned there," Adelson said.

"And the way these teeth were broken off and the wound inside the mouth, without any exterior wound, indicated that something had got into that mouth, hadn't it?" Corrigan asked.

"Certainly," Adelson said.[16] It was a small victory for Corrigan, who wanted to suggest that Marilyn had bitten her attacker.

At one point during the cross-examination, Corrigan posed a question that jolted the courtroom. He asked Adelson if he had heard on July 4 that Dr. Sam was supposedly sterile and that he had killed his wife because he discovered that she was pregnant.

Adelson admitted that he had heard such rumors, but wasn't sure if it was before he completed the Sheppard autopsy.

To some in the courtroom, it was not clear why Corrigan opened the door to rumors about Sam's sterility. Most likely he was trying to reinforce his theory that Gerber and company had rushed to judgment and embraced the false sterility theory, which in turn explained why they had failed to perform possibly exculpatory tests such as searching for seminal fluid on Marilyn's pajamas, body, and bedding. It could also explain a perfunctory attempt to find sperm in the vaginal swab of the victim. By putting the sterility rumor into the court record, however, Corrigan gave reporters free rein to write about it. Even worse, by indirection he had presented the jurors with a mo-

tive that could explain why a previously law-abiding husband might violently erupt: learning that his wife was pregnant by someone else.

After the first week of witnesses, the national press decided that the contest was even, both sides having scored points. It seemed as if the whole
world was following the Sheppard trial. In Havana, Ernest Hemingway
avidly read the coverage. "A trial like this, with its elements of doubt, is the
greatest human story of all," he told a London *Times* reporter. "They call
these girls 'sob-sisters' in the old fashioned Hearst tradition. But they're not.
They write well. And when you consider the speed at which they have to tell
their tales, it's good, very good. This Kilgallen is a good girl, don't you think
so? Not as good as Rebecca West. Nobody is as good as all that. But those
girls are damn good."[17]

The overheated local coverage, particularly that of the *Cleveland Press,*
alarmed editors running other newspapers. The news industry's trade magazine, *Editor & Publisher,* warned that reporters were "creating a circus of the
Dr. Sheppard trial. If the coverage continues in the same sensational vein of
the opening days, it could set the cause of courtroom photography back 20
years and do irreparable damage to the newspapers' fight against the charges
of 'trial by publicity.' "[18]

———

Assistant county prosecutor Thomas Parrino was ambitious and smart,
skilled at digging into the minutiae of testimony and evidence and finding interesting facts and contradictions that he could exploit when examining witnesses. He had served four years as an army combat-intelligence sergeant in
the war. After law school he had joined the county prosecutor's office and
quickly made his mark as a rising legal star. Unlike the other prosecutors on
the case, he was a bachelor. He lived with his mother and two of his sisters.
The Sheppard trial had become his life, and it showed; he was extremely
well prepared. He had black hair, a sharp nose, and a strong jaw that fit his
combative spirit.

He and the other prosecutors had planned to use a series of Sheppard
neighbors to portray Sam unsympathetically and show a troubled marriage.
Nancy Ahern was his first witness. She had come to believe that Sam probably was guilty, and her testimony would hurt the Sheppard cause.

Under Parrino's questioning, she admitted that she had at first tried to
keep some of Marilyn's secrets from authorities at the coroner's inquest. But
everybody in Bay Village seemed to know that she was Marilyn's confidante.
Immediately after her highly publicized inquest testimony, residents called
her at home and confronted her at the drugstore for supposedly hiding Mar-

ilyn's unhappy times with Sam. So she decided to tell all and called Dr. Gerber the next day. It wasn't the state's intent, but with her testimony Ahern revealed the large role community pressure played in building a case against Dr. Sheppard.

Parrino knew it was important to show that Sam Sheppard at some point had wanted a divorce. To get Nancy Ahern to reveal this, Parrino needed her to recount a conversation in which Marilyn had repeated what Dr. Chapman told her were Sam's comments about their marriage. Corrigan jumped to his feet, objecting to Ahern's answer as the basest, most obvious hearsay. Parrino cleverly argued that "we feel the dead Marilyn has a right to be heard here." Judge Blythin, to the surprise of many, allowed the hearsay.

Thus, the jurors heard from Nancy Ahern that Sam told Chapman who told Marilyn who told Nancy that Sam had considered a divorce, and that Chapman had convinced him otherwise, then informed Marilyn about their talk. Triple hearsay.

Another point Parrino made through Ahern was that she had chain-locked the living room door to the screened porch after dinner, a door through which Sam said he had chased the killer.

When Corrigan rose to repair Sam's reputation, he immediately asked Ahern if she had ever seen Dr. Sheppard display a temper.

No, she said.

They were in love?

Marilyn was in love, but "I wasn't so sure about Dr. Sheppard."

That night Sam wrote another letter to his son and had it sent from his cell.

Dearest Chip,

How are you? Fine I hope! Did you see the picture of you on the horse? My friend, the artist here, made it just for you.

Someday, Chip, I'll tell you all about what I'm going through now and why you and I are kept apart when we need each other the very most. Mommie always said you and I were the toughest guys she knew and now we must prove her right. It is up to us to be everything she expected of us. If we are ever in question as to what to do just think—how would Mommie want it—and the answer will be there.

I know you are doing your part in every way, which gives me more strength to carry my end of things. Remember that I think of you constantly and I am loving you every minute of the day and night.

Daddy.

The letter was shown to the *Cleveland Press,* which ran it on page 1.

The next morning, the arrival of state witness Spencer Houk caused a commotion among the reporters crowding the courtroom, and the judge had to
ask for quiet. Houk had the potential to help or hurt Sam. Corrigan and the
Sheppards wondered if he was still furious at Steve Sheppard for naming
him as a suspect and a possible romancer of Marilyn. Sam had not seen
Houk since the summer. Recently, the mayor had spent nearly a month in
Lakeside Hospital, incommunicado and far from Bay Village, recovering
from nervous exhaustion. He looked terrible. His eyes were sunken and life-
less. He refused to look at Sam.

Houk went over familiar ground, describing their friendship and what
he saw at the Sheppard house on July 4. He spoke so slowly that he seemed
drugged, and the prosecutor showed impatience with his barely audible answers. Suddenly, Houk created a stir by disclosing a sharp piece of new information: after Dr. Richard determined that Marilyn was dead, he came
downstairs to the den, leaned over Sam on the floor, and asked his brother
"if he had anything to do with this," Houk testified. To which Sam replied,
"Hell no!"

It was a damaging bit of hearsay. Commotion ensued as reporters ran out
of the courtroom to phone in breaking news. Blythin ended up rapping for
order four times during Houk's painfully slow testimony. Neither Corrigan
nor the local reporters noted a problem with Houk's remark: under oath at
the coroner's inquest in August, Houk had given a similar account of Dr.
Richard's returning downstairs and talking to Sam in the den. But Houk testified then that "I didn't hear the conversation. I don't know what was said."[19]
His damaging remarks stood unchallenged and led the next day's news.

Mahon then asked the mayor, over Corrigan's objections, if Dr. Steve
Sheppard had made accusations about him.

Yes, Houk said. Mahon then asked Houk if he had taken a lie detector
test.

Corrigan jumped up, furious. "John Mahon is going to be a judge!" Corrigan shouted. "How does he expect to get away with questions like that?"
The Ohio Court of Appeals had ruled that lie detector tests were inadmissible. Again, to the surprise of many, Blythin overruled Corrigan's objection.

Houk answered, yes, he had taken a polygraph examination, and the
prosecutor moved on to other areas. The implication was that Houk had
passed the test and therefore was cleared of any knowledge about Marilyn's
murder.

Houk's wife testified next. Esther Houk's face was thin and pinched, and she said she was ready to fall apart once she got off the stand. She was asked questions intended to show that Sam and Marilyn lived a battle-scarred marriage, but her answers only provided everyday disagreements. Esther said Marilyn wanted to buy more furniture for the house and Sam did not approve. Also, Sam "wasn't very happy" when he returned from a Boston business trip to learn that Marilyn had bought a dishwasher without consulting him. The only time Esther Houk rose above the mundane was discussing her sister's minor head injury from a car crash.[20] Sam treated the woman, and Esther said he had mentioned how difficult it was to diagnose brain injuries. They were easy to fake, which frustrated insurance companies that had to pay claims. The state's implication was clear—that Sam knew how to fake a head injury and therefore must be faking it now. Sam wrote a note for Corrigan. "As a matter of fact, a head injury is not easy to simulate. I merely advised to wait before making a rapid settlement."

Again, at the end of Esther Houk's direct testimony, reporters rushed noisily out of the courtroom, angering the judge. Their "constant movement" was "creating a disturbance," he told the press. It had better stop or he'd change their seating.

Esther Houk was an easy cross-examination for Corrigan because she was not as hostile or tongue-tied as her husband. Corrigan brought out details that helped his client: Chip had always been a deep sleeper and was difficult to awaken that morning. There was a puddle of water on the back porch along with smaller wet spots that trailed like footprints on the stairs.

———

On November 16, Cuyahoga County coroner Sam Gerber carried a small piece of paper to the witness stand. It said, "Don't let defense counsel make you lose your temper."

Gerber had testified in court dozens of times as the county coroner and had learned how to be an extremely effective witness. He even shared his expertise with other doctors in a book he cowrote, *Physician in the Courtroom.* But he had a weakness, his temper, and he hated to be challenged. His poker buddies nicknamed him "Torchy" because he would lash out when he lost a pot he thought he was going to win.

Gerber and the prosecutors had set a clever ambush for Sam Sheppard and his lawyers. Assistant prosecutor Saul Danaceau, a bald, short, round man with thick black-rimmed glasses, conducted Gerber's crucial direct examination. First, the coroner described everything he saw on the morning of July 4—the blood-spattered bedroom, Marilyn's body, its rigor mortis. He said he had lifted sheets to help move her body to a stretcher and also moved her crimson-stained pillow to the other twin bed. At that point, he told the jury, he turned over her bloody pillow and saw a smaller, darker outline of crimson overlaying the large bloodstain. The impression, Gerber said, was of "an instrument."

What kind of instrument? the prosecutor asked.

With deliberate effect, Gerber said: "A surgical instrument."

The courtroom buzzed, and Corrigan and Garmone exploded with objections. Blythin overruled.

A color slide of the pillowcase stain was projected on a screen in the darkened courtroom. Gerber stepped up with a pointer. "This impression here represents the blades," he said, "and the blade on each side is about three inches long and the two blades together, its widest part, measure about two and three-quarter inches, and there is a space between the two blades indicating the fact that these blades do—"

Garmone objected to "all this about indication." Judge Blythin said the coroner could describe what he saw.

"There is a tooth-like, a tooth-like indentation at the end of each blade." Then Gerber handed the pillowcase to the jurors, who passed it around, staring at the dark impression. It was an abstract shape with feathery, irregular edges that suggested the pillowcase had been wrinkled and bunched as it collected Marilyn's blood.

To many who studied the pillow stain, it resembled a large clot of blood that had been creased and flattened by something folding or bunching the pillow. Like a Rorschach test, the abstract shape allowed you to see what you wanted to see. It looked like a pair of crab claws bisected by a line of darker blood along a crease in the pillowcase. The state's theory was that the killer, sometime after murder, had rested a blood-soaked weapon on the pillow, leaving an outline on top of a larger, dried bloodstain.

Even Judge Blythin seemed doubtful. After Gerber's direct examination, the judge asked him if he was saying that *only* a surgical instrument could have made such an impression on the pillow. Gerber backed off a bit. He said the stain could have been caused by some other object "similar to a surgical instrument."

Gerber's performance was audacious. He was not an expert in bloodstain analysis, an emerging specialty in criminalistics that used the laws of fluid physics to reach conclusions as to whether crime-scene blood had been smeared, spattered, wiped, or applied by some other means. But he was confident and unflappable in his beliefs, a popular elected official with a carefully burnished image as a man of science. Gerber's testimony was a turning point for the prosecution.

While Gerber was testifying, Sam squirted ink from his fountain pen, again and again, onto scraps of paper and folded them, trying frantically to replicate the impression Gerber just described. Some of Sam's attempts began to resemble the disputed shape, and he showed them to Corrigan. They got into a heated disagreement. Sam insisted that the crab-clawed impression didn't resemble any surgical tool he or Steve had ever seen. Gerber wasn't a surgeon. What did he know? Make him bring in such a tool, Sam insisted. He can't.[21]

Corrigan disagreed. He said he "didn't want to glorify" the accusation. Corrigan insisted that the jurors were smart. They'd figure out that the prosecutors didn't have such a murder weapon or they would have presented it.

Corrigan probably did not want to risk making a demand for the tool. The prosecutors might be holding back the weapon, only to introduce it during rebuttal. If he argued, as Sam wanted, that the surgical tool was a fiction, their defense might be devastated when the prosecutors presented a tool that fit the bloody outline. It might be a trap.

Corrigan knew he had to damage Dr. Gerber. He planned to goad the coroner and get him to flash his famous temper, which could undercut his testimony. Corrigan ended up conducting a two-day cross-examination, an over-the-top performance, full of shouted questions, withering insinuations, furious objections.

He attacked the surgical-instrument theory, tiptoeing in. You knew he did a bit of surgery? Corrigan asked.

"Oh, yes," Gerber said.

There were surgical instruments in the home?

"Yes."

Did you compare those to the impression?

No, just a "casual inspection," Gerber admitted.

And there were surgical instruments at Bay View Hospital—did you look at those and compare them to the pillow impression? Corrigan asked.

"No."

Corrigan hoped that the jury would wonder why the police didn't compare Sam's medical instruments with the imprint, but he could not risk asking, "Why not?" A smart cross-examiner never asked an open-ended question, especially "Why?"

What Corrigan didn't have the benefit of knowing was that Cleveland detectives had called medical-supply houses across the country, pored through thick instrument catalogs with hundreds of pictures of surgery tools, and had come up empty-handed.[22] Nor was he aware that not even Mary Cowan was convinced of her boss's interpretation. Just after he testified she passed along a tip to Cleveland detectives that the imprint was made from a special tool for a Johnson outboard motor, which Sam had ordered that summer. A Cleveland homicide detective visited a Jaguar dealer in hopes of finding a tool specific to foreign cars that matched the crab-claw stain. Nothing could be found to match.[23]

Corrigan stepped close, doing his best to try to get under Gerber's skin. He repeatedly referred to Gerber's office as "the morgue," knowing that it irritated him. Corrigan even used Gerber's *Physician in the Courtroom* against him.

"One of the rules of conduct that you have here is, 'Do not argue,' isn't it?" Corrigan asked.

"Yes, and I'm not arguing. I'm merely stating a fact."

"And 'Do not talk too much'?" Corrigan asked.

"I'm not," Gerber protested.

The courtroom was thrown into an uproar when Corrigan asked Gerber about his thinking that Sam Sheppard might be sterile. Mahon objected and the judge agreed. Corrigan shouted, "I'm going to get it in the record even if I'm not permitted to!" Blythin told him to calm down; Corrigan walked away, saying over his shoulder, "Let me alone."

He calmed down and asked Gerber, "Did you assert that the murder resulted from the pregnancy of Marilyn Sheppard?"

"Never."

"Did you ever hear of it?"

"No," Gerber said, a lie. He and his staff had tried to discover the blood type of Marilyn's fetus the day after the murder, but Corrigan did not know this.

"Did you at one time make a statement that the Sheppards may have met someone who was a schizophrenic, without realizing it, and that Mrs. Sheppard had been built up in that person's mind as someone to be destroyed? Did you make that statement?"[24]

"I made a statement, but I don't know if those are the exact words, but at least the substance is correct," Gerber admitted.

Overall, the coroner had been convincing.

———

Even when he successfully undercut the police investigation, Corrigan wondered whether the jury or the press corps was paying attention. This seemed to be the case with prosecution witness Michael Grabowski, a fingerprint technician of the Cleveland Detective Bureau.

The accepted wisdom in Cleveland was that somebody had wiped all the fingerprints from the Sheppard home at the time of Marilyn's murder. Under

Tom Parrino's crafty questioning, Grabowski explained that he could not obtain usable fingerprints in the house because the surfaces he looked at were covered with fine scratches.

Parrino walked Grabowski through his work in the Sheppard living room. Were there any identifiable prints?

"No, sir."

"Any place in the room were there fingerprints?"

"No, sir."

Parrino went room by room, asking Grabowski, again and again, if he found "any identifiable prints," and Grabowski each time said no. Instead he found fine scratches, particularly on the broken trophies and the two metal boxes in Sam's den.

"Could these have been made by a cloth?" Parrino asked.

"Yes."

The state wanted to suggest that someone had cleaned up the house and wiped away evidence. The only cloth, though, that could have made scratches in metal was an emery cloth or perhaps a dishcloth full of an abrasive cleanser. The likely explanation for scratches was that Marilyn or Sam had scoured these treasured items after they were covered by smoke or soot during their recent house fire.

On cross-examination, Corrigan forced Grabowksi to present an accurate picture. "The question that was given to you by Mr. Parrino and which you answered a number of times, was that you did not find any *identifiable* fingerprints at certain places where you made examination?"

Grabowski replied, "He specified the places, if I recall correctly."

"Well," Corrigan asked, "did you—in those places that were specified in his question—find *any* fingerprints that were *not* identifiable?"

"Yes," the detective admitted.

"So you found fingerprints?"

"Yes."

Corrigan took him through the areas he tested. He was able to get the fingerprint technician to admit that—contrary to popular belief—partial or smudged prints were found in almost every place he looked. Grabowski found them on doorknobs, window latches, broken trophies, a desktop, and inside the medical bag, among other places. Grabowski had to admit that he did not attempt to lift prints from the banister to the second floor, the doorjambs, the beds, or the two watches.

Grabowski's admissions destroyed the authorities' early assertions that the Sheppard house had been wiped clean, making it look like a cover-up for an inside job. Even so, the Cleveland newspapers ignored the day's revela-

tions. Instead, the *Press*'s page 1 banner headline read, FINGERPRINT MAN
TELLS OF CLEANUP IN HOUSE.

Prosecutors used their next witness, Cleveland detective Jerome Poel-
king, to try to make something out of his discovery on July 23 of Sam's
thumbprint on the headboard of Marilyn's bed.

On cross-examination Corrigan asked a question he knew would be dis-
allowed, but he didn't need it answered to make his point. "Did you ever hear
of a man coming into a bedroom and kissing his wife good night?" Prosecutors objected, the judge agreed, and Corrigan said, "That is all."

Mary Cowan was called to testify. Cowan said she "dreaded" Corrigan's
cross-examination. She took the stand carrying a deck of three-by-five index
cards on which she had noted, in near-perfect Palmer cursive, the results of
various chemical tests and microscopic examinations of the evidence.

Despite the difficulty of testing older, dried blood, she said she had obtained a positive result for human blood in five locations on the stairs and
floor, thereby destroying Corrigan's dog-blood defense.

The table in front of the judge's bench was piled with bloody sheets and
a quilt, pillows, sneakers, moccasins, Sam's sports coat, his pants, and other
items. Corrigan pulled out a bloody white glove and put it on with a flourish,
captivating the jury at the beginning of the cross-examination.

One of the points Corrigan wanted to make with Cowan was that she did
not know how old the blood was or who it belonged to. She admitted that she
did not try to type what remained of the blood scrapings after her tests determined it was human. She said she didn't have enough dried blood to get
good results.

Corrigan, who decided to question her politely, did not make much of
this admission. Cowan should have at least attempted to type the blood; in
other cities, serologists had successfully typed a pinhead-size drop of dried
blood. All along, the police and Gerber had assumed that the drops on the
stairways and floors were Marilyn's blood. If the blood drops had been
tested and were determined to be group A or group B, something other than
Marilyn's group O, the state's case against Sam Sheppard would have been
seriously undercut. Sam hadn't been bleeding that day, so whose blood
would it be?

Cowan should have at least attempted grouping tests on the blood trail.
Some of the spots were three eighths of an inch in diameter, larger than anything she found on the watches. In Cowan's defense, the blood was more

than two weeks old and had been lifted from pathways that had been crossed by many people. It would have been difficult to get a good result.

Next, Corrigan tried to use Cowan to counter the state's theory that Sam had washed blood from himself by jumping into the lake. Corrigan cited the work of Dr. Paul Kirk, a criminalist at the University of California, who had conducted scientific experiments on washing blood from different fabrics. His textbook, *Crime Investigation,* was used as a reference by the coroner's office.

Mary Cowan, who had read some of the textbook, admitted that blood cannot be completely removed once it contacts fabric. Microscopic traces would remain.[25] Corrigan felt her revelation helped Sam's case immensely. There should have been a few dozen spatters of blood on the front of Sam's pants if he had killed Marilyn, not just the one large stain at the knee.

———

The prosecutors still had a couple of large holes to fill in its case. One involved premeditation. To send Sam Sheppard to the electric chair on a first-degree murder conviction, prosecutors had to prove that he planned to kill his wife. They hoped to show this through the testimony of Elnora Helms, the Sheppards' maid. They already had Helms inspect the blood-flecked bedroom, which she presumably was familiar with, having cleaned and dusted it weekly for two years. Under oath, Helms said nothing was missing from the room. This enabled prosecutor Mahon to argue that the killer brought the unknown murder weapon into the room—an act of premeditation.

Another weakness in the state's case was Sam's temperament. Whoever smashed Marilyn's head into a bloody mess did so in a rage. Sam Sheppard had no history of domestic violence.[26] The state's own witnesses—the Houks, the Aherns, patrolman Drenkhan—all said Sam was even-tempered. They had never seen him explode in anger.

To overcome this, prosecutors exploited a rift among Marilyn's relatives. Those closest to her believed that Sam was innocent. The others felt that he was a killer, and secretly dished rumors about Sam and his brothers to Cleveland detectives.

Tom Weigle, Marilyn's twenty-six-year-old first cousin, testified for the prosecution on the day the *Press* ran what was perhaps its most damaging story about Sam Sheppard. SAYS MARILYN CALLED SAM A "JEKYLL-HYDE" read the page 1 banner headline.[27] The article promised a "bombshell witness" who would say that two days before she was murdered Marilyn called her husband a Dr. Jekyll and Mr. Hyde.

There was no bombshell witness. Instead Weigle was left to paint Sam as violent and erratic. In March 1952, he testified, he visited the Sheppards and was watching a Western with Sam when Chip, overstimulated, ran by and hit his father's shoulder with a toy tomahawk. Sam put the five-year-old over his knee and spanked him. Weigle called it "an unmerciful beating. He landed repeated blows, and Sam began yelling, 'Don't do that, don't ever hit me again.' "[28] The state hoped this was sufficient to convince a jury that Sam Sheppard could turn violent.

The last of the state's thirty witnesses took the stand amid great anticipation, practically halting Weigle's testimony by simply stepping into the courtroom. Susan Hayes represented the sex appeal and the emotional pay-off that trial watchers and the press had been waiting for.

She did not appear to be the same free-spirited California woman who had lied to Los Angeles police about sleeping with Sam. She wore a black wool dress with a Peter Pan collar, matching shoes and handbag, and a small shell of black velvet on the back of her head. She had lost her tan and looked thin. At least one New York reporter couldn't go against the typecasting and described her as "a sexy-looking brunette." Parrino took her testimony.

Staring straight ahead, speaking with little expression, Hayes described working on emergency calls with Sheppard, then making love to him in his sports car and at different apartments. She listed the gifts he had given her: a ring, a suede jacket, a replacement watch for the one she had lost in his company.

"He did mention something about divorce?" Parrino asked.

"Yes, he did."

"And what did he say?"

"I remember him saying that he loved his wife very much, but not so much as a wife. He was thinking of getting a divorce, but that he wasn't sure that his father would approve."

"He said he loved his wife very much?" the prosecutor asked, almost surprised.

"Yes."

Recovering, Parrino asked, "He was thinking about a divorce?"

"Yes," Hayes said.

On cross-examination, Fred Garmone questioned her gingerly. He knew it would backfire for a man to treat her roughly when the popular view of Susan Hayes was one of a naive young woman, heart-struck by a rich, handsome doctor. Under questioning, Hayes recounted how she had lied at first to the Los Angeles district attorney about having sex with Sam.

Garmone saved his toughest question for last. He wanted her to share the blame for the affair. "In all this period you have told us about, in which your activities with Sam were going on, you were aware, were you not, that he was a married man?"

"Yes," she said.

Hayes was excused. She had not cried or looked at Sheppard. She put on her mink coat and left the courthouse with her father and a police escort, refusing questions from reporters on her trail. Her testimony turned out to be a letdown.

Moments later, the State of Ohio rested its case.

18

THE DEFENSE

AFTER THE STATE rested its case, the sob sisters weighed in. They were not impressed. Margaret Parton of the *New York Herald Tribune* thought the state's case "seemed to me extremely weak. . . . The Susan Hayes matter . . . was blown up way beyond its importance—it was as if no one concerned in the case (or writing about it for the newspapers) had ever heard of *Sexual Behavior in the Human Male*."[1] Kilgallen also was unconvinced. It was clear to her that at least on Sam's part the two enjoyed a casual sexual relationship. Hayes's testimony made the state's case seem weaker by offering a motive that "is gossamer-flimsy and undebatably remote from the crime."

Sam Sheppard was not giving interviews—Corrigan's orders. But brother Richard told Kilgallen that Sam had appreciated her story putting the Susan Hayes affair into a favorable context. Kilgallen spun Richard's retelling of his brother's reactions into a story that the *New York Journal-American* bannered as "Dorothy Kilgallen Exclusive: Dr. Sheppard Says: "I didn't love Susan.' "[2]

———

For their defense, Corrigan and Garmone followed the game plan outlined in opening statements: first, that Sam was not the kind of man who would kill; second, the evidence proved that he could not have done it; and, finally, evidence pointed to a third party at the crime scene—in particular two independent witnesses who saw a strange man near the Sheppard home about the time of Marilyn's murder.

The burning question for the press and the prosecutors was whether Dr. Sheppard would take the stand as a witness in his own defense. It was risky.

A smart criminal defense lawyer allowed a client to testify only when convinced of his innocence and certain he would not lose his temper under vicious questioning. On the other hand, testimony of a likable and convincing defendant could outweigh troublesome facts and inconsistencies.

Dr. Steve Sheppard was the first defense witness. He wore a dark, expensive suit accented with a pocket square and carried a journal to the stand. Ever since Marilyn's murder, he had taken notes on pages in the prescription pads he carried, then transferred those notes into the journal. He spoke with the precision and confidence of a board-certified surgeon, laying out medical facts such as how a concussion affects short-term memory. In answer to Corrigan's questions, Steve tried to defuse the controversy over the location of Sam's brown corduroy sports coat on the morning of the murder. Steve testified that the coat was on the floor near the couch and he remembered stepping over it twice the morning of July 4.

Many times, witnesses can hide their personality on the stand. Gerber had kept his cool. But Steve Sheppard couldn't hide his anger and his sharp-edged sarcasm during cross-examination.

Parrino did get Steve Sheppard to admit that he didn't know why, upon arriving at the murder scene, he ran directly to Marilyn in the guest bedroom without being told where she was. Parrino made this small act seems suspicious.

Again and again, Steve Sheppard refused to give Parrino yes-or-no answers to his well-crafted, leading questions. In the end he may have won the battle of wits with the prosecutor, but the jurors got the impression of a smart, cunning doctor who would do anything to help his brother.

With his wildly popular TV show, radio broadcast, and syndicated gossip column in hundreds of newspapers, Walter Winchell reached nearly every household. He was the most influential broadcaster in the country. Over the weekend he broadcasted a report about a New York City woman who claimed to be Dr. Sam Sheppard's mistress and mother of his illegitimate child. Winchell's attack on Sheppard's reputation, already in tatters, could not have come at a more unfortunate time for the defense. The woman was a convicted prostitute named Carol Beasley who was serving time for robbing a customer at gunpoint. Five days earlier, the Cleveland police had received an anonymous tip about Beasley and eagerly checked it out with the help of the New York City police. Within forty-eight hours, they discounted Beasley. In the words of one detective, she was a "psycho." But Winchell, with police sources ranging the gamut from FBI director J. Edgar Hoover down to beat cops, ran the unsubstantiated allegation even though detectives had easily proven it false.

The next day in court Bill Corrigan was furious. Before the jury was brought in, he demanded that Judge Blythin poll the jurors to see who had heard the inflammatory broadcast.

Blythin was not eager to accommodate him. "Well, even so, Mr. Corrigan, how are you ever going to prevent those things, in any event?" he asked. "I don't justify them at all. I think it is outrageous, even if there were not a trial here. The trial has nothing to do with it in the court's mind, as far as its outrage is concerned but—"

Corrigan demanded to know if any jurors had heard the Winchell broadcasts and how it affected them.

"How could you ever, in any jury, avoid that kind of a thing?" Blythin asked. Eventually he relented and agreed to poll the jurors.[3] Two of the them, both women, admitted that they had seen Winchell's show and had heard the damaging allegations. In answer to the judge's questions, they said that the broadcast would not influence their judgment about Dr. Sam's guilt. Blythin liked their answers. "Pay no attention to that kind of information," he told them. "That's a type of scavenging that has no place on the air." Surprisingly, he decided to keep them on the jury; Corrigan shouted protests—to no avail.

Dr. Richard Sheppard, the next defense witness, was much more easygoing than his brother Stephen. He made the important point that it would have been impossible for anyone to batter Marilyn to death without getting his pants spattered with blood, at least from the knees up to the belt. At this, Corrigan displayed Sam's pants to the jurors. They saw only one large blood spot on the knee.

On cross-examination, John Mahon ignored the blood evidence and focused instead on what Richard Sheppard knew about disagreements between Sam and Marilyn, trying to buttress the state's motive for the homicide.

Oh, there were minor spats, Richard explained, the sorts of arguments that might occur in any marriage. For example, Sam and Marilyn routinely disagreed over where to spend the day on Thanksgiving and Christmas—with Marilyn's relatives, more than an hour away in the eastern suburbs of Cleveland, or in Bay Village with the Sheppard families, near the hospital, where Sam invariably was on call for holiday emergencies. "Marilyn had difficulty in adjusting to the life of a doctor's wife," Richard explained. He mentioned the long and unpredictable hours and nights Sam had to spend in the emergency room. "She wanted Sam to spend all of his free time with her," Richard went on. "Dr. Sam would return to the hospital and try to help as much as possible and learn as much as he could, and I don't think Marilyn quite understood that situation, that so often in a doctor's life the profession has to come first, and I think she was a bit jealous of Sam's profession."[4]

Mahon brought up the remark of Mayor Houk that had electrified the courtroom a month earlier. When you came into the den to attend to your brother, Mahon asked, did you not ask, "Sam, did you do this?"

Richard Sheppard denied this emphatically.

————

For two months, the jurors sat a few feet away from Dr. Sam, scrutinizing his face, his reactions to testimony, his little waves to family in the back, his sobs at unsettling photos of Marilyn. Finally, they got to hear his voice. This was the climax of the trial—for him, his lawyers, the prosecutors, and the press. His challenge was to win the sympathy of the jury. There was no other reason to testify. The jury had already heard, through witnesses and cross-examination, Sheppard's explanations of the evidence. If they believed him, they would exonerate him.

He turned in the witness box and looked at the jurors. For the first time, they swiveled their chairs toward a witness as he answered questions. Given that he was such a tall, strapping man, Sheppard's voice was something of a surprise—high, nasal, with a hint of a whine. His language seemed unnatural, deliberately elevated, pedantic. He apologized when he used slang, as if it was offensive or beneath him.

Immediately, Corrigan asked him about Tom Weigle's account of having severely spanked Chip. It was a spanking, not a beating, Sam insisted. Chip had been misbehaving all week and not responding to his mother. He had pushed down Weigle's two-year-old son a couple of times. When Chip hit him with the tomahawk in front of guests, Sam said he decided that his son needed to be taught a lesson.

Corrigan asked about his reaction when he discovered Marilyn's body. "I was horrified, shaken beyond explanation. And I felt that maybe I'd wake up and find all of this a horrible nightmare."

What was his condition after he was attacked? Corrigan asked.

"I was very confused. It might be called punchy in the language used as slang. I was stimulated or driven to try to chase the person, which I did."

"What did you do?"

"I tried to pursue it as well as I could under the circumstances."

"Where did you pursue it?" Corrigan asked.

"Toward the steps to the beach. Then I lost visualization of the form."

"Was it dark?'

"Yes. It was dark—but there was enough light for me to see this form. I descended the stairway to the landing and I visualized the form going down or as he came on the beach. It was at this time I felt I could visualize a silhouette that was describable."

"What happened on the beach?"

"I descended as rapidly as I could. I lunged or lurched and grasped this individual from behind. Whether I caught up to him or he waited for me, I don't know. I felt as though I had grasped an invisible object. I was conscious thereafter only of a choking sensation. That is all I remember until I have some vague recollection of having a sensation of being in the water."

"What did you determine about this person?"

"He had a relatively large form. His clothing was dark. He had a good-sized head—with a bushy appearance at the top of his head—his hair."

The doctor gave the jury a picture of the good-cop, bad-cop interrogation he underwent. At one point Sam showed how a detective reenacted the murder while accusing him. He held his hands high, holding a piece of folded paper, then hammered it down, showing how the detective yelled, "Down, down, down, down!" with each blow. The jury seemed startled.

He related how police had examined him for hypodermic-needle marks on his arms, thinking he was a drug addict, and doubted whether he was the father of the baby Marilyn had been carrying.

Corrigan asked him to describe Dr. Gerber at their first encounter on July 4.

"Well, I remember he was smiling and I couldn't understand why a person would be smiling at a time like that. He asked me if I had any chipped teeth."

"Did he look in your mouth?"

"No, he looked at me, how carefully I cannot say. He looked closely at my hands. I held my hands out for him. He looked at them on one side and then turned them over."

Sheppard's defense team had presented conflicting theories about the blood evidence. In grilling deputy coroner Lester Adelson, Corrigan had built the case that Marilyn Sheppard may have bitten her attacker. However, when Sam testified Corrigan made him recount each person or pet who may have innocuously shed blood in Dr. Sam's home. It was a long list—his niece Margaret, the previous owner of the home, various neighborhood boys, Koke the dog, Chip, even Marilyn. "There was a period that she was under Dr. Steve's care," Sheppard explained, "and she had difficulty with her periods and she had quite a bit of flow and she did have trouble."

"She could not or did not control it?" Corrigan asked.

"Yes, sir." Sam added that she had been on a "medication to stimulate blood formation."[5]

This last testimony offended some courtroom spectators, particularly some of the women reporters. "He seemed like such a cad," one said. As a doctor, Sheppard was comfortable talking about bodily functions. But in a 1950s courtroom, his talk about his wife's messy menstrual periods made him appear desperate and uncaring.

John Mahon, in the cross-examination of his career, needed Sam Sheppard to show his temper or to appear devious. Mahon focused on Sheppard's relationships with Julee Lossman and Susan Hayes. Corrigan objected repeatedly, but Blythin overruled his objections. "When this man is accused of murdering his wife, certainly his relations with other women are material," the judge stated.

Sheppard was well prepared. He answered earnestly and coolly. But in back of each answer, there was an excuse: Marilyn suggested that he look up Susan Hayes in Los Angeles; Julee Lossman pursued him.

In a tactic that by the next decade would be considered improper, Mahon made Sheppard seem guilty for hiring lawyers and making detectives wait for his lawyers before questioning him. You did not turn on a light as you ran upstairs, did you? Mahon asked. Did you not fail to grab a weapon when you chased "the form," even though you passed the fireplace tools?

Sam Sheppard had been grilled harshly many times before. He stayed calm. He seemed indignant. It seemed the only time he was directly hurt by a question was when he had to answer, near the end of cross-examination, that he had lied under oath about sleeping with Susan Hayes. Mahon also asked hundreds of questions, some with slightly different wording, that had Dr. Sam responding, "I don't know," "I can't say," or "I don't recall"—328 times.

Building to an emotional conclusion, Mahon placed his final shots: "Doctor, what is the best way to remove blood from clothing?" Mahon was suggesting that Sam ran down to the lake to wash off blood.

"I couldn't tell you, sir," Sam replied.

"Is cold water more effective to remove blood from clothing than hot water?"

"I am certainly no authority on that, and I have never tried to remove blood from clothing, sir."

"Now, Doctor, the injuries that you received, didn't you receive those injuries from jumping off of the platform down on the beach?"

"No, sir, I think that would be impossible, sir."

Mahon, his voice louder, demanded, "Now, Doctor, isn't this the fact: that you beat your wife that morning?"

"No, sir.

"And that after you had killed her you rushed down to that lake and either fell on those stairs or jumped off of the platform down there out to the beach and thereby obtained your injuries."

"That is absolutely untrue, sir. And unfair."

"That is all," the prosecutor said.[6]

Sam's lawyers and family were sure he had done a good job. He had not gotten angry or slipped up. But lawyer Paul Holmes, the Chicago reporter, felt that his performance might not be good enough. The doctor seemed a bit self-serving. "Perhaps he tried too hard to be lily white in everything, to shift blame unnecessarily for his own mistakes, and, worst of all, to project his keen intelligence in his answers." There was a tinge of self-righteousness in his responses. "Sam on the stand was a man who feared he might be convicted but deep down inside himself was sure that this would not happen." He failed at "giving the jurors what they wanted most to see, a look into his bared soul. He aroused pity in his jurors but got no understanding. He commanded attention but never put across to the jury an impression that he would come out with unvarnished truth no matter how much it hurt him."[7]

———

Dr. Charles Elkins was a strong witness for the defense, its only independent expert. An M.D. and a professor at a prestigious medical school, Elkins had served as chief of surgery with the rank of captain at a U.S. Army base hospital in Australia during the war. He could not be dismissed as an osteopathic doctor with connections to Bay View Hospital. His firm opinion was that Sam Sheppard had been injured. Elkins cited objective evidence: Sam was missing several reflexes on the left side; when pressed, his neck muscles had gone into involuntary spasms.

Sam Sheppard's injuries alone did not prove his innocence; Marilyn could have swung a bat and caught him at the back of his neck. But it was unlikely that he had staged his injuries, as authorities argued. Any doctor would know that a self-administered injury to the spinal cord was too risky.

But Dr. Elkins's scientific assessment came after the main event: Sam's three days of testimony. The newspapers gave Elkins little space. The jurors who were interviewed after the verdict seemed to have missed what he had to say.

———

Before the day of closing arguments, the out-of-town reporters believed that Dr. Sam would be exonerated. The state had not proven its case. "We were sure, then, that he would be acquitted," Margaret Parton wrote. "The faces of his relatives shone with pride and faith."

But assistant county prosecutor Tom Parrino changed that. Each side had five hours to deliver a closing argument. He went first for the state, using nearly two hours to make a logical, pointed, and merciless attack on the morality of Sam Sheppard and his account of the early hours of July 4, 1954. Making "fair inferences" from the evidence (as the judge had told the jury that each side was now allowed to do), Parrino spun the circumstantial evidence into a story that seemed to make sense. He started by asking the jurors to be logical, to take their own experiences in life into account and apply them to Dr. Sheppard's version of events.

"Here we have a man supposed to be covered in a cold, clammy sweat. It is such a state of shock that he is supposed to be out of touch with the surroundings. Have you jurors ever seen a person in shock from some injury? How did they react? Do you feel that the person has the ability to go to a telephone, dial a number of a friend and ask for help? I feel that he does not. What do you think? Is he in the state of shock? That's food for thought.

"We know Dr. Richard lived only a short distance away, maybe only three minutes away, but Dr. Sam did not call his brother. He knew his phone number better than he knew Mayor Houk's. He didn't call his brother Steve nor any member of his family. Does that seem reasonable and logical? . . .

"Mrs. Houk comes, and tried to give Dr. Sam some whiskey. That wasn't anything unusual. It's the common thing. But what did the defendant do when this offer was made to him? He refused the whiskey. I wonder why? Does he feel that he should not drink the whiskey because when the police come they will smell the whiskey on his breath and maybe think that at the time of the crime he was under the influence of liquor?

"I think the testimony of Dr. Richard is certainly important. You will recall that Dr. Richard comes into that home, goes over to the defendant, his brother, and asks, 'Sam, did you do this? Or did you have anything to do with this?' To which Sam replied, 'Hell, no!'

"The brother of the defendant, asking him, 'Did you do this or did you have anything to do with it?' Now what was his state of mind at that time as to the relationship between Marilyn and Sam? What would prompt a brother to make a statement like that? A statement that, in its import, is so severe that words alone cannot describe. What was the true relationship between the defendant and his wife? Why would a brother immediately ask the defendant that ominous question unless there was something in their background that would immediately make him question that perhaps his brother had committed this most foul, vicious and brutal act? It practically amounted to a direct accusation, did it not?"

Parrino turned his attack on Steve Sheppard. "As you appraise the testimony of Dr. Steve, I want you to ask yourselves, Have you ever heard such a story in all your lives? Have you? You could not tell what that man was going to say from one moment to the next, from one day to the next, now, could you? And the record will prove it. We are dealing with a foul, brutal and vicious murder. We must call a spade a spade. You cannot perfume it." Parrino was shouting now. "It is there. These are the facts. . . .

"So Dr. Steve comes to the scene. He doesn't bring his medical bag but packs his gun on his person. He comes into the house and sees his brother for no more than 60 seconds. In this courtroom he does not recall having any conversation with the defendant. At the inquest he testified that Sam said to him, 'They've killed Marilyn.' Dr. Steve didn't speak to the Houks, to the police, to anyone. No one spoke to him. So after seeing Sam for one minute, what does he do? He immediately rushed through the living room. Where did he go? Directly to the room of Marilyn Sheppard. Ask yourself. You see Sam wet. Isn't it logical that if Sam is wet, that if anyone killed Marilyn she might be down in the lake? But Dr. Steve runs directly without hesitation, upstairs to Marilyn's room."

Parrino attacked Steve for rushing Sam to the hospital, without using the stretcher and not asking permission from the police. "If this was a burglary, then this was the neatest burglar in history. There was no burglary, ladies and gentlemen. Someone had a desire to make it look like burglary."

Parrino pointed out that two policemen, Drenkhan and Eaton, said that Sam's sports jacket was folded on the daybed. "You remember Steve's testimony. He's going to cure all of these things. As he ran upstairs, he saw a jacket lying on the floor.

"Now, it is for you to decide. Does that sound reasonable to you, if Sam threw it off during the course of the night, that the jacket was going to be neatly folded? Or in this instance, is Dr. Stephen attempting to help his brother in a way that he has in so many instances in this case? . . . Is this jacket just another example of an attempt to assist his brother?"

Parrino ridiculed Sam Sheppard's testimony. "Who do we have as a defendant? We have a man 30 years old, six feet and 180 pounds, in the prime of life, active in football, basketball, water skiing, the punching bag. This man was rendered senseless with a single blow?

"There is a mark on his face but nothing on his hands or knuckles that would indicate combat. You men on the jury, if you rushed into such a room, how much strength could you muster up under that situation, where it is a matter of life and death, to possibly kill or be killed? How much strength can a normal man work up in a situation such as that? And exactly what force did the defendant work up on this night in that room? Where were the signs of a struggle in the room, other than the condition of Marilyn's bed? Where was Sam while 35 blows were being struck?" Parrino acted out the slaying, swinging his arm, again and again. "Where was he? What was he doing? How long did it take to strike 35 blows? Try it in your jury room and see, certainly thirty seconds, maybe more."

Why didn't Sam pick up a weapon when he heard his wife cry out? Parrino asked. "Now here is something of tremendous importance in this case. Is there any doubt that the assailant used a vicious instrument to commit this violent act? The assailant struck Marilyn many blows on the head. So here is Sam Sheppard in the same room as this unknown phantom. There is light shining in from the dressing room. If the burglar was in that room and took the time and the trouble to strike all those vicious blows on Marilyn, I ask you why the assailant did not use that same instrument, not to hit Sam 35 times but to strike just one single blow against him. Why did the murderer hit Sam just one single blow? Was he being charitable to Sam? Can you answer that question?"

Parrino ridiculed the vagueness and the apparent contradictions in part of Sam Sheppard's account. "Here is a man apparently with one blow, out. And how long is he out? An hour? But when he does awaken to reality again, he is sitting there in that room, he sits up, and he has the memory to recall—this man who was in a state of shock—he has the memory to recall that there is his wallet, that there is a badge apparently shining from that wallet. . . . But as he is running up those stairs prior to that moment he does not recall whether he had his jacket on or his T-shirt on."

Why can't he remember if he had on his jacket or T-shirt when he ran upstairs? "He wasn't hit yet. Why can't he remember that, this convenient memory of this defendant?

"It made no sense for him to run downstairs after the phantom killer. He doesn't call police on a bedroom phone. He carries no weapon. . . . You are not going to destroy this man with your bare hands, are you? You are not going to destroy this man that felled you with one blow with your bare hands, are you? Everything you love is upstairs, and he is downstairs. What could you possibly do unless you have a gun or an instrument to use in destroying that evil person?"

Out in the courtroom press section, Theo Wilson wrote a note to Parton:

"My God, I think he might be convicted after all." Parton scribbled back, "Tom's really wrapping it up."[8]

Parrino continued through the affairs, arguing that Sam didn't love his family, and disrespected his wife by publicly flaunting his affair with Susan Hayes in Los Angeles. "For a few paltry dollars, he could have gone to a motel and enjoyed himself to his heart's desire in some obscure motel on the highways of California where no one would know, but, no, he goes to the home of a friend in the presence of all these people."

Two weeks after they returned, Parrino noted, Sam and Marilyn moved from the double bed to twin beds in the guest bedroom. "What does that mean in this case, you married people? Does that mean something, maybe?"

And Dr. Sheppard lied under oath at the inquest, Parrino said. "If this defendant is such a person who would lie under oath to protect the name of a lady, which he has admitted, how many lies would he utter to protect his own skin?"

———

The Sheppard defense argued next. Pete Petersilge presented a low-key, businesslike summation, without Corrigan's passion or Parrino's biting edge.

After five months of investigation and nine weeks of trial, Petersilge pointed out, "the state still does not know how she was killed, the State still does not know with what weapon she was killed, the state still doesn't know why she was killed. And yet on the basis of that rather flimsy evidence, the State of Ohio is asking you to send Sam Sheppard to the electric chair."

Petersilge countered many of Parrino's questions about why Sam Sheppard didn't act as you might expect. He wouldn't turn on the light when he ran upstairs because he knew the house and had enough light to see, Petersilge said.

Dr. Sam's supposedly confused story had its own internal consistency, Petersilge argued. "If Sam had been clear-headed and thinking clearly and had deliberately killed his wife, as the State is charging, and if Sam had then tried to cover up, he could have done a lot better than he did. Sam is a smart man. You have seen him on the stand. It certainly would have been a very easy thing to put on another T-shirt."

Houk was the proper person to call, not his brother, he argued. Houk was closer, only two doors way. He was the head of public safety for Bay Village, the police chief's boss. "All this talk about the brothers removing Sam from the house in a hurry and without the permission of the police is perfectly silly. Why wouldn't they take him? He was an injured man."

It doesn't make sense that Dr. Sam would wake up to the sounds of the first blow or Marilyn's first cry, Petersilge said. He was a deep sleeper. "It might have been the sixth or eighth or ninth call for help that Sam heard, we don't know."

Petersilge criticized Detective Grabowski, the fingerprint man, for not trying to lift prints from the stairway railing. After all, the killer presumably went up and down the stairs.

Petersilge undercut the significance of the blood trail, saying it was dog blood. And even if that wasn't the case, the trail could not have been caused by a dripping weapon because blood coagulated. Heavier drips would be in the upstairs hallway—there were none—and then would taper off before getting to the living room and basement. That the slayer was walking throughout the house with a weapon dripping blood "is perfectly fantastic."

"Whoever killed Marilyn, standing beside that bed striking her, inevitably was sprayed with blood," the lawyer continued. "You just couldn't get away from it, and that blood wouldn't come in great big gobs. It would come just as it came on the other surfaces around there, a myriad of small spots." Mary Cowan had testified that the pants were not sprayed with blood and that blood cannot be washed off. The absence of blood on Sam's belt, shoes, and socks was "mute evidence, but very powerful evidence, that Sam Sheppard did not kill his wife, because the person who killed Marilyn certainly had the blood on him."

Sam's neatly folded jacket on the daybed likely was put there by Esther Houk or Betty Sheppard. "It doesn't seem like the sort of thing a man would do," Petersilge said.

The sand in Dr. Sheppard's pockets and cuffs and packed into the fabric of his socks backed up his story as well, the lawyer pointed out.

"Then there is one other thing which I think is important," Petersilge said, "and that is that the State hasn't shown any motive for this crime. And after all, people don't go out and kill one another without some reason."

Bill Corrigan took over. He was tired and afraid. He had started out defending Sam Sheppard thinking he was guilty; then he had become convinced that he was representing an innocent man.

Corrigan apologized to the jury for his bombast. Don't hold that against Dr. Sheppard, he implored. He hoped the jurors believed his outrage was tied to the injustice he felt Sam had endured. Corrigan tried to be spellbinding, moving from point to point. He dismissed Sam's affair. "Susan Hayes said they were together and when the discussion [of divorce] took place, Sam said to her, 'I love my wife, I love my son.' That's what he was saying to his paramour." How could there be "any talk about divorce and marriage when a man is lying with his paramour and telling her at the same time that he loves his wife and he loves his child? Was Susan Hayes deceived?

"He loved his wife!" he roared. "That he strayed was no proof that Sam Sheppard did not love his wife, his child and his home." He begged the jury not to disbelieve Sam because he happened to lie at the inquest about sleeping with Hayes. "I'd lie under oath too"—he jabbed his fingers at the jury—"and so would you" rather than "confess private sins to a hostile mob" at the coroner's inquest.

Corrigan felt it important to portray Dr. Gerber and Dr. Adelson as unfeeling and vengeful. He had to stir emotions, push the jurors toward outrage. He brought up Marilyn's fetus. "Why would they take that little baby that was unborn, that little baby and put it in a bottle in the morgue without consulting the father of that child? And they kept it out there, and they have kept it since in a bottle in the morgue for the curiosity of students and others. Why, they are to be condemned, they are to be condemned, Adelson and Gerber are to be condemned for that kind of tactic as public officials of this community. The only reason they did it is because they were going to work on the theory that they had evolved that very morning that he had killed his wife because she was pregnant."

As proof of the coroner's rush to judgment, Corrigan pointed to evidence that could not be tied to Sam—a tooth chip found on the bedroom floor and fibers from Marilyn's fingernail scrapings. Since these did not implicate Dr. Sheppard, Gerber "filed it away in the morgue to be forgotten until we brought it into court."

Furthermore, his client had been grilled expertly and repeatedly, night and day, Corrigan said. Sam Sheppard would have cracked and confessed if he were the slayer. "There would be a compulsion within his soul to give that off and tell about that, just as much as if he had taken some poison in his stomach."

It was wrong and unfair to interpret the doctor's hazy recall as a sign of guilt. "The man who was cross-examining him was calling for the reactions of a normal man, of a man who had sat down and figured things out and knew just what he was going to do from spot to spot. Sam was giving you the reactions of a man that had been blacked out twice."

Corrigan scorned the prosecutor's claims that after a day of saving lives Sam took his wife's life. How could they believe such a claim, he asked, his voice rising. Corrigan stood behind Sam and gripped the wrist of his client's left hand and raised a surgeon's hand to the jury, the pose at once beatific and surrendering. Can you believe he killed his pregnant wife, the lawyer asked, "with these beautiful hands, hands that worked over the sick and the wounded, hands trained to cure and not to kill?"

Corrigan read a letter that Sam had written to him.

" 'There is only one judge any of us should truly fear and I face Him without apprehension. I am completely free of any desire for revenge. I have no anger in my heart. . . . Marilyn is with me now. That is why I can withstand this ordeal.' "

Four jurors were crying at this point. Did they believe it, or were they moved by courtroom stagecraft?

Corrigan could not erase what the jurors had read about the case or what they had heard from friends, family, and even strangers. These everyday citizens were now at least low-wattage celebrities. This made it tougher for them to render an unpopular decision. Could they return to their neighborhoods if they had voted to acquit public enemy number one?

Christmas was coming up. Hotel lobbies and downtown department-store windows were wreathed in green and red. Corrigan hoped to benefit from generous hearts. "Sam's father couldn't be here," he said. "His mother was sick. And his little boy, I wouldn't bring into this courtroom because I have no idea of trying to arouse sympathy in your hearts, and that is the only reason that little Chip would be brought in here. But he exists, you know that."

Corrigan turned to the reporters just a few feet away and thundered, "Write this if you want to," then lashed at them for "lurid headlines, misleading headlines."[9] He begged the jurors to consider only what they had heard in the courtroom, knowing that emptying their minds of the summer's relentless coverage was nearly impossible. He demanded justice. He begged for justice. He warned that freedom would die in America if Dr. Sam was not acquitted.

———

The second half of the state's closing argument was handled by Saul Danaceau, then John Mahon. Danaceau spun out a scenario that questioned what had happened between the time Marilyn died and the time Sam called Spencer Houk. "We know that certain things were wiped off with either sandpaper or a cloth. . . . There was opportunity at that time to go around from room to room to simulate or fake a burglary. There was an opportunity at that time to get rid of whatever instruments were used. Dr. Gerber said a surgical instrument or another instrument similar to it. There was opportunity for hours to do things in that house, but only Dr. Sam Sheppard was there and could tell."

The state used the hiring of Corrigan against Sam, "Would an innocent man act that way? Why was the foremost criminal lawyer in our community summoned out there so hurriedly if this man was innocent? Why did he refuse to take the lie detector test?"

Mahon argued a new theory. That Sam had thrown himself off the bluff, a suicide attempt, which injured his neck. He was trying to kill himself, "pursued by his own conscience as he ran away from the foul act that he had just committed," Mahon argued. But soon "the cold water changed his mind," and he returned to the house and put a cover-up in place.

"Ladies and gentlemen, at your hands may rest the life—does rest the life—of this defendant, and so you do have a serious job." He asked that "full and complete justice be done, justice for this defendant, and equal justice for the people of this community."

Blythin gave instructions to the jury. He explained that they may draw inferences from facts, but that they must accept the one more favorable to the defendant. And, the judge noted, you may convict Dr. Sheppard even though the prosecution doesn't convince you of a motive. By law, proving a motive is not necessary for a murder conviction.

The judge ran through the five possible verdicts—not guilty, manslaughter, second-degree murder, first-degree murder with mercy, and: "If you do find the defendant guilty of murder in the first degree and do not recommend mercy, it will be the obligation of the court to sentence the defendant to death." At this, Sheppard appeared to gulp, then bit his lip.

At 10:15 A.M. on December 17, after forty-three days of testimony, the jury retired from the courtroom. The fate of a well-to-do young doctor rested in the hands of a hardware-store manager, a construction foreman, a steel-mill timekeeper, a railroad-ticket salesman, a receiving clerk, two factory workers, and five housewives.

If they took a final image of Dr. Sam with them to the deliberation room, it was probably as he last appeared in the courtroom—a handsome, imploring face, his eyes flitting from juror to juror, while his well-trained surgeon's fingers clasping a large gold crucifix.

Walter Winchell was stumped at first. He was combing for an exclusive, but with the jury locked up, he had nothing to report. It was December 19. Two days earlier, in a column entitled "A Reporter's Report on the Nation," he had written, "No matter the verdict—the defense counsel cannot be over concerned. . . . Because legal experts—are *sure*—the case has at least one reversible error—which would require a new trial. Legal experts I talked with—are astonished . . . over the admission of hearsay evidence. They say— it is not legal—and that no judge ever allows hearsay—especially when a life is at stake. . . . The dubious evidence the Cleveland judge allowed was the hearsay testimony of an alleged conversation—by Mrs. Sheppard and a neighbor. No corroboration—no proof—no SIR!!!"

Local reporters and editors had not expected the jurors to take long to make up their minds. "Their Verdict Is Possible by Nightfall," read a *Cleveland Press* afternoon edition. But deliberations dragged on all day. The next morning Sheppard searched the faces of the jurors as they were ushered into court before being sent to deliberate. Only three of them looked at him. His hopes for an acquittal faded. It seemed the best he could wish for was a hung jury, which would mean an expensive retrial.

Deliberations dragged into a fourth, then a fifth day. He waited in his cell, its walls covered with Chip's crayoned drawings, listening to classical music on a tiny radio. He tried to read medical journals and slog through a biography of Dr. George Crile, the founder of the Cleveland Clinic. At night he could hear prisoners yelling out windows to family members standing in the snow on sidewalks four stories below.

His family and lawyers decided to consider the long delay as good news. The *Cleveland Press* had made up its mind hastily; so had the public. Perhaps the jurors had been swayed by the two hundred exhibits and Corrigan's lawyering.

After five days of deliberations, lawyers on both sides were talking about a retrial. It had been long enough for jurors to thrash out positions and then reach a compromise verdict. A hung jury would be a victory for Sheppard. Now that he and his lawyers had seen the state's case, they could correct mistakes, search for new evidence, hire experts, find new ways to attack the prosecution's case.

By December 21, the jury had taken eighteen written ballots. At first they had voted 7 to 5 for conviction. Now only two jurors held out for acquittal. After each vote, the jury foreman tore up the ballots and flushed them down a toilet. The last holdout was Louise K. Feuchter, juror number five.

———

Later on in the afternoon of December 21, the jury buzzed the court. They had a verdict. In the crowded, smoky courtroom, Sam waited next to Corrigan. Judge Blythin read the form. "We find the defendant not guilty of first degree murder"—Sam smiled and sighed—"but guilty of murder in the second degree."

Sam seemed stunned beyond belief. Blythin asked him if he had anything to say before he was sentenced.

"I'd like to say, sir, I am not guilty, and I feel that there has been proof presented before this court that has definitely proven that I couldn't have performed this crime."

Blythin gave him a life sentence. He would be eligible for parole in ten years.

The Sheppard brothers, of course, were outraged. "This is a great miscarriage of justice," Dr. Richard said. "My brother is innocent. We will appeal to the highest court in the land."

"We'll never quit this fight," said Dr. Steve.[10]

———

The jurors agreed among themselves not to talk to reporters afterward, which nearly sparked a brawl as they tried to push through the reporters and camera crews gathered outside. "After the verdict, we were escorted down to our taxis, and I have never seen a group of people act like that—it was a shame to the human race!" juror Anne Foote recalled recently. "They were clambering all over the car, to get in, get information. It was terrible. I'll never forget that part, so many people you couldn't see trying to get to us."[11]

Within weeks, a couple of jurors eventually broke the silence and were quoted anonymously in news stories. They said Sheppard's account was "fantastic." They felt that for some reason he had become enraged at Marilyn, began striking her and was unable to stop, swept up in fury, until he had beaten her to death. Hence, murder in the second degree.

All of the surviving jurors, five people, were tracked down and interviewed for this book. Their opinions are eye-opening, even shocking. They based their guilty verdict, in large part, on several assumptions that have now been disproved as well as on information they retained—before the trial— from news articles or from other people.

In general, these five jurors said they convicted Sheppard because they didn't believe his testimony, felt that he was arrogant, and thought his extramarital affairs provided a motive. They based their decision on several things they assumed to be true: the long time between Marilyn's death and Sam's call for help; someone removing blood and fingerprints from the scene; the Sheppards' dog not barking. Furthermore, they each said they knew Sam Sheppard had had several affairs, even though just one, with Susan Hayes, was established in court. Clearly, the jury had been contaminated by press accounts before the trial and perhaps during it.

William Lamb, a construction foreman, was convinced that Sam and his brothers were guilty of a crime-scene cover-up. "The house was washed down, wiped down, the walls, doors . . . with a solution of some nature used for cleaning the house. It left vertical streaks and there were no fingerprints in the whole house—that tells you something." Sam was "a kind of spoiled brat. Brother Stephen ran the show, you know. Sam was very kind to the jury, smiled every day." Also, Lamb said, "it was admitted to us that he did have many lady friends. He was cheating on his wife."[12]

Howard Barrish, who worked at Republic Steel, reached his guilty vote easily. "He was the only one there besides his wife and a boy and a dog in the house. Everything was locked up. Everything. There was no forcible entry anyplace. The stories they came up with—the intruder and all that—it just didn't gel."

Anne Foote, a homemaker, should not have been seated as a juror. "Their reputation in their hospital was not the greatest," she said. "It happened that somebody I knew had an abortion there and at that time abortions were out, and they were done secretly." Foote was most convinced of Sam's guilt by the time lapse between Marilyn's death and Sam's call for help. "That's what really made us think it couldn't have been anyone else. If it was anyone else, why did it take so long for him to call the police? Why didn't he call the police right away? Why did he call his brother and have him come over to take care of things and clean things up?"[13]

No evidence was presented at the trial that showed that Dr. Steve Sheppard had cleaned up the murder scene. As we now know, Gerber's 3 A.M. time of death was contradicted by the written report of his own deputy coroner, who performed the Marilyn Sheppard autopsy and placed her death at around 4:30 A.M.

Lois Mancini, seated as an alternate juror, thought Sheppard was guilty from the start. "I read the first story and said, 'I bet he did it.' " She too felt that Sheppard "was a spoiled brat" because he had two sports cars but "was having a fit" when Marilyn bought a new appliance. "One thing I always remember, the prosecution asked if he knew how to remove blood from an item and he said no. A doctor doesn't know how to get blood out of something? Cold water! Anybody knows that." Mancini was mistaken; Sheppard was asked on cross-examination if he knew that the *best* way to remove blood was with cold water, and he said he didn't know. Furthermore, as Marilyn had complained to friends, Sam was clueless about domestic maintenance.

Asked about a possible motive, Mancini replied, "Well, he was going out with some of these gals. . . . He used to go and meet gals at the bar there in Rocky River." There was nothing presented in court about Sheppard and a bar in Rocky River.

The Sheppard case shows that once you've read or formed an opinion about a suspect, it is nearly impossible to erase it from your mind. In celebrated trials, jurors are often sanctified, by the winning side usually, as exemplars of common sense. Often, however, they base their decisions on misinformation or impressions, not upon the direct evidence before them.

———

Many people—editors at large and small outlets included—were shocked by the verdict. They had read the neutral coverage of the New York *Daily News,* the wire-service reports, and others, and believed that the case against Sheppard had not been proven. The *Citizen* of Asheville, North Carolina, a Bible Belt town that harshly condemned adultery, called the verdict "utterly preposterous" and disparaged "Ohio justice, if that is what it is. . . . Of course, Dr. Sheppard was not really tried for murder. He was tried for manifold and specified sins and indiscretions which while offensive to society, do not rate a murder rap. . . . The Sheppard case was set up for the sob sisters and the little minds who write suggestive headlines. . . . The Lothario-doctor-ne'er-do-well was a gone goose from the time the trial got into its second week. The 12 men and women, who were more a Greek chorus than a trial jury, gave back just what they were fed in as notorious and vulgar a travesty on justice as ever affronted the dignity of the law in America."[14]

Kilgallen was astounded. Perhaps the doctor had killed his wife, but the prosecutors had not proven it. "It was a verdict wrongly arrived at and therefore frightening," she wrote in a column for the next day. "I heard the same evidence the jury heard. I saw Dr. Sheppard on the stand. I listened to the summation by both sides. I could not have convicted him of anything except the possible negligence in not locking his back door." The prosecutors did not explain what happened between midnight and six in the morning, she complained, even though they all had private theories that they had shared with reporters. Kilgallen revealed their out-of-court musings: police inspector McArthur felt Sam went upstairs, tried to make love to Marilyn, she made a flippant remark about Susan Hayes, and he flew into a rage. Deputy coroner Adelson thought Sheppard was a psychopath or a schizophrenic. Prosecutor Mahon said the couple got into an argument, Marilyn struck first, detonating her husband into a murderous rage. "This is the first time I have ever seen what I believed to be a miscarriage of justice in a murder case,"

Kilgallen wrote. "It is the first time I have ever been scared by the jury system, and I mean scared."[15] Usually, the *Cleveland News* prominently displayed Kilgallen's column. Its editors killed this one.

The next day Chief Eaton turned over the keys to Sheppards' house to Bill Corrigan.

Seltzer said the *Cleveland Press* sold thirty thousand extra copies the night of the verdict.[16] With the case over, his newspaper suddenly decided it was time to back away from the monstrous sensation. In an editorial, the *Press* said: "Somehow, in some dark way, this case became too much a part of all our lives. Too interesting. Too important. Let the tragic episode end now. For always." But the beast it spawned would not trot meekly into a cage.

PART 2

Any theory that is contradicted
by a proven fact has to be incorrect.

—PAUL KIRK, PH.D.

19

THE SCIENCE OF MURDER

DR. PAUL KIRK had not followed the Sheppard murder trial even though
he was a famous criminalist and the San Francisco newspapers had lavished
space on the case. He had been busy teaching at the University of California
at Berkeley and performing pro bono crime-scene analysis for police departments and prosecutors. He had not even heard that his 1953 textbook, *Crime
Investigation: Physical Evidence and the Police Laboratory,* had been cited
as an authority during testimony.

That all changed in early January 1955. Bill Corrigan telephoned Kirk at
his home in Berkeley and asked him to reinvestigate the homicide. Kirk was
not sure he wanted to get involved. From his cursory reading of the local
newspapers, he recalled that Sam Sheppard supposedly had faked a head injury to throw police off the track, then had refused to undergo a polygraph
exam. Though he had consulted on defense cases several times, Kirk usually
analyzed evidence for prosecutors and police agencies; the hurly-burly of the
Sheppard murder did not immediately appeal to him.

By this point, Corrigan had to realize what a large mistake he had made
in not presenting an expert witness to try to counter the shaky findings of Dr.
Gerber and the incomplete work of Mary Cowan. He might have been feeling guilty as he pleaded with Kirk to take a look at the evidence. A great injustice had been done, the lawyer insisted to Kirk, and a man is wrongfully
imprisoned. Without your wisdom, this injustice will remain unchallenged.

Kirk said he needed to think about it.

He never expected to work as a crime solver. He had earned a chemistry
degree at Ohio State University in 1924 and a doctorate in chemistry at the
University of California three years later. He taught biochemistry to medical

students at the University of California and published journal articles with such titles as "A Volumetric Modification of the Pregl Halogen Micro Combustion Method for Organic Iodine." In 1935, by neighborhood circumstance, he was drawn into a life of crime study. A twelve-year-old girl had been raped and left unconscious in the brushy Berkeley hills. Kirk was known as a diligent microchemist to an adjunct professor at Berkeley who was also the city's police chief, August Vollmer, a pioneer in modern police methods. (Vollmer, dubbed "the Best Police Chief in America," was the first to link patrol cars by radio and to collect and use crime statistics to deploy manpower, among other innovations.) Vollmer asked Kirk to make a scientific analysis of the crime scene.

Kirk and a graduate assistant with a zoology background noted crushed poison-oak leaves, matted milkweed nettle, cotton fibers snagged in the brush, and other clues. Kirk reconstructed the crime based on these and other observations and asked police to stake out the remote site. They detained a suspicious visitor to the area and searched his home to seize his clothes. Once Kirk matched nettles, fibers, and snags from the man's clothes to what he found at the crime scene, the man confessed. Case closed. Though his methods seem obvious today, his techniques were little used by police departments in the United States at the time.

Word of Kirk's success spread, and soon he was taking on lab assignments for police departments throughout the Bay Area, working on cases evenings and weekends. He became hooked on using the laws of chemistry, physics, and other hard sciences to examine evidence and solve crimes, making it a life's work. He was often called upon for help by Alameda County district attorney Earl Warren, who later became the chief justice of the United States Supreme Court.

In his university laboratory Kirk developed standard analytical techniques that could be taught and used by crime-lab workers anywhere. He interrupted his work for two years during World War II when he helped conduct plutonium research for the Manhattan Project, the team of scientists who built the first atomic bomb.

Kirk became known as the founding father of criminalistics, a term he coined. By the time Corrigan telephoned him, Kirk had worked on 630 criminal cases, including some that put men on death row. The Sheppard case intrigued Kirk. Before becoming involved, he told Corrigan that Corrigan would need to understand the way he worked: once he took on a case, no one was to tell him what to look for or what to expect to find. In fact, Kirk said, he might end up building a case *against* Dr. Sheppard.[1] He was a scientist; his only loyalty was to the evidence.

Corrigan replied that he understood the possible danger but wanted to hire him nonetheless. His client said he was innocent. Kirk, the gifted criminalist, could prove it one way or the other.

In the wake of the Sheppard guilty verdict, a reassuring popular opinion took hold in Cleveland: that a wealthy man could not get away with murder—even if he employed skilled lawyers and was a member of a powerful, protective family. In other words, the system worked. Beneath this sentiment flowed a strong current of dissatisfaction. Dr. Sam was denying the public a more satisfying victory by refusing to confess. People could not "put an end to it," as the *Press* had urged, and get back to their lives.

Seltzer, Gerber, and the police, perhaps hoping to erase nagging doubts, began exerting pressure to force Sheppard to admit his guilt. A week after the verdict, the *Press* ran an article, based on anonymous sources, titled "Sam to Get Chance to Clear Mysteries." It reported that "authorities" would make a "final effort" to "clear up the mysteries in the case."[2] They wanted to know what happened to the murder weapon and Dr. Sam's missing T-shirt and "what was the spark that caused the suburban osteopath to pound his wife to death, as the jury ruled he did."[3] The newspaper reported that the police offered an inducement to Sheppard—a shorter prison term. Admitting guilt would help him win relief from the Ohio Parole Board because its members would want to know if he "has repented and expressed regret at his crime—or whether he holds a grudge against society."

Sam Sheppard and his lawyer had no intention of giving the police what they wanted. In addition to trying to hire Paul Kirk, Corrigan filed a motion for a new trial, saying that his client had been treated unfairly. In the motion, the lawyer attacked the judge for failing to protect the jury from the poisonous news coverage. Corrigan also accused prosecutors of concealing four pieces of evidence that suggested an intruder in the Sheppard house: red threads under Marilyn's fingernails that didn't match Sam's clothing; a piece of dark red leather that matched nothing in the home; a third fragment of human tooth found next to Marilyn's bed; and an unfiltered cigarette butt from the second-floor toilet.

It seemed as if a toxin had been released into the Sheppard family. Dr. Richard A. Sheppard was hospitalized with pleurisy during jury deliberations. It fell to Dr. Steve to intubate his father's chest and drain fluid every several days. He wasn't recovering and kept losing weight. By January, tests at the Cleveland Clinic showed that he had stomach cancer. Little could be done medically.

Janet Sheppard, Steve and Betty's nine-year-old daughter, suffered in ways familiar to her sister and cousins. After the trial she felt shunned at school. Behind her back, she could make out others whispering about terrible things her uncle had done. "I overheard or imagined such remarks while choking back the tears, horrified, unable to breathe, move or speak, and just wishing I could totally disappear," she wrote decades later. She did not fight back because she so desperately wanted to fit in and have friends. "It seemed to me that everybody outside of my family was convinced that Uncle Sam was guilty and therefore they all thought that my family was bad, which meant that I was bad. The most terrible thing was that I believed them. I was certain that I must be, indeed, a very bad, unlovable person."[4]

The family burden grew heavier on January 7, 1955. Ethel Sheppard was staying in Rocky River with Steve and Betty while her husband was treated at Bay View. Considering the trauma of the past six months, Ethel had put on a good front for the children and the public. After breakfast that day, Steve left for work, the girls walked to school, and Betty went grocery shopping. Chip had a cold and stayed home with his grandmother.

Betty returned in time to fix lunch. She asked Janet, who had walked home for the meal, to call her grandmother to the table. Janet could not get an answer at the bedroom door, which was locked. Betty ran up and opened it with a key. Ethel Sheppard was lying faceup on the bed, wearing her glasses, and still holding a snub-nosed .38-caliber revolver in her hand. A bullet had pierced her skull near the right ear. When police arrived, they found a note she had written on Dr. Steve's stationery and left on a card table. "Dear Steve: I can't manage without Dad—thanks for everything. Mother." She had left a signed, blank check to pay for cleanup and repair to the room.

Before her son's trial for murder, it was Ethel Sheppard who had urged Sam to be strong and to show faith. She had sent him self-help pamphlets that promoted positive thinking through prayer. But by midfall, she herself had fallen into a deep depression and tried to kill herself by swallowing a bottle of sleeping pills. Steve and his father had managed to find her, get her stomach pumped, and cover up her sad suicide attempt. When asked by reporters why Mrs. Sheppard had been hospitalized, Steve said that she had suffered a stroke. Not even Betty or Sam knew the truth.[5]

Steve Sheppard blamed himself for his mother's suicide. She had spotted his revolver in the handkerchief drawer of his dresser while putting away freshly laundered clothes. It was the weapon he had carried for protection to the murder scene on July 4.

"Mother had really been dead for two months," Steve later wrote. "We had pulled her back and she had resumed a pretense of living because she had accepted the suggestion that her suicide would hurt Sam's chances at his trial. Now the trial was over and the worst had happened and there was no longer a need, as she saw it, for her to live with her pain."[6]

In the county jail, Sam knew something was up. His jailers abruptly arrived at his cell block and removed his radio. He depended on it for news and classical music. What is going on? he demanded. His jailers said they couldn't explain at the moment.

Soon Steve, Betty, and Dorothy Sheppard arrived. "Who is it?" Sam demanded before they could speak. Steve told him. He was unprepared for Sam's reaction. He broke down and sobbed for several minutes. He was inconsolable. Within hours, the news went over the airwaves and made the front page of the afternoon *Press* under the large headline LOCKS DOOR AND PENS DEATH NOTE.

Sitting in jail, Sam felt frustrated that he could do nothing to help his family. He was a surgeon, someone whose modus operandi was taking action, being in charge, exuding confidence to whoever asked for help. After he controlled himself, he composed a statement for the press.

Today my mother . . . took her life as a result of American injustice. Though no person had more faith in Sam Sheppard's innocence, no person had lost more faith in her fellow man and U.S. law than she. Mother found the unjust court and outright public persecution more than she could endure.

Personal loss and hardship was something that she had experienced in her share due to her constant effort in a cause for others. This was the great person who was a mother to Marilyn as well as to her immediate family. She taught Marilyn to cook, sew, keep house, and care for her baby as a newborn and as he grew. It was Mother Sheppard who flew to Marilyn's assistance when she had Chip and when she later suffered surgical disease.

Mother and Marilyn now are both wrongfully gone from us. As we think of them both we realize they were very much alike in many many ways, both psychologically and physically, down to their small feet and their self-demanding perfectionism.

They are now spared this "Hell on Earth" and may be fortunate.

However, I can and will never stop fighting in the name of the truth for their sake, if for nothing else. —S. Sheppard

Later that day Sheriff Sweeney put Sam on suicide watch in a solitary cell, with bed checks every quarter hour. Sam had argued, unsuccessfully, to stay in his cell block, "where I know all the fellows and have friends." The next day, he was allowed to leave the county jail for a few hours to attend the funeral. Kneeling at the service, he prayed with one hand over his heart, the other at his knee. He did not want to be photographed handcuffed at the wrist to a deputy sheriff.

Steve Sheppard was bitter, consumed by rage. As he continued to care for his father at Bay View, he talked openly about seeking revenge for the injustices he felt had been rained on their families.

"You're too intelligent for that," he recalled his father saying. "Violence, if that's what you're talking about, cannot possibly solve anything—only make things worse. You are just bitter and upset. And a little hot-headed, too, I'm afraid. Maybe this veneer we call civilization wears a little thinner on you than on the others. But, Steve, revenge is not our business, nor your business. 'Vengeance is mine, saith the Lord.' I really believe that."

Steve was surly. There's no evidence God gives a damn about us, he argued, if there even is a God.

"Don't be in such a hurry," his father replied. " 'He works in mysterious ways, His wonder to perform.' Meanwhile let him continue to run the world, Steve. He's been at it for quite a while and you aren't ready to take over yet."[7]

Ten days later Richard Allen Sheppard, sixty-four, died in the hospital that he'd built. *The New York Times* ran an eight-inch obituary, noting that he had served as president of both the National Osteopathic Hospital Association and the American College of Osteopathic Surgeons.

Sam went to the funeral in handcuffs. Again, there was a mob of curiosity seekers, reporters, and photographers. For the second time in ten days, he and his brothers buried a parent and found their grief on public display. "We could not bury our dead in respectful privacy," Steve raged. "We had to walk in a prying, obscene spotlight."[8]

―――――

When Paul Leland Kirk arrived at the Cleveland airport on January 22, 1955, reporters were waiting for him. He was easy to spot. He was a bland-looking man, fifty-two years old, of small build. He was pulling a large, sturdy trunk of carefully packed scientific equipment. Kirk favored gray suits with white dress shirts and dark neckties. He had short silver hair, wire-rimmed spectacles, and a thin, almost invisible mustache. His only stylistic tic was that he liked to smoke a large curved pipe that reminded people of Sherlock Holmes.

Corrigan had already vexed the scientist by telling reporters that "a renowned expert" had been hired who thought the case was "a miscarriage of justice." Kirk contradicted Corrigan, to the delight of the press. "I have no fixed opinion on the case," Kirk said. He would simply look into it and "marshal the facts."

At the murder scene Kirk went inside, took off his suit coat, and got to work. He ignored reporters who rang the doorbell and peered into windows. Moments after entering the murder room and seeing its walls, Kirk was stunned. He had gathered evidence at scores of crime scenes; until now, he had never encountered blood patterns so richly detailed and at the same time so elegantly simple. It was a crime-scene analyst's dream, a showcase for applying the techniques of blood-pattern analysis.

First, Kirk vacuumed the bedroom floor with a small, high-powered sweeper with a customized filter to trap minute particles. Then he photographed every corner and angle of the room and made measurements. The twin beds were eighteen inches apart. Their headboards were against the south wall. To the left, along the east wall, were the entrance door and a closet door. Windows were on the west and north walls.

Kirk measured the size and noted the shapes of scores of blood drops. He had experimented in and written extensively about the ballistics of blood—how it traveled through the air and how it reacted when it struck various materials at different angles and velocities. By the 1940s, he and other forensic scientists had established principles that were widely accepted.[9] He outlined many of them in his textbook *Crime Investigation*. For example, "impact spatter"—airborne blood that strikes a surface—looks much different from "contact transfer"—blood that is smeared on. Flying blood starts to coagulate as soon as it is shed and leaves beaded droplets. A drop falling perpendicular to the floor makes a round spot. A drop flying to a flat surface at an angle leaves a bowling-pin shape, a bead with a tail. The more acute the striking angle, the longer the tail. The line of the tail shows the trajectory of flight.

On the room's bloodstained walls Kirk noted two broad, overlapping patterns. First, smallish drops of blood radiated out from a hub in straight lines like spokes in a wheel; one blood drop had skimmed across the top of a radiator cover like a stone skipping across the surface of a pond. The hub or source of the blood was Marilyn's battered head, positioned near the center of her mattress.

Studying the trajectories, Kirk was certain that her head had been stationary when the beating started and stopped. Practically all the blood spots in the room and on the bedsheets radiated in straight lines from her head. She was either knocked out or stunned by an early blow or the killer perhaps held her by the hair so he could be certain to strike her face.

All four walls were spattered—except for a sharply defined gap starting in the northeast corner and extending a few feet along the east and north walls, where no spatter was found. How to account for this? Kirk ran strings from each boundary of the gap back to the hub, creating a pie shape. The pie shape was two feet wide where it cut across the edge of the mattress, the width of an average man. Kirk determined that the killer was positioned to the left of the foot of the bed. As he battered Marilyn, his clothes intercepted scores of blood drops, sparing a portion of the wall behind him.

The east wall displayed another distinctive pattern: a horizontal arc of larger blood spots that cut across the bedroom and closet doors, parallel to and about three and a half feet above the floor. These larger drops were cast-off blood from the murder weapon, Kirk determined. As the killer struck Marilyn, again and again, he coated his weapon in blood. At the end of his backswings, he inadvertently flipped some of the blood collected on the weapon against the wall. No blood was found on the ceiling or high on the east wall. This horizontal arc of cast-off blood showed that the killer used a level, left-handed swing to strike Marilyn's head.

Taking into account these patterns, the position of Marilyn Sheppard's head, and the span of an average man's arm, Kirk estimated the length of the murder weapon: about one foot.

One blood spot in the room begged for attention. It was the largest by far, one inch in diameter and nearly round. It adhered to the lower third of the wood closet door, about three feet from where Marilyn's head rested, and did not display the beading characteristic of impact spatter. Kirk had never seen a volume of blood this large travel through the air in a compact mass; it would normally break apart into smaller droplets. So how did this unique blood spot get there?

It took him four days in Cleveland to gather evidence, reconstruct the crime, and test parts of Sam's story. One night, for example, Kirk had Dr. Richard Sheppard dress in a white shirt and dark slacks and stand at the foot of Marilyn's bed. All the lights were off except a fifty-watt lamp in the dressing room off the master bedroom, which served as the second-floor nightlight and was kept on when Sam left for emergency calls. Kirk pretended that he was asleep on the living room daybed, eyes closed. Then he jumped up and ran upstairs as fast as he could.

As he climbed, Kirk saw Dr. Richard's white shirt but little else. It was an indistinguishable white form, just as Sam had described. Kirk repeated the experiment with a one-hundred watt bulb in the lamp. Kirk again saw a whitish form, with a more discernible outline, but he was still not able to tell if it was human or a mannequin or something altogether different.

Before he returned to Berkeley, Kirk visited the Cuyahoga County prosecutor's office to look at the physical evidence used in the case. He found several surprises. Among them, the spatter stains on Marilyn's thin cotton pajama bottoms were not across the thighs and waist, as you would expect if she was wearing them when she was battered. The pattern was consistent with the position of the pants shown in crime photos: removed from one leg, pulled down and bunched below the knee of the other leg. Spatter patterns on the bedspread showed that it had been moved after the killing. The quilt had not been arranged as the photographs showed. It was rumpled and pushed toward the foot of the bed, not spread over the bed, when the beating unfolded. This confirmed another aspect of Dr. Sheppard's story—after returning to the bedroom from the lake, he had covered Marilyn's lower body because "she was a modest woman." "To any experienced investigator, such a condition is direct and forceful evidence" of sexual attack, Kirk explained.[10]

He was surprised by the size of the pieces of Marilyn's teeth. From having read the trial transcript, he expected enamel chips. Instead one piece was an entire incisor except for its root. Another fragment was half that size. The third tooth piece was one quarter inch long and had not been tied to Marilyn Sheppard during testimony.

The broken teeth puzzled Kirk at first. A blow to the mouth, one strong enough to snap teeth, would cause bleeding or bruises. Marilyn's lips and chin were not bruised, swollen, or cut.

Kirk theorized that the killer covered Marilyn's mouth with his hand to keep her quiet during a rape. At some point she bit down in terror, breaking her teeth on a finger bone or having them snapped as her attacker yanked back his bleeding hand. Awash in pain, enraged, he clubbed her again and again, gouging her head, smashing her hands that were thrown up in defense.

By the time Kirk left Cleveland, he said he "was astonished at first to find how much emotion and lynch spirit there was in Cleveland." This mood helped him understand, at that point, why the jury returned the verdict it did. He was captivated by unanswered questions. He knew he needed to do some scientific sleuthing in his lab.

———

Back on the Berkeley campus in his lab in the Life Sciences Building, Kirk squeezed the Sheppard analysis around his teaching and pro bono police-lab work. He and his lab assistants kept meticulous notes.

He ran an experiment that Dr. Sam had asked his lawyers to try: seeing how long blood would drip from a weapon before drying. Kirk dipped the ends of possible murder weapons—a length of pipe, a flashlight, a hammer—into a large beaker of human blood, then walked across a runner of paper, making a trail. Kirk's results confirmed Sam's original hunch. At first, a couple of large drops fell, then a few more smaller ones. All the blood was congealed by about fifteen feet. Kirk concluded that the blood trail in the house must have been placed there by a different mechanism, certainly not by the weapon.

Next Kirk dipped different weapons in blood and swung them, one by one, toward a paper sheet covering a wall a few feet away. No matter how quickly or carefully Kirk swung a weapon, its cast-off blood did not replicate the one-inch stain on the closet door. The blood broke up in the air, rather than staying in a compact mass that made a one-inch spot. Finally, Kirk cupped a bit of blood in his hand and, from only a couple of inches away, gently tossed the blood in a pouring motion to the wall. Eureka! Virtually the same spot. This supported his thesis that the killer was bleeding, probably from a bite wound on his hand.

Kirk and his graduate students tested the time it took for blood smears to dry on a similar watchband and found that it took about ninety seconds. It would be easy for someone to pick up a watch, find the green bag, and put the watch inside without getting additional blood on the outside of the bag. This finding did not eliminate Sam Sheppard as a suspect, but it sharply reduced the shortest possible time between the killing and stashing the watches to a few minutes.

To complete his analysis, Kirk needed to test the unique blood spot. Steve Sheppard, with his minister as a witness, scraped off some of this blood as well as a nearby "control" spot, carefully collecting them in separate vials.

Kirk had already typed some of Sam's blood smuggled from the jail by his brother. It was group A. Marilyn's blood from the mattress cover dissolved and reacted quickly to show group O, which confirmed Mary Cowan's assessment.

Sam's brothers and lawyers, of course, hoped that Kirk would determine that the unique spot was group B or group AB blood—neither Marilyn's nor Sam's. They believed such a finding definitely would prove that someone else had killed Marilyn.

Kirk, of course, was aware of the possibility. In the quiet of his graduate laboratory, far from reporters or lawyers or interested Sheppard relatives, Kirk directed his lab assistant to make the tests. The control spot, which Kirk called stain B, dissolved quickly, turning distilled water pink in a series of test tubes. Using reagents that test for the absence of type A and type B antibodies in the samples, he got quick results. Group O blood, likely that of Marilyn Sheppard.

The dried flakes of the unique spot—stain A, Kirk called it—did not dissolve at all. He left the tube overnight in a lab refrigerator. The next day he noted a slight ring around the test tube. The two reagents reacted slowly, taking a couple of hours. It seemed to be group O blood.

Kirk was puzzled. Both stain samples were shed at the same time and dried under the same conditions. Even though both were group O blood, they showed remarkably different properties. Kirk made the highly debatable conclusion that two persons had shed blood in the murder room.

Mary Cowan had testified to having had trouble typing the blood on Dr. Sam's watch. She would say later she believed it to be group O, but without a strong reaction she could not make the call. Kirk thought his troubles typing the "unique spot" were similar to Cowan's experiences. "Could the blood on the watch have come from the murderer's bleeding hand as he stripped it from Sam's wrist?" Kirk wondered.[11]

Kirk studied photos of Marilyn Sheppard's head wounds. Many of them were crescent-shaped and, based on the cast-off-blood pattern, at right angles to the axis of the weapon. This suggested to Kirk that the murder weapon may have been cylindrical, and flared at the end. Coroner Gerber may have had the same idea before he settled on his surgical-instrument theory. Days after the murder Gerber told reporters the weapon might have been a short length of pipe.

The murderer either picked up the weapon in the bedroom or carried it in with him. Kirk didn't believe it had been a "weapon of opportunity," often used when a domestic killing erupts and one partner uses a handy object as a club. According to interviews with Chip Sheppard, Sam's brothers, and housemaid Elnora Helms, nothing was missing from the bedroom.

Kirk theorized that the weapon could have been a heavy three-cell flashlight, something that an outsider might carry into the home. The killer might have held the flashlight by its light and swung the heavier, battery-loaded end at his victim's skull. The weapon must not have been heavy; pieces of the victim's skull bones, though fractured, had not been pushed into the dura, the leathery outermost membrane surrounding the brain and spinal cord.

He turned his attention to the red particles vacuumed from the bedroom floor. They seemed to match Mary Cowan's description of what had been scraped from the body's fingernails. Kirk analyzed the chemical composition of the red nail polishes from Marilyn's vanity, "Cherries in the Snow" and "Bachelor's Carnation." Neither matched that of the tiny red flecks. After more testing, he concluded that the red flecks were commercial lacquer, not translucent nail polish. Early in the murder investigation, Dr. Gerber himself had said a larger chip of red paint from the bedroom floor could have come from the murder weapon.[12] Kirk wondered whether the red flecks had come from a lacquered surface of a flashlight.

He had come to Cleveland with an impression that Dr. Sheppard probably was guilty. He left believing that the prosecution got much of its case wrong. Operating under the belief that someone else killed Marilyn Sheppard, Kirk began to look at all of the evidence in a different light. "Any theory that is contradicted by a proven fact has to be incorrect," he told his students. He began testing facts against his new theory. His crime-scene analysis was grounded solidly by the science of blood-pattern interpretation. Assuming that foundation to be accurate, Kirk moved into a more subjective analysis of the behavior of the killer. These insights were less science and more commonsense impressions.

The first time he heard the account Sam Sheppard told and retold, Kirk felt the story made no sense. That alone was the single most convincing reason he and others felt that the doctor was guilty. "Why an obviously intelligent person would tell so vague and indefinite a story was puzzling until it occurred to me that the reason must be that it was true," Kirk said. "Beyond a doubt, Dr. Sam knew that he would have to account for himself that night. Had he been making up a story, surely he could have done better."[13]

Kirk thought about the apparent staging of a burglary, an effort perhaps to throw police off track. If a complete stranger had killed Marilyn, he had little reason to stage a burglary and point suspicion elsewhere, since no one knew him. This analysis pushed suspicion toward Sam. But Kirk puzzled over the broken athletic trophies. If Sam was the killer, breaking the trophies would add little to pulling off a hasty cover-up. Sam was proud of his athletic ability and cherished the trophies. It was a stretch to believe he would destroy them. But someone jealous of Sam's athletic prowess or annoyed by his bare-chested displays of waterskiing and pickup basketball might take pleasure in smashing them.

Nor did Kirk believe that Sam had dumped out his medical bag in the hallway. "A doctor has a personal feeling for this necessary item, and would instinctively avoid damaging it, or its costly contents," Kirk noted. "For another person this, too, could have been a retaliatory act."[14] Perhaps the handiwork of someone who fantasized about becoming a doctor but had failed to do so.

———

In late April 1955 Bill Corrigan received Kirk's report, nineteen single-spaced pages that laid out his scientific testing and reasoned scenarios that

built a seemingly irrefutable case that someone other than Dr. Sam had killed
Marilyn Sheppard. Corrigan became more excited as he read.

Kirk's report noted that the killer swung the weapon, probably a flashlight, with a level, left-handed swing. He was certainly misted with blood on
his pants and shirt. The blood trail in the home came from a flowing wound,
maybe from being bitten by Marilyn.

"It was entirely possible that the defendant was struck on the back of the
neck by the same weapon used to kill Marilyn Sheppard." Kirk described his
experiment in the darkened Sheppard home, running up the steps into the
murder room, where his assistant

> merely moved around as [I] arrived at the door, and delivered a slight
> blow to the back of the neck without the movement being seen or antici-
> pated by [me].
>
> The method and clumsiness of removal of the watch and key chain
> from the defendant's pocket certainly appears to be the work of another
> person. As pointed out earlier, it would be difficult and completely un-
> natural for a person to rip his own trousers pocket downward in remov-
> ing a key chain, but this would be extremely probable if someone else
> stripped it from a prone body. It is also unlikely that a person removes his
> own watch so as to damage the band, even if he were faking a burglary.
>
> The abandonment of the green bag in the woods is not the work of a
> person who is deliberately setting a scene as it was postulated that the de-
> fendant did. If he took time to wash off all the blood, to sponge the stairs
> and take the other precautions attributed to him, he would not carelessly
> throw away the green bag where it would not reasonably be in a real bur-
> glary. Rather, its abandonment was the act of a person in an unnatural
> hurry, as would be true of an intruder being pursued as claimed by the de-
> fendant.
>
> Another point of importance . . . is the question of the amount of
> sand in the defendant's shoes. If he waded out into the lake to wash off
> blood, he would not sink into the wet sand very far, and would pick up in
> the shoes minimal quantities of sand. Also, he would not pick up any
> sand in the pockets. If he were lying on beach, as he stated, he would ac-
> cumulate large quantities of sand in his shoes, and some in his pockets,
> as was the case. . . .
>
> It is not reasonable to believe that the defendant would deliberately
> break his own and his wife's trophies, as occurred. Under no conditions
> would this assist in establishing the event as the work of a burglar, for it
> is equally unreasonable for a true burglar. It is completely consistent only

for someone who hated the Sheppards, or who was jealous of their athletic abilities.

It is not reasonable that the defendant would mistreat his surgical and medical equipment, as was done. Even to establish the event as the work of a burglar, a doctor who likes his work (as it appears he did) would have faked the theft from the bag entirely differently.

By no stretch of the imagination can it be conceived that the injuries to the defendant were self-inflicted. As a person who was fully aware of the danger associated with a blow to the back of the neck, and faced with the almost insurmountable difficulty of delivering such a blow at all, and certainly of doing it under control, no doctor would ever risk trying it. It is also peculiarly difficult to deliver a blow of any force to one's own face. Neither of these injuries can be reconciled with self-infliction.

It is equally ridiculous to assume that these injuries were sustained in falling from the landing platform at the beach. That type of fall would inflict many abrasions, bruises and secondary injuries to the limbs, with the serious possibility of broken bones. It could not under any circumstances select the back of his neck and his face for the only injury. No satisfactory explanation except THAT GIVEN BY THE DEFENDANT has been advanced for his injuries.[15]

The Marilyn Sheppard murder, in Kirk's opinion, was a sex crime. It was "completely out of character for a husband bent on murdering his wife."

And finally, Kirk noted, his tests of the large, one-inch blood spot on the closet door in the murder room reacted so differently from Marilyn's blood and Sam's blood that, in his opinion, it came from a third person—the likely killer.

Corrigan had to wonder what would have happened at the trial if Kirk had testified. Half the jurors had voted for acquittal in the first ballot. Kirk's findings almost certainly would have set Sam free.

Corrigan rushed a copy of the report to Sam in jail. "It is terrific," Sam wrote in his journal that night. "It proves my innocence beyond all questions. His complete thoroughness is that of only a great scientist, which he is. I'm so fired up now (2 A.M. 4/24/55) that I can not think of sleep. I want to show this report to the whole cockeyed world. . . . I want them to open these doors!!"

Corrigan filed a motion for a new trial, citing new evidence discovered by Kirk, noting in particular that a third person's blood had been found at the crime scene. Steve and Sam felt it wouldn't be long before he was granted a new trial.

Gerber was stung by Kirk's findings, even though Kirk's report did not criticize him by name. He already had taken his slide show about the case on the lecture circuit. Gerber knew that to maintain his standing in national forensic circles he had to destroy Kirk's credibility.

In a hearing before Judge Blythin, the prosecutors and Gerber savagely attacked Kirk's experiments, blood work, and overall conclusions. Blythin ruled against the Sheppard motion, saying that even if there was new information, it had come too late. Corrigan appealed.

Behind the scenes, Gerber blackballed Kirk, who was seeking membership in the American Academy of Forensic Sciences, of which Gerber was an officer. Kirk soon lost the editorship of a journal in criminology as well as some grants. After nearly twenty years of helping the police, Kirk was wounded by the attacks on his scientific credibility. He was no match for Gerber, whose political skills were forged in Cleveland's feisty machine politics. "A lot of people think I'm some kind of a mountebank who sold out for money to try to get a rich man out of prison," Kirk complained bitterly.[16]

Sam Sheppard should have been prepared for the attacks, but he wasn't. "Reaction of the Pros. Attys. to Dr. Kirk's work is absolutely a disgrace to the State of Ohio," he wrote. "If the people or judges don't do something about their slanderous remarks toward Dr. Kirk, I'll say there's no justice left around here at all. Dr. Kirk should sue the sons of bitches."[17]

That summer, the Ohio Appeals Court, a panel of three elected judges, turned down the motion for a new trial, saying Kirk's blood typing and other interpretations were "highly speculative and fallacious." When reporters telephoned Kirk for his reaction, he said: "I'm just as positive as I am of my own name that Dr. Sam didn't do it." Corrigan said that they would appeal the decision to the Ohio Supreme Court.

If the Kirk affidavit could not achieve results, Sam wondered in jail, what else could possibly be done to help him? He slipped into a depression. He asked to be transferred to the Ohio Penitentiary, rather than wait for another court ruling. "I have been so bounced and battered by this type of injustice that at this point I'm really numb. I don't dare hope and count in any way on honesty and justice for fear the hammer will fall again and knock me apart. I'm planning on the O.P. This 'wait until the decision' is the worst yet."[18]

20

THE WALLS

ABOUT A YEAR after the murder Sam Sheppard found himself shuttled to the Ohio Penitentiary in Columbus. Just west of the capital city's downtown, he spotted the outlines of the notorious prison. It was an ancient Gothic monstrosity, with stone walls thirty feet high and three feet thick. Nicknamed "the Walls," the prison was built in 1835 and encompassed eight square blocks. Inside were ranges of cells, a machine shop, a clothing mill, sports fields, a hospital, vegetable gardens—essentially a small brutal city in sight of the capitol. The Walls had witnessed some of the lowest moments in U.S. penal history: riots, breakouts, a 1930 fire that killed 322 inmates. Sam Sheppard was incarcerated when the Ohio Pen was at its peak overpopulation, 5,230 inmates, roughly twice its designed capacity.

About fifty reporters, photographers, and TV-camera operators gathered near the prison entrance as Sheppard passed. Once inside the massive gate, he was struck by the prison's vast, manicured green yard. Marching in formation across it was a ragtag prison band, men in rough striped shirts, playing out-of-tune instruments, the black band members relegated to the rear. Outside the warden's office were beds of beautiful roses, some of them prizewinners, lovingly tended by the prison doctor, Dr. Denton Engstrom. The Catholic chapel nearby was still in disrepair, the aftermath of a prison riot two years earlier.

The new inmate was frisked, then marched down a five-hundred-foot hall to the deputy warden's office. Guards checked the few items he brought with him—a comb, handkerchief, safety razor, billfold, and a large photo of Chip. His medical books were confiscated. He was handed a bundle of prison clothes.

At the intake room Sheppard was asked for his version of the crime. It was assumed by prison officials that he had tried to save his skin with expensive lawyers and protestations of innocence. His court battle would not be held against him; he had played the legal game and lost. Now he was expected to accept his punishment, admit his crime, and express remorse so that society could forgive him. An inmate who made excuses and denied guilt was not considered a good candidate for parole.

Sheppard denied killing his wife. His opposition was noted in his permanent file.

The high point of his first day was supper. In the county jail he had been served slop, and had subsisted instead on the fruit, nuts, and candy bars his family brought him. His first evening at the Walls, Sheppard ate fried eggs, bacon, Jell-O, cole slaw, and ice cream. He hadn't eaten an egg since Easter, bacon in a year, and had never been served ice cream. "It tasted like the Waldorf Astoria," he said.[1]

He was quarantined in a hospital ward for a month, a routine procedure. There he was struck by the stupidity of the medical setup. The hospital wards were on the first floor, near the most foot traffic, making cross-contamination likely. The tuberculosis ward was close to the surgical and postsurgery wards, which was madness. He could not stop thinking like a doctor.

As he did with all new inmates, the prison sociologist, Ernest D. Gilbert, performed a clinical evaluation of Sheppard.

The most noticeable thing about the subject was his seriously flattened affect; he showed the effects of a series of shocks that he has suffered. Consequently, there were none of the flashes of insight, quick comprehension of concepts or moments of scintillation that one usually encounters when conversing with an individual with a trained mind. Only once did he brighten up and that was when he spoke of his innocence of the charge which sent him here, declaring that if there were any justice he would be out very soon. Partly because of this flattening of affect and partly because he was on guard, he spoke slowly weighing each word. He appeared to try to discover the reason why the examiner asked each question before answering it. One soon gains the impression that he is very compulsive, overdoing everything that he undertakes. . . . He became almost paranoid on the subject of his innocence, stating among other things that his rights as an American citizen had been abridged. . . .

There were no outward signs of mental stress other than the flattened affect already mentioned. Consequently it seems very unlikely that either a severe psychoneurosis or a psychosis may develop in the immediate future. Things may take a different turn however should his appeal be denied.[2]

Back in Bay Village a week later, Karl Schuele took an evening swim in Lake Erie. He lived next door to Sam Sheppard's empty house on Lake Road. In shallow water Schuele came across a three-cell flashlight. Thinking it might be evidence in the Sheppard murder case, he turned over the corroded flashlight to Bay Village police chief John Eaton. Eaton filed a report, noting that the flashlight was dented and battered at one end as if someone had used it for "striking something repeatedly." He gave a copy of his report and the flashlight to his neighbor, Cleveland homicide detective Adelbert O'Hara, who in turn filed his own report, then turned the evidence over to coroner Sam Gerber "for further examination." No mention was made in the police reports of Paul Kirk's widely publicized theory that the murder weapon was a flashlight. There was no attempt by Mary Cowan or anyone else in the coroner's office to examine it for trace evidence, the files would later show.

Dr. Sam's brothers kept fighting for him, despite the hopes by many at Bay View Hospital that the murder case would vanish. Steve took it upon himself to keep up Sam's spirits, writing and visiting more frequently than Richard. "From this distance," Steve told Sam in a typical letter, "I want you to know that no matter where you are—jail or elsewhere—I think you are the finest man I have ever met and I wouldn't change our life or relationship one tiny bit even if I could. Keep punching, boy—we're all with you!" A few weeks later, Steve wrote: "Your courage and faith have been truly inspirational to all who have had the sense to see the injustices heaped one upon the other. Your supporters and sympathizers are gaining both in strength and numbers while your detractors are becoming less effective and fewer. Now we must *all* guard against the destructive bitterness that we may feel as the full story finally comes out. Hate is all we have to fear now and I do not refer to the hate of others for us. To seek revenge would be both unchristian and inconsistent with our stand to date."[3] Sam depended on the letters. They were "like a shot of epinephrine or a half time pep talk . . . only better."[4]

Later that summer Richard Sheppard wrote to Gerber and demanded that Marilyn's fetus be returned to the family so that it could be buried with Marilyn. "I had seen it in a jar in his office," said Doris O'Donnell, a *Cleveland News* reporter who married Gerber's close friend Howard Beaufait, the *News*'s lead reporter at the trial. "Doc showed it to us. It was a boy. You could tell that. If you shook the jar a little bit, it swirled around and you could see his hand up by his face. It looked just like he was thumbing his nose at you." Richard Sheppard's quiet demand of Gerber never made the newspapers. In late August the coroner sent a specimen jar containing the four-month fetus to Knollwood Cemetery, where it was entombed with Marilyn Sheppard's body.

———

Back in Columbus, Sam Sheppard left quarantine and was housed with three other convicts in a small cell originally intended for two men. He was assigned at first to a job in the clothing mill. If he behaved, he was told, he would get to be a teacher. The handful of inmates with college degrees—better educated than the warden and his executives—usually taught reading and arithmetic to inmates. Sam later was told to teach auto mechanics.

One night, soon after his confinement, Sam awoke to loud, prolonged screams of pain and terror. It was a new young inmate, barely twenty, being raped by his cell mates. "He was torn and had to be taken to city hospital and have several stitches and have his rectum packed," Sam said. "It was a terrible thing."[5]

In his free time, Sam worked out in the weight room with a fury. Once he tore a pectoral muscle pumping iron, trying too quickly to create an intimidating jailhouse build that might give attackers hesitation.

To his family and to prison officials, Sam Sheppard seemed to adjust well to prison life. Outwardly, he appeared hopeful and cooperative. Guards and inmates gave him greater courtesy and respect because of who he was. But Sheppard knew that he was fair game for any inmate seeking the status and notoriety that would come from stabbing the Walls' internationally famous inmate.

His diaries give a more reliable snapshot of his mental health. By late 1955, he noted mostly mundane details about his workouts and his meals. He seemed depressed and recorded little emotion, except for an incident in November. An inmate had tried to hang himself using strips of his sheets. A week later he tried again and succeeded. Sam was profoundly disturbed, mostly because the man's parole date was in a few weeks and he was likely to be released.

Why couldn't he wait? Sam wondered. Did the Ohio Penitentiary eventually drive everyone crazy?

———

Over the next two years, William Corrigan exhausted nearly all of the legal appeals available to his famous client. At every turn he lost. In desperation,

Steve Sheppard turned to the Court of Last Resort, a project of Erle Stanley Gardner, the wildly prolific millionaire author of the Perry Mason legal mystery series. Several years earlier, Gardner, a lawyer, had assembled a dream team of forensic experts—polygraph examiners, criminalists, pathologists—that would reinvestigate, pro bono, selected cases in which the defendant appeared to be wrongfully convicted. Gardner wrote about his findings in *Argosy,* a middlebrow men's magazine that featured crime, sports, outdoor writing, and popular fiction.

Typically, the experts went into prisons to polygraph convicts and jailhouse snitches, obtain blood samples and fingerprints, reinvestigating the parts of a criminal that could be tested or measured.[6]

What Steve Sheppard didn't know when he begged for help from Gardner was that the author was a good friend of Dr. Gerber and had even dedicated one of his mysteries to the Cuyahoga County coroner.

Gardner was intrigued by the idea of giving Dr. Sam a lie detector test. He worried that he was being "used as bait" by the Sheppards, who he thought might employ the Court of Last of Resort as a public platform to shout his brother's innocence, then, at the last minute, come up with an excuse for not going through with the polygraph. Gardner shared his misgivings with Gerber in a January 1957 letter. Gerber wrote back, saying he would like to see "the Sheppard flock" submit to testing; then perhaps the alleged crime-scene tampering could be proven.

In Ohio, Gardner had no success convincing the warden at the Ohio Penitentiary to allow Sam to be examined by Gardner's experts. So Gardner proceeded with a backup plan. On May 4, 1957, Drs. Steve and Richard Sheppard and their wives traveled to Chicago and underwent several hours of polygraphing by John Reid, Alex Gregory, C. B. Hanscomb, and Lamoyne Snyder, M.D., all top experts.

Going into the exams, these four men, perhaps swayed by newspaper coverage, believed that Sam was guilty of murdering Marilyn and that his brothers had helped him cover up his crime. The four Sheppard family members were tested separately. Steve remembers it as a cold affair until the court's examiners were finished. Then the experts, all smiles, brought them together and said that each had conclusively passed the tests. Erle Stanley Gardner had abandoned the cover-up theory of Gerber and the Cleveland police. He became convinced that Dr. Sam was probably innocent. To Gerber's chagrin, Gardner wrote about clearing the Sheppard brothers and sisters-in-law of conspiracy. Doubts about Sam Sheppard's guilt began to grow, at least outside of Cleveland.

Back in Columbus, behind the walls of the Ohio Pen, Sam Sheppard was pleased with Gardner's results. But it was frustrating because it had no impact on his freedom. He tried to keep up his spirits by writing letters to Steve and Chip. He lifted weights for hours a day; he read medical journals. The mid-1950s were an unfettered gilded age of medical research, with federal funds flowing to teaching hospitals and universities, which sparked a wave of human experiments on prison inmates. Sam took part in perhaps the most controversial and dangerous experiment of the time. He and several dozen inmates volunteered to be injected with live cancer cells.[7]

Dr. Chester M. Southam of Manhattan's Sloan-Kettering Institute and Dr. Charles A. Doan, director of medical research at Ohio State University's College of Medicine, directed the research. They wanted to learn whether a healthy person would reject the cancer cells more quickly than a patient with cancer. At the Ohio Pen, the warden asked for twenty-five healthy volunteers and ninety-six inmates responded. They were not truly "volunteers." These inmates hoped their humanitarian contribution would count in their favor when they were considered for parole. They were willing to risk anything. Dr. Sam turned out to be an important recruit because he could allay inmates' fears that the experiment might injure them. Along with other inmate subjects, Sam was injected several times in the upper arm with three to five million cancer cells, which created a large nodule. It turned out that he and other inmates rejected the cancer cells at a rate about twice as fast as those already suffering from cancer.[8] He was an ideal guinea pig. He kept dated notes about the nodule, describing its changes in color and size. After taking his second injection on March 27, 1958, he went into the prison yard to watch a baseball game.

"Within 2 minutes," Sam wrote in his journal, "R. Harris struck area hard with his very bony fist. (Friendly punch! Some fun! He didn't know, or did he?)"

21

DEAD GIRL'S STONES

MORE THAN ONCE Dorothy Sheppard's window washer told her, "You know, people always tell me I look like Dr. Sam."

The remark did not strike her as odd. The man, Richard Eberling, *did* look like Sam—six feet one, 180 pounds, sinewy from manual labor, carrying ladders, working on his feet all day. Like Sam, Eberling had a handsome face, tanned, with full lips, a strong jaw, and a receding hairline. He sometimes wore a hairpiece.

He was an ambitious, hardworking man. Abandoned by his single mother when he was six months old, he had grown up in foster homes. As a child, he enjoyed rearranging furniture. Later, he taught himself to appreciate fine fabrics, antiques, and interior decorating. His expertise came in handy as he gathered customers for his small company, Dick's Window Cleaning. Eberling was comfortable talking to women about decorating. His company's motto was "We're expensive, but we care."

"We thought very highly of him," Dorothy Sheppard, Sam's sister-in-law, later would say. "He seemed like an intelligent person, well read, and interesting. He seemed completely trustworthy. I never hesitated to leave the house while he was working inside."[1]

Dorothy had recommended Dick's Window Cleaning to Marilyn. After the first job, sometime in the early 1950s, "my men came back and all they could talk about was what a beauty she was," Eberling said. He decided to pick up payment from the new customer and check her out. "Oh, she had that California look," he said dreamily, years later. "Tight little brief shorts and a very little blouse. She was immaculate, all in white." Sexy *and* virginal, in other words.[2]

He enjoyed working for Marilyn, who was only a few years older than he was. Once, when Marilyn and Chip were having brownies and milk on the porch, she gave him some, he recalled fondly. Dr. Sam Sheppard left early for surgery and was not home during the days. Eberling said he saw him only once in the morning and he didn't talk to him. After Marilyn's murder, police found his name in the Sheppards' checkbook ledger. Cleveland detectives and prosecutor Parrino questioned him, but he was not considered a serious suspect.

Over the next two years there were a series of thefts throughout the upper-middle-class homes in Bay Village, Rocky River, and Westlake. The only common denominator, other than unforced entry, was Dick's Window Cleaning. Police detained Eberling several times on suspicion of grand theft, but they could never make a case against him. They tried to catch him by asking homeowners to leave out marked bills, but on those few occasions that they did, he didn't take the bait.

Cleaning windows gave Eberling an excuse to be in a house's every room. He found his decorator's eye drawn to jewelry and figurines. He slipped his *objets de désir* into his ever-present pail of wash water and went about his cleaning, walking out when the job was done. Mostly he stole inexpensive keepsakes, jewelry, pitchers, and bowls, items with personal meaning rather than of great value, such as pottery figurines of Tiny Tim and Little Nell, the Charles Dickens characters.

In 1957 Dr. Richard and Dorothy Sheppard hired Eberling to clean their house so that it would be ready for new wallpaper and paint. At the time he had already relieved them of a sterling serving bowl, a vase, and a Belleek pitcher. In a master-bedroom closet, Eberling spotted a box labeled "Personal Property of Marilyn Sheppard" on a high shelf. Inside he found two of Marilyn's rings, her engagement ring and a larger, diamond-clustered cocktail ring. These were the rings on the hands Marilyn had raised to deflect the blows on the morning she was murdered. Eberling slipped them into his pocket. The rings weren't missed for months.

On a Sunday afternoon in November 1959 Eberling washed windows at a fine home in Rocky River while the owner was downstairs watching a Cleveland Browns football game on television. The man heard a creak from the second floor. He knew his house, and the creak told him that his window washer had walked into an area where he shouldn't have. After Eberling left, the man checked, found ninety dollars missing, and called the Rocky River police. Detective George Jindra and his partner were assigned to the case. Jindra said they called Eberling and accused him over the telephone, and "the damn fool admitted to it."[3]

Jindra and another detective quickly went to the Eberling farmhouse in Westlake. There, spread out on the heat register, was a soggy blanket of bills, drying out after Eberling had hidden them in his wash pail. They began to grill him about various burglaries all over Rocky River.

Christine Eberling, his foster mother, now nearly seventy, lashed out at the detectives and tried to throw them out of her house. "The old lady, she was a tiger," Jindra remembered. "She said, 'How dare you accuse my son of something like that. I'll call my attorney. You can't prove it.' "

Eberling acted like he was relieved to be caught. With little prodding, he made a confession that would haunt him for life. "He kicked into the whole business," Jindra said. He showed them his loot. "He plucked the diamonds out of settings," the detective said. "He had Royal Doultons up the ass, two trunks full. These little Oriental rugs."

Two of the rings, Eberling admitted, belonged to Marilyn Sheppard. Usually he took the gems from the settings and sold them, but he had kept her cocktail ring intact, seemingly cherishing it, why he didn't know. He had first noticed it on her dressing table a year before she was murdered. He said he still had the setting and stones from her engagement ring, too, long after having stolen them.

"As time went on," Eberling told the detectives, "it started to bother me, for two reasons. One, that the stones had belonged to a dead girl. And secondly, as to the trouble I could get into or cause in case something should happen to me and the stones would be found."

"I was trying to be caught," he would say years later. "I said I took the ring. That whole dumb thing, I wanted it all out. I don't know why."[4]

Eberling admitted to scores of larcenies in Bay Village, Westlake, and Rocky River, and detectives from each suburb took turns running down the various thefts. It's unclear what happened next. Either Eberling volunteered, wanting to get it all out, or one of the detectives, knowing about Marilyn's rings and playing a hunch, asked Eberling why his blood was at the Sheppard murder scene. What he said next stunned the detectives: he cut himself a few days before the murder and dripped blood throughout the Sheppard home. On July 2, 1954, a Friday morning, he was alone there, putting in screen windows. The last window, over the kitchen sink, was the toughest. A pair of sliding metal pins held the storm-window sash into the jamb, but the pins were stuck. He gripped a pin with pliers and pulled, lost his hold, and slashed a finger. The wound bled freely. He dripped blood in the kitchen, mostly around the window and sink. He said he wiped the blood up immediately because Marilyn "was a very meticulous housekeeper."[5]

Could the blood trail have been his? the detectives wondered. Dr. Sam still was insisting he was innocent. Might Dr. Sam have been telling the truth all along?

As preposterous as it may have seemed, some detectives from Cleveland's western suburbs like Rocky River or Bay Village were not convinced that Sam was guilty. To them, the idea of reopening the famous case was intoxicating. Here was a criminal who said his blood was at the murder scene of Marilyn Sheppard. Was he the bushy-haired stranger?

On November 11, Bay Village police lieutenant Jay Hubach and detective Ronald B. DuPerow picked up Eberling at the Rocky River jail to move him to the Bay Village lockup. Eberling kept changing his story when he was requestioned. "After stating that he cut his finger about four days prior to the murder and had dripped blood all over the downstairs of the Sheppard home he changed his statement—that he was all over the house with his finger dripping blood. He also said that he went to bed at 11:30 P.M. the night of the murder and changed his story and said that it was after 1 A.M."[6] Bay Village policemen were suspicious and asked if he would take a polygraph test. Eberling, in his confessional mode for the moment, agreed to take the test.

Bringing Eberling to a polygraph examiner became a political problem for Bay Village. The small suburban police department did not have a qualified examiner. The much larger and wealthier Shaker Heights Police Department did. It is telling that Chief Eaton and his lieutenant, Jay Hubach, bypassed the Cleveland police. When Hubach arrived in Shaker Heights with Eberling, they were told that the Shaker Heights police chief had changed his mind. Authorization was first needed from either coroner Gerber or new county prosecutor John T. Corrigan (no relation to Bill Corrigan). Patrick Gareau, one of the lead Cleveland detectives in the Sheppard case, was now an assistant county prosecutor. He brought Eberling's statements to prosecutor Corrigan, who said to drop the whole matter. He would not approve a polygraph examination for a thief named Richard Eberling.[7]

Lieutenant Hubach, who harbored doubts about Sam Sheppard's guilt, pushed for the test with Gerber. The coroner agreed to talk to the suspect. Gerber knew the Sheppard case intimately and knew he could quickly dismiss a charlatan or liar, as he had done several times in the past. He spent three and a half hours with Eberling. No report or notes of the interview have turned up since then, but Dr. Gerber, a busy man, decided that Eberling should be subjected to a polygraph exam.

A day later Gerber reversed himself. He decided not to give Eberling a polygraph. He was indicted for grand larceny.

"I was hoping to get caught," Eberling later admitted, "so I could unload myself."[8]

22

UNLOADING

RICHARD EBERLING WAS BORN unwanted at St. Ann's Hospital in Cleveland on December 8, 1929. Two weeks premature, he was jittery, underweight, and cried day and night from colic.

His mother, Louise Lenardic, was little help. She was an unmarried twenty-year-old immigrant from Yugoslavia with only eight years of schooling. She told the nuns at St. Ann's that no one had instructed her about babies or birth control. She had no one to turn to. Her mother had died when she was a baby, then she and her eight older brothers and sisters were scattered among relatives and foster homes. Above all, she did not want anyone at St. Ann's to tell her father that he had a new grandson.

Louise's father spoke scant English. He drank heavily and, when he could hold a job, worked in a nearby factory. A few years earlier, after living without his children for a decade, he insisted on reuniting his family. He gathered Louise, an older daughter, and two sons to live with him on East Thirty-third Street in a poor factory district on Cleveland's near East Side. Louise was overwhelmed by Cleveland, a teeming industrial city with a world-class symphony and library and museums, and streetcar lines linking every neighborhood. She took a streetcar to clean houses in the city's middle-class sections, making six dollars in a good week.

Before he drew his first breath, Richard George Lenardic was trouble. He was a breech baby, coming down the birth canal feetfirst. Louise labored for fourteen hours. Richard weighed more than six pounds, large enough for his premature lungs to survive without difficulty.

At St. Ann's, the nuns insisted on knowing about the father. Was he a

Catholic? Was he feeble-minded? Would he marry her? The father, Louise finally admitted, was a Cleveland Heights policeman named George Anderson.

Anderson, twenty-nine years old, was a tall, charming, handsome man. He conceived his son at a Cleveland Heights home that Louise regularly cleaned. As it happens, Dr. Richard A. Sheppard and his family lived not far away. Anderson drank with relish, borrowed money from other officers, and "was in one scrape after another." His police chief fired him, reluctantly, because George was smart, personable, and, most of the time, a good officer. He left town, leaving behind his son and his debts.

Louise had seen what happened to the illegitimate children of her older sisters—they were taken away. When a county welfare worker arrived to talk to her about her infant, she proved to be smarter than she let on. The child-welfare system was set up to place Richard for adoption. She was determined to fight that. When pressed about her "fitness as a mother," she knew what they were after. She insisted that she had sex only one other time, with a Cleveland cop.

To the Catholic church and to her family, Louise had committed the mortal sin of adultery. As was customary, she was expected to give up her baby so that he would be adopted by a "good Catholic couple" unable to have children. Louise was shuttled to an unmarried mothers' home, the Humane Society Boarding Home for Babies. It was now the task of county welfare workers, mostly well-educated women, to find a foster family to adopt Cuyahoga County's ward no. 1575, otherwise known as Richard Lenardic.[1]

Louise went back to cleaning houses and agreed to pay the welfare society a small sum to board her baby. In effect, she abandoned him and rarely visited, records show. Decades later neurologists would establish a link between antisocial behavior and the lack of sensory stimulation and parental bonding during the first months of life. Cooing, hugging, and simple touching are crucial to an infant's emotional and mental development. For his first few months, Richard's feedings and diaper changes were all the attention he received.

During the Depression, many families were willing to take in a foster child for a while. The county paid about four dollars a week for his room and board, and for some families, this extra income offered a fair standard of living. At six months, Richard Lenardic was placed with a family. He was underweight, unable to flip over, but capable of terrible tantrums when upset or when left alone after a feeding, in which he would hold his breath until his face turned blue. To get him to stop these fits, his astonished foster mother threw cold water in his face. After two weeks, the woman returned Richard to the welfare agency, saying he was too difficult for her.

Meanwhile, Louise Lenardic had neither found a husband nor returned for her son, as her county caseworker had hoped she would. Unfortunately, Louise was "quite unattractive. She had large bones, with high cheekbones and a long, rather vacant face. She seemed to be afraid to say the things that she was thinking and would search about for ways of expressing herself."[2] When Richard was ten months old Louise Lenardic officially abandoned him. She wrote a note saying that she could not afford to pay $2.50 a week for his care. Keep him or let him be adopted—he's yours, her letter said in summary.

But there was one complication. Later on, once a couple had been found to adopt her son, Louise Lenardic would have to sign a notarized probate document giving up her legal rights as a mother.

———

In June 1930 Richard was placed with a new foster family. He still held his breath and threw fits, especially when his routine changed, but he seemed to have normal intelligence, and the parents persevered with him. Over the next two years he learned to walk, rather unsteadily, and talk somewhat, jabbering babyishly. Richard was "small and very much in the puppy stage," his file noted. "He has large brown eyes and long, black curling eyelashes. He has a peculiar way of looking out of the corners of his eyes at you to coax you to do something for him. He has a sweet smile and pretty teeth."[3]

His caseworker recorded her theories about Richard's fits. They were not due to a serious medical condition such as epilepsy, but were caused by becoming terrified when left alone or overloaded with new sensations from a change in routine. Richard's current foster mother, a woman named Dynes, was an old hand at raising foster children. She didn't allow him to scream out but instead held him. Child-welfare workers believed that her restraining hug reinforced his screams; they talked her into trying something else. "Richard is not holding his breath since his foster mother spanked him for it with a small ruler," a caseworker wrote in May 1932.

Despite this seeming success, the Cuyahoga County child-welfare system decided that Richard had to be moved. He had been born to a Catholic mother and should be put in a Catholic home. The Dynes family was Protestant.

In June 1932 Richard was placed in the Roman Catholic home of Mrs. J. Hogan. Richard remembers liking the Hogans, but he still held his breath when upset, passing out and emptying his bladder as well. After five days with the Hogans, his spells became more intense, almost like epileptic seizures. Mrs. Hogan noticed that when Richard did something wrong—

spilled a drink, made a mess, knocked something over in his usual hyperactive state—he held his breath, anticipating punishment. Maybe, she thought, he had been severely punished in a previous home and he was holding his breath out of fear. Even so, she dunked his head under cold water or spanked him to break the spells. Sometimes Richard went weeks without an attack, then had three in a day. Mrs. Hogan began to feel that he tried to fight off the spells, which encouraged her. Her own doctor, not the county welfare doctor who treated Richard without charge, felt that Richard had epilepsy and should be treated as if he had an illness, not a temper tantrum.

She brought this to the caseworkers' attention. To rule out epilepsy, Richard was sent to Rainbow Children's and Baby Hospital, part of University Hospitals, a teaching and research hospital. He was placed in a crib and restrained for two weeks. He did not have unconscious spells, but he screamed and ranted when faced with a new routine such as taking a different route when being walked to the bathroom. Still, pediatricians suspected epilepsy and kept him there for six weeks, mostly confined to a bed. At night he often wet the bed. It was hard for him to fall asleep, and he woke up early. He masturbated. He developed a "peculiar" gait and fell frequently. His speech was almost impossible for outsiders to understand. Doctors were mystified.

Despite all this, the Hogans said they wanted to adopt Richard. They had grown to love this difficult child. This was wonderful news at child-welfare offices—a successful placement for a particularly demanding child. Quickly, Richard's caseworker tracked Louise Lenardic to a home she cleaned in suburban South Euclid, a middle-income suburb east of Cleveland, and gave her the good news.

Lenardic had not seen Richard in three years. She had not paid a cent toward his upkeep, never sent a card, and never called to ask about his health. Now she confirmed the agency's worst fear. She refused to give up Richard. She would not give permission for him to be adopted.

This development devastated the Hogans. As adoptive parents, they could not risk falling in love with a child who months or years later could be torn from them on short notice by the whim of an errant birth mother.

Meanwhile, the social worker had placed an eleven-month-old boy with the Hogans, in the event that Richard's adoption did not work out. At first Richard seemed to like the baby, but soon he began to mimic him. He stopped walking; he crawled and baby-talked. At night he masturbated more than usual, rubbing himself up and down on his sheets until he broke into cold sweats. He taxed the Hogans. He required enormous attention and diverted his foster parents' attention from the younger child.

"The drive for attention which the child showed was perfectly terrific," his caseworker wrote after a visit. "When there are guests in the home, regardless of whether they were talking business or not, the child made a most tremendous effort to get the interest of the entire group. He crawled over everyone, brought all his toys out, made a great deal of fuss, until it was practically impossible to talk."

The Hogans had become attached to Richard and once said he was "the best boy in the world." But now that they could not adopt him, they decided to return him to the foster home. To prepare him for the breakup, Mrs. Hogan lied and told Richard he was going on a vacation. When the caseworker arrived, Richard beamed. He said he was excited about going on a vacation. He took a big teddy bear he had received at Christmas. Pauline Hogan gave him some Hershey bars and all-day suckers, then went into the kitchen and cried.

———

Louise Lenardic told social workers that she dreamed of getting married and rearing Richard herself. They were not convinced. She was too eccentric. She showed up at the child-welfare offices in outlandish outfits, one time in "a billowy chiffon dress" with a "peculiar hat with a nose veil," but she was wearing worn, flat shoes "entirely out of keeping with the dress," a caseworker noted.

Another time, Richard's caseworker, Alice Hart, spotted Louise's name in a Cleveland newspaper's daily list of marriage licenses and asked Louise to come to the office. This time Louise was decked out in a stylish brown coat and dress, with matching purse, gloves, and accessories. Asked about the marriage license, Louise giggled and said, "Oh, that's me. But I'm single again." She said her husband, a semipro baseball player, had left her after two days.

"She shrugged her shoulders and grinned in a rather silly manner. Did not seem to accept the seriousness of the situation," Alice Hart noted.

"Is Richard still acting insane?" Louise asked.

Actually, he is doing much better, no more tantrums now that he has been placed with the new foster family, Hart told her.

Louise Lenardic replied that she would never allow Richard to be adopted. "I will never give consent."[4]

———

Richard's next home was with John and Catherine Lacy in rural North Ridgeville. This turned out to be the happiest of his seven foster-home placements. "They were great to me," he said later. "They gave me my head."

As a first-grader at St. Peter's, a Catholic elementary school, Richard had his most satisfying childhood experiences. He was allowed to go door to door, unsupervised, selling raffle tickets for the parish. He loved looking inside strangers' homes and seeing how they lived. With his handsome face, clear skin, and diffident style, he was the epitome of soft sell. For several nights in a row, the Lacys let him peddle his wares, street to street, ranging so far from home he did not know where he was, feeling free. He won the prize as the top seller.[5]

Richard had problems at school. He was effeminate, interested in cleaning and decorating, and dressed up in his foster mother's clothes. He had no interest in sports. Boys called him a sissy and pushed him around. When Mr. Lacy told him to strike back, he replied, "Dad, I don't like to fight." He got in trouble by stealing from other children's lunch boxes—a tangerine, money, candy. When he was caught, he flatly lied, unaware of the absurdity of his denials.

Soon enough the Lacys' two teenage daughters began to resent Richard. They complained that he was "not normal," and stopped talking to him. Rather than work out these difficult problems, Catherine Lacy asked the child-welfare bureau to start to look for another home for him. Her husband was opposed. He had always wanted a son and had grown fond of him. Also, their pastor thought the boy should stay at school and in the home with the family. Your daughters have boyfriends; they will marry and move out soon, the pastor said.

Richard's caseworker started looking for another home for him. She visited him and told him that he might have to leave the Lacys. "The foster mother seemed rather upset that the child had not broken down and cried," she noted in the file. "His reaction was one of indifference."[6]

Richard was placed with a family in Clyde, a small farming town of about five thousand people some seventy miles west of Cleveland. He hated it there. "She was a witch," Eberling said of that foster mother. Her husband put him to work, weeding flower beds and cleaning animal pens. He felt more like a farmhand than a nine-year-old boy. One afternoon when he and the foster father were alone in the house, Eberling recalled, the foster father tied him up in the basement and sexually abused him. "I had blood all over my pants," he said. He said that the man raped him a second time, and he ran from the foster home and hid in the confessional of the parish church.[7]

Eberling's voluminous county welfare files contain no suggestion of child abuse. Over the years, in several separate retellings, Eberling's account of the abuse has been consistent. However, a forensic psychiatrist who listened to an audiotape of Eberling talking about the abuse said the violent descriptions may have been Eberling's own fantasies.[8]

———

Richard was moved into a large Children's Aid Society foster home, where many of the children had been abandoned, abused, or rejected after placement. Unfortunately, Richard fit right in. He quickly impressed the staff with his constant striving for attention. He was a bundle of nervous activity and hard to settle down at night. He bounced on other kids' beds, danced around, and "paraded in an exhibitionistic manner." By spring 1939, at age nine and a half, he was caught engaging in sex play with two other boys in his dorm, children whom staffers had already punished for homosexual behavior. No amount of punishment had an effect on Richard. He showed an incredible tolerance for pain, almost as if he could remove his mind to another place.

He showed no interest in the typical activities of the other boys. Mostly, he enjoyed cleaning up, rearranging furniture, and commenting on the clothing and jewelry of the women who worked there. During weekly interviews with a social worker, he was asked to finger-paint, a method used to assess his psychological well-being. Richard crafted extraordinary, obsessively detailed abstract designs, and "showed an exaggerated drive for attention concerning his paintings," according to his caseworker. "These demonstrate attention to decorative detail which is a tendency of schizophrenic patients and show no artistic ability although Richard has great interest in drawing and decoration of all kinds."[9]

His homosexuality stumped them. A few months earlier, a doctor had noted that one of Richard's testicles was smaller in size and slightly retracted. Perhaps this accounted for his thinness and effeminate manner. The doctor prescribed a daily ten-milligram dose of gonadal growth hormones, antuitrin-A and antuitrin-S, to enlarge the boy's testes and counteract "his tendencies." And although he took the growth hormone for several months, Richard did not become more masculine or less outwardly homosexual. The doctor recommended larger doses and observation. Some of the social workers felt that his girlish nature "is something organically fixed and is not due to training."

Since he was "a moral hazard," likely to "become involved in homosexual difficulties," he would not be accepted by the average welfare home. "He would be a liability if placed with other children who would probably tease him and yet be annoyed by him. He is also difficult in the school environment. Perhaps it is best to make up our minds that this boy is institutional material for the rest of his life and therefore that he should be placed now."[10]

But Cuyahoga County did not have such a children's home. The alternative, they decided, was to place him in a small town where people could closely watch him and with foster parents who would not mind that he seemed to be a homosexual. The foster parents might let him achieve satisfaction from doing housework. As a vocation (and to get him off the county welfare roll), "perhaps he might work into some sort of interior decorator's helper." Even so, his prognosis was poor. "We may see this child develop a definite psychotic state, and there is nothing we can do at the present to help him."

Richard got lucky. A farm couple in Dover Township, just west of Cleveland and south of Bay Village, agreed to consider him. In the summer of 1939 Alice Hart drove him out to Dover Township to meet George and Christine Eberling. An older couple with grown children, George and Christine lived on a sixty-acre farm on Bradley Road. They grew fruit and vegetables, raised dairy cows, and made a decent living. At the end of the 1930s, there were nearly twenty-five hundred such farms in Cuyahoga County. Hardtop roads and cheap land—about $350 an acre—made small-scale farming a viable livelihood.

The Eberlings were not liked by their neighbors. One nearby farmer said that George Eberling was "a slave driver" who used foster boys as free labor while getting paid by the taxpayers to house and feed them. The Eberlings already had two other foster boys in their home. Christine Eberling, George's younger, childless second wife, was said to be "evil" and a meddler in church and civic affairs. For example, she threw a fit whenever a priest at their Catholic church was reassigned. She battled the school district over school bus schedules. Neighbors said she felt she was better than all the rest of them.

In July 1939 Hart brought Richard to the Eberlings' farm. She warned them about his homosexual tendencies, and that they would have to supervise him around other boys. His birth mother was alive but had abandoned him, and Hart asked them to keep this secret from Richard, who thought that both of his parents were dead. The Eberlings agreed to accept him.

Christine Eberling doted on Richard. She nicknamed him Dickie and clearly favored him over the teenage foster boys who lived on the farm. He could do no wrong. On the first day after school, he alit from the school bus miles from home, wandered through the woods, and arrived at the Eberling farm hours late, worrying his new foster parents. He blamed the bus driver, but his caseworker later suspected that Richard just wanted to see if his new parents would be alarmed. Christine, true to form, blamed the bus driver and called the school superintendent to complain.

Christine Eberling loved having a young boy who enjoyed helping her clean house. She hugged and kissed him like a moonstruck teen, calling him "her baby," rewarding him with extra desserts and privileges. The older foster boys resented it. They picked on him and called him a sissy.

In a follow-up visit to Richard's school, Alice Hart learned that he had created trouble his first day by putting his arms around several girls and kissing them on the playground. Maybe he thought this was how to make friends. The school superintendent said he was afraid that the boy might develop into "a sex problem." He did not like the Eberlings and the foster children they brought into the school system.

Later Hart visited the Eberling farm unannounced. Richard had always brought hardship into homes—bedwetting, stealing, being unable to fit in at school—but she was surprised. Christine sang Dickie's praises. She said she was tickled by the way he came downstairs in the morning, announcing "Here I am, Mom!" He played jokes on her, hiding under tables. He tended to a few goats and helped her clean and dust. She admitted that he still wet his bed and flitted around the farm, a tangle of nervous energy. He also woke up earlier than everyone else and climbed into bed with her. "He must have been beaten because he is always so afraid," Christine Eberling said.[11]

Hart, alarmed at this practice, said allowing him into her bed was a terrible idea. Richard was near adolescence. This behavior was terribly inappropriate. After the caseworker left, Christine Eberling ignored her warnings. She enjoyed babying Dickie.

Richard learned to give his foster mother what she wanted: a babyish, submissive child who, at least outwardly, loved her and did what he could to please her. But secretly he resented her oppressive control, he admitted later. She wouldn't let him play with other children in the neighborhood; they weren't good enough for him. She refused to let him join in school activities or sports, fearing he'd get hurt. "The Hogans were good to me, the Lacys were wonderful to me," Eberling once admitted. "With the Eberlings I was owned, I was possessed. I wasn't allowed to play with other children. When somebody on a bicycle was out in front on the road, my mother would come out and call me in. She wouldn't let me talk to him."[12]

She had grandiose plans for him. Within a year, she decided he should learn to play the piano, and insisted to Alice Hart that the county pay for his lessons. He must go on to college, she insisted, and perhaps become a doctor.

LEFT: Sam and Marilyn on a tennis court in Los Angeles circa 1946. BELOW: Marilyn and Sam on the beach during Sam's medical school days in the mid-1940s.

Sam and Chip, 1947.

Marilyn and Chip at the beach in 1948.

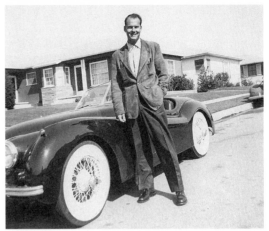

RIGHT: Dr. Sam and his used Jaguar convertible, 1953.
BELOW: The Dr. Sam Sheppard family, February 1951, just before leaving California.

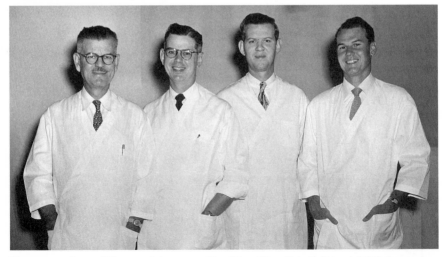

Two generations of Sheppard doctors at Bay View Hospital: (left to right) father Richard A., Steve, Richard N., and Sam.

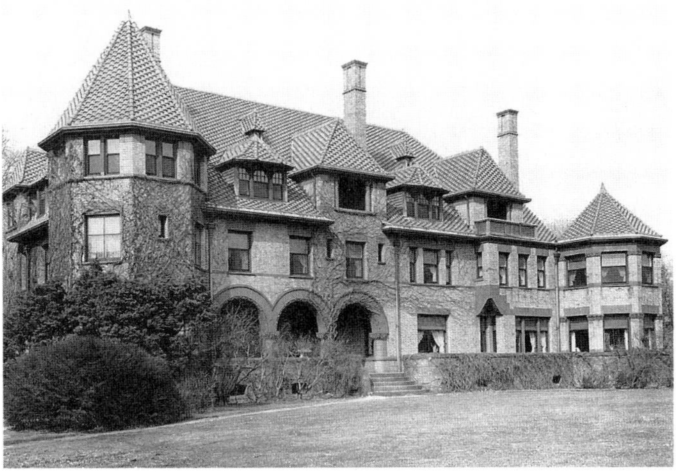

Bay View Hospital, founded by Sam's father.

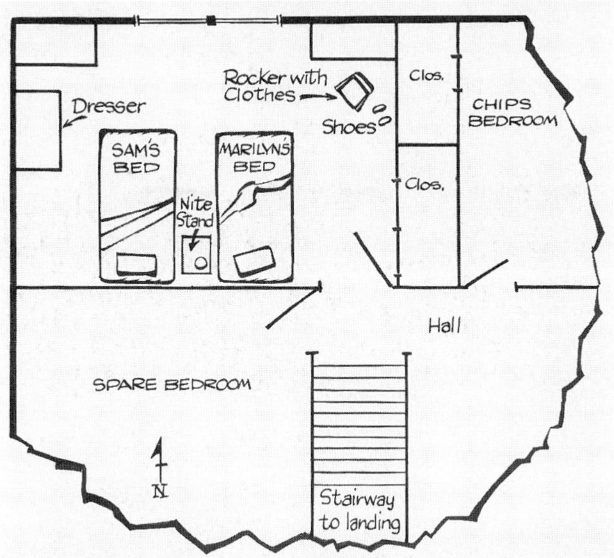

Rocker with Clothes
Dresser
Shoes
Clos.
CHIPS BEDROOM
SAM'S BED
MARILYN'S BED
Nite Stand
Clos.
Hall
SPARE BEDROOM
N
Stairway to landing

LEFT: Diagram of the second floor of the Sheppard house. BELOW: Diagram of the first floor of the Sheppard house, used as a court exhibit.

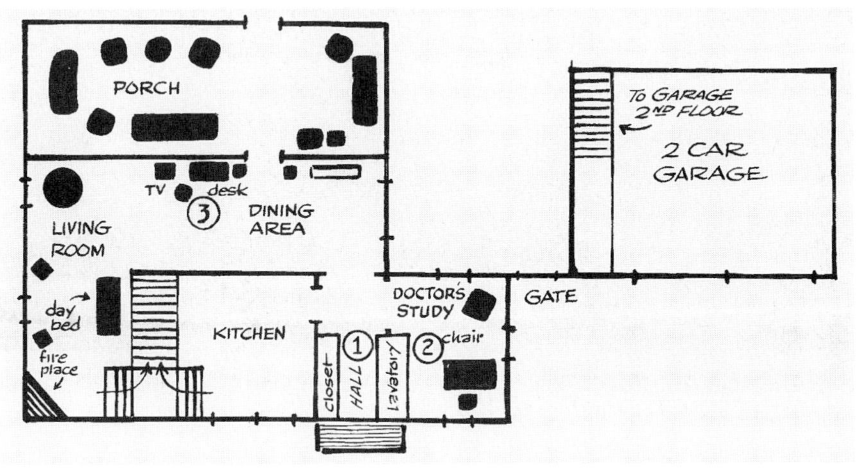

PORCH
TO GARAGE 2ND FLOOR
2 CAR GARAGE
TV
desk
3
DINING AREA
LIVING ROOM
DOCTOR'S STUDY
GATE
day bed
KITCHEN
1
2
chair
fire place
closet
HALL
Lavatory

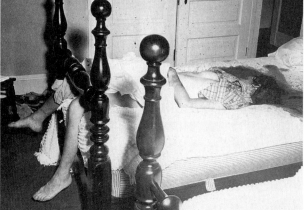

ABOVE: The Sheppard living room on July 4, 1954. Police say the scene was staged.
LEFT: Police photograph of Marilyn Sheppard's body, mid-morning, July 4, 1954.

Neighborhood boys search Lake Erie for the unknown murder weapon, as viewed from the Sheppards' deck at the bottom of the stairs.

Coroner Samuel R. Gerber poses with bloodstained work gloves found by Dr. Steve Sheppard under the stairs near the Sheppard beach on July 4, 1954.

LEFT: Ethel Sheppard and Dr. Richard Sheppard, with daughter-in-law Dorothy, on their way into Normandy School for the coroner's inquest, July 1954. BELOW: Dr. Sam, with sister-in-law Betty and her husband, Steve Sheppard, entering the inquest.

LEFT: Defense attorney William Corrigan (seated), surrounded in the courthouse by a crush of news photographers. ABOVE: Susan Hayes, the "other woman," testifies before a grand jury in August 1954 about her affair with Dr. Sam.

A detective, concealing the handcuffs with a coat, walks Dr. Sam past the press into the police station.

Sam Sheppard and the inmate wrestling team at the Ohio Penitentiary.

RIGHT: While his father was in prison, Chip lived with his uncle Steve and aunt Betty. BELOW: Sam Reese Sheppard, no longer called Chip, in his dress uniform at Indiana's Culver Military Academy.

Sam and Ariane: their first Christmas after his release from prison.

Sam and second wife, Ariane—"my goddess!"

In 1989, Sam Reese Sheppard began talking publicly about his mother's murder and eventually becomes an anti–death penalty activist.

ABOVE: Richard Lenardic (left), about eleven years old, at the Eberling farm, before he changed his name to Eberling. RIGHT: Richard Eberling at his arrest in 1959 for burglary, including the theft of Marilyn Sheppard's rings.

POLICE DEPARTMENT
ROCKY RIVER   OHIO
11 - 8 - 59   NO-1058
  29   6-0   180   GL

problems, after being confined to his bed for nine months. Christine, exhausted, took to her own bed. Richard was afraid that he would be sent away, and slept on the couch outside her room for three weeks. When Alice Hart visited him a few days after the funeral, Christine wailed to her that Dick was all she had now, please let him stay. Hart took Richard aside for a moment, and he told her, "Now more than ever, I want to remain on here."

George Eberling had willed Christine the house and farm. His children expected to inherit the land eventually. John Eberling and a cousin decided to farm the land on a share basis, so Christine would have some income.

With the death of George Eberling, Richard felt he was the man of the house. "He seemed to take it for granted that everything would be given him as a spoiled only child and was most egocentric," his case file noted. Christine still pushed him toward medicine, even though he earned D's in biology. The high school counselor felt that she was "using the child to satisfy her own needs."

Despite their problems with Christine Eberling, the county children's welfare bureau still needed foster homes for children, and so they placed an eight-year-old boy with her. Richard told his caseworker that he looked forward to the new arrangement, but quickly he resented him. Christine Eberling seemed to enjoy being the object of competition, fanning flames of jealousy. Within a month the boy was reassigned.

During the next two years Richard worked hard cleaning and decorating other houses in the area. He and an older teen started a company, Dick's Cleaning Service, and bought a small ad in the local newspaper. Christine was furious when she saw it. Such work was beneath him. He had college to think about.

Soon Richard was making ten to fourteen dollars a day, and banking most of it. He bought Christine two chairs and a Deepfreeze, and redecorated part of the farm. He graduated from high school in the summer of 1949, at nineteen. His yearbook picture was captioned, "He has a way with the ladies." Alice Hart came to the graduation and later wrote in his case file, "He developed into a very good looking young man, tall and broad shouldered with a clear complexion and a nice manner toward women."

Christine talked of selling the farm and moving, but Richard told her no, he would buy it first. Over the next few years, he eventually paid her about twenty-five thousand dollars, parcel by parcel, for the sixty-acre farm and farmhouse. He had control over the house, the farm, and her.

In August 1948 he went to court and legally changed his name to Richard George Eberling. A year later Christine Eberling inquired about legally adopting him once he turned twenty-one. Alice Hart said this would not work. "Richard is a sensitive, tense young man and the foster mother is demanding and plays upon his emotions," his file noted.

Later Richard Eberling made it clear that he had hated his foster mother. He resented her because she possessed him, choosing his activities and friends, making him get into bed with her, even as a teenage boy. He loved the power he felt being the surrogate man of the house. But he also despised himself because he could not pull away from her.

23

POLYGRAPH

THE BAY VILLAGE POLICE did not give up trying to make Richard Eberling take a polygraph test. In mid-November 1959, Lt. Jay Hubach arranged for an examination by the state's Bureau of Criminal Investigation, an hour's drive south in Mansfield, Ohio. Officially, the Bay Village police had reopened the Sheppard murder case and were treating Eberling as a suspect.

At about the same time, Eberling was sent to the Cleveland Clinic for a court-ordered psychiatric evaluation following his grand-larceny indictment. Dr. Louis J. Karnosh examined and tested him, particularly about his childhood and the behaviors that led to the crimes. "Since 1953, he has been subject to compulsive stealing, which is one form of kleptomania," Karnosh's report read in part. "The temptation to this type of misdemeanor came to him frequently during the time of his job which was that of a window-washer of private homes. Since that time he has taken something like 100 various objects including diamond pins and rings and various art objects which he secreted in his own home. He admitted a certain peculiar pleasure in obtaining the stolen material and obtains a certain degree of security in possessing these objects—none of which he has converted into cash. He admits that the impulse to take the stolen material is not normal and that the objects which he stole were all symbolic of some craving which he, himself, is quite unable to crystalize."

Eberling had no masculine interests, and his foster mother was "demanding, domineering, possessive," Karnosh wrote. He diagnosed Eberling as an "immature personality, with obsessive compulsive disorder, manifested by kleptomania. I believe that he is in dire need of prolonged psychiatric care which we recommend."

A week later polygraph examiner A. S. Kimball hooked Eberling to the lie box: girding his chest was a constrictor that measured respiration; a blood-pressure cuff circled an arm; attached galvanic skin-response sensors were clamped on a fingertip. As Eberling was asked questions, the machine graphed his body's responses.

A polygraph machine doesn't actually detect lies. It records stress as certain questions are asked. A skilled examiner interprets the results. In the hands of a highly trained examiner, the polygraph is a fairly reliable investigative tool. Its strength is in excluding suspects who passed. Interrogation afterward leads to confessions. It is a forensic version of a stethoscope.

Kimball asked control questions—Do you live in Ohio? Is today Thursday?—and established a baseline for a truthful answer.

"Are you positive that you deposited your own blood in the Sheppard residence prior to Marilyn's death?"

Yes.

"Are you positive that the French door to the study was left unlocked?"

Yes.

"Did you kill Marilyn Sheppard?"

No.

"Do you know what weapon was used to kill Marilyn?"

No.

"Did you set the Sheppard residence on fire?"

No.

Kimball repeated the test two more times, asking the same questions. He concluded that Eberling did not show deception in his answers.

In the hands of an inexperienced examiner, the polygraph is a dangerous crime-fighting tool. Years later, the director of the Department of Defense's Polygraph Institute studied the tracings and questions and said that Eberling's tests were inconclusive. There were several problems with the testing: many questions were ambiguous; the examiner asked too many questions with the blood-pressure cuff inflated to 87 millimeters; and several times Eberling was allowed to answer just after taking a deep breath.[1] Furthermore, Leonard Harrelson, the retired director of the respected Keeler Polygraph Institute in Chicago, studied the test data at the author's request. He stated flatly that Eberling showed deception when answering questions about Marilyn's murder.[2]

A few months later Eberling's grand-larceny case was brought to court. Eberling was a well-to-do, white, first-time, nonviolent offender facing judgment in an era long before mandatory minimum sentences. He had hired a good, well-connected lawyer, and a plea arrangement was struck. Faced with his confession to a chain of thefts, Eberling pleaded guilty to petty larceny. The judge fined him three hundred dollars and costs, gave him a ninety-day sentence in the Cleveland Workhouse, then suspended it. It was April Fools' Day 1960.[3]

24

F. LEE BAILEY

BILL CORRIGAN WAS SPENT. He had fired all the postconviction weapons available for Sam Sheppard, and the higher courts said the various appeals all missed the mark. It was the summer of 1961, and he was seventy-five and watching his health slip away. He had suffered a slight stroke, had heart problems, and, despite doctor's orders, continued to smoke, favoring a brand of nasty brown "midget cigars."

Like Corrigan, Sam Sheppard's family and friends were exhausted from the seven-year war for his freedom. Steve seemed to be the only one left who wanted to charge ahead. He visited Sam regularly in prison and kept him posted on Chip's progress in school, but even he was getting discouraged. In a meeting that summer, Corrigan explained to Steve Sheppard that the only strategy left was publicity. Publicity put your brother in prison; perhaps it could help get him out. Corrigan outlined his thinking: "Tell the public at every opportunity that your brother is in prison for a crime he did not commit." The killer wants to forget the crime. Every time he reads or hears about your brother, he feels guilt and comes closer to unburdening himself. "If you understand psychology as well as I think you do," the old lawyer said, "you will know why we get so many letters and telephone tips about the crime each time it is mentioned in the papers or on radio or on television programs. Someone in this town knows what happened out there at your brother's house the night Marilyn was killed and some day he will be compelled to tell of it. I only wish I might still be here when that happens."[1] Several weeks later, on July 31, Corrigan walked back from court to his downtown office, then collapsed. He died on the way to a hospital.

The only bright spot for the Sheppards in 1961 was a book written by

Paul Holmes, *The Sheppard Murder Case,* which spent weeks on national best-sellers lists. Holmes, the *Chicago Tribune* reporter, made the case that Dr. Sheppard was innocent. Until then, many people felt that the case against Sheppard had been weak and his trial shockingly unfair, but they also believed that he probably killed his wife. Holmes's book presented Kirk's findings about the blood trail and the blood from a third party, which began to change public opinion.

Meanwhile, Steve Sheppard tried to resurrect a plan to have Sam take a lie detector test. His strategy was to have Sam pass the test, then tell the world the positive result, hoping to sway public opinion and to provide political cover for Ohio governor Mike DiSalle to commute Sam's sentence to seven years. Steve needed a lawyer who knew about the polygraph to oversee the procedure. He called his new friend, Paul Holmes. Chicago was home to the respected Keeler Polygraph Institute, which trained polygraph operators and was run by Leonard Harrelson, one of the nation's top examiners and interrogators. Harrelson recommended a young Boston lawyer named Francis Lee Bailey, who was in town teaching a seminar on the legal aspects of the polygraph. When he was a legal officer in the U.S. Marines in the mid-1950s, Bailey relied on polygraph exams extensively, as did most of the military, and he was a proselytizer for its wide but careful use as an investigative tool. Thanks to his fascination with the polygraph, Bailey ended up in the Sheppard case as a fluke, which soon enough turned him into the most famous defense lawyer in the world.

In late November 1961, Bailey routed a return trip to Boston through Cleveland and spent several hours at the home of Steve and Betty Sheppard. By then, Bailey had read the Holmes book and was persuaded of Sam's likely innocence, and wanted to take the case. Steve Sheppard met Bailey at the airport and convinced him to stay the night. They talked until midnight, and Betty listened and added her opinion while trying to cover the seat of a small stool with her crochet work. After watching her struggle, Bailey asked for the hammer and nails and sat cross-legged on the floor, the stool in his lap, and expertly finished the upholstering. "I had to work a lot of different jobs to get through school," he said.

Betty Sheppard could see that both men were getting excited talking about the legal battles ahead. After Bailey retired to the guest room, she asked her husband whether hiring a new lawyer to aid Sam was worth the heartache and reprisals. Things had quieted down, finally. Wouldn't it be better to lie low, wait for Sam's eventual parole, while hoping for a semblance of a normal life? Each new development in the case brought headlines, harassing phone calls, and cruel remarks to their daughters at school. "Do we have to stir everything up again?" she asked Steve. "What kind of family life can we have?" When you weren't busy with surgery or seeing patients, she told him, you were making calls across the country, writing letters, talking to the press, waging a public relations campaign for Sam. "What do you have left for me and the girls?"[2]

Steve was torn. Richard and Dorothy Sheppard had already reached the point that Betty had just described; they had pulled back. After a while Steve replied, "What would you want Sam to do if our roles were reversed?" Betty answered that she'd support him no matter what he did, but at least he knew the depth of her feelings.

———

Several months earlier Sam Sheppard had been transferred to Marion Correctional Institute, a medium-security prison between Cleveland and Columbus. He lived in an honor dorm, the reward for seven years of good behavior. When Bailey made his unexpected visit, he had been a lawyer for one year and two days. He was trying to build a practice as a personal-injury lawyer, not defending criminals. Even so, at a time when lawyers were barred by professional ethics from soliciting clients or running advertisements, Bailey understood the economic benefit of publicity to a little-known lawyer.

Until they met, Sam knew nothing about Bailey, a barrel-chested man in a three-piece suit and gold vest chain that was supposed to make him look older than his twenty-seven years. He was a heavy smoker and drinker, and had a deep, mellifluous voice. He struck Sam as confident, smart, and aggressive. He could see that Bailey and his brother already were fast friends.

"By the time I met Sam I said to myself, 'This guy Steve is the brains and backbone of the family,' " Bailey said. "Number one, if his brother did it, he would know it. Number two, he wouldn't be putting the family through all this if Sam did it. If Sam did it, Steve would know it. He would have gotten the truth out of him. Sam was very intimidated by Steve."[3]

Bailey's strategy, which had excited Steve the night before, was simple. An inmate is entitled to effective counsel. To represent his client, Bailey needed to give him a lie detector test so that he could best determine how to represent him. A recent California higher-court opinion held that a prisoner awaiting trial was entitled to have his lawyer arrange a polygraph. Why should Ohio be any different? Bailey reasoned.

Bailey would soon find out how passionately the courts and law enforcement in Ohio felt about the Sheppard case. "I was young, I was idealistic, and I was naive,"[4] he said. And of course he had no idea that representing Sam Sheppard would lead him to a landmark U.S. Supreme Court decision and far beyond.

F. Lee Bailey grew up in Boston, the son of a struggling advertising man and a nursery school teacher. He was short, brilliant in school, and won a prep school scholarship, then admission to Harvard. He planned on being a writer but was a restless student, an outsider. He dropped out after two years of getting gentleman's C's, and joined the service to be a fighter pilot. He passed flight school and officer school and ended up flying FJ-2 Furies out of a marine base in Cherry Point, North Carolina. The military shaped Bailey more profoundly than law school would. The marines had an efficient, in-house justice system that relied heavily on polygraph exams to help officers eliminate suspects and decide who to court-martial or punish. When the base's legal officer died in a plane crash, Bailey, only twenty-one, was asked to step in. Despite his lack of training, Bailey took part in nearly two hundred quasi-trials as the base legal officer. In 1956 he finished his tour of duty as a captain and entered law school at Boston University. He put himself through school working full-time as a private investigator in civil cases for law firms, and found time to attend the Keeler Polygraph Institute, becoming an examiner.

Bailey agreed to accept the Sheppard case working pro bono, with his expenses reimbursed. Within a month he set up meetings with the two most important political figures in the state, *Cleveland Press* editor Louis Seltzer and Governor Mike DiSalle. Bailey knew that court decisions did not take place in a vacuum and hoped to convince the *Press* to call off the dogs. A December meeting with Seltzer quickly turned ugly. Bailey started out asking, "Why don't you give my client a break for a change?" That was perhaps the friendliest exchange. Seltzer stayed seated, flanked by two younger editors. One of them criticized Bailey, telling him he was ignorant of the real truth about the Sheppard case and that he wouldn't last ten days in town before running back to the East Coast. The former marine captain enjoyed this sort of macho sparring. Looking at the smaller Seltzer, Bailey vowed to set Sam free, and promised that when he did, he and his client would sue Seltzer and the *Press* for millions of dollars. "I'm a much younger man," Bailey told Seltzer, who was sixty-four. "If you die before I do, then I'll go after your reputation." There was nothing left for Seltzer to do but kick the lawyer out of his office.[5]

Bailey's meeting with Governor DiSalle was cordial but fruitless. DiSalle said he was not about to let Dr. Sam take a lie detector test. As an elected official, he had public opinion and the editorial page of the *Cleveland Press* to worry about. If he commuted Sam's sentence, DiSalle told Bailey, Seltzer and the *Press* would savage him. The governor already had been attacked for reducing the sentence of murderer Edythe Klumpp to life in prison, sparing

her from Ol' Sparky, the state's antiquated electric chair. DiSalle was running for reelection in a year and could not risk another display of mercy. He
referred Bailey to the Ohio Pardon and Parole Commission.

Throughout his tumultuous legal career, Bailey would employ novel
legal arguments and investigative techniques. He asked both the parole commissioner and the director of Ohio prisons to allow Sheppard to take a lie detector test and to undergo hypnosis. His client had been struck on the head
and knocked unconscious, Bailey argued, and these procedures were needed
to see if he could recall the details of July 4, 1954, maybe even identify the
killer or killers. To deny his request was to deny Sam Sheppard his right to
effective counsel. Hidden behind the legal arguments was Bailey's true purpose: "We thought the polygraph would be useful not judicially but elsewhere to convince the public. And that's the principal purpose for which the
polygraph was proposed," he admitted recently.[6]

Both men turned Bailey down. He appealed to the Ohio Supreme Court
and lost that battle as well.

Meanwhile, he and Steve Sheppard took every opportunity to argue Sam's
case on television, radio, and at civic forums. In November 1962 Governor
DiSalle lost to his Republican opponent, state auditor Jim Rhodes. Bailey and
Steve hoped that DiSalle, a decent man who opposed the death penalty, might
change his mind during his lame-duck period and commute Sam's sentence
to manslaughter, making him eligible for parole. Bailey wrote a long, passionate letter to DiSalle, citing Sam's good works in prison—saving inmates'
lives, volunteering as a human guinea pig for Sloan-Kettering cancer experiments, working as a nurse and putting in long hours during the 1957 flu epi-
demic, not getting ticketed for infractions. From Chicago, Paul Holmes
abandoned his reporter's neutrality and pleaded in a letter to DiSalle: "The
eventual emergence of truth in the Sheppard case—and it will emerge—will
provide the gauge by which posterity will evaluate your courage, your independence, your wisdom, your integrity, and your greatness—if any. I think
you have it in you to be great." Cuyahoga County prosecutor John T. Corrigan
opposed a break for Sheppard. With his crime reduced to manslaughter, Dr.
Sam would be able to reclaim his medical license, and he did not deserve to
be a doctor, Corrigan said.[7]

DiSalle refused to change his mind. However, the Ohio Pardon and Parole Commission said it would hold a parole hearing for inmate Sheppard on
January 29, 1963.

25

A R I A N E

IN DECEMBER 1962 Bailey had unexpectedly received a $250 check for Sam's defense from a woman in Düsseldorf, Germany. He called Steve Sheppard and asked, "Do you know a woman by the name of Ariane Tebbenjohanns?"[1]

Indeed he did, Steve replied. She was a wealthy divorcée who had been corresponding with Sam for a couple of years. Judging from her snapshot, she was young and attractive, and her letters had been boosting Sam's spirits.

Bailey, working without the promise of a fee, hoped that she would send more.

As he would learn, Ariane Tebbenjohanns had closely followed the Sheppard murder trial from Düsseldorf, fascinated by accounts of the handsome American doctor accused of killing his pregnant wife. A year after Sheppard's conviction, she met an American couple vacationing near her family's vacation home on the Côte d'Azur on the French Riviera. The Americans told her they thought Dr. Sheppard was innocent and had been railroaded by the press. Afterward, Tebbenjohanns followed the Sheppard case even more obsessively, feeling sorry for the young doctor who had lost his wife, then both parents, his career, everything. Two years later, just after her divorce, she composed a letter to Dr. Sam, then tore it up before sending it. In 1960 she forced herself to write again, this time to Dr. Steve Sheppard, the family spokesman. Each year he received scores of letters intended for his brother, some of them from women seeking to strike up a relationship with Sam. Steve threw out the abusive letters and passed along the supportive ones during prison visits. At the Ohio Pen, Sam was allowed to correspond only with his lawyers and family. After reading the Tebbenjohanns letter, he relayed comments to Steve, who forwarded them to Germany. Between 1960 and 1962, with Steve as intermediary, Ariane Tebbenjohanns sent Sam long letters and photos of herself and her family. She became his lifeline to the outside world and a fantasy to indulge. He pinned a snapshot of her to his small radio—a sultry pose of Ariane in a tight skirt, sitting on the hood of a Volkswagen, displaying her tanned legs like a model.

Ariane Tebbenjohanns was wealthy and bored, the daughter of industrialist Oskar Ritschel, an inventor and the owner of a company, Magno Ltd., that made complicated water-purification systems. She lived the fast life in Düsseldorf's flashy high society, a German version of Beverly Hills. After her divorce, she enjoyed being outrageous, swearing in German "like a beer-barrel transporter" and drinking top-drawer vodka all night.[2] She lived on the Riviera from March to October and skied in Switzerland each winter. By 1960, she had tired of the frivolous life and sought meaning by doing whatever it took to free an innocent man from prison. Her altruistic mission surprised her fast-life friends. "People accused me of all kinds of things, saying that it was impossible that a good-looking woman—who has been a playgirl up to now, just worrying about her next adventure—could possibly fall in love with Sam Sheppard. Because they think you have to be ugly, a thousand years old and bowlegged to have human feelings in your heart and the guts to stand up and fight for what you think is right and good."

Once Sam was transferred to Marion Correctional in 1962, he was able to write to her directly. Soon he finagled her onto his approved-visitors list (he later said he had to bribe a prison official) and begged her to visit him. She arrived in Cleveland on January 23, 1963, and stayed with Steve and Betty Sheppard. That night their house was surrounded by local newspaper and television reporters. From Chicago, Paul Holmes had already broken a story in the *Tribune* about a beautiful woman who had fallen for Sam Sheppard from across the Atlantic and had journeyed thousands of miles to see him.

The next day at Marion Correctional, a guard awakened Sam Sheppard and told him, "There's a blond stunner in a mink coat out to see you." Sam, always slow to awaken, mumbled that this better not be a joke. He snatched one of Ariane's photos and was passed through a series of locked doors into the visiting room. He was stunned. There stood a slim, blond woman in a beautifully tailored suit, wearing high heels and a nervous smile. Despite the winter storm outside, her platinum hair was perfectly in place. She wore giant earrings and emerald rings. In all, she was a rare sight in the middle of Ohio's farm country, let alone in a state prison.

"How about giving me a big kiss?" Sam asked, but she turned and offered her cheek. For more than four hours they talked about their lives, holding hands, professing love. Sam had made a silver necklace with a dove pendant in a crafts class. He put it around her neck and asked Ariane to marry him. She said yes, with little idea of the enormous role she would play in his turbulent life over the next seven years.

Ariane charmed nearly everyone in her path—Steve, Bailey, even Sam's prison minister, who told her that Sam had been depressed but now seemed more alive. "He was changing from a vegetable into a man again since I came," Ariane wrote to a friend. "I gave him something to look forward to. [Before] he really didn't have anything that he wanted to be out for. His reputation ruined, his home gone, his profession gone, his son a stranger."

More than ever, Sam wanted to get out of prison—under any circumstances. After being denied the right to polygraph him and losing twice on a governor's commutation, F. Lee Bailey planned to file a writ of habeas corpus in federal court, arguing that Sheppard was wrongfully imprisoned because his civil rights to a fair trial had been violated in 1954. Bill Corrigan had tried a habeas writ twice. However, in the mid-1950s Corrigan had to file the motion in Ohio courts. Only after exhausting those appeals was he able to file before the U.S. Supreme Court. At the time, the Court accepted only one in sixty cases for written arguments, and he lost. By the early 1960s, however, the Supreme Court, under Chief Justice Earl Warren, had begun its dramatic expansion of the constitutional protections of the accused. Suddenly, the Court authorized federal courts at the district level to hear writs on constitutional claims, in theory giving every defendant an immediate chance at a new trial. By 1962, with its appointees by President Kennedy, the Warren Court achieved what was later termed a liberal majority. The court clearly wanted to use worthy habeas corpus writs as a way to police state judges, who were shown to be hostile to the new criminal procedures established by the Court.

Meanwhile, Bailey had to represent his famous client based on his wishes. Sam didn't want to spend another day locked up, and wanted a sentence reduction even if it didn't clear his name and meant that most of the world still would view him as a murderer. He simply wanted to be with Ariane. "You are the most wonderful thing that has ever happened to me!!!!!" he wrote not long after her visit. "The words 'I Love You' are so inadequate, but they will have to do until I take you in my arms when we are finally alone. This love for you, Ariane, which is beyond what I thought was possible, is intensified by separation!! Never leave me. SAM."

———

The Ohio Parole Commission heard Sheppard's case on January 29, 1963, in Columbus. While Sam waited in Marion, Lee Bailey argued persuasively to the commissioners that his client deserved a break. Ever inventive, Bailey had floated the idea that Sam, if let out, would work in a health clinic in India that would be funded by a philanthropist friend. Bailey said he had asked Senator Ted Kennedy to clear the way with the Indian government. There was a chance for success.

Bailey's problem that day was that everyone seemed to be ignoring his arguments and focusing attention on Ariane. Usually surefooted with the media, he had allowed her to attend the public hearing. It took only moments before the pack of journalists descended on her. Reporters, especially television reporters, loved Ariane because she would say whatever came to mind without worrying about its consequences. "Ariane was very attractive," said a woman journalist who befriended her. "She wore these very high-heeled shoes and had beautiful clothes that fit her like a second skin. She just had this aura. She was sexy. When she walked into a room, every man stopped and looked at her."[3]

Before and after the hearing, Ariane proclaimed her love for Sam and her contempt for the American justice system. She talked to anyone who would listen, then made the rounds by taxi to each of Columbus's three television stations, finishing up well into the evening. She gave nearly manic performances, saying she would write about the great injustice to Sam in a German magazine and appeal to President Kennedy with a personal White House visit, if necessary.

News of Ariane's engagement and her sharp comments created headlines all over the world, and reporters in Germany dug into her background. As had happened with each new revelation about Dr. Sam, the story exploded into bizarre sensationalism. Unknown to Sam and Steve, Ariane had a half sister who was about twenty years older, Magda. She was the daughter of her father's first wife. Like Ariane, Magda had married a multimillionaire, then was divorced. Magda's second husband was Joseph Goebbels, Hitler's minister of propaganda for the Third Reich. Ariane insisted that her father, Oskar Ritschel, was not a Nazi true believer and privately had told Goebbels his feelings. Ariane's mother, Ritschel's second wife, was his maid, a fact that caused Ariane some insecurity in Düsseldorf society. It was revealed that Ariane also had a mentally handicapped eleven-year-old daughter who lived in a group home.

Even though these facts, on their own, were juicy enough to entertain readers, one newspaper referred to Ariane's prison visit to Sam as a "tryst," suggesting a sexual encounter. The mix of sex, Dr. Sam, and Nazism made for sensational coverage. Returning from a Jamaican vacation, Dr. Richard and Dorothy Sheppard read about Ariane's engagement to Sam in Miami newspapers. They were furious at Steve, blaming him for allowing Ariane to make a mockery of Sam's efforts for early release. It took several weeks before the brothers would speak to each other at Bay View Hospital.

In February, the Ohio Pardon and Parole Commission ruled against Sam and took away Ariane's visiting and writing privileges. Undaunted, she impetuously sent a love letter to one of Columbus's dailies, the *Dispatch,* and asked for it to be printed so Sam could read her words from prison. Overjoyed to have an exclusive dumped in its lap, the newspaper obliged her with a front-page story.

It was not surprising that the director of Ohio prisons, Maury Koblentz, was incensed. The brouhaha made his prison system appear out of control; its most notorious convict seemed to enjoy special favors, becoming engaged while incarcerated, having letters broadcast to him via the daily newspaper. Governor Rhodes had even called him to complain about Ariane's behavior. Koblentz drove up to Marion to deal with what was turning into a public relations fiasco. He quickly learned that Ariane was not officially on Sheppard's visitors list, that strings had been pulled. Along with the warden and an assistant as witnesses, Koblentz called Sam into a meeting.

This publicity is unacceptable, Sam recalled Koblentz telling him. You need to get rid of the "blond bitch," your "damned brother," and the "S.O.B. Bailey." If you do, you'll soon be out on parole, Koblentz promised. If you don't, you'll get buried.

"If you call her 'that blonde' again, your wife is a whore," Sam later recounted.

"I'll put you in the hole for that."

"Be my guest, you'll get no cheering."[4]

Even before his retort, Sam probably knew he would be punished. On February 5, he was put in leg chains and handcuffs and transferred to the Ohio Penitentiary to serve the hardest time the prison system could deliver. He arrived in Columbus at 4 A.M. and quickly found himself in the Hole, a narrow space between two walls of bars, with barely enough room to stand. "There was no food," Sheppard later testified in a congressional hearing. "There was no light and little air, and I felt I would suffocate. I couldn't sleep. I was allowed to wear my shorts, shoes and socks. I had no toilet privileges and just stood in my own excrement." He said he was beaten by guards with rubber hoses before being locked up. When he was released after six days, "my ankles had swollen so large the shoe strings had split on my shoes."

Why, the question has long been asked, did media-savvy Lee Bailey allow Ariane to attend the parole hearing? Perhaps Bailey thought the story of her engagement to Sam would be viewed as heartwarming and help Sam's cause. Others accused Bailey of preferring to wipe out Sam's conviction by winning a new trial through the federal courts and achieve exoneration rather than the empty victory of a state parole. But he had no assurance of what the Warren Court would decide eventually. Most likely, he and Steve made a severe miscalculation.

Paul Holmes, by now clearly a Sheppard partisan, was sorry he didn't incidentally mention the Goebbels connection in his profile of Ariane. If he had, "the damaging effect would have been largely if not entirely obviated," he wrote to Steve Sheppard. But even so, Ariane was making matters worse, Holmes advised. She "is a fighter, with a scrappy, volatile nature, and she lacks both judgment and experience about the backfire possibilities of her ill-considered public statements." Public opinion had quickly turned against Dr. Sam's cause, Holmes wrote, and the *Chicago Tribune* was less interested in the case. "Where there used to be indignant concern over injustice to Sam this now seems to replaced in the public mind with indifference. He is no longer to the public a martyr suffering with dignity but a person who seems to have lent himself to some conniving—a trickster who might be guilty of anything."[5]

———

Sam's celebrity, along with Ariane's wealth and tenuous ties to the Third Reich, made their romance seem extraordinary. Stripped of those distractions, their relationship was fairly commonplace to the psychologists and academics who study prisons. Women like Ariane Tebbenjohanns were familiar figures. Across the country, certain types of women fell in love with convicted killers, generally convinced that their partner was innocent or had changed for the better. Many, like Ariane, were divorced and had experienced disappointing relationships or had low opinions of themselves. For complex reasons, they needed to be in total control in their relationships. Who better to provide that than a prisoner, especially one likely never to be released? Psychologists typically saw such women in the role of the "controlling mother" or "the redeemer," who believed that she alone could change the man for the better. Other women targeted high-profile criminals by bombarding them with letters and latching on, driven by a need for "reflected notoriety," basking in the perverse glory of their mate's misdeeds.[6]

To whoever would listen, Ariane said she felt guilty that she had intruded on Sam's life and had played a part in sending him to the Hole. But Sam sent messages back to her through his brother, saying that he didn't blame her, he loved her, and he wanted her to keep up the fight. They were forced to write to each other in a secret code and sent the letters through Steve and young Sam, now a high school student at Culver Military Academy in Indiana.

Ariane decided to stay in the United States. She bought a town house in suburban Rocky River, near Steve and Betty Sheppard's home, and decorated it in eighteenth-century French style with a royal purple color scheme. In a guest bedroom to be used for visits from young Sam, she hung two pictures of Marilyn Sheppard. She even bought Sam a car for when he "wins his freedom," and stored it in a garage.

Inmates were allowed to carry a handkerchief. Just before visits by Steve and his son, Sam put on aftershave, then rubbed the handkerchief over his face and neck, soaking it with his scent. When the visiting room guard wasn't looking, Steve or young Sam would pocket the handkerchief and deliver it to Ariane. She slept with it under her pillow until the scent wore off, then returned the handkerchief with her body perfume.

Even though she was not allowed to visit, Ariane sometimes accompanied Steve and young Sam to the Ohio Pen and positioned herself on the sidewalk so Sam could spot her from a window. The other prisoners would hoot as Ariane, wrapped in a fur coat with her jewelry flashing, blew steamy kisses toward the window. Once she wrote to Sam that he seemed a bit heavier. He began dieting furiously and snapping off hundreds of push-ups a day.

Meanwhile, Ariane enjoyed "getting real blind," she wrote to a friend. "Don't get me wrong. I could never drink more than I like, but I like a lot. But liquor does not change me. My friends only realize when I tell them the next day that I was completely blind. When I am sad, liquor does not make me happy. When I'm happy, I'll be the same with it."[7] Sam, she worried, might not be enough of a drinker for her. "My Sam never did [drink] very much, so far. I hope he will change his mind about it."

MOCKERY OF JUSTICE

BACK IN BOSTON, F. Lee Bailey rounded up three Harvard Law School students to help him prepare Sheppard's writ of habeas corpus for federal district court in Ohio. Fortunately, he was able to build on the crate of pleadings that Bill Corrigan had crafted, including five scrapbooks of articles, cartoons, and editorials about the case.

Bailey knew the moment was ripe for convincing the Warren Court that Sheppard deserved a new trial. The Court was continuing to expand individual constitutional rights—poor defendants were entitled to court-appointed lawyers—which in turn multiplied the constitutional issues that could be raised in a habeas writ. A decade earlier the Supreme Court required a grave constitutional flaw, such as a forced confession, before overturning a conviction on a writ of habeas corpus. In March 1963, with the case of *Townsend* v. *Sain,* the U.S. Supreme Court again expanded prisoners' habeas rights. The Court held that if the facts alleged about a constitutional violation were in dispute, a federal judge had to hold a hearing and determine the facts. The *Townsend* case proved to be Sheppard's life raft.

Bailey looked forward to "trying the trial" before a federal judge, someone with lifetime tenure who was insulated from Cleveland politics. The named defendant was the warden of the Ohio Penitentiary, E. L. Maxwell, but in fact Bailey, with the habeas writ, was attacking coroner Gerber, the Cleveland police, editor Seltzer, and especially Judge Blythin. The case was assigned to federal judge Carl A. Weinman of the Southern District of Ohio.

Defending the State of Ohio fell to William B. Saxbe, the Ohio attorney general and future U.S. attorney general under President Nixon. Bill Saxbe began in politics as a popular state lawmaker from rural Ohio. He owned a farm, favored rumpled suits, and exuded down-home charm. When insulting an opponent's intelligence, for instance, he would say the man "couldn't chase a chicken down the stairs with a broom." He and his assistants underestimated Sheppard's chances of winning. (It was a miscalculation Saxbe would not make when, as U.S. attorney, the Justice Department opposed Bailey at the bank robbery trial of another famous client, heiress Patty Hearst.)

Bailey reduced the constitutional claims to twenty-three issues for Judge Weinman to consider. This catalog described judicial conduct that today seems out of bounds even to a layman: Dr. Sheppard was arraigned without his lawyer, despite asking for a short delay so he could arrive. The trial judge refused to move the trial to another city despite venomous pretrial publicity. A month before trial, the potential jurors' names and addresses were published in the newspapers, subjecting them to prejudicial comments and community pressure. Sheppard's home was confiscated by authorities and not released to him until after trial. Detectives testified repeatedly about Sheppard's refusal to take a lie detector test. In violation of Ohio law and without the judge's permission, jurors, while deliberating, were allowed to make unmonitored telephone calls. The list went on.

Shortly after the habeas writ was filed and it appeared that Judge Weinman was taking it seriously, an amazing development took place. Coroner Samuel Gerber changed his mind about the man whom he once described as "the most brilliant murderer in the annals of Greater Cleveland crime." In February 1964 Dr. Gerber, seemingly unprovoked, told reporters that he supported Sam Sheppard's early release on parole by reducing his conviction to manslaughter. All along, Gerber said, he had believed Sheppard guilty only of manslaughter, not murder. The osteopath had paid his debt to society and was not going to kill again.

In a letter to Saxbe, Gerber wrote that "no one could have an honest basis for criticizing Governor Rhodes if he should pardon Sam Sheppard, if the parole board should so recommend."

Gerber's stunning turnabout puzzled many people. None of the news stories explained why he had never mentioned this belief at the 1954 trial or even at the Sheppard parole hearing he had attended a year earlier, when Ariane had created a sensation. Retired Cleveland police chief Frank Story announced that he, too, had felt all along that Sheppard was guilty only of manslaughter. Even more remarkable, the *Cleveland Press* ran an editorial supporting Gerber's position.

The abrupt about-face caused whiplash in the community. Sheppard's public support had dipped after news of his unusual romance with Ariane Tebbenjohanns, then began to climb after Gerber suggested mercy. How to explain Gerber's change of heart?

By 1964, Gerber realized that Bailey was not going to disappear but instead was one of the new breed of aggressive defense lawyers who not only were empowered by the Warren Court but also used the news media to make their cases. As an outsider from Boston, Bailey didn't need to make a living in Cleveland. He felt no social pressure to tame his act. Perhaps the most significant reason for Gerber's new position was Bailey's threat of civil lawsuits against Gerber (and Seltzer) once Sam Sheppard was freed. Gerber cared tremendously about his reputation in the city and in forensic-science circles, and he wanted the Sheppard case to be over. If Sam Sheppard was paroled, it would end his shot at winning a new trial on constitutional grounds. Without a new trial and exoneration, Sheppard would not have legal ammunition to win damages against Gerber and Seltzer in civil court—as Gerber, a lawyer, was well aware.

Lee Bailey and Steve Sheppard wanted to see Sam win his freedom by getting his conviction overturned in federal court, not giving away possible exoneration for an immediate parole. But they had not counted on Sam's desperation.

After nearly a decade in prison, Sam was hardened and impatient and suspicious of everyone's good intentions, except for Ariane's. Within the prison's caste system, he had thrown his lot in with the smarter, tougher bank robbers and organized-crime figures, men who held power within the Walls. The warden and his administrators were used to having the educated, middle-class felons—they were few—acting friendly and open to them. They were disappointed that Sheppard hung out with career criminals. They did not understand that he viewed the prison brass as part of a system that kept him wrongfully imprisoned.

Dr. Sam complicated his incarceration by reinjuring his back with weight lifting and wrestling. To deaden the pain, he used drugs from the prison hospital, beginning a habit that grew into a problem. It was no secret that anything could be smuggled into the Ohio Pen. The inmates with opportunity and money, such as Dr. Sam, could numb their imprisonment with pills and booze. He faced other problems. Some convicts wanted him to steal drugs for them; if he did not, they would kill him. Another convict, a few months before his parole date, threatened to kidnap young Sam.[1]

After Gerber's remarkable change of heart, Sam sent a letter on February 28, 1964, to the Ohio Parole Board, asking for a rehearing of his failed request for executive clemency. He did not tell Bailey what he had done. Even worse, Sam said that if he was paroled, he would drop the federal-court lawsuit.[2] Gerber was certainly pleased. Suddenly, the mood of the press and the public became "let Sam out." Bailey was upset by Sam's impetuousness. It was a lawyer's nightmare, especially in a high-profile case, to have a client who was hard to control.

A couple of weeks later F. Lee Bailey got lucky again. He was a guest at an Overseas Press Club dinner and discussion that featured lawyer William Kunstler, columnist Dorothy Kilgallen, and NBC newsman Gabe Pressman. The discussion that evening focused on the clash between a defendant's right to a fair trial and the press's supposedly unfettered right to publish the news and inform the public. Kunstler favored restrictions on the press. The moderator turned to Kilgallen and said, "Dorothy, you were at the Sheppard trial. What do you think?"

Kilgallen quickly replied that the Sheppard trial had been "a farce" not because of the press but because of the trial judge. Before the trial, he had told her that Dr. Sam "was guilty as hell."

Her story electrified the audience, especially Bailey. One reporter jumped up and blistered Kilgallen. "If you are the journalist that you are supposed to be, why wasn't your headline the next day, 'Judge Says Sheppard Guilty as Hell!'? Is it not the duty of a journalist to tell the public things as they really are? If you had come forth with this information years ago you could have changed the venue and complexion of the entire case. Why did you not do this?"[3]

Kilgallen, stung, gave an excuse. "Things said to a reporter in confidence should be kept in confidence."

Bailey couldn't believe his good fortune. He talked to Kilgallen afterward, and she enthusiastically agreed to help the Sheppard cause. Since Blythin had died, Kilgallen reasoned, she was released from keeping his remarks private. She ended up being deposed by Bailey and a lawyer from the Ohio attorney general's staff. At the last minute Bailey was able to attach a transcript of her deposition to the habeas motion and argue yet another issue, that Blythin, who held a strong opinion about Sheppard's guilt, had violated Sheppard's rights to a fair trial by not recusing himself.

———

Normally, Lee Bailey assumed the unflappable coolness of a fighter pilot. On July 15, 1964, Steve Sheppard answered the telephone and heard the lawyer shouting, "Steve, we won! We won!"

Judge Weinman had thrown out Sam Sheppard's conviction on constitutional grounds. In an eighty-six-page opinion, the judge called the 1954 trial a "mockery of justice" that shredded Sheppard's Fourteenth Amendment rights to due process. Weinman ordered Sheppard released on a ten-thousand-dollar bond and gave the Cuyahoga County prosecutor sixty days to bring charges against Dr. Sheppard. Otherwise, the case would be dismissed permanently.

When Ariane heard the news, she screamed and drove to Columbus to try to see Sam. Bailey flew in from Boston. A media whirligig collected near the Ohio Pen.

Weinman took pains to point out that his ruling did not address whether Sheppard was guilty or innocent, only whether he had been denied his constitutional rights to a fair trial. The decision, Weinman wrote, had been an easy one to make. He cited five reasons for overturning the verdict, each one sufficient by itself to require a new trial: Judge Blythin's failure to disqualify himself after making biased remarks about the case; Blythin's failure to move the trial to another city; allowing detectives to testify that Sheppard refused to take a lie detector test; letting jurors make unsupervised phone calls in the middle of their deliberations; and Blythin's failure to shield the jurors from slanted news coverage.

Weinman focused his sharpest criticism on the news media. "If ever there was a trial by newspaper, this is a perfect example," he wrote. "And the most insidious example was the *Cleveland Press*. For some reason that newspaper took upon itself the role of accuser, judge and jury."

Before Ariane could arrive, Sam strode out of prison dressed in a tacky gray suit. It had been custom-made for him months earlier by a prison tailor. His face was tanned. His arms and chest were puffed up from weight lifting. At the gate Warden Maxwell, the man Sam had sued to get his freedom, shook his hand and wished him luck. Bailey took him to a hotel, where he was to wait for Ariane and meet with the press.

In a high-pitched voice, Sam demanded orange juice and a steak. More than anything, he wanted to have sex with Ariane, but was afraid that the Ohio authorities would arrest him for fornication, still a misdemeanor in Ohio. Ariane arrived that afternoon and ran a gauntlet of photographers and reporters before getting to hug and kiss Sam. They decided to solve the adultery problem by getting married immediately. Steve Sheppard opposed the instant wedding; he insisted they first get to know each other better. Sam would have none of it. At any time, the federal appeals court could overturn Weinman's decision and send him sent back to prison. At least if they were married, Ariane would be admitted for visits.

Paul Holmes was among the press corps in Columbus. He enjoyed favored status with Bailey and Steve Sheppard. To scoop his competitors, he hatched a scheme as old-fashioned as a city-room cuspidor. Holmes had cut his teeth as a newspaperman during Chicago's rollicking Front Page Era, with its fierce circulation wars, when reporters were known to capture a fugitive suspect and hide him or her from their competitors *and* the police until their newspaper published exclusive photos and an interview, preferably a teary confession.

Holmes outlined his plan to the anxious couple: the *Chicago Tribune* would pay for Sam and Ariane's wedding—bridal suite, champagne, meals, blood test, fees—in exchange for exclusive wedding photos and a story. Illinois had no waiting period. They could marry the same day they obtained a license.

Bailey, who was traveling with his wife, went along with the scheme. They looked forward to tricking the press. That night Sam and Ariane made sure to stay in separate rooms. The next morning at a short press conference they announced their wedding plans, hinted it would take place in North Carolina, then hit the road. Ariane drove her rented Lincoln Continental, accompanied by Sam, Bailey, his wife, Wicki, and an exuberant Paul Holmes. Keep it under the speed limit until you're out of Ohio, Bailey commanded. Ohio authorities would love nothing better than to arrest you for speeding.

A dozen cars with reporters and photographers pursued them. Outside of town, they twisted and turned down rural back roads, trying to conceal their ultimate destination. Above, an Ohio Highway Patrol helicopter followed the entourage, clocking the Lincoln's speed. Photographers and their drivers took turns pulling up alongside the Sheppard car and snapping pictures. At the Indiana line, the helicopter peeled off and the pursuers were down to four cars. Overjoyed to be out of Ohio, Sam led the car through a round of convict songs such as "I'm a Bird in a Gilded Cage" and "The Prisoner's Song." Spirits were high. After nearly two hundred miles of driving, they reached Indianapolis, and the last pursuing press car dropped off. That night they roared into Chicago in a blinding rain. Holmes brought them inside the Tribune Tower, where Sam and Ariane drank coffee and sat for photographers and a camera crew from the *Tribune*'s WGN-TV newsroom. To sneak them over to the Conrad Hilton's bridal suite, Holmes had Sam and Ariane ride down a freight elevator and climb in the dark into a newspaper delivery truck. On the short ride to their hideout, they sat on bales of the next day's newspapers.

Maintaining the *Tribune*'s exclusive was trickier and more dangerous the next day. First, Sam and Ariane were forced into public at the county clerk's office, where marriage licenses could only be picked up in person. Afterward, reporters tried to tail them to find out where they were getting married.

Sam and his companions embarked on "as frantic a chase through the Loop streets and alleys as had been seen in Chicago since Al Capone's gangsters were running wild in the 1920s."[4]

As the Sheppard party sped off, reporter Virginia Kay of the *Chicago American* hailed a cab and got the chance to shout with all seriousness, "Follow that car!" Several other reporters gave chase. They raced through the Loop, making U-turns, wheels squealing, as the Sheppard party backtracked, sped through red lights and past the massive support pillars on narrow, twisting Lower Wacker Drive underneath the Loop. Kay and her cabbie stayed on Sam and Ariane's tail for nearly an hour. "Sam proved himself a connoisseur of good chase-driving, turning around during one of our insane U-turns to salute my driver," Kay wrote. Bailey, always resourceful and aggressive, finally enabled the getaway. "Bailey jumped out of his cab to place himself in front of mine. Every time we tried to move, he maneuvered with us. The lovebirds roared off while we were debating the judiciousness of running down a lawyer."[5]

By the time the vows were over and the champagne corks popped, the Chicago press corps had located them at the Hilton. They threw open the doors and let them in. Holmes had already dictated a news story over the telephone; an early edition with the exclusive photos was coming off the presses. Ariane was disappointed with the ceremony. The experience was not as romantic as she had hoped, and the Hilton seemed shabby compared with the finer European hotels to which she was accustomed. Neither she nor Sam had family at the service, so Lee and Wicki Bailey were the best man and matron of honor.

It seemed odd that Sam Sheppard would expose his life to the news media during a private moment, especially since he blamed the newspapers for causing him to suffer in prison. But he knew he could not escape the reporters, so he decided to exploit the press as it exploited him. Their second evening in Chicago, the newlyweds dined at the Pump Room, guests of Chicago *Sun-Times* columnist Irv Kupcinet. The next day, they flew to New York and stayed at the Pierre Hotel, courtesy of *Parade* magazine. They dined well and walked hand in hand in Central Park.

Their frantic honeymoon was soon over because Sam had to be back in Ohio. The State of Ohio had appealed his release, and a panel of federal appeals court judges was going to decide whether he was entitled to bond while it took its time reconsider Weinman's decision.

27

SHANGRI-LA

SAM SHEPPARD'S LIFE was clouded by the chance of being returned to prison at any time. "A tension develops that is beyond description," he once explained.

An Ohio prison psychologist who tested Sam earlier as part of the parole process found "controlled hostility" and "syndromes of manic behavior."[1] After Sam's release, he displayed both traits in spades. Steve Sheppard tried to ground his younger brother, but with little success. Sam could not pick up where he had left off ten years earlier. His life had not been put on hold while he was gone. It was twisted into a new shape entirely. Gone were the physician's temperament and judgment. He was filled instead with rage and a self-pitying sense of entitlement. Sam could not slipstream into the lives of his brothers and their families or the routine at Bay View Hospital. Steve had suggested that Sam give neurosurgery lectures to Bay View interns, but Bailey overruled the idea.

The court ruled that Sam could stay out on bond, which gave the newly-weds time together. Sam moved into Ariane's apartment. At first he was practically a courtesan for her. He gave her expert rubdowns. He shaved her legs. He massaged her feet. He trimmed her toenails. Ariane preferred to have a beautician wash and style her pale blond hair every day, so Sam drove her to and from the beauty salon. No moment with Ariane was too mundane. They went out to dinner or cooked at home, usually late, Sam drinking Scotch, Ariane smoking Kents, Sinatra albums playing softly in the background.

In a diary he kept from September to November 1964, Sam recorded a few details of his life—where and what they ate for dinner, clothes purchased and tailored, medical problems (mostly Ariane's teeth), severity of hangovers. It was a hurriedly scrawled catalog of Sam's life on the edge— workouts, sessions under the sunlamp, passionate sex. Typical entries: "Bed, sex 16 times woweeeeee!" "I love Ariane desperately!" "Home in Shangri-La all day! WOW. . . . My goddess!!"[2]

Sam also had a decade of American life to catch up on. Ariane showed him how to dance the Twist, but he disliked the new rock music and pre-ferred Perry Como or Tony Bennett. They watched a lot of television, in-cluding some of the medical dramas. He thought *Dr. Kildare,* with its physician hero sitting around and neatly solving everybody's problems, was far-fetched. He did enjoy *Ben Casey,* which starred a young resident doctor in Los Angeles and used actual shots of Los Angeles County General Hospi-tal, where Sam and his brothers had trained. Sam used the television episodes to instruct Ariane about how he used to practice medicine in Los Angeles and later at Bay View Hospital. A hit show in 1964 was *The Fugi-tive,* a drama about a doctor named Richard Kimble who had been wrong-fully convicted of murdering his wife and was on his way to the electric chair when a train crash allowed him to escape. As the "Fugitive," Dr. Kimble hunted his wife's killer, a one-armed man, while he in turn was hunted by a relentless detective named Lieutenant Gerard. For Sam, the drama perhaps struck too close to home. "It doesn't catch me at all," he said.[3]

Eventually, the popular notion took hold that *The Fugitive* was based on the life of Dr. Sam Sheppard. The parallels were striking: like Sheppard, Dr. Kimble was from the Midwest and accused of murdering his wife. Instead of pursuing a bushy-haired stranger, Kimble chased a one-armed man. Articles noted the similarities, and ABC's publicity department took advantage of the connection. Once again, another dose of fiction was injected into the Shep-pard case.

In 1960, when news of Sam Sheppard was at an all-time low, a success-ful television writer named Roy Huggins had written a treatment for a po-tential TV series called *The Fugitive.* Huggins had produced TV's first hourlong western drama, *Cheyenne.* He created *Maverick* and *77 Sunset Strip* and in the 1970s would go on to create *The Rockford Files.* He wrote novels and screenplays. In 1960, however, he wanted to leave the industry, finish his doctorate in political philosophy at UCLA, and teach. But first he wanted to create one last television series, a swan song and a retirement fund. As a writer, he had always been fascinated with the Western hero, a man running from a mysterious past, alone, drifting from town to town, en-countering new situations. What if he put this hero into a contemporary set-ting? Huggins needed to give him a good reason for roaming from town to town, and came up with the idea of making Kimble a wrongfully convicted man who escapes his captors during a train crash and now seeks his wife's real killer. If Kimble was caught, he'd be sent to the electric chair. It was an inspired concept—a cop show, a doctor show, and a chase show all in one, with new characters and settings each week.

"I was not at all influenced by the Sam Sheppard case," Huggins insisted.[4] "The only reason people think it's based on the Sheppard case is I made him a doctor." He made Kimble a doctor because it created more dramatic plot turns. Faced with an injured child, Kimble would have to save a life, which would blow his cover and put him in jeopardy.

Unfortunately for Huggins, everyone—his agent, his writer friends, producers at the networks—hated his concept. "It's a slap in the face of American justice every week," one TV executive told him. Huggins put his three-page treatment of *The Fugitive* in a file drawer and tried to forget about it. "It was 1960, which was still the 1950s. Everybody was very conservative and suspicious." Two years later ABC Television, desperate for ideas, called top writers and producers. Huggins dusted off *The Fugitive,* pitched his idea, and the show was off and running by the fall of 1963. The brooding drama became an international phenomenon, airing in seventy countries.

The fictional television story gripped the nation for many of the same reasons that the Sheppard story did. Though not known for his introspection, Sam understood why his life had captured the popular imagination. "I'm a professional man, a guy who went to college and was brought up in a neighborhood consistent with the average citizen—the gray flannel suit, the white-collar worker—and all of a sudden a lot of these people thought, 'Well, goddamn, this could happen to me. But for the grace of God, there go I.' And of course many of them are playing around, having a little extra sex on the side. . . . Because the average Joe could be Sam Sheppard, he wants to read about me and he thinks, 'What the hell would I do under these circumstances?' "[5]

———

Meanwhile, Bailey prepared for a possible retrial. Early on, he had decided to point to someone else as the killer of Marilyn Sheppard. It went against his nature to simply argue at a murder trial that the state's evidence against the defendant did not rise to the standard of "beyond a reasonable doubt." He knew that jurors were unsatisfied with mysteries. It was easier to win an acquittal if the jury could at least consider someone other than the defendant as a possible suspect.

Bailey got a huge head start on this aggressive strategy by relying on Paul

Holmes's book, which laid out the holes in the case against Sam Sheppard as well as concluded with a plausible scenario that a woman and a man killed Marilyn. Holmes based his theory on Kirk's work, which eliminated Sam and pointed to tantalizing evidence: the fibers under Marilyn's nails that didn't match Sam's clothing; a chip of red nail enamel from the floor; the less-than-powerful blows to Marilyn's skull. Holmes's hypothesis was that Marilyn had a lover, a neighbor who knew the layout of the house and who had misinterpreted a dressing-room light that was on as a signal that Sam was out on an emergency call. The neighbor crept in through the kitchen and went upstairs, unable to see Sam on the daybed. Meanwhile, the man's wife noticed that her husband was missing and suspected his whereabouts. She walked to the Sheppard home carrying a flashlight. She caught Marilyn and her husband flagrante delicto, turned her fury on her rival while her husband pulled up his pants. Hearing Sam coming up the stairs and realizing the jeopardy they were in, he knocked Sam out from behind. His wife fled in a panic. He didn't know if Marilyn was dead, but he was not a killer, so he didn't finish off Sam. The neighbor staged a burglary as a way to throw suspicion to a stranger. During this hasty cover-up, Sam recovered, chased the intruder to the beach. Already weak from a head injury, Sam got knocked out again. It was pure hypothesis, Holmes wrote, but more satisfactory than what either the prosecutors or the defense offered at the 1954 trial.

Holmes did not name suspects in his book, but it was clear to anyone familiar with the facts that he was suggesting Spencer and Esther Houk.

Bailey was also excited about another possible murder suspect: Richard Eberling. Eberling was brought to his attention in 1962 by a prominent lawyer and Bay Village councilman, Guy Hardy, who knew about Bay Village's frustrating efforts to have Eberling polygraphed after he was arrested with Marilyn's rings and admitted to bleeding in the Sheppard house. These facts, just on their face, were startling and made Eberling a prime suspect. Bailey assigned cocounsel Russell Sherman to check out Eberling but cautioned, "I do not wish to have it publicly known that we are perhaps going to be in a position to contradict the results of the polygraph test he took."[6]

However, by August 1964, a month after Sam had been released from prison, Bailey rejected Eberling as a suspect. Bailey believed that Marilyn's pajamas—half removed, not torn—and the absence of vaginal wounds showed consensual sex, and "I didn't think she would have anything to do with the likes of Eberling." He settled instead on the Houk theory.

As another element of Sheppard's defense, Bailey wanted to film an expert conducting a hypnosis interrogation of Sam on videotape. Bailey thought Sheppard might recover memories or details of the crime. He reassured Sam that he had no need to worry about "what may pop out." Not only were results privileged, but "as you know, I am personally satisfied that Esther Houk murdered Marilyn in the presence of Spencer. If the information derived from hypno-interrogation is sufficient to demonstrate this as fact, we will see that the blame is lifted from you and properly placed—one way or the other. This is the only result—even though it is beyond my duty as a defense lawyer—that will settle my mind on the Sheppard case. So long as there is one individual on the face of the earth who believes that you are guilty, my job—in this case only—is unfinished."[7]

By September 1964 Ariane was pregnant (so much for rumors of Sam's sterility), and she stopped drinking for a while. On October 8 Bailey flew his plane to Cleveland and ferried Sam and Ariane to Cincinnati for the federal court of appeals hearing. Young Sam joined them at Bailey's suggestion. "I think psychologically it might be a little difficult for the judges to look down at a boy who was deprived of his father for ten years due to a 'mockery of justice' and turn around a few days later to perpetuate that deprivation. You and Sam and Ariane make up an attractive family, and I think that your appearance together could do you no harm at all."[8]

Beyond appearances, the new family was frought with tension. Ariane's pregnancy pleased Sam, but young Sam was upset. He and his father had talked during prison visits about all the great times they would have when they were reunited—fishing, camping in Canada, being father-and-son buddies, repairing ten years of separation with a flood of togetherness. His father was free, but Ariane was enveloping him in ways that shut out a teenage boy.

At the court of appeals hearing, Bailey and the prosecutors assumed their usual positions: Bailey's, that a fair trial was impossible in face of the prejudicial publicity; Saxbe's, that there was no evidence that the publicity affected the jury, and besides, it would not have mattered how open-minded the jurors started out because the evidence overwhelmingly supported a guilty verdict. Bailey performed well, but the appeals judges were sharply critical, especially presiding judge O'Sullivan. Sam couldn't stand the tension and ran off "to pee, like a school kid," Bailey wrote. "I expect a reversal."[9]

Two days later Sam scrawled in his journal, "Ariane finally fell off the horse. I love that gal." He still drank heavily, knowing that it was hurting him. Like Ariane, he tried to cut back. "Very little booze in the last few days 'cause I feel so good!" he wrote in November. He tried to stay busy, but he was in limbo, unable to practice medicine. Ariane no longer dominated the relationship, though she tried. Sam depended on her for money—his inheritance had all gone to pay defense lawyer Bill Corrigan and to support young Sam. He allowed Ariane to buy him clothes and tell him how to behave in public, but he still resented the arrangement. He had survived the Walls, the Hole, prison gangs. With his lawyers, at least for the moment, he had slammed the justice system to the mat. After a decade behind bars, he did not want to be controlled by anyone.

On Christmas Day 1964, Ariane suffered a miscarriage. Sam blamed it on the stress she felt not knowing whether he would have to return to prison. He had not been spreading comfort and joy, either. "I'm nervous, and I'm not as tender and calm toward Ariane as I want to be," he said, "and I don't even know it."[10]

On March 4, 1965, seven months after hearing arguments, the U.S. Court of Appeals for the Sixth Circuit in Cincinnati released its long-awaited opinion. Bailey was in Massachusetts, having just met with a new client named Albert De Salvo, a young convicted rapist who would confess to being the Boston Strangler. By now, Bailey had built a lucrative law practice, thanks in large part to becoming a celebrity through such famous clients as Dr. Sam.

Bailey was shocked by the panel's decision. The three-judge panel voted 2 to 1 to reverse Judge Weinman's release of Dr. Sheppard.

In Cleveland, Sam and Ariane were preparing to move from her apartment into a newly purchased home in Bay Village. They received a call from Bailey moments before reporters and photographers knocked on their apartment door. Sam was devastated. As a small consolation, he was allowed twenty days before turning himself in to serve his life sentence. Bailey filed for bail while he appealed to the U.S. Supreme Court. County prosecutor John T. Corrigan opposed him; he believed that Sam should serve the rest of his prison term while waiting to see what the U.S. Supreme Court would do.

Bailey was deeply troubled. Out of the flood of appeals to the Warren Court, the justices agreed to review fewer than one out of a hundred. It was debatable whether the constitutional issues in the Sheppard case were weighty enough to convince the justices to review the lower court.

Sam won permission to stay out on bail, but it was a small victory.

A DECISION

IN AUGUST BAILEY FILED a writ of certiorari with the U.S. Supreme Court, the first step to obtaining a full hearing before the Court. Bailey hoped to convince four of the nine justices that the core question of the Sheppard case—that his constitutional right to a fair trial had been violated by a judge's failure to insulate jurors from prejudicial news coverage—was broad and important enough for the full Court's consideration. Lawyers for the State of Ohio argued against it. "I was not confident," Bailey admitted.

Sheppard was fortunate because his appeal to the Supreme Court came at an unusually opportune time. The justices had been seeing more and more cases of "unfair and prejudicial news comment on pending trials," Justice Tom Clark would say later. Furthermore, Chief Justice Warren had reached the point where he was fed up with the blanketing, visceral power of television news. Several months before, Warren had wrapped up a blue-ribbon investigation into the Kennedy assassination and had issued the *Warren Commission Report,* which concluded that Lee Harvey Oswald had acted alone. Largely overlooked was the report's attack on the press for making it impossible for Oswald, if he had survived, to get a fair trial. Privately, Warren had come to the conclusion that courtroom television coverage and justice were incompatible.

In November 1965, to Bailey's delight, the Supreme Court granted certiorari—agreed to hear the Sheppard appeal—a tremendous breakthrough for Sheppard and a disappointing setback for the state. Sam was allowed to stay out on bond, which meant several more months of freedom.

Bailey had never appeared before the U.S. Supreme Court. He was an excellent cross-examiner, but this skill would not help him with the justices. He needed to craft a compelling piece of appellate argument. As it turned out, Bailey, the aspiring writer and legal mind, crafted what one academic study described as "Bailey's finest work."[1] The Ohio Attorney General's Office was overmatched and outmaneuvered.

On February 28, 1966, Bailey and Ohio attorney general Bill Saxbe faced off in front of the Supreme Court justices. Each side had one hour to present its arguments. Bailey was joined by Bernard Berkman, a lawyer with the Cleveland ACLU who successfully argued *Mapp* v. *Ohio,* the landmark case that required police to obtain warrants before searching a home for evidence. Saxbe was joined by county prosecutor John T. Corrigan. Sitting in the first row of public seats were Dr. Sam, young Sam, and Ariane, surprisingly subdued.

With his thumbs in the vest pockets of his custom-made suit, Bailey launched his main argument. Dr. Sheppard "was so thoroughly tried and convicted by the news media that a fair trial in the courtroom could not and in fact did not occur."[2] Bailey danced on the edge of calling for press restrictions, something Justices Black and Douglas adamantly opposed. Reporters should indeed "cast their single or collective harsh light upon shady official conduct," Bailey said. But there must be some perimeter within which the press could function without diminishing its power to "to attack and expose when the public is being duped."

Bailey was interrupted. What new evidence do you bring to the case since the Court refused to hear this case in 1956? he was asked.

Bailey pointed to columnist Dorothy Kilgallen's deposition in which the trial judge had told her Sheppard "was guilty as hell," the case "open and shut."

Why didn't Dr. Sheppard's lawyers challenge on bias? Chief Justice Warren asked.

The lawyers would have challenged, Bailey answered, if they had only known the judge's prejudice, which came out ten years after the fact.

———

"This was a trial by the book," Saxbe told the Court during his time. "It was a good trial. To allow Sheppard to attack his conviction now with an emotional issue that obscured the overwhelming proof of guilt subverts the jury system." In his brief, Saxbe listed the proof: there was no burglar in the home, the scene was "faked," Sheppard was in the murder room at the time of the murder, and he "had a reason and temperament to commit murder. The ultimate conclusion . . . Dr. Samuel H. Sheppard murdered his wife, Marilyn, by brutally beating her to death with 35 crushing blows to the head."[3]

As the justices asked him questions, Saxbe, a popular Republican office-holder, fumbled around. He was not as well prepared as Bailey. He had difficulty answering some of the questions from the bench. As the state attorney general, he ran a huge two-hundred-person law firm and aspired to higher office, but he hadn't spent the time to know the case as Bailey did. Instead, Saxbe relied on assistant David L. Kessler, who had prepared many of the motions and who had been wrangling with Bailey for years.

Saxbe compared the Sheppard murder to another controversial case, Sacco and Vanzetti, two anarchists who were executed in 1927 for the murder of a Massachusetts bank guard. Like the Sheppard case, Sacco and Vanzetti also unfolded in the midst of a red scare (this one after World War I, and it also divided the community). The controversial murder trial caught the eye of a Harvard law professor named Felix Frankfurter, who later became a U.S. Supreme Court justice.

Frankfurter wrote a book about the case, arguing persuasively that the two immigrants were innocent, Saxbe noted. Then he made a dumb statement: "Sacco and Vanzetti were guilty, and so is Sheppard, regardless of everything the 'bleeding hearts' think, like Felix Frankfurter said."

Judging from their faces, the justices were unhappy with the attack on their former colleague, who had died nine months earlier after having presided for twenty-three years on the Court. "I hope you don't want us to reexamine the evidence in Sacco and Vanzetti," Justice Black told Saxbe. "The Sheppard case is difficult enough."[4] Saxbe, a powerful vote-getter in rural Ohio, had miscalculated with this more sophisticated audience.

Associate Justice Hugo Black asked Saxbe, Should the conviction stand if the trial judge was prejudiced?

"But he wasn't prejudiced," Saxbe insisted. "Even if he had been, the conviction should stand unless prejudice was passed on to the jury." He dismissed Kilgallen's meeting with the judge as something that had "come out accidentally at a cocktail party ten years ago."

Suddenly, time was up and the black-robed justices disappeared behind heavy red drapes and headed to their offices.

———

By May 1966 Sheppard still had not heard from the U.S. Supreme Court. Often, he awoke at night, heart pumping, sweating, unsure whether he was at home or bunked behind bars. He'd slip into the living room, angry at being awake, edgy, go to the liquor cabinet, and pour a tumbler of vodka. After ten years in prison, he found freedom almost as tense. "He was bitter and angry, hostile and unpredictable," Steve Sheppard said. "There's no doubt he was taking uppers to get up in the morning and downers to go to bed at night and drinking his share of vodka."[5]

For several weeks on Monday mornings, the day the Supreme Court released new opinions, news reporters camped outside the Sheppard house. It was just before noon on Monday, June 6, 1966, when Sam heard, almost simultaneously, a knock on the front door and the phone ringing. He had been resting in bed. Nearby was a bag packed with underwear and supplies he could bring with him if the justices said he had to go back to prison. Ariane snatched the telephone, and young Sam ran to the front door. A moment later, he bounded up the carpeted stairs, shouting, "Acquittal or retrial, Dad!"

"Thank God," Sam said. They were strangely quiet as the news sank in. The U.S. Supreme Court, by an 8-to-1 vote, had struck down his murder conviction, saying that he had not received a fair trial. The State of Ohio could retry him within a reasonable time. Otherwise, he was free forever.

An associate from Bailey's office rang next and passed on a warning from Lee: You're still under indictment and could be arrested. Leave the house while we clarify your status.

To get to the car, the three Sheppards had to pass camera crews and numerous reporters asking, "Are you happy?" "Do you want a retrial?"

"I'm relatively happy," Sheppard said. "I want what is proper for complete vindication. However, I don't wish to put my family through the tremendous ordeal of another trial." On her husband's big day, Ariane entered into the act by wearing a brunette wig, which prompted attention and questions from reporters. Sam didn't mind. To avoid an immediate arrest, he left the county and took his family to a restaurant suitably named the Castle.

———

For several years, lawyers had been presenting Bailey with variations on a theme: "Sheppard's probably innocent, but you'll never get him out." Springing Sheppard had been the tricky part, and Bailey felt tremendously vindicated. Now more than anything, he wanted to cap off his accomplishment with a trial victory. He had been goading the Cuyahoga County prosecutor, even in remarks before the U.S. Supreme Court. He had challenged Corrigan to televised debates, drawing lines in the sand, hoping to spark a rematch. He believed he could outwork and outprepare the county prosecutors. If he could get an open-minded jury, he would bet anything that Sam would be acquitted.

The day after the Supreme Court decision, however, John Corrigan struck a reasonable tone, saying that he might not retry the Sheppard murder case. He doubted that he could find twelve jurors "who would convict this man again after he spent nine years in prison" and one in county jail. Corrigan was less likely than other county elected officials to be swayed by public opinion. He had held the office for nearly a decade, had won reelection with huge margins, and had a reputation for personal honesty. "If I feel we can't get a jury and we can't get our witnesses and our evidence together, I'm not going to give him a new trial."

Meanwhile, the landmark *Sheppard* decision landed on the news industry with a crash, jangling the nerves of editors who wondered if the rules were changing. For the first time, the Supreme Court recognized that prejudicial press coverage—including stories *before* a trial—could deprive a defendant of a fair trial guaranteed under the due process clause of the Fourteenth Amendment. Associate Justice Tom Clark, a sixty-six-year-old Texan who had been appointed by President Truman and was the swing vote on the Warren Court, wrote the majority opinion. He said "virulent publicity" violated Sheppard's fair-trial rights. In a phrase that would resonate for decades, Clark placed blame on a "carnival atmosphere" at the trial that "could easily have been avoided since the courtroom and the courthouse are subject to control of the court." Without naming Blythin, Clark gave a litany of the trial judge's sins: failing to protect the jurors from Bob Considine's weekly radio report during trial that compared Sheppard's testimony to the perjury of Soviet agent Alger Hiss; failing to protect the jurors from Walter Winchell's false television scoop about a female felon who claimed to have given birth to Sam's illegitimate child; and so on.

Clark faulted Blythin for not sequestering the jurors, especially after the newspapers had turned them into local celebrities. Even worse, Clark felt, were efforts by the prosecutor to try the case in the newspapers by dishing exclusives to reporters about what witnesses were going to testify about. These leaks exposed jurors to such headlines as SAM CALLED A JEKYLL-HYDE BY MARILYN, COUSIN TO TESTIFY. No such testimony was ever produced at trial, Clark noted. Furthermore, Judge Blythin insufficiently warned jurors not to read or listen to stories about the case. Though they had no direct proof that the jury was contaminated by the press, the justices assumed that was the case. In his opinion, Clark noted the highly prejudicial article "Tie Sam to Five Women," an irresponsible story based on an anonymous official source. Court testimony, however, proved only that Sheppard had a sexual affair with one woman. This multimistress allegation leached into the jury room from outside the courtroom, something prosecutors denied in appeals briefs but that interviews with jurors now prove. "It was admitted to us that he did have many lady friends," said juror William Lamb. "Family values meant something back then."[6]

The Warren Court's decision did not sit well in Cleveland. The *Plain Dealer*'s editors buried the story on page 7 and criticized the decision in an editorial. The *Press* played the story on page 1 of the afternoon edition under a one-column headline, the narrowest possible. The national press reacted quite differently. Fred Graham, the *New York Times* legal correspondent, wrote, "It is clear that such 'circus' proceedings will be happily relegated to the past." (There was no way Graham could have foreseen Court TV, CNN, tabloid TV shows, and the tangle of competitors that would drive sensational murder trials in years to come.)

The national reporters who covered the 1954 Sheppard trial, particularly Theo Wilson of the New York *Daily News,* were stunned by language in the opinion about "commotion within the bar" and the courtroom's Roman-holiday atmosphere. Wilson rounded up nearly a dozen of her colleagues from the trial—fellow "sob sister" Margaret Parton, columnist Bob Considine, Alvin Davis of the *New York Post,* Doc Quigley of the United Press, Jack Lotto of Hearst Newspapers—and sent the Court a letter of protest.[7] Blythin's courtroom had been orderly and quiet. Reporters with midday deadlines left and reentered the courtroom quietly. The national press corps showed restraint and professionalism. If anything, the Cleveland reporters created the problem. "We never believed that the American press as a whole would be condemned 12 years later for local stories about revelations made by police, defense and prosecuting attorney and the coroner in one city in the Middle West."

The Warren Court's opinion has created a popular image of bedlam throughout the courtroom at the 1954 trial. But that is inaccurate. The bedlam was mostly outside the courtroom and at the coroner's inquest. As Wilson and her colleagues noted, Sheppard lawyer Bill Corrigan complained to *The New York Times,* two days after the guilty verdict, about the "carnival atmosphere" at the inquest—not at trial. In the twelve years of appeals in various courts, "the description of a 'carnival atmosphere' has slowly moved from a description of the inquest three months before the trial to the trial room itself," Wilson wrote.

What commotion did unfold inside the Sheppard courtroom took place in the first days of jury selection, was short-lived, and can be blamed in part on the bulky, unwieldy technology of a courtroom newcomer, local television news. "Flashbulbs were popping and the lighting devices backed by powerful reflectors were sprouting from chairs, tables, and the floor to near-ceiling height, their cables twisting and coiling over the carpet," reporter Paul Holmes wrote. Defense lawyer Bill Corrigan protested to the judge that no trial could be carried on amid such hubbub. "They're standing on tables, sitting on railings, and hanging from the chandeliers. They're even taking pictures of the jurors—that is, when they can get their lenses past the assistant prosecuting attorneys trying to get into the picture."

Blythin quickly banned filming and photographs during court sessions. Camera crews had to be content with rushing in and out before and after court was in session.[8]

Two days after the U.S. Supreme Court's decision, prosecutor Corrigan shed all signs of uncertainty about taking Sam Sheppard to trial. His office had learned from coroner Gerber and others that the evidence had been carefully preserved. At a press conference timed to coincide with the local noon newscasts, Corrigan sternly announced on live television, "We will retry Sam Sheppard. He will be arrested or he can come in voluntarily."[9]

RETRIAL OF THE CENTURY

WHEN HE FIRST VISITED Sam Sheppard in prison, F. Lee Bailey was a little-known civil attorney only a year out of law school. Five years later, as he prepared for the Retrial of the Century, Bailey rushed about the country handling a flurry of high-profile cases. The Sheppard case brought him vast amounts of free publicity at a time when lawyers were barred from advertising their services. Bailey prospered. He now represented the Boston Strangler; a leader of the Plymouth Mail Robbery gang; double-murder suspect Dr. Carl Coppolino (a physician accused of poisoning a mistress in New Jersey and his wife in Florida); and many others. To keep up with his crushing trial schedule, Bailey leased and flew small airplanes.

In the intervening years, Bailey expanded the legal frontiers staked out by his idol Edward Bennett Williams, a charming, politically connected Washington, D.C., lawyer. Williams and now Bailey had changed the popular image of the criminal defense lawyer as a shabby, somewhat disreputable poor cousin of the legal bar into a heroic battler for justice. Bailey realized that image mattered, and he played the part of a swashbuckling James Bond character. He traveled on occasion with a beautiful female private investigator. He bought the latest high-tech communications and security gear. Once, when landing at a small airport in the winter, he spotted a waiting reporter and photographer on the tarmac. He changed from an aviator jacket into his full-length mink coat and made a theatrical exit. He waved the two men over, opened a tiny bar in the plane, pulled out a bottle of Scotch, and said, "Libation, gentlemen?"

The day after Bailey passed the bar exam he had the opportunity to talk to Williams. "How do you always manage to pull a rabbit out of the hat at trial?" the young lawyer asked.

To pull a rabbit out of the hat at a trial, you need fifty hats and fifty rabbits, and luck, Williams replied. In other words, prepare obsessively, much as large law firms did in complex civil litigation. Bailey took the advice to heart. He spared no necessary expense in preparing for trial. He hired forensic experts and private investigators, reinterviewed witnesses, and searched for new ones. For the Sheppard case, he retained Dr. William Bryan, a physician and expert in hypnosis, to help him select jurors. It was one of the earliest uses of a jury consultant, now standard practice at important trials.

Going into the trial, Bailey was supremely confident. He underestimated the abilities of the two Cuyahoga County prosecutors who were handling the case.

Sam Sheppard's fate rested with Cuyahoga County prosecutor John T. Corrigan, a tall, broad-shouldered man who had played tackle at St. Ignatius, a Jesuit prep school. Corrigan had lost an eye and hearing in one ear from shrapnel in World War II's Battle of the Bulge. The glass eye made him appear forbidding. He had built a small political machine with his office of lawyers, many of them Irish Catholic, some of whom went on to become judges. He was the son of a retired Cleveland policeman, the brother of a Cleveland police detective. A devout Catholic, Corrigan had a reputation as a law-and-order hard-liner. Because of his poor hearing, he learned to read lips as he worked his way through college and law school. It was a skill that served him well in the courtroom, enabling him to anticipate surprise moves by opposing counsel.

Corrigan decided to try the Sheppard case himself. For his cocounsel, he selected a thirty-three-year-old assistant prosecutor, Leo Spellacy, another smart, rangy Irish Catholic from St. Ignatius and a Georgetown University graduate. For investigative support, Corrigan borrowed Cleveland police sergeant Harold Lockwood, who had worked on the 1954 homicide.

A few days after Corrigan announced that Sam Sheppard would stand trial again, the prosecutor sent Harold Lockwood to reinterview an inmate informer who, two years earlier, had claimed to have some dirt on Sheppard. Edmund "Frenchy" Flott was a muscular career criminal who'd robbed banks and occasionally traded information with authorities when it served his interests. Flott had served time with Sam in county jail and later in state prison. Flott said Sam had paid him for protection. They'd had a falling-out and now Flott despised him.

In early February 1964, after Dr. Gerber's public recommendation of mercy, when it appeared that Sam would win an early release, Flott made contact with Lockwood. On Valentine's Day and again three days later, the two men met and Flott dished up damaging allegations against Sheppard. The information made its way to the Ohio Pardon and Parole Commission, which turned down his early release.

Now, more than two years later on June 14, 1966, Sergeant Lockwood traveled to Leavenworth federal prison in Kansas, where Flott was serving the third year of a bank-robbery sentence. They met in a private room at 11 A.M. and talked for five hours. Later Lockwood wrote a nine-page report, assessing Flott as a witness and relaying his information.

> [Flott] is apparently quite intelligent. He appears to be able to make him-self appear sincere and believable, and it is my thought that his sincerity is NOT an act, that he is firmly convinced that what he is doing at any one time is for the best of interests for himself and/or his friends. . . . He was the "buffer" for SAM SHEPPARD, warding off many of the other inmates who attempted to get friendly with SAM SHEPPARD for reasons of the wealth SHEPPARD supposedly represented, for professional reasons (the word was that SHEPPARD was truly a good and capable doctor) as well as many other reasons, least of which was not the fact that many inmates resented DR. SAM SHEPPARD because of the fact that SHEPPARD could buy a great number of favors inside the Ohio State Penitentiary, which they could not. Other inmates apparently felt that by possibly causing physical harm to DR. SAM SHEPPARD that they, themselves, would be covered with the notoriety surrounding the SHEP-PARD case. It was FLOTT'S duty to protect SAM SHEPPARD against intrusions by unwelcome inmates.[1]

Lockwood and Flott danced a tricky dance. Each needed the other; Flott hoped for a break when he came up for his next parole hearing in 1967, and Lockwood wanted solid information to use against Sheppard. Flott ended up telling a fantastic story that, if believed by a jury, could sink Sam Sheppard.

According to Flott, around 1960 Sam asked him to kidnap Dr. Lester Hoversten and force him to write a confession saying that he, not Sam, had killed Marilyn. Flott said he then was supposed to kill Hoversten and make it look like a suicide. The confession would be found, and Sam would be re-leased. To accomplish all this, Sam was going to bribe a prison administra-tor to transfer Flott to Marion Correctional, a low-security honor camp. Flott would then escape, make his way to California, and seek out Dr. Arthur Miller, one of Sam's staunch supporters. Miller, unaware of the illegal scheme, would give Flott cash and tell him where Hoversten was residing.

Flott would then kidnap Dr. Hoversten, force him to write a confession, then either fake a fatal heart attack with an injection of curare, a deadly poison, into the mucous membranes of his nose or fake a suicide by putting a gun in Hoversten's hand, forcing it to his head, and pulling the trigger. Flott said Hoversten was selected because he did not have a good alibi for his whereabouts when Marilyn was murdered.

Once he was freed, Sam was going to perform plastic surgery on Frenchy's large protruding ears. With glasses, dyed hair, and a fake mustache, Flott could conceal his identity when he met Dr. Miller—just in case he became suspicious when he heard about Hoversten's death. "After everything had been accomplished and SAM had been released, SAM planned on taking FLOTT out in DR. STEVE SHEPPARD's boat and thereupon perform a second series of operations which would reverse the previous operations and return FLOTT'S features to their normal appearance," Lockwood reported. "I suggested to FLOTT that possibly SAM meant to kill him during the above operation since anesthetics would have to be used and he agreed, stating that he had given it considerable thought." Flott also outlined to Lockwood a variation on the kidnap-confess-kill routine that employed former Bay Village mayor Spencer Houk as the victim.

Flott's account of the murder for hire should have struck Lockwood and Corrigan as far-fetched. If Sheppard wanted Hoversten killed, why select an assassin who required a prison transfer and a jail break? Sheppard knew many ex-cons on the outside. Wouldn't one of them be more likely to succeed? How was Flott, a convict on the lam, going to get to California? Wouldn't Sam know Hoversten's address or obtain it first, rather than allow Flott to tip off Dr. Miller by asking for it? Where was Flott going to get the curare? Curare, an active ingredient in tetanus shots, causes paralysis, not heart attacks, something that Dr. Sam would know but a clever convict might not.

Also striking about Flott's exchange with Lockwood was Lockwood's pursuit of details about Sam's sex life. Had Sheppard engaged in any "deviant sexual activities"? Once, Flott remembered, Sheppard told him about Susan Hayes fellating him while he was driving. Flott also recalled the time he stood outside an infirmary door while Dr. Sam and a "punk boy" went inside. But even so, Lockwood wrote, "discussions about any abnormalities in SHEPPARD'S sex life . . . specifically as to whether SHEPPARD was 'queer,' produced nothing of a definite nature, FLOTT declaring he had no reason to believe this to be the truth." Perhaps the police were searching to find a new motive behind Marilyn's murder.

Informants, like trace evidence, were the building blocks of criminal convictions. Even so, the subspecies known as jailhouse informants were "remarkably unreliable."[2] They had tremendous motivation to lie—trading testimony for months or years of freedom—and little chance of being punished for perjury. Lies larded with truth are difficult to detect. Some industrious jailhouse informants were known to keep files of news articles on sensational cases; others stole legal documents from the cells of inmates they planned to implicate. Some were known to act as jailhouse lawyers, offering free advice, which allowed them a long look inside a prison mate's criminal case, giving them the details to con authorities.

At trial, defense lawyers attacked the character and credibility of informant witnesses. Prosecutor Corrigan had a retort: Who would you expect to know what criminals are up to? "We don't see too many nuns involved with criminals."

It was Flott's word against Sam's. Did authorities really believe what he was telling them? Was he credible? Corrigan and Spellacy had until late fall to decide whether to put Frenchy Flott on the witness stand.

———

On September 8, 1966, Sam Sheppard was arraigned on second-degree murder charges. Asked by the judge how he pleaded, Sam impulsively shouted, "Not guilty!"

Reporters asked why he shouted.

"I've always shouted 'I'm not guilty,' many times," Sam said. "I've always said it that loud, but nobody would listen."

In contrast with the first trial, now Sam's brothers were noticeably scarce during the weeks before the retrial. Steve Sheppard had reached his limit with Sam. "He called me at all hours demanding that I meet him in downtown Cleveland in order to help him find where he had left his automobile," Steve recalled sadly. "His tales of intrigue were imaginary and his suspicions global. He was convinced he was under constant surveillance and he reassured those who would listen that he had powerful friends among the Mafia who would protect him."[3]

In fact, Sam Sheppard was under surveillance.[4] The Bay Village Police Department was writing down the license plate numbers of and running checks on whoever was visiting at Sam and Ariane's home on Lake Road. Several cars were traced back to felons he knew from prison. Since his conviction had been tossed out, he was not on probation, and therefore not breaking any rules by hanging out with ex-cons. It was reckless behavior nonetheless. If Sam were to get tangled up in even a minor infraction with a felon, the resulting headlines would be devastating, tainting the jury pool within a month of trial.

That fall Ariane and Sam quietly agreed to a separation, and she left for Germany. The cover story was that Ariane had to return to Düsseldorf to care for her ailing father. In fact, Sam was fed up with "her insatiable need to dominate," and she was tired of his erratic behavior. In addition, Ariane was furious at Bailey. He wisely had ordered her to shut up and quit talking to reporters. As part of his strategy, he had been manipulating the press to set up an expectation, a false one, that Sam would testify in his own defense. Ariane could undermine this and other careful plans with one impulsive remark. On her way to Germany, she first stopped in New York City. There she complained to a friend, "Nobody can stop me from talking to the press if I want to. Not even the great Lee Bailey. . . . Every time he comes to Cleveland, he has the press meet him at the airport before he ever sees us. But what I can't forgive Lee for is the way he makes fun of us behind our backs, and he even makes jokes about how Sam walks. Sam had an injury—he knows that. Lee is short. Maybe that's why he has to make compensation."[5]

With the trial only weeks away, the Sheppards and Bailey should have been pulling together as a team. But Sam was paranoid and didn't trust his lawyer. At Bailey's request, Sam had assigned him the movie rights to his forthcoming autobiography, *Endure and Conquer,* to pay for part of his legal fee. Bailey was able to get $125,000 for movie rights from Robert Evans, who later produced such classics as *Bonnie and Clyde* and *Chinatown.* Sam, who was broke, was angry at Bailey for his "overwhelming greed for money," a charge that would be flung at him in years to come.[6] Even so, Sheppard seemed to forget that Bailey had represented him since 1961 without a fee and had achieved remarkable results. Bailey had little in common with his client other than celebrity status and a fondness for strong drink. Once, after downing a few drinks, Bailey referred to the couple as "the bitch and the blockhead."[7]

———

Cuyahoga County common pleas judge Francis J. Talty had served two years before being assigned the Sheppard retrial. He was a boyish-looking forty-six-year-old bachelor who had grown up in a large Irish Catholic family, one of nine children. His parents had immigrated from Ireland's County Clare. In school, Talty excelled at sports. He was captain of the John Carroll University basketball team and later worked there as an assistant coach. A Democrat, Talty was more of a politician than a legal thinker. He was determined not to make a mistake with this closely watched trial. Until the mid-1960s, state judges did not have to worry about federal judges correcting their courtroom behavior. Now Talty, like many judges across the country, was uncertain about how to apply the guidance coming from recent court decisions that overturned convictions because judges failed to protect jurors from poisonous publicity.[8] One such recently overturned case was the death penalty conviction of Jack Ruby, who had killed presidential assassin Lee Harvey Oswald in front of the police and the press. Complicating matters, the American Bar Association overreacted to *Sheppard* v. *Maxwell* and these other decisions by proposing, seriously, that the news media be restricted from publishing or broadcasting background information about suspects accused of crimes. In a spasm of self-examination, journalists heatedly argued that such a ban was unconstitutional and unneeded because they would police themselves instead.

Against this backdrop, national attention focused on how Talty would handle the Sheppard courtroom. In keeping with the monomania, the judge set up severe restrictions: news reporters could not use cameras or tape recorders in the courtroom or even employ sketch artists. They could not install teletypes or special phones on the second and third floors of the county courthouse, as had been done in 1954. Seats would be distributed on a first-come, first-served basis. If reporters left the courtroom to meet deadlines—wire-service and radio reporters, typically—they would have to stay out until the next recess. Talty set aside no seats for out-of-town newspapers, merely one each for the Associated Press and United Press International wire services. This rule sparked howls of protest. Improvising, a *New York Times* reporter hired someone to stand in line for him. The reporter, Sidney Zion, got caught and kicked out of the courtroom. *The New York Times,* in an editorial, said a reporter, unlike other courtroom spectators, "fills a special role as the public's eyes" and should not have his seat in court left to chance.

Judge Talty did set aside assigned seats for the local media: the two remaining Cleveland newspapers (two seats each), five local radio stations, and three TV stations. In other words, Talty rewarded the local news outlets that contributed to the problem that the U.S. Supreme Court later had to fix. Even so, Theo Wilson of the New York *Daily News* and Paul Holmes of the *Chicago Tribune* somehow managed to find seats every day in the small courtroom.

The courthouse atmosphere could not have been more different. Gone were the cuspidor and cigar smoke, the hoary rhetoric, the after-hours joie de vivre. The prosecutors and police were all business. The key players were much younger than the gray-haired gang of 1954. At forty-six, Talty was the oldest lawyer in the room. He had gagged the lawyers. They could not comment on the trial as it unfolded. This suited the taciturn John Corrigan. With only one good ear, he hated questions shouted at him by a scrum of reporters.

Unlike Bailey, he did not need publicity to generate clients and cash. Bailey had already waged a five-year public relations campaign for his client and had won a new trial. Talty's gag order only hamstrung the news media.

As expected, Bailey asked the judge to move the murder trial to another city. Talty refused to rule on the motion. First, see if a jury can be picked here, the judge said. Talty decided to take no chances and sequestered the jurors—they would have to stay in a hotel at nights during the trial. They could call their families, but only with deputies monitoring the calls.

Jury selection took a week. The prosecutors wanted older, better-educated jurors, people who had lived in Cleveland during the first trial. Bailey also selected better-educated jurors, which violated a criminal defense canard that poor, less-educated jurors favored criminal suspects. But he wanted jurors who were young or new to Cleveland.

During jury selection, Bailey decided that Ariane was needed back in Cleveland to quash rumors that she and Sam were getting divorced. Bailey wanted the jury to see her standing by her man. Furthermore, she was bringing back twenty-five thousand dollars as a down payment on his fee.[9]

On November 1, 1966, the retrial of Samuel H. Sheppard commenced with a bus trip by the jury to the murder scene, where the recent owners of the house allowed access. There were no helicopters or boisterous crowds. It was a chilly, drizzly day. From off the lake, a crisp wind blew dead leaves across the yard.

Later, back at the courthouse, prosecutor Corrigan made perhaps the briefest opening statement ever for such a celebrated case. He stood tall, with black-framed glasses and receding wavy hair. Corrigan confidently recited the familiar details of Marilyn's murder and what the State of Ohio expected to prove. In a switch from the first trial, Corrigan described the murder weapon as "an instrument capable of making more than one wound at a time."[10] Clearly, he and Spellacy wanted to eliminate an intruder's flashlight as a possible weapon. They also jettisoned Dr. Gerber's questionable "surgical instrument" interpretation of the bloodstain on the pillow. The prosecutors at this trial did not say that the defendant faked his neck injury. No mention was made of Sam's sex life. After seventeen minutes, Corrigan sat down.

Bailey was nearly as brief in his opening statement. He began with the usual flattery of the jurors and moved quickly to suggest an alternative killer. This aggressive approach typified Bailey's lawyering. By law, he needed only to create reasonable doubt among the jurors about the prosecution's case. "The jurors don't like to go away unsatisfied," he would explain years later. "Too many people have watched *Perry Mason,* where the culprit is always identified. If we can give alternative theories, it's a good tactic. But you need some credence to your theory, or it can backfire."[11]

In theory, the prosecution had the easier motive to sell. People understood, at least intuitively, that spouses might grow to hate each other. From there, it was possible that an enraged spouse might simply snap and do something deplorable.

As Sam sat scribbling on a legal pad, Bailey moved to casting suspicions on what Spencer Houk said and did on the day of the murder. After getting a call for help, Bailey said, "the evidence will show that Spencer Houk did not call the police, he did not pick up a weapon." Instead, he drove unarmed to the Sheppard home, accompanied by his wife, without knowing whether a killer still lurked.

Someone familiar with the Sheppards' routine might have assumed that Dr. Sheppard was not at home, Bailey said. One of their cars was gone, borrowed by a houseguest, Dr. Lester Hoversten, who was staying elsewhere for the night. A light could be seen shining from a second-floor window of the dressing room off the master bedroom. "Those who were close to him knew what that light meant, that Sam was not at home," Bailey said. The murder weapon was something resembling a flashlight, swung by someone "whose physical strength was compatible with that of a woman." Someone else "killed Marilyn Sheppard for reasons that may become apparent to you as the case unfolds."

———

Dr. Lester Adelson, the deputy coroner of Cuyahoga County, was the state's first witness. He had been roughed up by Sam's defense lawyer in the first trial and was apprehensive about facing Bailey, who for years had been bashing the coroner's office in the newspapers.

Under Spellacy's questioning, Dr. Adelson noted that most of Marilyn Sheppard's injuries were on the left side of her head. There was a sharp puncture on the right side. Adelson said he looked at her wounds and found nothing in the blood, no foreign matter. He had looked for sperm in her vagina and found none. The killer landed twenty-five blows, give or take a couple. As he had in the first trial, Adelson showed gruesome color slides of the victim. This time spectators were not as shocked.

"Did you have occasion to do anything else insofar as blood was concerned?"

"I sent some of her blood up to be blood grouped or blood typed." Adelson did not volunteer that just after the murder he sent blood from Marilyn

Sheppard's fetus to be typed, back when authorities, in search of a motive, tried to learn if the housewife had been unfaithful.

During a brief, low-key cross-examination, Bailey got Adelson to say it was possible that Marilyn's two broken teeth had been snapped by being pulled from the inside out. During a break afterward, Dr. Adelson came up to Bailey in the hall and thanked him for his "gentlemanly" examination.

———

Limping slightly, his full hair now gray, Spencer Houk took the stand. The twelve years since he last testified had been trying. He was no longer the Bay Village mayor. He had closed down his butcher's business and now sold cars for a living. He and Esther were divorced.

Answering questions from Corrigan, Houk, his voice timid and soft, recounted what he saw on July 4, 1954. In Sheppard's hospital room that evening, Sam told Houk that two Cleveland detectives accused him of the murder. Houk testified, "He said, 'You don't think I could have done that?' I said, 'No, I don't.' "

The prosecutor steered Houk closely to pay dirt—Houk's surprise testimony in the 1954 trial that he overheard Dr. Richard Sheppard, moments after seeing Marilyn's body, ask Sam, "Did you have anything to do with this?" Before Houk struck, Bailey asked for a sidebar with the judge and objected to the anticipated answer. It was highly prejudicial. It was not an admission, which might be allowed in evidence, but a denial. The judge overruled, and Bailey again asked for a mistrial.

On cross-examination, Bailey quickly established that Houk had visited Marilyn two or three times a week when Sam was working. Houk delivered meat from his butcher shop or cashed checks.

When Dr. Sheppard said, "They've killed Marilyn," did you know how many people "they" were? Bailey asked.

Houk said no.

Did you know whether they had gone?

No.

Was your phone working so that you could have called the police?

Yes.

Did you bring your shotgun?

No.

Did Mrs. Houk bring a weapon?

No.

Did you have a reason to believe the killers were gone?

"I just, I didn't give it any thought," Houk said.

Houk's voice was barely above a whisper, and the judge repeatedly told him to speak up.

Bailey established that the Sheppard brothers had pointed to Houk as a suspect. "Did you make any effort to find out why this was being done?"

"Not that I recall."

"You never asked Sam, 'What are you bringing my name in as a suspect for?' "

"I did on one occasion."

"You asked him to cut it out?"

"No."

"You didn't."

"No."

Bailey used Houk to set up a witness he planned to call later. Do you remember a driver from Spang Bakery at the house?

"Quite possibly," Houk said.

Had you ever been in Marilyn's bedroom before July 4?

No, Houk said.

Didn't you go into her bedroom with a meal on a tray when she was sick?

Yes, but it was a different bedroom.

John Corrigan repaired some of the damage with a redirect examination of the former mayor. The reason he had visited Marilyn in bed was because Dr. Sam had called and asked him to check on her, Houk said.

Next his former wife, Esther, answered questions from Corrigan. She described the gore shrouding Marilyn's body. "Her hair was a tangled mass of dried blood, and it was lying in a large area of bloodstain, and her face was completely covered with blood. Her pajama tops were up under her chin. A sheet was pulled up to about her hip, and her arm was extended out. The right arm was extended out over the side of the bed."

Bailey did not like Esther Houk; he once described her as "an unusually unsightly woman." Even though he suspected her of killing Marilyn, he did not attack her harshly. He simply needed to cast suspicion on her and her husband's actions on July 4.

Esther Houk admitted that her husband had suffered a nervous breakdown and was hospitalized for two or three weeks after the murder. "He was crushed to think his very closest friend would intimate that he had anything to do with that," she said.

At the Sheppard house, she noticed water on the stairs to the second floor as well as a puddle on the screened porch. She admitted that she had ignited a coal fire in her living room fireplace in the early morning. Bailey put into evidence national weather reports that the air temperature never dropped below 69 degrees F. that night. He hoped to suggest that the fire may have been used to burn evidence such as bloody clothing.

———

This time, news coverage of the Sheppard retrial was restrained. Not only had the judge's restrictions kept out many reporters, but prosecutors did not delve deeply into Dr. Sam's sex life, which failed to ignite reader interest. Corrigan had decided not to have Susan Hayes reprise her role as the Other Woman. After the first trial, Hayes stayed in California. On St. Patrick's Day 1956, she was married in San Juan Capistrano, near the famous Spanish mission where swallows return each year. Her husband, Kenneth Wilhoit, was a thirty-two-year-old sound editor who collected art and, like Sheppard, drove a British sports car. In a coincidence that furthered the misconception about origins of *The Fugitive,* Hayes's husband worked as a music editor for several seasons on that television drama.

"Corrigan didn't want to get into the sex stuff," Leo Spellacy explained years later. "His concern was that her life had gone on. She got married, had children. He didn't want to drag them through all that."[12] Bailey felt the prosecutors dropped Hayes as a tactical decision. In 1966, when miniskirts, contraceptives, and youthful rebellion against the status quo were part of the culture, Sam's dalliances were less likely to inflame jurors. The notion that Sheppard eliminated his wife to be with Hayes, Bailey insisted, "was passé" and foolish—Sam had not seen the woman for four months, and didn't plan to. The Other Woman argument, if heavily relied upon, might undermine the stronger parts of the prosecution's case.

Even so, Spellacy and Corrigan realized that they needed to give the jurors a motive for the killing. They settled on a more plausible theory: that Sam and Marilyn got into a violent argument about his philandering.

Robert Schottke, the Cleveland homicide detective who had first accused Dr. Sam of murder, was called upon to do the heavy lifting for the prosecutors, including getting Sheppard's denial of adultery before the jury. Schottke had questioned Sheppard at least five times, including one interrogation on July 10, 1954, that was summarized in a nine-page signed statement. Corrigan wanted to enter it into evidence.

In a series of questions from the county prosecutor, Schottke recounted his questioning of Sheppard.

"We asked him how the screams sounded to him at the time he woke up. He said they were loud screams. We asked him how long the screams lasted. He stated all the while that he ran up the steps. We asked him if he turned any lights on in the home. He stated no. We asked him if there were any lights on in the home. He said he didn't know, he didn't recall. We asked him if he could give us a description of the form he had seen going out the door, whether the man was white or colored. He said that he thought the man was white because the dog always barks at colored people. He said he was a large man, about six foot three, dressed in dark clothing, was larger than he was, and was a dark complected white man. We asked him as to the condition of the beach and light and darkness when he woke up, and he claimed it seemed as though day was just breaking, that it was just a little bit lighter than dark.

"We told him we heard rumors to the effect that Dr. Hoversten may be infatuated with his wife. And he said yes, he had heard those rumors, but he didn't believe them because he knew his wife was true to him. We asked him if there were any men callers during the day, at the home while he was away, and he said there could have been men callers calling at the home. We asked him if he knew the names of these men callers, and he said at this particular time he could not recall any names.

"We asked him if he was having any affairs with women. He stated no. We asked him if his wife was having any affairs with men, and he stated no."

Schottke authenticated Sam Sheppard's nine-page statement, then Corrigan, over Bailey's objection, read several pages of it to the jury. They learned about Sam's close friendship with Hayes, his denial that they were lovers, and his reason for buying her a watch during a California vacation.

The statement didn't prove that Sam had committed adultery, just that he denied it. The jurors were left to rely on memories of the original case, if they had any, and to make a small leap and conclude that Sheppard was unfaithful.

During Schottke's cross-examination, Bailey prodded the detective into admitting that he didn't know how badly injured Sam was before accusing him of murder. Answering Bailey's fast-paced questions, Schottke said that since Sheppard talked freely to him and his partner, they assumed that he was fine. What Schottke did not say was that he already believed Sam murdered Marilyn, and therefore the thought that Sheppard was seriously hurt had never entered his mind as a possibility.

Dr. Samuel R. Gerber took the witness stand with trepidation. He was sixty-eight, more than twice Bailey's age, and weary of defending his interpretation of the Sheppard evidence. At first Gerber had enjoyed taking much of the credit for Dr. Sheppard's 1954 murder conviction. But then Dr. Paul

Kirk's crime reconstruction circulated widely in forensic circles. Kirk's work challenged every aspect of Gerber's case. Some of his colleagues at the American Academy of Forensic Sciences were happy to see the egotistical Dr. Gerber get a comeuppance. To blunt Kirk's critique, Gerber took his case on the road, accepting invitations to conferences of lawyers, doctors, and forensic specialists, where he spun through a carousel of slides, making the case that Dr. Sam was a vicious murderer who nearly escaped justice. F. Lee Bailey even attended one of these presentations in Boston and went up to Gerber afterward and introduced himself, rattling the coroner. Time and again, Bailey had challenged him to debate the evidence (he always declined). After Sheppard was freed and given a new trial, Bailey threatened to sue Gerber for violating his client's constitutional rights. Gerber tried to hide his feelings, but he clearly was annoyed by and disgusted with Bailey.

Gerber was not getting star billing in the retrial. In pruning the case to its strongest elements and changing arguments, Corrigan and Spellacy reduced Gerber's role to establishing several important points: that Sam's folded sports coat lay on the daybed the morning of the murder; that Sam's watch had been found in a green bag in the underbrush; and that Marilyn's bed pillow displayed a bloody impression.

Spellacy wanted no part of Gerber's theory that the bloody impression was made by a surgical instrument. "We didn't have the weapon," Spellacy later explained. "It could have been anything." Identifying the weapon and then not producing it in court could undercut the prosecution's case, Spellacy felt. Gerber, a lawyer, may have disagreed with Spellacy's restriction, but he went along with the plan at first. Under Spellacy's careful questions, Gerber made all the points he was asked to make. He said the impression in the pillow was made by "an object."

Bailey relished the chance, finally, to tangle with Dr. Gerber. Steve Sheppard had blamed Gerber more than Seltzer for his brother's conviction and the smearing of the Sheppard family name, and his animosity had rubbed off on Sam's lawyer. Poring over Gerber's testimony, Bailey found a few glaring weaknesses. Cross-examining is a skill, much like a golf swing, with standard techniques, and Bailey was a master. It had little to do with Perry Mason–like tricks and accusations. The cross-examiner, Bailey once wrote, must pin down all the witness claims to know about the topic and all that he says he doesn't know. "Until a witness is firmly committed to a position or statement, he can parry a question or sidestep it with an explanation." With Gerber already locked into his account from the 1954 trial, Bailey found his job much easier.

The first point Bailey wanted to make was this: since Gerber had assumed that Sam was the killer, then Sam therefore could not be seriously hurt. As he had with Detective Schottke, Bailey pressed Gerber on why he believed Sheppard was not injured. "You felt this without an examination?"

"By my observation and I took his pulse," the coroner replied.

"When you were practicing medicine, Doctor, did you make determinations and diagnoses without examinations of your patient?"

"No, I did not."

"Why didn't you do that to Dr. Sam Sheppard?"

"I wouldn't think he was hurt very badly."

"Dr. Gerber, did you determine that he had no injury to the back of his neck by taking his pulse?"

No, Gerber said. He didn't. He had no right to.

Bailey asked Gerber about having dinner with an editor and reporter from the *Lorain Journal,* a daily newspaper in nearby Lorain, Ohio. "Did you say on that date, 'I'm satisfied Marilyn Sheppard's killer is a woman'?"

Gerber denied it. "That was their theory." He probably said it could have been any adult, man or woman.

Bailey brought up Gerber's encounter with H. Max Don, a young Bay View osteopath whom he met on June 4, 1954, at an autopsy of a man shot in the spine. "Did you ever tell Max Don that you were going to get the Sheppard family?"

Gerber was caught off guard. "No," he shot back, furious. "Whoever said that is a liar!"

"But you deny that you said it?"

"I deny it."

With Gerber riled a bit, Bailey moved to the so-called imprint in Marilyn's pillow. Spellacy hoped the witness would not slip up and say "surgical instrument."

Bailey creased the pillow. "How do you suppose this impression was made—by the folding of the pillow, like that?" he asked Gerber.

No, sir.

"Would you explain to the jury how you are satisfied that it was not made in that fashion?"

"I'd be glad to," Gerber said. "I would have to—do you mind—" The coroner pointed to the pillow.

Bailey, feigning magnanimity, said, "Do whatever is necessary to explain it, please, Doctor."

"This impression of this object is similar to a pair of pliers or a surgical instrument or something that has two blades that opens on a fulcrum," Gerber said.

Bailey pounced. "You have indicated that it might be a surgical instrument?"

"I have."

"Do you have such an instrument available for us to look at, Doctor?"

Corrigan and Spellacy looked dejected. "No, sir," Gerber said.

Tell the jury the name of the surgical instrument you see impressed in that pillow, please.

"I can't give you the name of it, because I don't know what it is. It could be one of many, but it's something that weighs about eight, nine, ten, eleven ounces."

Bailey, smiling, had pinned him like an insect in a specimen tray. He proceeded to pull off the legs, one by one. "Now, you know Sam Sheppard is a doctor, don't you?"

"Yes," Gerber said.

"And you knew it at the time you testified at the first trial?"

"Yes, sir."

"And you testified then that it was a surgical instrument, didn't you?"

"I did."

"And you never produced one, did you, did you?"

No, Gerber had to admit.

"Produce one now if you can."

"I can't," Gerber said, but quickly added that a bone spreader or cast cutter, instruments used in bone surgery, may have made the stain.

Did you find anything that fit the impression?

Again, the coroner had to say the word "no."

"Doctor, could you tell us where we could find one of the instruments compatible with what you believe you may see there?"

"Any surgical store, but I hunted all over the United States and I couldn't find one."

Bailey couldn't believe his good fortune. "Was the search after the last trial?"

No, before.

So you never had it at the 1954 trial? Bailey asked eagerly.

No.

"So that when you testified at the last trial about a surgical instrument, you didn't suggest that just because the defendant was a doctor, did you? Did you?"

Gerber said no, feebly. He had been humiliated and discredited in front of the jury. It was as effective as a cross-examination could get. During the rest of his testimony, Gerber could barely keep his voice up. Several times, Judge Talty told him to speak louder.

To repair all the damage was impossible, but Spellacy tried. On his re-direct examination, he tossed Gerber a clever lifeline: "In the course of your investigation from manufacturers of surgical instruments, did you learn that many doctors and surgeons have their own instruments tailor-made to their own specifications?"

Yes, Gerber said. He had heard of that.

———

Detective Grabowski testified for the prosecution about photographing the crime scene and looking for usable fingerprints on July 4. His account at this trial differed slightly from his testimony in 1954. He said he arrived at 8:30 A.M., looked around, then took photographs. After that he looked for prints. Later in his testimony he said he took photos of the footprints at about 10 A.M. That would leave only thirty minutes to identify and lift fingerprints, since the day's assignment log shows that he left for another assignment at 10:30 A.M. Either way, he did a perfunctory job.

Under questioning, Grabowski carefully said that he did "not find any fingerprints of value" on the two broken athletic trophies or the file boxes in the den, or on the windows in the bedroom. He gave the impression that the surfaces were free of fingerprints and therefore somehow wiped clean. This misconception took hold in the early days following the murder, after Grabowski's supervisors told reporters of a fingerprint cleanup, even though it was completely false. The doorknob and doorjamb were layered with fingerprints, Grabowski had said under cross-examination in 1954. So were many other parts of the house that he looked at. The Sheppards' broken tro-phies displayed fingerprints, too, but Grabowski could not get *identifiable* fingerprints because of the finely etched lines that cut across the whorls and ridges of the fingerprints. As a result, people who are familiar with the case and convinced of Sheppard's guilt cite the so-called fingerprint cleanup as proof that Dr. Sam must be guilty. The police's cleanup theory was unbe-lievable if anyone seriously thought about it. At a minimum under this the-ory, the killer executed a clever cover-up by wiping nearly all of his prints from most of house.

Grabowski backed off from the cleanup theory when questioned by Bai-ley. "All wiped?" Bailey asked at one point.

"Well, I couldn't say all wiped. I mean, all got those lines which could have been," Grabowski said. "Could have been" was a far cry from the damaging police accusations in 1954.

The next witness the state called also presented scientific evidence. Sgt. Henry Dombrowski, who had testified at length in the first trial, had collected and analyzed evidence from the crime scene. He was the Cleveland police equivalent of the coroner's trace-evidence supervisor, Mary Cowan: he held a college degree in science, and he was confident and experienced. The prosecution's strategy with this witness was to undercut the expected defense testimony of Dr. Paul Kirk about the large "unique blood spot" on the bedroom door. It was crucial for the prosecutors to show that it was cast-off blood from the murder weapon, not a contact stain from the bleeding hand of the killer, as Kirk believed. Dombrowski described his nine visits to the crime scene—mostly tracking down dozens of blood spots and collecting trace evidence from the bedroom floor, in particular a piece of tooth.

Bailey tried to make an issue out of the steps that the police had not taken: Dombrowski never attempted to type the blood in the murder room, which may have revealed a third party. The tooth chip was not checked against the teeth of Sam Sheppard. Through Bailey's questions, Dombrowski did explain one puzzling aspect of the blood trail—why he and Mary Cowan found much of the trail on stair risers, rather than the steps. People had gone up and down the bare wood stairs dozens of times, scuffing off some of the blood evidence.

Again, Dombrowski was forced to admit that no one thought to type the large spot or any other blood in the room because they assumed it was all Marilyn's blood. But he presented a plausible explanation of the large "unique" spot on the closet door. "One large spot appeared to be at least two or perhaps more spots accumulated together. There is definitely in the lower section of the one spot an obvious loop that indicates that a second spot had struck in the same area." As Marilyn was beaten, blood in her hair had started to coagulate. This thicker blood may have become stuck to the weapon. When the killer swung it back, an inch-wide blood spot was cast onto the closet door.

————

The prosecutor had one more witness to present before resting the state's case. Bailey could taste victory, though he had learned never to underestimate a jury's whimsy. So far, as he saw it, the state had developed no new evidence, nothing directly connecting Sam to Marilyn's murder other than that he was home at the time. He was unprepared for the surprise that Spellacy had waiting.

A couple of months earlier, Spellacy had reviewed physical evidence at the coroner's office. Mary Cowan had explained it to him piece by piece. Spellacy noticed a color photograph of Sam's watch with a couple of blood spots on its rim. Cowan explained that the tiny brown crusts were blood spatter—flying blood. She could tell by the shape of two of the tiny flecks. "That is your opinion?" Spellacy asked her. Yes, she said.

Spellacy was familiar with the 1954 trial transcript; there was no mention then about blood spatter on Dr. Sam's watch. Spellacy realized that if Cowan's interpretation was accurate, the photograph put Sam's watch, and presumably him, in the murder room while the crime took place, since he had testified that he was wearing it when he fell asleep the night before.[13] It was a devastating opinion.

On November 9, 1966, Mary Cowan, now fifty-eight, took the witness stand. Since the first Sheppard trial, she had testified scores of times, smiling sweetly at jurors like a favorite aunt, but she was unshakable and tough. Cowan held an advantage: criminal defense lawyers, practically an all-male club in the 1960s, came off as rude and bullying if they cross-examined her sharply.

Spellacy asked her to describe the crime-scene blood that she tested. He had her offer an opinion that cold water worked best at removing blood from clothing. She defined the term "spatter" as flying blood and described different kinds of spatter in the murder room: cast-off spatter from the weapon, impact spatter from the victim, and so on. Spellacy asked about her examination of Sam Sheppard's watch.

The metal band was broken, she said. A film of blood was smeared over the watch crystal.

What else did you see? he asked.

"On the rim and on the wristband there were numerous spatter type staining of large and small drops of varying sizes, some drops coalescing with each other, and some drops, fine drops, superimposed on them."[14]

A color picture of a man's Swiss-made watch was projected onto a large screen. Cowan stepped down and picked up a pointer.

Spellacy said, "Calling your attention now to just directly underneath the numeral six on the watch portion itself, what is that?"

"These are—this is the rim of the watch, and these are individual spatter type stains." The blood she described was not on Sam's watch anymore. She had removed much of it with a small, sterile spatula in July 1954 when she tried to determine a blood type.

Cowan said she had looked at the broken watch on July 5 under a microscope and remembered seeing tiny blood droplets that had landed on larger, partially congealed drops. "One was deposited first then another was deposited on top of it."

She described another tiny drop near the number eleven on the watch face. It was shaped like a tadpole, she said, which indicated that the blood had traveled through the air, then struck the watch at an angle.

In other words, someone wearing Sam's watch was in the murder room while blood was flying.

Bailey and his cocounsel were rocked by Cowan's testimony. "This is a switch," Bailey whispered to Sherman. "I don't like this."

"Nothing further," Spellacy said, resting on the high point of the state's case.

Bailey was fortunate that Dr. Paul Kirk had arrived in Cleveland the night before. While the jurors went to lunch, Bailey arranged for Kirk to view the color slides of Sam's bloodstained watch. Bailey listened to a few observations from Kirk as he prepared, on the fly, to cross-examine Cowan.

30

THE VERDICT

MARY COWAN DID NOT OFFER her devastating opinion about airborne blood landing on Sheppard's watch in 1954. If county prosecutors had known about it, they certainly would have used it. What could explain the vast difference between Cowan's recent and past testimonies?

Cowan almost certainly reached this new opinion after the 1954 trial, according to her lab notes, trial testimony, and coroner's photographs. Whenever she tested blood or examined a hair, she diligently recorded her findings in tiny cursive handwriting on three-by-five index cards, one card per procedure. She made no notes about airborne blood in 1954. Even more surprising, her twenty-seven-page trace-evidence report was filled with minute, detailed observations about the evidence—the watches, Sam's pants, hairs from the bed, blood from the stairs—but nothing was noted about spatter on the watch. A longer draft of this report, including typed-over lines and lengthy penciled-out passages, was obtained recently. Again Cowan made no mention of blood spatter. At the 1954 trial Cowan described Dr. Sheppard's watch: "There were crusts on the watch itself, blood into the crevices and on the wrist band."[1] She testified that she had examined the watch with a stereomicroscope, hoping to find fingerprints; she made no mention of analyzing the blood droplets.

In fairness, Cowan was not a blood-pattern analyst.[2] In 1954 that work fell to the crime-scene investigators such as Detective Henry Dombrowski. Even so, blood-pattern analysis was an accepted technique among better-informed crime labs and police departments, and Cowan and her colleagues had been exposed to the techniques. A standard reference at the time, Paul Kirk's introductory textbook, *Crime Investigation,* outlined the basics of bloodstain analysis. Cowan was familiar with the book. Also, Dr. Alan Moritz, a widely known professor of forensic medicine at Cleveland's Western Reserve University who worked closely with the coroner's office, gave a seminar in 1952 about crime-scene blood patterns to an association of Cleveland serologists in which Cowan was active. If the blood on Sam Sheppard's watch had been striking or probative, detectives and technicians should have noticed it at the time.

In April 1955, once criminalist Paul Kirk used blood-pattern analysis to argue for Dr. Sam's innocence, Cowan and her colleagues began paying attention to blood spatter. Unfortunately, by then much of the blood evidence on Sheppard's watch had been scraped off or swabbed up with moistened cotton and used in Cowan's blood-typing tests. The first step of blood-pattern analysis is to consider the overall pattern. Are there enough distinct spots to even proceed to an analysis? Often the answer is no. With the Sheppard watch, the pattern was destroyed; only isolated spots remained. The best evidence upon which to base an opinion was the three color photos taken of the watch before Cowan removed any blood. They showed only a few tiny spots that might be spatter.

On October 27, 1966, as the jury was being selected, Cowan once again examined the brass-plated watch. Under a microscope, she found mostly pinpoints of blood in the grooves of the band's expandable metal links as well as "remnants" of blood spots on the watch case. Many spots were of "irregular" shape. At least one "suggests the outline of an ellipse."[3] She made no note of one spot being on top of another.

When he rose to cross-examine Cowan, Lee Bailey did not have the benefit of her notes or original reports. He started out by asking her about tests she did *not* do with the evidence, returning to his theme that authorities rushed to judgment and therefore performed an incompetent investigation.

No, Cowan was forced to admit that she had not tried to type the blood from the murder-room walls.

Why not? Bailey asked.

"The blood was 'throw off' and the general pattern is the important fact here," Cowan said.

"In other words, you could tell by looking at that blood that all of it was Marilyn Sheppard's?"

"No."

"But you made no examination to determine whether that was in fact the case, true?"

"True."

About an hour earlier, under direct examination, Cowan had said that when she first looked at Sam's watch she saw blood droplets deposited on top of larger drops. Bailey had nothing with which to contradict her memory or undercut her damaging analysis. The best he could muster was asking Cowan if she had looked for blood inside a rivet hole on a broken link of the watch's expandable metal band. Blood inside the hole would show that blood had gotten to Sam's watch after it was broken.

Cowan said, no, she had not looked there.

Bailey was finished. Corrigan and Spellacy immediately rested the state's case, ending with a strong showing by their most important witness. Suddenly, Sam was concerned.

———

As expected, Bailey asked Judge Talty for a directed acquittal, arguing at length that the state's circumstantial case was weak and failed to reach the sufficiency standard set by Ohio law.

John Corrigan spent about three breaths answering him. Plenty of evidence exists to show Sheppard guilty, Corrigan said. "The most telling evidence came from Sam Sheppard's watch. It not only told the time, it told that the killer wore that watch, that this watch was on the arm of the man who wielded the weapon, that this watch was on Sam Sheppard's wrist when he went to sleep that night."

Judge Talty overruled Bailey's motion for a directed acquittal.

At this point, Leo Spellacy felt the prosecution had a winning case while still holding a weapon in reserve: Edmund "Frenchy" Flott had been shuttled to Cleveland from Leavenworth federal prison and was stashed in the county jail, several floors above the courtroom. The prosecution's plan was to wait until after Sam Sheppard had testified and was cross-examined about his conduct in prison. After Sam made his expected denials of Flott's corrosive accusations, the prosecutors would put on Flott to rebut Sam's testimony.

Corrigan and Spellacy could have put Flott on the witness stand earlier, but such a move would have eliminated the element of surprise. They would have had to put Flott's name on their witness list given to the defense before trial. Bailey's investigators would have time to dig up details to damage Flott's credibility.

The prosecutors faced a risk in holding back Flott. If Sam Sheppard did not testify, Flott could not later be presented to the jury because there would be no witness testimony to rebut. Spellacy and Corrigan truly believed that Sam was going to testify.[4] "I thought he had to," Spellacy said years later. "If your wife is found in that condition and all this stuff he said about running up and down stairs. His story was so different, so odd, he had to come in and explain."

Meanwhile, Dr. Sam sat at the trial table in his suit, white shirt, and skinny tie, scrawling notes on a yellow legal pad, trying to help his ghost-writer come up with the final pages for his instant hardcover autobiography, *Endure and Conquer,* which was set to go except for a final chapter on the re-trial. Occasionally he glared at Spellacy. When one side or the other seemed to score a tactical point, Sam swiveled in his chair and caught Ariane's eye, three rows back. She would purse her lips, sending him a tiny smooch.

———

Bailey had promised to show the jurors that someone other than Sam killed Marilyn for "reasons that may become apparent as the trial unfolds." He wasted no time. As the first defense witness, Bailey called Jack Krakan, a dark-haired, long-faced man who used to deliver bread to the Sheppard home.

The reporters who had covered the first trial, Theo Wilson in particular, came to attention. Finally, a new witness.

At the 1954 trial, both sides held up Marilyn Sheppard as a paragon of virtue, the Eisenhower-age ideal of a perfect housewife and mother. "Sam decided back then to withhold evidence that would have impugned his wife's reputation," Bailey later explained. "He felt he could do that because he knew he hadn't committed the crime and he couldn't imagine that any jury would convict him." This time, the defense tainted Marilyn's reputation by suggesting that she was having an affair that may have sent the wife of her paramour into retaliatory rage. Krakan had the job of painting the scarlet letter. The father of two, he had held odd jobs since 1954: watchman, amusement-park worker, deliveryman for Spang Bakery. He suffered from diabetes and had not worked in the 1960s. Under Bailey's questioning, he told about delivering bread to the Sheppard house. His routine was to knock, let himself into the hallway just outside the kitchen entrance, pick up his money, and leave Marilyn's order, usually one loaf of Aunt Mary's Bread. One morning, looking in, Krakan saw Marilyn at the kitchen table drinking coffee with a "distinguished older man" with graying hair, dressed in a suit without a tie. Krakan assumed, at first, that the man was Dr. Sam Sheppard.

During another delivery in early 1954, he walked in as Marilyn handed the same man a key, saying, "Don't tell Sam."

Krakan testified that he identified the man from an array of five photos. But Krakan was not allowed to name him; Judge Talty had sharply restricted what he could testify about. (Later, out of court, Bailey said Krakan had picked out Spencer Houk.) Nor was Krakan allowed to testify that he saw Houk embracing Marilyn, who was dressed in a sleeveless nightgown.

Such restrictions probably mattered little to the jurors. They had already heard from Houk's own lips that he frequently visited Marilyn in the mornings and drank coffee in the kitchen. They did not have to jump far to figure out who Bailey was trying to implicate.

Professor Paul Kirk, Sam Sheppard's potential savior, was waiting outside the courtroom, eager to testify and end a frustrating eleven-year odyssey. Many days, Kirk regretted ever getting involved in the controversial case. He had not counted on being blackballed by Dr. Gerber, who in the 1960s was still a powerful figure in the American Academy of Forensic Sciences. "I have taken a very bad beating over the case, as you probably do not realize," Kirk wrote to Sheppard's lawyer, Bill Corrigan, in 1956. "I've lost membership in organizations, lost a large research fund, editorship of a journal, and have been denounced in public meetings, one by Coroner Gerber before the American Academy of Forensic Sciences."[5] Some forensic examiners went along with Gerber, glad to see Kirk get a comeuppance. They were annoyed that he voraciously applied the principles of physical chemistry to just about every field of police science, from dating inks on disputed documents to expounding on how human teeth shattered under force. To some, Kirk was as stubborn, overreaching, and certain of his brilliance as Gerber.

Kirk took the witness stand in an off-the-rack suit, his silver hair slicked down. Bailey took him through his qualifications: four books, 240 scientific articles, degrees from Ohio State University and the University of California at Berkeley. Some of the older jurors perked up when Kirk said he had worked on the Manhattan Project, helping create the atomic bomb for the United States.

Next, Bailey set up the defense theory of the "unique blood spot"—that blood from a third party had been spilled in the murder room.

You've had experience in dried blood? Bailey asked Kirk.

Yes, since 1937, he replied.

"Now, in a case where two blood samples have exactly the same history in the same area and been given identical treatment, and are tested at about the same time, is there any significance if a difference in the rate of agglutination between those two samples appears?"

"In my opinion there is very definite significance to it." Kirk explained that the large spot on the closet door reacted differently from Marilyn Sheppard's blood, even though both were type O. Dr. Sheppard was type A.

Kirk explained the simple, commonsense steps he took to investigate the crime. He had vacuumed the carpet and found red paint flecks that were not nail polish. He had measured and photographed the room. Using a blackboard, he showed the jury that a blood drop falling perpendicular to a surface would make a round shape. A drop striking at an angle would make a bowling-pin shape. Much of the blood pattern in the murder room radiated out from the victim's head in straight lines "like spokes of a wheel," Kirk said. The pattern abruptly stopped in a corner because the killer's body intercepted the flying blood. A line of larger blood drops along the east wall, closest to Marilyn's bed, was made by blood cast off from the weapon and corresponded to the arc of the weapon's swing. It was a fairly level, left-handed swing. A right-handed swing would have to be backhanded, Kirk said, leaving a slanted arc across the door, which he did not find.

From Sam Sheppard's point of view, Kirk's most important task was to undercut Mary Cowan's opinion about blood spatter on his watch. However, Kirk was at a disadvantage. He had not examined the watch under a microscope before most of its blood had been removed.

In the courtroom, Bailey projected a color slide of the watch from early July 1954, before Cowan removed the blood. "For the most part it looks like contact transfer," Kirk said. Someone or something covered with tacky blood had pressed against the watch.

Bailey directed Kirk to the spot that Cowan described as a blood spot on top of a blood spot. Kirk disagreed with her flying-blood opinion, calling it instead a "contact transfer." "If blood is clotted or partially clotted, it can go on in thicker form, becomes very viscous, very tenacious, very jelly-like."

Bailey pointed to the tiny, tadpole-shaped bloodstain on the rim near the numeral eleven on the watch face. This spot was the linchpin of Cowan's opinion.

"When you get that shape, you always suspect flying blood," Kirk said. ". . . Now, examining this particular spot leaves the issues somewhat in doubt. It appears that it is not a symmetrical tail on the blood spot, and flying blood invariably leaves a totally symmetrical tail. It cannot come off one side or the other. It has to come off the exact center."[6] It was possible that someone with blood on his fingers handled the watch and transferred clotting blood, making the tail. "If you touch it, and pull your finger away you will pull a string out of it," Kirk said, as you would if you touched glue.

Then Kirk added a qualifier, words that some expert witnesses only concede after being pinned down after a skillful examination by the opposing lawyers: "I wouldn't want to say this is my definite and final and irrevocable opinion." It was an honest answer, one that showed scientific integrity, the best he could offer since he had not examined Sheppard's watch in its original condition.

Sam was left to wonder if Kirk's nuanced opinion would be enough to discredit Mary Cowan's wholesale testimony.

———

Long before the retrial, Bailey and private investigator Andy Tuney had carefully gone over the transcript from the 1954 trial, sifting for witnesses to reinterview. Bailey thought some of Sheppard's witnesses had been thrown up on the stand with little preparation, for instance, Dr. H. Max Don, the Bay View physician who had overheard Sam Gerber threaten "to get" the Sheppards. Bill Corrigan had not had Dr. Don testify about Gerber's possible vendetta. Bailey, on the other hand, made certain that Don told the story to the jury.

Another defense witness asked to play a larger role was neurosurgeon Charles Elkins, M.D. In 1954, Elkins's testimony that Sam suffered a spinal contusion got lost in the commotion. Bailey's argument, an appeal to common sense, with no science behind it, was that Dr. Sheppard could not be Marilyn's murderer since he was injured himself. As a physician, Sheppard would not selectively injure his spinal cord or chip his teeth to mislead detectives. To blunt this defense, prosecutors admitted that Sam was injured, but argued, without any supporting evidence, that Sam's injuries were caused by Marilyn's having fought back.

This trial moved rapidly. A series of defense witnesses testified for only a few minutes, nailing down any loose ends and unanswered questions the jurors might have later.

Jay Hubach, retired from the Bay Village Police Department, told the jurors he saw a bloody fingerprint on the banister at the Sheppard house. Katherine Post, a reporter for the *Lorain Journal,* said Dr. Gerber told her over a dinner with her editor that a woman may have been the killer because it was a messy overkill.

Samuel Reese Sheppard—he no longer went by the name Chip now that he was a nineteen-year-old freshman at Boston University—gave fifty-three words of testimony. He was home on the morning of July 4, 1954, and remembered little. "Well, I was taken away from the house in a slight state of confusion."

"Have you ever had any memory from that day right up until today of being awakened at any time during the night?" Bailey asked.

"No, I do not," young Sam said. The prosecutors had no questions for him.

At about 9:30 A.M. on November 14, Richard Eberling stepped to the witness stand and swore to tell the truth. Bailey had abandoned Eberling as a possible murder suspect at least two years earlier, mainly because Bailey believed that the window washer had passed a polygraph test clearing him of the crime. Bailey did not review the graphs or have an expert evaluate them. If he had, he may have felt differently about Eberling. Furthermore, Eberling did not fit into Bailey's theory of the case: that Marilyn Sheppard was killed just after hurried, consensual sex. To Bailey's eyes, the working-class Eberling was an unimpressive suitor for Marilyn Sheppard.

By 1966, however, Eberling was a well-to-do landowner in Westlake. He had bought the farm from his foster mother and several parcels nearby. Westlake was turning into a bedroom community, and Eberling would eventually become a millionaire by selling his land to developers and the local school board. With little overhead other than taxes, Eberling poured his income into furnishing and decorating the farmhouse. He also ran in better social circles, thanks to his companion of the past few years, Oscar Buford "Obie" Henderson, a handsome, outgoing man who taught shorthand and typing at a secretarial school and worked as the executive assistant to the managing editor of the Cleveland *Plain Dealer,* a perfect perch for learning how the powerful elite ran the city.

On the witness stand, Eberling said that he had told authorities, just after Marilyn's murder, that he cut himself changing storm windows on July 1 (a day earlier than he told police in 1959) and bled in the Sheppard home. His remark was ignored, the defense suggested, because it contradicted the state's theory in 1954 that the blood trail dripped from the murder weapon.

"Do you know Dr. Sheppard?" Russell Sherman asked.

"I met him once at the breakfast table, briefly."

"I take it then all your contacts were with Marilyn Sheppard?"

"Yes." Eberling testified that he worked at the house six to eight days a year. If no one answered his knock, he let himself in.

Sherman asked him about the reaction of the Sheppards' dog to his visits.

"One time in the winter, I recall, when I went in, the dog was in the chair sleeping and never got out of the chair."

"Never so much as bothered that you were roaming around the house?" Sherman, posing his final question, asked.

"No."

Bailey had dropped hints that he would call Sam Sheppard as witness, but that was a bluff. Sam was short-tempered and unstable, drinking heavily and taking pills. It would be malpractice to let him testify. Bailey rested the defense.

The prosecutors were disappointed that Dr. Sam didn't testify and they had to send Frenchy Flott back to Leavenworth prison. Since Paul Kirk had been a strong witness for the defense, Corrigan and Spellacy presented a rebuttal witness, chemist Roger Marsters, to undercut Kirk's opinion about a third person's blood being in the bedroom.

Marsters held a doctorate in chemistry and was a friend of Mary Cowan's and Gerber's. He had directed the blood banks at several Cleveland hospitals. Much of his work involved elaborate subtyping of fresh whole blood as a way to settle disputed paternity cases. Back in 1955, during Sam's appeals for a new trial, Marsters provided prosecutors with an affidavit that attacked the validity of Kirk's opinion that the closet-door blood, though type O, was not Marilyn's because it dissolved and agglutinated more slowly. He also insisted that Kirk's tests of that stain were invalid because it had been contaminated with fingerprint powder.

Until the Sheppard case, Marsters had never attempted to type dried blood. Nonetheless, he attacked Kirk's findings on the closet stain, as well as just about every other aspect of the noted criminalist's work.

Questioned by prosecutor Spellacy, Marsters, who had no training in blood-pattern analysis, backed up Cowan's theory about flying blood on Sam's watch.

Bailey jumped up to object. "He is not a criminalist!" Judge Talty allowed the chemist's remark to stand.

Expert witnesses who push their opinions to the limit or state them without nuance or qualifiers are often easy targets for cross-examiners such as Bailey. He got Marsters to admit that he had never attempted to type dried blood until the Sheppard case.

Next, Bailey embarrassed Marsters by asking him about a 1958 journal article the chemist cowrote, his only publication, about experiments he had participated in that sought to learn whether semen, gunpowder residue, and other crime-scene substances interfered with blood-grouping tests. The study concluded that police fingerprint powder did *not* prevent the grouping of dried blood into A, B, AB, or O types, which contradicted his earlier affidavit.

Marsters resisted Bailey's attempt to pin him down. Kirk's results were unreliable because blood from the closet door might instead have been "contaminated by body secretions," Marsters insisted.

"Do you know of any body secretions ever being placed upon or contaminating the blood samples in question?" Bailey asked.

"No, I don't. I think it is perfectly probable, certainly possible."

"No, I am sorry, please don't speculate," Bailey said. "I asked you if you *knew* of any contamination by body secretions, personal knowledge?"

"I assume it to be present."

"Why would you assume body secretions to be present on the closet door?"

"I assume that a closet door in a bedroom, that inevitably human skin would be in contact, people being in the process of disrobing, and all you need to do is brush against the painted wood surface to leave a smear of perspiration."

Do you know how many inches off the floor the large blood spot was?

"No, I can't tell you in inches."

"Then how were you able to make assumptions about what portions of the body might or might not touch the door, without any idea where they were located?"

"I just assume in a bedroom that human skin is from time to time going to come in contact with the paint of a closet door," Marsters said.

"Tell us what portions would be covered in a matter of course, from your experience on human secretions," Bailey said.

Marsters tried to give an answer, perhaps hoping it would mollify Bailey. "I would say about a foot above the doorknob would be an area reasonable to suspect that would be contaminated with human secretions."

"You mean from the very bottom to above the doorknob you expect to find on this closet door human secretions?"

"I would not want to rule out the possibility," Marsters said.

"Did you ever make tests on closet doors to find out what human secretions were present on that area?"

"No," Marsters insisted, digging himself in deeper. "I am assuming it from our work on human secretions."

"You are able to understand from your work on human secretions the probability that they would be found on bedroom doors?"

"Well, just from living, I assume that."

Bailey continued his slashing attack with glee. "Well, from your experience with living—you are referring now to your own closet doors—they probably have secretions?"

"Perspiration, yes, I would suppose that," Marsters said.

"You brush up against your doors, then, in your own experience when you perspire?"

Spellacy could stand it no longer and objected. "Sustained," Talty said. Enough was enough.

Bailey moved to the coup de grâce. He picked up the watch with its broken band and wrapped it around his left wrist, then asked, Did you examine the spots to see that they were all on surfaces exposed when the watch is worn like this?

No, Marsters admitted.

Then you didn't make an examination to see if spots were there that could land on the watch if it were off the wrist and the inner side of the wrist-band exposed?

No, Marsters said.

Bailey pointed to the projected image of Sam's watch, with its band folded against the back of its watch case. He directed Marsters to the gap between the rim at the number twelve and the pin anchoring the first link of the band.

Everyone in the courtroom could easily see through the gap to the inside of the band, the surface against the skin. Staring back like a pair of dull, far-set eyes were two small rust-colored spots that resembled other tiny spots that Mary Cowan said were flying blood.

Bailey's point was obvious to all even before he asked the next question: It was impossible for a watch worn on the wrist to be spattered on the inside of its band. Did you ever notice the blood spots on the *inside* of the band?

"No, I honestly can't say that I did," Marsters said.

"That is all. Thank you."

Sam Sheppard was elated and broke into a smile. So much for "my watch as being proof of my guilt," he said later.[7]

———

On November 15 both sides rested. Again, without the jury present, Bailey asked Judge Talty for a directed verdict, arguing that the state's presentation of evidence did not rise to a level that deserved the jury's consideration.

Judge Talty threw a scare into the Sheppard side. This time, Talty said, the state's circumstantial evidence was "stronger in some areas" than what prosecutors offered in 1954. He denied the defense motion.

———

Closing arguments commenced with Leo Spellacy attacking the plausibility of Sam's account on the morning of the murder. Why did he call Houk from downstairs? Spellacy wondered. "Right beside the bed was a telephone, on the night stand. Was that used when he found that Marilyn was beaten so badly? No. Were the police called at that time? No. Were the police ever called by Sam Sheppard? No."

Sheppard added details to his stories as he went along, Spellacy said. He couldn't keep his stories straight. His attacker changed from "a large form" into a bushy-haired man, six feet three with broad shoulders.

And think about the so-called burglary. "What burglar pulls out drawers in a desk and leaves them all even? This is just a make-believe burglary."

Russ Sherman, Sam's lanky, crew-cut cocounsel, briefly argued next. "I would ask each of you to think, if this happened to you, after all this happened, after being knocked out twice, could you get up and repeat a story, bing, bing, bing, bing, right down the line, and never leave a thing out, add a thing, subtract a thing, or change a thing? If you could you would be lying, because you had a memorized story."

Next Bailey began his fifty-minute argument by flattering the jury, the prosecutors, the judge. In all his cases in different places, said Bailey, "I have never met lawyers of any greater caliber than you have seen representing the State of Ohio in this case. When Mr. Spellacy concluded his closing argument, it took me a while to realize that this was not a strong case, but it was a very good lawyer describing it."

Please remember, he told the jury, there was direct evidence of someone else in the house: Dr. Sam's own account, found in a July 1954 police statement that prosecutors entered into evidence. Sheppard said "they," meaning two persons, the lawyer pointed out.

"Behind every deed there is a why somewhere," Bailey said. The state doesn't have to prove a motive, but you still may consider it when deciding the case. "A murder was done in the room. Somebody had an awful hate for Marilyn Sheppard. I am sure that none of you had ever experienced this, but try to conceive of the kind of hate that would not cool down before you had butchered a woman's head with twenty-five smashes to the face. Somebody had hate that this defendant could never have known, and they sprayed that hate all around that bedroom with her own blood."

Then the police assumed that Dr. Sam was not hurt, Bailey said, but never checked his medical condition and accused him of murder. "Throwing out the filthy accusation while he is lying in bed hurt."

Bailey showed the jurors the slide of Dr. Sam's watch. If this watch supposedly displays flying blood, how can you explain a droplet inside the metal accordion band? The only explanation is that Sam could not have been wearing it when the killing took place.

There is no doubt that Dr. Sheppard was injured, Bailey went on. The prosecution called no doctors or medical experts to contradict that. But Dr. Elkins, who was unassailable, certainly showed that Sam had lost reflexes and had a spinal cord injury. Elkins "wasn't any ringer for the Sheppards. He was no part of the plan to cover up this deed by phonying a hospital record."

Bailey dismissed Dr. Marsters, the blood-bank director. "Someone who

saw fit to undertake his training, his first experience in grouping dried blood
in a case as immense as this cannot carry much weight, especially when he
is forgetful of his own article on the subject."

He concluded by suggesting that Marilyn had an affair that angered her
lover's wife. "Behind every killing, ladies and gentlemen, there must be a
reason. This is very difficult to suggest to you and I am going to skirt it as
delicately as possible, but the evidence is before you. I don't have to slap it
down on the rail. Someone was angry, angry enough to kill, someone who
didn't have the strength in her arm that Sam Sheppard had, for indeed he
would have crushed that skull like an egg shell, with the frenzy that was taking place, just as any of you would. Twenty-five blows and you would have
found nothing left but bits. Why was that person so angry? What had happened? What had Marilyn done to anger that person? We will never really
know."

———

Prosecutor John T. Corrigan had survived Nazi soldiers and overcome dis-
abilities to hold his elected office for a decade. He would have no regrets if
he lost the case, nor would he gloat if he won. He had nothing to lose, which
made him a dangerous adversary. He was offended that Bailey said detectives made a "filthy accusation" against Sheppard. "With the very first witness, the character and reputation of Marilyn Sheppard was put in issue in
this trial," he said. "You remember the first witness, Mr. Jack Krakan. He
said he saw Marilyn give a gentleman a key and say, 'Don't let Sam know
about this.'

"What could the reason be for bringing that testimony before this jury,
other than to put in issue the reputation and make a filthy accusation as re-
gards the character of Marilyn Sheppard?"

Corrigan argued against Bailey's thesis that Sheppard would not wipe
away his fingerprints because you would expect to find them throughout
his own house. "Except wouldn't it be strange if we went to each one of
those drawers and alongside of the drawers that were pulled out, we find
Sam's prints on the first drawer, on the second drawer, on the third drawer.
Wouldn't it be peculiar if we found Sam's prints on the trophies, on the metal
file boxes, and on the furnishings? In these areas wherein there is some reason to suspect something. And if we found Sam's and nobody else's, then the
story about somebody else being in there would be a little bit difficult to buy,
wouldn't it?"

Corrigan admitted that Dr. Sam was injured. But not by an intruder.
"When Marilyn met her death, she didn't lay there and permit her assailant to

bludgeon her into Kingdom Come. Her arms were flailing, as is indicated by the defense wounds she had on her hands, and her legs were kicking. And it was the assailant, Dr. Sam, who forced those legs down under that crossbar, and in the course of doing so he got clipped and he got clipped good. These are where the injuries and the chipped teeth came from." Corrigan swung his right arm viciously, blow after blow, twenty-five times, re-creating a version of the crime, his face red with intensity.

Twenty minutes into his argument, Corrigan signaled that he was wrapping up. His voice rose as he pointed to Sam's bloody watch. "The watch tells more than time," the prosecutor said. "The watch clearly tells who the murderer of Marilyn Sheppard is." It was an effective slogan. Had Bailey, by pointing out blood drops on the underside of the band, eviscerated the strongest element of the prosecution's case?

"And I say to you, ladies and gentlemen, bring back a verdict consistent with the facts in this case. A verdict that will tell Sam Sheppard that he can't hide from the truth."

———

On November 16 at 10:30 A.M., Judge Francis Talty instructed the Sheppard jurors about the legal elements of second-degree murder and reasonable doubt and sent them to deliberate.

It had been a compact, crisply run trial in front of a hobbled news media in a small courtroom. The jurors heard from thirty-one witnesses (there were seventy in the bloated 1954 trial) in two weeks of testimony (one third the length of the original trial). The jurors got along well. As their foreman, they selected Ralph J. Vichill, a thirty-three-year-old industrial engineer, a good sign for the Sheppard team. Bailey believed that someone with Vichill's background might appreciate the science behind Paul Kirk's methods.

Sam Sheppard spent the rest of the day at the Hollenden Hotel, where he and Bill Levy, his ghostwriter, pounded out pages for *Endure and Conquer,* an autobiography scheduled for hardcover publication in fifteen days. Bailey took a few hours to knock out a draft of a final chapter, in Sam's voice, that explained his legal strategy. The book also offered such tidbits as "Lee Bailey went down to the hotel cocktail lounge to pursue his favorite jury-waiting pastime, slowly sipping scotch for the nerves."[8]

Sam had told himself he was not going back to prison if found guilty again. After reexperiencing life outside, he felt he could not take another day locked down. He hatched a reckless plan to avoid such a fate. He would smuggle a handgun into the courtroom. He alone would know it was unloaded. If convicted, he would pull it out at once, yell that he was never going back to jail, and pretend to be more unhinged than he already was. He hoped to provoke deadly gunfire from the courthouse's armed deputies: a police-assisted suicide. He told his son of his plans, supposedly seeking approval but perhaps hoping to be told, No, I can't live without you. "We talked about it beforehand," Sam Reese Sheppard said years later. "He wanted to make sure I was okay with it."[9] The young man didn't know how to reply. He understood his father's desperation and didn't oppose his plan. "I didn't see a weapon," Sam Reese said, "but I believe he had it."

Later that evening, at about ten o'clock, Talty summoned lawyers for both sides to the courtroom. He had decided to send the jurors to their hotel for the night and needed the parties in the court for his official adjournment. Before they arrived, the jury foreman sent a message to Talty. They had reached a verdict.

Sam and Ariane walked in with Bailey, his wife, and Russell Sherman. They heard the news instantly. Sam had been drinking heavily. Sherman and Bailey sat on either side of him. They didn't know what he would do. Ariane took a seat a few feet behind him in a spectators' row, wearing her familiar leopard-skin fur coat. Either way she knew she was going to break down.

Sam took out his wallet, flipped through it, then gave it to Bailey. He gave two of his pipes to a deputy sheriff. He closed his eyes and bit his knuckles and waited. It seemed forever. At about 10:45 P.M., the jurors filed in looking straight ahead, grim. Russell Sherman, scanning faces for eye contact, thought he caught the briefest smile. "You're all right, Sam," he whispered.

Vichill handed the verdict to Talty, who read it instantly. "We find the defendant . . . not guilty."

Sheppard slammed his hand on the table, a startling crack. Talty glared at him, then thanked and dismissed the jury.

Ariane burst into tears. Sam, sobbing, jumped up and leaned over the polished wood rail that separated him from the public seats. Arms out, he cried, "Baby!" and they fell into each other.

Reporters surrounded him. Was this a full vindication, Dr. Sheppard?

"Aw, for christsakes, give me a break, will you?" he said, still crying.

What are your plans?

"I'm going home with my wife. Let's go, honey." He turned and tried to leave.

"How do you feel?"

"Whatta you think?"

"What about the last twelve years?" he was asked.

"What about them? Are you gonna bring my mother back?"

"Let's go," Bailey told him. "Let's get out of here."

With his wife in tow, Bailey bulled his way out to their car, but they were surrounded in the parking lot by reporters. "The prosecutors were able," Bailey said. "They did a lot of things that we didn't expect. I didn't think that they would be as good as they were."[10]

Before the jurors were bussed back to the hotel to pack their suitcases and go home, foreman Ralph Vichill said his views were typical of the group. "I had the impression he wasn't guilty beyond a reasonable doubt," he said.

The Sheppard team held a midnight press conference at the Hollenden Hotel. One of the first questions was, "Why didn't Sam testify in his defense?"

"We made the decision last June" over Sam's "vehement objections," Bailey said. It was a message to the prosecutors that he felt he had outfoxed them.

Years later, prosecutor Spellacy, attorney general William Saxbe, coroner Gerber, and others would say that the jurors in the retrial voted to acquit because they felt that Sheppard, having served ten years, had been punished enough. But the jurors tracked down and interviewed for this book say that that was not the case. They simply were not persuaded by the state's case and had doubts that Sheppard was Marilyn's killer. They had been impressed with Bailey and believed that the police investigation was flawed. Several jurors said Dr. Kirk's analysis of the blood pattern and his opinion that a third person bled in the house persuaded them to vote not guilty.

On their first balloting, they voted 8 to 4 for acquittal. Carl Lindblom, a twenty-seven-year-old Internal Revenue Service agent when he served on the jury, lived in Detroit during 1954. "There was a lot of emotion in the discussion because some of the older people had been in the Cleveland area when the murder occurred and they had certain opinions that they just couldn't shake." After half a month of togetherness, the jurors had grown fond of one another. Three of the four jurors who at first voted guilty were hard to persuade otherwise, Lindblom said. "In the jury room it was so emotional because we had all developed somewhat of a bond and we were friends. We wanted everything to come out right. So there was not animosity between people, there was just emotion." Even so, this jury's not-guilty verdict was not a ringing endorsement of Sheppard's innocence. "I can't say that I know he *didn't* do it," said juror Charles Stephens, a mail carrier.

Shortly after the verdict, one juror said that he had received telephone calls at home from people who denounced him for acquitting Sheppard when "ninety percent of the people know he's guilty."[11] It made that juror understand why Sam Sheppard wanted his trial held in a different Ohio city in the first place.

31

DEMISE

ON THE EVENING OF August 29, 1967, in three out of every four house-
holds, people were transfixed by the televised clash of Dr. Richard Kimble
and the one-armed killer of his wife. It was the final, pervasively hyped
episode of *The Fugitive,* the highest-rated hour in TV history until the "Who
Shot J.R.?" episode of *Dallas* years later. Just as *The Fugitive*'s creator had
dreamed it up seven years earlier, the series ended with freedom and justice
and emotional release for Dr. Kimble, the wronged man.

There was no such neat solution for Dr. Sam Sheppard despite his acquittal and the instant, best-selling success of his autobiography. Being
found not guilty meant to many that Dr. Sam simply beat the rap, thanks to a
skilled lawyer and a justice system softened by the Warren Court. Sheppard
found that his courtroom victory set him adrift. He had nothing anchoring
his life. He could not practice medicine because his Ohio license was suspended. He and Ariane reconciled after the retrial but were not getting along,
and she wanted to try living in Germany. His son lived hundreds of miles
away in Boston. Sam's brother Richard, drinking heavily himself, had pulled
away years earlier, which left only Steve, the brother's keeper.

———

Lee Bailey had sent Bay Village police chief Fred Drenkhan a long, confidential letter that outlined why he thought Esther and Spencer Houk were responsible for the murder. In speeches in Cleveland just after Sam's acquittal,
Bailey said that the two murderers were walking free around Cleveland and
should be arrested. Prosecutor John T. Corrigan took affront. Within a week

Corrigan convened a grand jury in Cuyahoga County that the media por-trayed as a reinvestigation of the Sheppard murder, a vast overstatement.

Corrigan called Bailey, Dr. Sam, and three detectives to testify. At the end of the day, the grand-jury foreman, in an outrageous breach of secrecy, told reporters that Dr. Sheppard "appeared evasive at times and not clear at other times." The panel spent another day looking at crime-scene photographs and asking questions of prosecutor Corrigan. The last witness was Robert Kelley, the retired police chief of Rocky River. Corrigan used Kelley to undercut Bailey's theory about the Houks. Kelley said that Bailey, a few years earlier, had had another murder suspect in mind, a burglar who had stolen Marilyn Sheppard's rings. Corrigan used Bailey's short-lived pursuit of Eberling to suggest that the Boston lawyer went shopping for suspects, doing whatever was necessary for the defense.

The grand-jury performance was more a public relations effort than a murder investigation. A more diligent grand-jury investigation might have eliminated the Houks as suspects by checking their medical records, inter-viewing the Houks and others. But Corrigan treated it all like a waste of time, since he was convinced that Dr. Sheppard was the killer. The three-page grand-jury report in particular echoed Corrigan's outrage at injecting a woman's infidelity into the retrial: "We find the motive ascribed to the killers by Mr. Bailey to be wholly unwarranted. His charge that Marilyn Sheppard was killed by the jealous wife of Marilyn's lover has no basis in truth or fact and we hasten to protect her good name. . . . Marilyn Sheppard's reputation, character and fidelity were of the highest. We deplore the besmirching of her name and good reputation." Furthermore, the report said, the county coroner, sheriff, prosecutors, and police all did an "outstanding job of discovering, tracking down and presenting evidence before both trial juries."[1]

Bailey was awaiting what turned out to be a not-guilty verdict in the Dr. Coppolino case in Freehold, New Jersey, when he heard about the grand-jury report. "It's ridiculous," he fumed. "A damn whitewash! Exactly what I ex-pected. Cleveland is protecting itself for twelve years of sin."[2]

———

Sam was broke and struggled to scrape together cash. Steve Sheppard set up a program at Bay View Hospital that would have enabled Sam to get his sur-gical license back by serving as a full-time surgical resident under Steve's supervision. But a week before the program was to start, in November 1967, Sam and Ariane suddenly moved to Germany, hoping European life would somehow solve their problems. Sam sold his used Jaguar convertible to his son for twenty-five hundred dollars, to be paid later. While in Europe, he pressured young Sam for payment, urging him to spend part of his remaining inheritance from Marilyn's side of the family. Bailey told him that as a minor he didn't have to pay the debt until he was twenty-one. Regardless, Dr. Sheppard kept up the pressure on young Sam, who sent his father an anguished letter. "This seems such a triviality to come between us but all this has really, really upset me so please, please try to understand my predicament. I wish we could talk this out. All this, I would assume, will make you upset with me but you have no idea the effects of all this in the past year upon my mental and emotional stability."[3] At Boston University, young Sam had grown his hair longer, begun playing the guitar, and had experimented with drugs. In addition, without the structure of Culver Military Academy, he too was unraveling.

Dr. Sam came into some money by suing ABC Television and Walter Winchell for broadcasting a false story in 1954 that Dr. Sam had an illegitimate two-year-old daughter. They reached a fifteen-thousand-dollar settlement. In November 1967, Sheppard sued the *Cleveland Press,* Samuel Gerber, and Louis Seltzer for conspiring to violate his civil rights, but a federal judge dismissed the complaint several months later.[4] Film producer Robert Evans agreed to pay $125,000 for movie rights to Sheppard's *Endure and Conquer,* but Bailey held the rights until his legal bills were paid. Among the beneficiaries, Sam and Ariane ended up getting $20,000, the publisher and lawyer Russell Sherman about $10,000, coauthor William Levy $6,000, and Bailey about $75,000. Bailey now owned a Learjet, a fifteen-room home, a sailboat, and six cars. He needed a cash flow to cover his expenses and maintain his celebrity status. Paramount Pictures ended up making the film after changing the lead to a crusading defense lawyer named Tony Petrocelli. Released as *The Lawyer,* the movie starred Barry Newman and was adapted into a short-lived television series, *Petrocelli.* Sam complained bitterly to Bailey about keeping too much of the money from the book.

———

Out of pride and sheer cussedness, Steve Sheppard had refused to leave Cleveland while he and the Sheppard families were vilified in the 1950s and 1960s. With Sam's acquittal, Steve felt they could leave town with heads high. Their two daughters were away in college. Bay View Hospital was now run by trustees who preferred that no doctor named Sheppard was connected to the hospital.

"My own hopes and dreams were completely shattered by Marilyn's death and the situation which followed," Steve Sheppard wrote. "I had hopes our hospital would grow and in the process provide superior care for the citizens of Cleveland's western suburbs. When Dr. Sam went to prison with a life sentence and Richard went down the tubes, I knew all was lost. My parents' premature deaths, especially my mother's suicide using my gun in our guest bedroom, left a deep and indolent wound. My belief in religion, which was precarious to begin with, disappeared. My professional life, which had been busy and fulfilling, became a chore without the desire to be of real service to my patients. I felt like a technician performing the same old operations over and over. My enthusiasm for training residents and interns vanished. Community projects and services left me cold." Steve, angry at both brothers, suggested that they get professional help for their problems. When they did not, Steve said he realized "all was lost."[5]

He activated his medical license in California, where he had worked as an intern, and began a psychiatric residency at a San Francisco hospital. He wanted to be a psychiatrist, he said later, because he wanted to understand what sort of person could murder Marilyn in such a brutal way. He and Betty sold their house and forty-one-foot sailboat. Before they moved, Sam had his Ohio medical license restored, but not hospital privileges. Steve offered to give his half of the private practice in Fairview Park to Sam. "Most of the patients are friends of yours and many are people whom you have cared for in the past," he wrote to Sam. "They all would come to you for medical care rather than anyone else I know." The first year's rent was paid. Sam's share of the overhead—splitting utilities and office help with Dr. Richard—would cost four hundred dollars a month. Even without hospital privileges, Steve wrote, Sam could expect to gross forty thousand a year. Sam rejected the offer; he wanted to be a surgeon.

On May 10, 1968, the board of Youngstown Osteopathic Hospital reactivated Sam's admitting and surgical privileges, a huge mistake. Sam Sheppard's skills as a surgeon had deteriorated, and much of the time he was impaired by alcohol. Five days later Sheppard operated on Mary Duffy, forty years old, the mother of five children. She had a chronic back problem and agreed to have a disc removed. During the operation, Sheppard accidentally cut an artery and the woman lost four pints of blood. He repaired his mistake but didn't inform the patient or warn the nursing staff. She was left unattended in a recovery room, bleeding internally for four hours while her blood pressure dropped. She lapsed into a coma after sixteen hours, then died. Her family sued the Youngstown hospital and Sheppard.[6]

The hospital should have suspended his privileges but did not. On August 6, 1968, Dr. Sam tried to solve the back problems of a twenty-nine-year-old man, Samuel Lopez, by removing a spinal disc. During the operation, he

nicked the right iliac artery, didn't catch his mistake, and sewed up the patient. The man bled to death in three hours.[7] His family sued.

Sam and Ariane separated again, and on December 3, 1968, she filed for divorce. As usual, each development of the Sheppard story, however mundane,
spun into spectacle. She showed up in court wearing a white rabbit coat and
matching hat. It was winter in Cleveland, after all. Ariane's lawyer asked for
a restraining order, saying she was afraid of her husband, even though Sam
had been gone for days. A Cleveland newspaper trumpeted its "exclusive"
interview with Ariane, saying she was "in hiding." If so, she hid for only a
few hours; over the next two days, Ariane gorged herself on media attention,
trooping from television station to newspaper newsroom, telling how awful
her life had been with Sam. He had taken her money, acted crazy, and had
disappeared, she told reporters as she dabbed her teary eyes with a lavender
handkerchief. "Knives, knives, he kept them behind the bed and under the
bed." She said Sam never struck her but swore at her and threatened her. He
had even taken up with another woman, who "is considerably younger than
I am," Ariane said.

Joe Eszterhas, a *Plain Dealer* reporter who would later become a screen-
writer, asked her, "Do you feel now that you've been had?" Suddenly she
started to cry. "Yes, that is probably what makes me feel so bad. Because I
am not so dumb, I am not so stupid." She turned to the photographer. "Please
don't take pictures of me when I'm crying."

"Do you still love him?"

Ariane Sheppard was not asked why she felt it important to publicly air
her grievances or to engage in such histrionics. Many years later, she would
sadly say that if she had known better she would have gotten medical help
for her erratic husband, tried at least to get him into a treatment facility.

Sheriff deputies wanted to serve Sam Sheppard with divorce papers but
said they could not find him. It was a natural for the reporters: Dr. Sam is on
the run, the real-life Fugitive. In fact, he was in California, visiting an old
medical-school friend, Dr. Arthur Miller, relaxing in plain sight. Sam even
played a round of golf for the first time. "It was an ill-advised marriage,"
Sam said. "But I felt very indebted to Ariane. I looked on her as a 'partner-
savior.' I felt I had to marry her to justify all she had done for me, or said she
had done, while I was in prison. I still feel love for her. But we are two dominant people and we just aren't compatible."[8]

Ariane's lawyer said she wanted to settle without a public contest. To
force Sam to agree to a reasonable settlement, Ariane's lawyer listed eleven

allegations—in effect, legally permissible blackmail—that might come out if there was a public trial: "That her husband used barbiturates and alcohol to excess. . . . That he evidenced symptoms of kleptomania throughout their marriage which included stealing drugs from hospitals, surgical instruments, uniforms from interns, valuable jewelry. . . . That he continually had barbiturates hidden in the household and, at times, would hide some of them in her clothing and at one time inside her wig. That while in Youngstown and on the staff of the hospital there, he would awaken in the morning and drink vodka prior to performing surgery and that he did drink alcohol while on duty in the hospital and on days when surgery was scheduled."[9]

Much like his mother, Sam wanted to kill himself, only at a slower pace.

By 1969, Sam had moved to Columbus, Ohio, where he knew Benjamin Clark, a lawyer who had helped Bailey with the successful habeas corpus writ. Sam set up a small medical practice in Gahanna, a suburb of about twelve thousand. His office was a few doors from Slane's Gun Shop and Mama Nebb's Beer Wine & Pizza. He kept hours from midafternoon to the early evening, attending to whoever walked in with ailments. He disliked the work—he thought of himself as a surgical specialist—and the everyday complaints of his mostly female patients bored him. He treated about thirty patients a month and erratically collected payment.

———

In June 1969 Sam Sheppard walked into a beauty shop near his Gahanna office and found himself captivated by a petite, platinum-haired twenty-year-old named Colleen Strickland. He managed an introduction, and Colleen, a hairdresser, immediately called her father to announce the celebrity in their midst. George Strickland, a part-time professional wrestler and promoter, rushed over to meet Sam. It turned out they had met at a state track meet in the early 1940s. Before long, George Strickland was urging Sam to turn pro, promising to train and promote him. They could even wrestle as a tag team.

For the next six weeks Sam Sheppard ran, lifted weights, went on a diet, and got in decent shape for a forty-five-year-old. His first match, in August 1969, was greeted with disbelief by the Cleveland newspapers. "High on anybody's you-got-to-be-kidding list is the no-joke announcement that Dr. Sam Sheppard will make his debut as a professional wrestler."

Sheppard was a promoter's dream. Dressed in a doctor's white lab coat, the stethoscope around his neck, he posed for cameras holding the poster for the fight and told reporters that he had developed a special disabling nerve hold: he slipped two fingers under his opponent's tongue and pinched a nerve that disabled him. If he couldn't practice surgery, he said, there was nothing he'd rather do than wrestle. He took the name "Killer" Sheppard, a bleak, defiant joke that said he was beyond the sting of the media. His stage name was a ritual thumbing of his nose. He used the reporters, knowing the freak show that was his life would attract customers and enough cash for him to survive. He wanted no money from his brothers. He didn't want to see them. When Steve heard about Sam's bizarre new career, the psychiatrist in training wondered if Sam was subconsciously trying to compensate for the wrestling match he lost on the beach on July 4, 1954.

His divorce from Ariane went through in the fall of 1969, about when Sam, broke, moved into the Strickland home. George's wife, Betty, kept his books. Soon he and Colleen began dating. He gave her stuffed animals, which she thought was sweet. She accompanied her father and Sam on their matches throughout the country. That autumn in Los Angeles, Sam and George held a press conference to hype the event. At one point, he turned to Colleen and said, "Tell them we're going to get married." Embarrassed, she told reporters that she hadn't made up her mind. On October 21, 1969, Sam drove Colleen to Chihuahua, Mexico, and they eloped. "It happened very suddenly," Betty Strickland told reporters in Columbus. "We are very happy. They should get along fine. Dr. Sam is a man full of surprises."[10]

"We didn't have much in common," Colleen Sheppard would say later. "He always had his nose in a medical journal." Colleen liked rock music and dancing in clubs. "He liked to listen to Nat King Cole and Johnny Cash and I couldn't hack it. And he couldn't hack Jimi Hendrix." She said that she felt sorry for Sam. He was "like a little kid," always getting his feelings hurt when, out of frustration, she snapped at him. "He was like a little puppy dog."[11]

Sam Sheppard was hard on his son. Young Sam had grown his hair longer, protested the Vietnam War, and smoked pot. He played guitar and wrote anguished confessional folk songs. Dr. Sam disapproved of his son's transformation into a hippie, a stance rich in irony, since Dr. Sam himself took drugs, had practiced a version of free love, and was fiercely antiestablishment regarding the criminal justice system.

In the spring of 1970, Sam Reese brought a girlfriend to Ohio and visited his father. The three of them were in the Stricklands' yard when Dr. Sam took a cocklebur from the top of a thistle and stuck it on the crotch of his son's jeans. Sam Reese looked quizzically at his father.

"Because you're such a big prick," Dr. Sam said, smiling.

It was the last time he saw his father.

By March, Sam Sheppard was predicting his death. He said that he had it figured out to the day. His wife and her parents felt that his pronouncements were just his way of getting their attention. By April, Sheppard weighed 210 pounds, 25 pounds above his weight in prison. He ate little solid food, instead drinking a quart or more of vodka a day. On April 5 he collapsed at the Strickland home. He ran a high fever and was shaking. His wife later said that she thought he was suffering a terrible case of the flu. They were unable to get him into his bed, so they found pillows and blankets and made him comfortable on the living room floor. When Betty Strickland tried to call a doctor, Sam raged, saying that he was going to die anyway, do not call. At about 3 A.M., he asked Betty to give him a shot of Librium, a tranquilizer, which she did. Colleen remembers that Sam carried on imaginary conversations that night, talking about not wanting to go to prison. In the early morning he collapsed walking to the kitchen, then he vomited blood. This time the women called an emergency medical squad. Medics could not revive him. At 8:38 A.M., on April 6, 1970, Dr. Samuel H. Sheppard died at age forty-six.

Betty Strickland mentioned to authorities that she had given him a shot of Librium on his orders. Taking no chances, the coroner tested Sheppard's organs for poison. Had he been murdered? This was the Sheppard case, and anything was possible. Columbus's afternoon paper ran a huge page 1 story, SHEPPARD DEAD; CORONER PROBES.

On the coroner's copy of the death certificate were the notes "self-medication" and "100 mg of Librium, six Phenobarbitals and half a gallon of vodka." Later, the pathologist determined that Sam died of Wernicke's acute hemorrhagic encephalopathy, a liver disease triggered by acute lack of vitamins, particularly thiamine, which causes the nervous system to shut down. It was sometimes seen in alcoholics.

Colleen and Betty Strickland arranged the funeral. Sam was dressed in a green suit and dark glasses, looking like a mannequin in a trendy store. "He always wore sunglasses," said Colleen. "We decided he looked more natural with the glasses." Fifty people, including reporters, gathered at a local chapel for a service led by the Reverend Alan Davis of Cleveland. He was struck by the pathetic end of his promising, once wealthy boyhood friend. Davis recalled that days after the murder, hearing that Sam needed him, he visited him in the basement recreation room at Steve and Betty's home. They hugged, then wept together. "Either he was a great actor putting on a brilliant show for his naive friend, and I was a fool, or he was genuinely revealing the pain that could only come from the sudden death of a beloved wife," Davis would later write.[12]

Except for Richard and Dorothy Sheppard, the pews were filled with people who knew Sam only at his worst. Steve was studying on a medical fellowship in London, and he and Betty did not make the trip. Young Sam was in Spain and sent a telegram. F. Lee Bailey, in a dark suit, served as a pallbearer next to Colleen's long-haired brother, who wore an embroidered white leather outfit. Ariane, in dark glasses, cried throughout the service.

"In many ways," the minister said in his eulogy, "the life of Sam Sheppard has been an open book. Certainly parts of it are known to many. More important, other parts remain a mystery, as they should be. As with every life, the truth in full is known only to God."

Afterward, the funeral procession to Forest Lawn Cemetery included "four motorcycles driven by hippie-types" and "at least three ex-convicts at the services who had known Dr. Sam," the local paper noted.

Colleen placed mementos inside the casket—Sam's stethoscope, a few surgical tools, and a large plastic replica of a red-and-gray Darvon capsule, a mild narcotic painkiller. Colleen tucked the telegram from his son in a pocket of Dr. Sam's suit coat. Did young Sam have a death wish, too? His telegram, addressed to his father, said, "I am with you."

32

DICK AND OBIE

WHILE SAM SHEPPARD'S FORTUNE was fading, Richard Eberling's rose. A few years after Dr. Sam's death, Eberling had become an insider with Cleveland's new Republican mayor, Ralph Perk, who had hired Obie Henderson as a personal assistant.

Eberling went out of his way to cultivate Lucille Perk, the mayor's stay-at-home wife. She and the mayor had raised their six sons and a daughter in a small, inexpensive two-story house in a working-class neighborhood overlooking the city's vast industrial valley along the Cuyahoga River. A heavy-set woman, Lucille Perk was embarrassed to make public appearances as the city's first lady. Once, when her husband was invited to a state dinner at the Nixon White House, she refused to go, saying it conflicted with her ladies' league bowling night. Her turndown sparked a rash of jokes about Cleveland. Eberling urged her to go on a crash diet, and soon she became so comfortable around Dick and Obie that she attended one of their summer parties and cooked hamburgers and hot dogs for the crowd. Eberling, who now called himself an interior decorator, convinced Lucille Perk to let him redecorate their shabby home. Soon she had new drapes, wallpaper, and choice pieces of furniture, all for free. Eberling hoped that his pro bono work would soon pay dividends.

Henderson and Eberling were social climbers who wanted to be taken seriously as sophisticates, men of cultured tastes. Cleveland's conservative old-money crowd had no use for "Dick and Obie"—people referred to them as a couple—Obie with a slight West Virginia burr in his voice and a high school education; eccentric Dick with his corny, heavy-handed charm. So they volunteered at Cleveland's newer cultural institutions, the Cleveland Ballet and the Playhouse Square Foundation.

Through their friendship with the mayor, they were able to climb higher by cultivating those who were new to power, among them some of the state's most prominent black political figures: W. O. Walker, owner of the city's influential black weekly, *The Call & Post;* Cleveland City Council president George Forbes; Cleveland school board president Arnold Pinkney, who would run the Reverend Jesse Jackson's 1984 presidential campaign.

By the 1970s, Eberling's house on Bradley Road was a regular stop on Westlake's tour of homes, a Sunday event where half a dozen old homes were open to the public. Eberling had restored the four-bedroom, century-old home into a showcase, filled with antiques, art, china and crystal, loaded with lush, heavy drapes and brocaded chairs.

Behind the home was a one-acre, obsessively tended Japanese garden. Eberling had hired a master Japanese gardener who imbued the garden with *meigakure,* which means the quality of remaining hidden from ordinary view. As you walked the twisting path of Dick's garden, each feature—a massive rock, a tall, slender shrub, a miniature waterfall, a reflecting pool—came into view from partial concealment, creating a sense of mystery. You were supposed to feel yourself pulled along the winding path by the expectation of more concealed surprises.

Dick and Obie threw elaborate parties, which attracted clients, and soon Eberling landed decorating contracts with some of Cleveland's nouveaux riches. He constructed interiors that were classical yet startlingly original, combining rich, outrageously marked-up fabrics and wallpaper with objets d'art, Amish antiques, even a Communion rail from a nineteenth-century Catholic church. And like the partially hidden features in his gardens, he liked to leave hidden signatures behind. For instance, when he installed the Communion rail, he turned its crosses upside down, a sign of devil worship.

In 1973 Eberling was perfectly situated to take advantage of Mayor Perk's sudden interest in historic preservation. Perk had just toured Europe for the first time and was taken by the dignity and grandeur of the continent's ancient public buildings. After his return, the mayor established the Commission for the Preservation of City Hall and appointed Eberling, his personal interior decorator, to oversee the restoration and decoration of several rooms in the federally designated historic building. For Eberling, this assignment was the high point of his life.

Perk's reward to Eberling frightened the city's preservationists, aghast that an unschooled, self-described interior decorator would be restoring the grand rooms in one of the nation's beautifully designed municipal buildings.

Cleveland City Hall, with its majestic rotunda and wide marble stairs, was a Beaux Arts jewel of the City Beautiful movement from the 1910s.[1]

Eberling's first project was to restore the large, ceremonial Tapestry Room, often criticized as a dark cave. To his credit, he stayed true to its classical style and preserved the panoramic hand-painted scenes on the room's massive fifteen-foot tall draperies. Chemical dry cleaning, as previously planned, would have ruined them. He had dozens of layers of varnish stripped from the woodwork, which revealed beautiful, reddish Australian oak.

Eberling quickly made enemies within city hall. He hired outside contractors instead of using City of Cleveland carpenters and electricians, who could not perform up to his standards. Also, he ordered expensive materials and services without getting bids, and circumvented attempts to control his spending by the city's commissioner of accounts. Eberling waited until he had the mayor alone in the evening, ran his ideas by him, got approval, then told anyone who complained, "The mayor approved this."

It was no surprise that the *Press*'s city hall reporter soon was asking Eberling about his qualifications as an interior decorator and for a breakdown of costs. "Why are you asking these questions?" he snapped. "I'm donating my time, and we are not spending money on lavish items. Everything is done with the mayor's approval and he's the boss." The newspaper revealed his old 1960 conviction for stealing jewelry and money from his window-cleaning clients. Perk defended Eberling, saying his petty-larceny conviction was old and he was "donating his time. I think he deserves praise."[2] In fact, Eberling was paid thirty thousand dollars a year to oversee the work. After Perk lost the 1977 election, Henderson had to resign. The new mayor, Democrat Dennis Kucinich, fired Eberling. Dick and Obie's glorious run at city hall was over.

––––

Eberling had learned how to charm older women through years of practice on his suffocating, controlling foster mother, Christine Eberling. He knew that if he was patient and discreet, he could make a good living by taking advantage of older women who lived alone and, preferably, were estranged from their children. Considering his abandonment and his emotional manipulation as a child, it makes sense that Eberling was obsessed with gaining control over women, making them dependent on him. If they did not do what he wanted, he punished them with the silent treatment, pretending that he was hurt, withholding affection. They soon came around. His goal was to get himself written into their wills as a major heir.

By the 1970s, he had several women on the hook. One of them, a woman named Claire Miller, died without a will. Eberling told the probate court that he was her nephew, a bold lie. He filed in probate court, put up a bond, and took her possessions and house, valued conservatively at seventy-five thousand dollars. Another was Ethel May Durkin, whom he had befriended in 1960 after being hired to wash her windows. Durkin, a widow, lived in a beautiful home perched on Lake Erie in the older suburb of Lakewood, known for its tasteful shoreline mansions. She had a round, sad face and permed white hair, stood five feet three, and weighed more than two hundred pounds. She was a lonely woman. She and her late husband never had children. Of her two sisters, Durkin was closest to Myrtle Fray, a sixty-three-year-old widow. On May 20, 1962, at about 4:30 A.M., Fray was murdered in her bed, a brutal killing. She was beaten repeatedly in the head, suffocated with a pillow, and strangled. Ethel Durkin's other sister, Sarah Belle Farrow, seventy-nine, was living with Ethel in March 1970 when she fell down the basement stairs, broke both arms and legs, then died in a nursing home a month later.

The relatives of Ethel Durkin who did come around to visit were treated shabbily by Eberling. They tried to convince her to fire him. But Durkin had already been charmed by him. A cousin, Linda Newton, informed Durkin that when Eberling shopped for her groceries, he used her money for his own purchases as well. The old woman said she knew, but she didn't care. Don't worry, Durkin insisted, I'll keep an eye on him. She was lonely and wanted Dick around.

By the late 1970s, Eberling began pulling in cash from Ethel Durkin. She was aged, unable to get around, and needed full-time home care after breaking her knee in a fall. She paid him handsomely to be a nurse's aide for the second shift, 3 to 11 P.M. He had no medical training. Mostly, he prepared dinner for her, fixed her a stiff drink, urged her to take her medicines, parked her in front of the TV, then helped her into bed. He was reliable. He even left his own dinner parties to take her a meal and quickly check on her. Often Obie Henderson dropped by and cooked. They used Durkin's well-appointed home as a satellite social center, inviting their own friends, which amused Ethel Durkin, who had no social life of her own. Later it was obvious to her relatives that Eberling tried to turn Ethel Durkin against them. Each time one of the nurse's aides became close to Durkin, Eberling concocted a reason to have the aide fired.[3] He didn't want anyone interfering with a scheme he had in mind, one in which he needed, preferably, an unwitting accomplice.

In Patricia Bogar, Eberling met a woman he could not manipulate. She was good-looking in a hard way—brassy blond hair, a tanned face, leaving a trail of cigarette exhaust wherever she went. Fortyish and divorced, Bogar was on a mission: to settle down with a smart, easygoing, well-to-do man. He didn't have to be handsome or superrich or traditional; she was not a helpless, clinging female. Her only child, a son, was grown, and she did not want to live alone. Pat Bogar liked to tell people that she could be a real bitch, but delivered the warning in a likable, disarming way. Above all, she hated being conned because she was something of a con herself.

She met Obie Henderson in 1979 while working the election phone banks for Cleveland's Republican mayoral candidate, George Voinovich, now a U.S. senator.[4] Henderson, she decided, was worth flirting with. He dressed well and looked as if he had an education and maybe read a book now and then. She walked over, twitched the hair on the back of his neck, and said, "You have a cute behind."

Obie laughed and took her to lunch. Soon enough, she was invited to the home he shared with Eberling.

"They were like the odd couple," Bogar said. "Obie would lay Richard's clothes out." She and Obie became intimate friends, and after several months of dating, she was staying overnight at the farmhouse two or three nights a week. She was a night owl; after Obie fell asleep, she and Eberling stayed up talking until three in the morning.[5] When Dick and Obie threw their famous parties, Bogar worked as "a perfect little hostess," she said, greeting guests, taking coats, refilling drinks. She first met Ethel Durkin when Dick brought her to one of his parties.

Sometime during 1981, Eberling asked Bogar to sign her name at the bottom corner of a blank sheet of typing paper. Ethel Durkin's signature was in the other bottom corner. Eberling said he was going to his psychic and had promised Ethel to have her handwriting analyzed. Eberling told Bogar he wanted to get his money's worth and so he wanted to give her a free analysis, too.

Bogar smelled a ruse and was insulted. She knew then that he was trying to scam Durkin.

For a criminal, Eberling had a fatal weakness: he was so proud of his cunning that he wanted others to appreciate it. "He had a big mouth, and when he'd sit up long enough and drink enough, he'd say something stupid," Bogar recalled. Eventually, he admitted to her that he was constructing a will for "the old bat," which explained why he needed the signatures on a blank page. His admission made Bogar furious.

"I am your friend," she yelled at him. "Just come out and say what you want. Don't con me. I'm not one of your customers." Eberling said he would give her 10 percent of whatever he got from the Durkin estate. He planned on taking about $500,000. Bogar said she went along, acting "excited that I was going to be wealthy."[6]

But before that happened, Bogar came to despise Eberling. "I lived out there two or three nights a week," she said. "Obie and I talked about getting married. But then it turned sour. He was close to Richard and I started to resent that. Richard took precedence over me." The breaking point came when Obie invited her to the farmhouse to see some new purchases for the house: an Oriental rug, dishes, a new vase (he always drew out the word, saying *vaahhz*). As the two showed Bogar each new objet d'art they'd bought together, she grew more angry. She realized that Obie and Dick were inseparable; she was always going to be a third wheel. She walked out, telling Obie, "You can keep your Dick."[7]

She decided to move to Florida. Just before she left, Eberling came to her with a scam. "You've got everything all packed up," he said. "You should have a robbery."

Dick explained that he would break into her suburban house, and she could file a false insurance claim. He would boost the value of her claim by providing phony invoices on the letterhead of his interior-decorating business. The letterhead would list art and furniture he supposedly placed in her home, stamped "paid in full." As he explained to her, "What's a girl to do, out on the streets, with no money?"

Bogar was an opportunist when the crime was victimless and getting caught remote. She went along and ended up with thirty-five thousand dollars. Eberling secretly congratulated himself. If he ever needed to keep Bogar in line, he could threaten to expose her felony fraud.

While Eberling took comfort in his blackmail, Bogar was creating her own protection policy. He had promised her 10 percent of whatever he finagled from the Durkin estate, but Bogar didn't trust him to keep his word. She wrote a long account detailing Eberling's plan to defraud the Durkin estate, including her own role in the crime. She had the document notarized and mailed it to her lawyer, first telling him to keep it safe without opening it. If Eberling tried to double-cross her, she would use the document as a triple-cross "to hang Dick at the proper time," she would say later. "I'd wait until he got himself in so deep with no way out before I would reveal the true facts."[8]

Eberling needed other partners in the Durkin scheme; he found them in Beverly and Dale Scheidler. The Scheidlers owned a greenhouse where he bought flowers for decorating jobs, and he sensed an opportunity. They had bought thirteen Arabian horses, which in the early 1980s, if handled right, could be wise investments with huge tax write-offs.

Dale Scheidler was losing money on the horses. So Eberling came up with a plan: have a fancy party at his home, invite Cleveland's wealthy elite, then ask them to invest. They agreed. The party cost thirty thousand dollars, and the Scheidlers had to borrow money. It was a fabulous outdoor bash, with spectacular food and drinks and company. The horses were brought out one by one to prance along a runway through the middle of the festivities.

But no one chose to invest. So Eberling recommended his old standby, insurance fraud, as a way for the Scheidlers to hold off bankruptcy. They went along with it, and made ninety thousand dollars. Meanwhile, they gave Dick one of the horses, which he donated to the local public television station for its fund-raising auction. Bids on the stallion were to start at twenty thousand dollars. A story about Eberling's offer and a picture of the horse made the front page of the *Plain Dealer*. "This is the most unusual, most expensive thing ever donated to an auction," the station manager enthused.

Around this time, at a Cleveland Ballet function, Eberling met an attractive twenty-one-year-old named Kathy Wagner, who worked as a health aide. She was smart, ambitious, and desperate to rise above her troubled working-class past. She had joined the Mensa society; she volunteered at the Cleveland Ballet; she read novels to learn about other places and times. She also was blond and voluptuous, and had a husky laugh, the product of cigarettes and singing backup in bar bands.

Dick Eberling, though three decades older, recognized her as someone much like himself. Kathy Wagner wanted to be worldly and, although sexually experienced, was bored with dating men her age. She told everyone she liked older men. Eberling asked her to care for Ethel Durkin, and she agreed, starting in mid-1983. She made a fair wage, had a place to sleep, and still had time to be a part-time student at Cleveland State University. Mostly, she helped her obese client take a bath and get into bed. She would check vital signs and sleep in the same room, if needed.

After Kathy Wagner put Ethel to bed, Dick would invite her to talk in the kitchen. He'd work through several glasses of Scotch and water, and she'd have a cigarette and a Coke. Dick would expound on decorating, life, politicians he knew, and, mostly, sex. Kathy liked the talk. He flirted heavily, which she liked because she needed to know that she was attractive to men.[9] Dick talked of going to Japan and visiting the White House with Mayor Perk. He gave her such advice as that women should always wear sexy lingerie when taking a man to bed.

After working for Ethel Durkin for a few months, Wagner decided that Eberling was unbalanced. He told Durkin that she was beautiful, that her nightgown flattered her figure and accentuated her breasts, making her look sexy. Durkin, in her eighties, was moonstruck. To Wagner, Eberling practically winked behind the old woman's back, as if to say, "What a cow, and she falls for this."

"Ethel was in her eighties and wanted to be in her forties, and she was in love with him from the way that he led her on," Wagner would later say. "And when she would look at him you could see the longing and love in her eyes and it was pathetic. It was just really pathetic."[10]

Eberling's motives were clear to Durkin's niece, Arlene Campbell. He wanted to inherit her estate. Eberling defended himself by asking, so what? He took care of her and made her feel like a young woman. He was like the son she never had. None of her relatives stayed with her for nearly twenty years, as had he. Why shouldn't he be rewarded in her estate? So what if she allowed her fantasies to flourish because he teased her, he argued. What was the harm?

———

After drinks one evening in late 1983, Kathy Wagner told Eberling about being raped at fourteen by a friend of her father's. Eberling in turn described being raped as a boy by a foster parent in Clyde, Ohio. It was an emotional moment, and soon they were in each other's arms, sobbing. "After that we were bonded," Wagner said.[11]

Every evening, they talked, and his stories grew more violent. Once she brought up the movie *Apocalypse Now,* and its portrayal of the horrors of war.

"Wouldn't it be fun to watch someone die?" Eberling asked.

"No."

"Have you ever thought about how it would be to slit somebody's throat and watch their life slip away?"

"No, I haven't."

"Well, it's got to be extremely exciting."

Later, Wagner said he asked her if she had ever killed anyone. She said no. He replied, "Well, I have."

He asked if she knew the name Marilyn Sheppard. Wagner said no.

"Well, I did her."

"You mean, you killed her?"

"Yeah. And someone else paid the bill." She remembers that he said he had grappled with Dr. Sam the night of the killing, hitting him in the head with a steel pail.

Then he told her, You didn't hear that. Wagner says she looked at him as if he was insane and said dismissively, "Oh, Dick." A week or so later, she told her mother, Virginia Haskett, what he had said about Marilyn Sheppard. Haskett told her daughter the man was crazy and to forget about it.[12]

A week or so later Richard Eberling fired Kathy Wagner. With Durkin at his side, he confronted her with an empty Scotch bottle from Durkin's cabinet, saying she had a drinking problem and that she had to leave. She protested that she didn't drink and he knew she didn't drink. "I've been marking the bottle," he said. Kathy protested some more, but Durkin sided with Eberling. On her way out, Wagner warned Durkin, "I think you need to watch what's going on."[13]

On November 15, 1983, a paramedic named Al Davis answered a call to the home of Ethel Durkin on Maple Cliff Drive. She was found facedown on the hardwood floor between the dining room and living room, comatose. Davis and his partner flipped her over. Durkin's right eye was swollen and her face was bruised. Blood from her mouth had smeared her face.

She must have hit the floor hard, Davis thought. Her face was flattened as if she had been facedown for a while. He only had a few seconds to figure it out—heart attack, stroke, head trauma, insulin shock, drug overdose?

It looked more like head trauma than heart attack. He and his partner hooked Durkin to intravenous fluids and an EKG to monitor her vital signs. She was experiencing bradycardia, a very slow heart rate.

That is weird, he thought. With head trauma, the heart races up to 150 beats a minute, and only slows down after about fifteen minutes. A lot of time must have passed after she was injured and before someone called the emergency squad.

They suctioned blood from her throat, tried to slip in a tube but could not, so they cut an airhole in her windpipe and intubated her to get her breathing again. The paramedics didn't know what Durkin was dying from, so they pumped her with drugs to counteract several possibilities. Gradually the oxygen and intravenous drugs forced her heart to pump steadily enough so that she could be moved to a hospital emergency room.

Eberling, who identified himself as Durkin's nephew, informed Davis that she had pushed herself up out of a living room chair, taken a few steps, screamed, then fallen face forward onto the hardwood floor. He had called for an ambulance.

Eberling's explanation of how Durkin was hurt did not match their medical findings. "I can't pinpoint my feelings," Davis would say much later, "but there was something wrong that didn't add up."[14]

They rushed her to nearby Lakewood Hospital, where X rays showed that she had a fracture near the second vertebra in her neck, the same place Dr. Sam Sheppard was injured on July 4, 1954. Her doctor figured that she had broken her neck from the fall.

———

A few days later Eberling asked Dale and Beverly Scheidler to meet him at Durkin's home with a typewriter. He needed their help and would make it worth their while.

After they arrived, Eberling took Dale and a bottle of wine upstairs and told him to wait. Downstairs, he gave handwritten pages to Beverly and asked her to retype it on the sheet with Ethel and Pat Bogar's signatures at the bottom. Beverly was frightened, she said later, but he had them in a vise: they were accomplices in the insurance fraud that had netted them ninety thousand dollars. Now he was dangling the hopes of a big payoff if the phony will passed muster with Cuyahoga County Probate Court. She and her husband were desperate, about to lose their greenhouse and its surrounding fields. Beverly typed as Dale worked on the bottle of wine. The new will divided 30 percent of Durkin's estate among nine persons and gave 70 percent to "Richard G. Eberling, good friend and adviser, Westlake, O." Following this list was an unusual paragraph, "Item V," the only place in the will where Eberling put words into Durkin's voice: "Dearest Richard, a gentlemen who to me was the son I always wished for, who saved my life, and [has] given me the greatest happiness and comfort." In the heat of his biggest score, whether he knew it or not, Eberling was still trying to compensate for the fact that he was an orphan.

On January 3, 1984, after having spent six weeks in the hospital, Durkin died. The Cuyahoga County coroner did not perform an autopsy. Her death certificate put her cause of death as "natural."

On January 14 Dick and Obie held a funeral at Durkin's house. The flowers and service were tasteful and sparsely attended—some relatives, a few friends from the neighborhood and St. James Catholic Church. Durkin's body was laid out in a fur coat and adorned with diamond rings her husband had given her decades earlier. Eberling made sure the Scheidlers were there, since they had to continue the charade that they were friends of the old woman. Beverly brought the will and gave it to Francis Feighan, Durkin's lawyer. He was to handle the probate work.

After everyone left, Eberling stripped Durkin's corpse of the diamond rings and the fur coat. The mink had cost five thousand dollars originally, but it had not been well cared for and was now worth far less. He tossed it to Beverly, a bonus for all her help. Eberling kept the dead woman's rings.

33

REVENGE

AFTER SCORING THIRTY-FIVE thousand dollars on the faked burglary of her apartment, Patricia Bogar left Cleveland and settled in Pompano Beach, Florida. She opened a dress shop. She did not find a rich husband. She ran through the money, her business struggled, and within a few years she was desperate for cash. She had given Eberling 10 percent of her score, payment for providing the phony invoices on his letterhead that had fooled her insurance company; now she wanted her cut for helping him loot the Durkin estate.

She phoned Eberling and first asked for a five-thousand-dollar "loan." But Eberling put her off. He explained that Durkin's distant relatives were contesting the will in probate court, which technically was true. The relatives had hired lawyers and complained to the court that Aunt Ethel would not have left the bulk of her estate to Eberling, nor would she have made Obie Henderson her executor and rewarded him with 4 percent.

Bogar was suspicious of Eberling's evasions and asked a lawyer in Cleveland to check the probate record. She was infuriated to learn that Eberling was going to get 70 percent of Durkin's $1.4 million, and that he had already been paid $250,000 for "companionship 1965–1982" by a check signed by executor Obie Henderson.

In late September 1987 Pat Bogar made a final play for money. She called the two men and demanded fifty thousand dollars—she would have settled for far less. If she did not get payment, she would turn them in to the police. She swore she was serious.

Dick and Obie dismissed her. They reminded her that she had committed insurance fraud and that she was in no position to be talking to law enforcers.

Bogar wouldn't drop it. She called Dale and Beverly Scheidler, who she knew had signed the fake will. She explained that she was going to the police if she wasn't paid right away. "If Dick goes down, you'll go down with him," Bogar warned them. "Because you're going to be in a lot of trouble if you were in probate court and perjured yourself. If you've got an ounce of brains, you'll talk to him."

Instead, Dale Scheidler reached Henderson and asked for his and his wife's share of the plundered estate, the payoff for typing and signing the one-page document. Otherwise, they were going to join Bogar in going to the police. Their threat didn't faze Henderson. You perjured yourself in probate court, he reminded him. You forged a will. You'll be in just as much trouble as we will. Be smart about this.[1]

A con hates to be taken, but Bogar was more incensed that Eberling did not take her threats seriously. She felt disrespected. She called Eberling again and told him about the paper trail she had created years earlier, outlining their scheme. "Before you make your decision, you need to come down and see the copies of what I have," she said. "Trust me, sweetie, you will go to jail."

Eberling turned her down and put Obie on the line. He could not placate his former lover. Henderson finally said, "Pat, maybe you should just do what you feel you have to do."[2]

———

Sgt. Vince Kremperger of the Lakewood Police Department had thirty-one years on the job, the past fifteen as chief of detectives. He was tired of the work and, to the delight of his wife, planned to retire in a few weeks. It was September 4, 1987, and the last thing he needed to hear when he picked up the telephone was a complicated tale from an angry woman in Florida about a forged will from years ago.

One of the most important and least appreciated jobs in a detective bureau is fielding the unsolicited complaints that come in over the phone every day and deciding which ones to take seriously. The job requires experience, judgment, and an understanding of time management to cull out potential cases to pursue. Not all tips can be investigated. Some complaints are tossed aside because the statute of limitations on an alleged crime has expired or because of the difficulty of securing a conviction.

In her quest for revenge, Bogar was learning this hard truth. When she called an administrator at Cuyahoga County Probate Court to expose Eberling, the man brushed her off, wondering why she, not a legal party to the will, should have any concern. She slammed down the phone, enraged. She crashed around the room, screaming, "The son of a bitch, he's going to get away with it!"

She called the Cleveland police. A detective told her to call the police department in Lakewood, jurisdiction for crimes against resident Ethel May Durkin. Soon she found herself talking to Kremperger.

Kremperger was a blunt-spoken, old-school police officer, unlike the younger, weight-lifting, college-educated young cops found in suburban departments. He was burly, with ropy forearms and a desk-job gut. He was not known for being deferential to his police chiefs. Kremperger found himself touched by Bogar's story about the exploitation of a ninety-year-old woman, feeling a bit over the hill himself. He started digging.

Meanwhile, Eberling sold his ostentatious farmhouse in Westlake and moved with Obie to Lookout Mountain, Tennessee, a wealthy area near Chattanooga. They purchased a huge Mediterranean-style mansion with twenty-seven rooms and spectacular views of the mountains. Even by their neighborhood's high standards, they spent lavishly, redecorating their mansion. They had no idea that Bogar's revenge was uncoiling in Lakewood.

————

Kremperger learned that Ethel May Durkin had died after a six-week stay in Lakewood Hospital, that she had come in paralyzed from the neck down, and had been kept alive on a respirator until eventually she was unplugged, and that the coroner's office had not performed an autopsy. The cause of death stated was accidental, the result of blunt trauma to the head.

Probate-court records showed more promise. Ethel Durkin's will was contested, but her relatives settled with Eberling for sixty-five thousand dollars. Kremperger consulted a forensic-documents examiner who looked at the poorly typed will under a microscope and tested the inks of the four signatures.

Eberling, for all his caginess, had made some rookie mistakes. The will was signed by pens with different inks. This did not in itself prove forgery. The signature of Ethel May Durkin was determined to be hers. But the examiner, Dr. Phillip Bouffard, noticed that the bottom of the loop of the signature's lowercase Y was beneath a bit of typescript. In other words, Durkin signed first and the document was typed later, one keystroke landing on top of the signature. It was highly suspicious.

Bogar's testimony, combined with the expert's opinion, gave Kremperger and his partner, detective Kurt Fensel, a solid case. They decided to work their way to Eberling by pressuring his coconspirators, Dale and Beverly Scheidler. Not only had the couple helped type and witness the fraudulent will, but they had testified in probate court that it was authentic, committing felony perjury. In July 1988 the Scheidlers, Eberling, and Henderson were indicted for forgery, perjury, aggravated grand theft, tampering with evidence, and tampering with records. Bogar, who had simply signed a blank sheet of paper, was not charged with anything.

Dale and Beverly were bankrupt, could not afford lawyers, and felt betrayed by Eberling and Henderson. They quickly told Kremperger that they would inform on their former friends in hopes of lenient sentences.

———

A few weeks later Kremperger and Fensel visited Eberling and Henderson's mansion in Tennessee with a search warrant and a U-Haul trailer. They found several other wills for elderly women in other states, stolen art objects, a silver plate, and a huge painting stolen from Cleveland City Hall.

The Scheidlers were not yet in the clear. As a safeguard, Kremperger made them take polygraph exams. He and his partner wanted to smoke out any evasions or deceptions by the couple before putting them on a witness stand and subjecting them to cross-examination. Dale Scheidler passed, but Beverly showed deception, particularly on the broad question as to whether she was hiding anything about how Ethel Durkin had been hurt. Told that she had failed, Beverly Scheidler started sobbing, afraid she was going to prison.

Kremperger calmed her down and extracted the story. A few years after Durkin's death, she recounted, Eberling took her to dinner at a fancy restaurant, the Blue Fox, while her husband recuperated in a hospital from shoulder surgery. Eberling had several drinks and was feeling expansive. Beverly brought up Durkin, saying it was sad the way the woman died, lingering for weeks from a fall that was an accident.

"She didn't fall, I hit her," Eberling told her, somewhat proudly.

Shocked, Beverly Scheidler couldn't think of something to say. Suddenly she realized that she might be part of a murder scheme.

———

Upon hearing this, Vince Kremperger postponed his retirement indefinitely. He wasn't leaving until he and Fensel built a murder case against Eberling and, if warranted, Henderson. The investigation already was complicated and fascinating, and was certain to be the capstone of his career. Now he was even more determined.

He fought to have Durkin's body exhumed. The Cuyahoga County coroner's office agreed, and Durkin was dug up in an Erie, Pennsylvania, cemetery. This time, a pathologist noted a hematoma on the back of Durkin's head to go along with the broken neck. Also, the first and second vertebrae in Durkin's spinal column were mushy. The pathologist decided that Durkin was struck from behind, which broke her neck. The official cause of death was changed: homicide.

Within weeks, Eberling and Henderson were charged with aggravated murder. Their legal problems stunned Cleveland social circles, from the Cleveland Ballet to the Playhouse Square Foundation. Their many acquaintances knew the two men were social climbers and money grubbers, but no one ever suspected that they could be killers. They had been at Eberling's parties. Had they been rubbing shoulders with a murderer?

At a bond hearing, Eberling said he was worth $2.1 million. (Henderson said he was worth about $65,000.) For all their wealth and supposed sophistication, they blundered badly when it came to hiring lawyers to defend them. They started with Dan Gaul, who had eight years of experience and was the son of the politically connected Democrat Frank Gaul, the longtime Cuyahoga County treasurer. But Dan Gaul and Eberling clashed. "He wanted me to represent both of them, but Obie's interests would not be served," Gaul says. "I liked Obie, had dinner with him. He was not a whiner, he was loyal. He didn't have a dark side like Richard Eberling." Gaul withdrew, but not until he was handsomely paid.

Henderson had far less criminal liability because no evidence linked him directly to the murder. Eberling alone was with Durkin when her neck was broken. Like the Scheidlers, Henderson was in the position to cut a sweet deal and roll over on his companion of two decades. But the assistant county prosecutor, George Rukovena, didn't push for a plea bargain because he, like Kremperger, apparently wasn't certain which of the two men was the prime mover behind the crimes. Eventually, the authorities decided the two worked together "like finely meshed gears." Or as Bogar later explained, "Dick came up with the schemes, but Obie put the fine points on them."

After Gaul resigned, they hired two incompetent lawyers, one of whom later was disbarred. At one point their lawyers were bungling the defense so badly that the trial judge hearing the case, Donald Nugent, dismissed the jurors and asked what was going on. Eberling and Henderson's first two witnesses, a probate-court referee and an appraiser of the Durkin estate, gave damaging testimony. "By asking if it was a valid will, you opened it up for the prosecution to ask a line of questions about what if it was an invalid will," the judge lectured Eberling's lawyer. So inept were Eberling and Henderson's lawyers that one court watcher called them "Abbott and Costello."

Also, deep in the thick stack of Durkin's medical records from Lakewood Hospital were facts that suggested that Eberling was more likely guilty of at-

tempted murder, rather than first-degree murder. Shortly after Durkin's admission, a nurse asked her if she slipped and the old woman nodded yes. A
few days later, Durkin's doctor said that he had tried to convince Durkin's
relatives to unplug the paralyzed and now unconscious woman's respirator
and let her die. But Eberling had refused, saying, "Miracles have been
known to happen."

Eberling and Henderson were convicted of aggravated murder, forgery,
theft, and related crimes in July 1989 and sentenced to life in prison. They
had to give up everything they stole and pay huge fines. The Scheidlers received suspended sentences with no prison time. For her cooperation, Bogar
was not charged with the seven-year-old insurance fraud that she and Eberling pulled off.

"He gave up his life for five thousand dollars," Patricia Bogar would say
later. "If he gave me that, I would have gone away and they'd be living the
life of leisure."

Which is what Sgt. Vince Kremperger now had in mind. Days after the
successful conclusion of the Durkin case, he retired from the Lakewood Police Department.

Eberling was disgusted with himself. "I should have had her body cre-
mated," he told me.

PART 3

Be kind, Oh be kind to your dead
and give them a little encouragement
and help them to build their little ship of death.
For the soul has a long, long journey after death
to the sweet home of pure oblivion.

—D. H. LAWRENCE

34

THE PURSUIT

IN OCTOBER 1989 I sent a telegram to Richard Eberling in the Cuyahoga County jail. I identified myself as a journalist and asked to talk to him. During regular visiting hours the next day, I passed through a metal detector, signed in, and rode a padded elevator to the eighth floor of the jail tower. I had no idea whether Eberling would come out of his cell to talk to a stranger, especially since his recent murder conviction had made him a Cleveland celebrity.

During Eberling's trial, newspaper coverage touched on the same tantalizing details about his life that F. Lee Bailey had pursued two decades earlier: that he worked for the Sheppards, stole Marilyn's rings, and admitted bleeding in their home around the time of the murder. Since Eberling's trial, Dr. Steve Sheppard, Dorothy Sheppard, and others had publicly called for the Bay Village police to reopen an investigation into Marilyn's death. Steve Sheppard made the most compelling case in a long article published in the *Plain Dealer* on July 4, 1989. Now a psychiatrist, Sheppard explained that Eberling, as an abandoned, illegitimate child who had never met his father, fit a likely psychological profile of Marilyn's killer: "Eberling worked for Dr. Sam Sheppard and his wife Marilyn. Nothing could infuriate a man like Eberling more than to see a happily married couple with one child, a son, who received the benefits of loving parents. This young couple and their son, Chip, were symbolic of the family such a man would have liked to have been a member of and could well have triggered the kind of violent jealousy that could have resulted in a decision to take something from them. That something had to be of value. I think he would want them to be forced to experience the feelings of loss that he felt over the years."[1]

Nobody in the Cleveland-area law enforcement community rushed forward to take a crack at America's most famous unsolved murder. A Bay Village police lieutenant said, "There may a come a time . . . but I'm not sure where we go from here, unless someone would talk to us." But Eberling refused, repeatedly, to talk to detectives about anything.

———

It was easy to pick out Eberling from the two dozen men who shuffled into the visiting pen, all dressed in bright orange coveralls and floppy thongs. He was the oldest prisoner. He stood tall and carried himself with a haughty air, as if to suggest that it would only be a matter of time before he and his money overturned his convictions. He had a surprisingly unlined face for a man of fifty-eight, with full lips and a strong jaw. He might have been considered good-looking, except for a gray toupee that after a few months in jail now looked like roadkill. He sat across from me at a long table.

He started by denying that he murdered Ethel Durkin. She was kept alive for weeks at the hospital until a doctor unplugged her respirator. The real crime, he claimed, was that he and Obie had been framed by unethical detectives and prosecutors.

Since I hoped this to be the first of many conversations, I didn't challenge him. He switched topics abruptly, almost as if he were free-associating. I wanted him to keep talking until I figured out the right questions to ask.

Yes, he knew Marilyn Sheppard, Eberling went on. She hired him to clean windows shortly after she and Dr. Sam moved to their house on the lake. She had long, tanned legs and wore tight, white shorts and a little top, he said. She was a lovely lady, classy, a perfect mother.

His description sounded like a fantasy, Marilyn as virgin-vamp.

One summer day while working, he recalled, Marilyn brought out brownies and milk for Chip and him. The three of them ate the snack sitting at the top of the wood stairs leading to Lake Erie. She invited him to swim on their beach anytime; he could change in the bathhouse. He was describing an ideal mom—feeding him comfort food and making sure that he got to play.

Eberling resented Sam Sheppard. "I think he just was a prick," he said. Sheppard ignored him, treating him as a member of the service class, which Eberling even then was determined to rise above. What particularly galled him was that Sam Sheppard was "doctor to the high school boys" on Bay Village's football team who thought "he was a big shot, sitting on the bench during the games."[2] Working for free on Friday nights as a high school football-team physician may have been smart marketing for a doctor trying to build a practice, but it was hardly a prestigious position. It was striking that decades after the murder Eberling focused on this fact when first remembering Dr. Sam. Later, I wondered whether Eberling resented Sheppard because he achieved two things that young Dick Eberling wanted to be: a doctor (Christine Eberling had pushed him to become one) and a high school athlete (she refused to let him play).

Eberling told me how his blood ended up in the Sheppard home. On July 2, 1954, a Friday morning, he said that he was alone in the Sheppard house, taking out storm windows and putting in window screens. The last storm window, over the kitchen sink, was the toughest to remove. A pair of sliding metal pins held the storm-window sash into the jamb, but the pins were stuck. He squeezed one pin with pliers and yanked. He lost his grip on the pin and slashed a finger as his hand recoiled. The wound bled freely. He shed blood drops in the kitchen, mostly around the window, and wiped them up. "She was a very meticulous housekeeper," he explained.

Near the end of the visit, Eberling said something that stopped me cold. "I fully expect to be convicted of killing Marilyn Sheppard."[3]

He hadn't been asked if he killed her. Where did this come from? He had just tried to convince me that he and Henderson were wrongfully convicted of the Durkin murder. So perhaps in his mind it was not illogical to fear being tagged with another murder. Or was his remark a "tell," a psychological giveaway?

At the least, it meant that Richard Eberling had secrets. This was reassuring because it told me that there were still things to discover.

A week later Sam Reese Sheppard made his first visit to Cleveland in nearly twenty years. He was a part-time dental hygienist, living in Boston, and had stayed away because Cleveland held nothing but painful memories. Recently, however, Sam Reese had become active in the anti-death-penalty movement. His father's friend the Reverend Alan Davis, director of the influential City Club of Cleveland, the city's "Citadel of Free Speech," had convinced Sam to give a speech about capital punishment at the forum, which would be broadcast over Ohio's public radio network.

The news that Sam Reese Sheppard would make a speech created waves of excitement in Cleveland because young Sam—he took offense at being called Chip—had never talked publicly about his life. Steve and Betty Sheppard had sheltered him from the media, but there was only so much they could accomplish. As a child during the first trial, Sam had nightmares about his father being set on fire. He would awaken and call out, "Make them stop!

My dad is frying." His classmates had heard discussions that Dr. Sam was "going to fry" in the electric chair. The death penalty, filtered through children's retelling, terrified young Sam.[4]

Sam Reese suffered from what would later be diagnosed as untreated chronic posttraumatic stress syndrome. He exhibited classic symptoms, depression and suicidal thoughts, as his grandmother and father had before him. Shortly after Christmas 1971, he deliberately injured himself and was hospitalized at Napa State Hospital in Napa, California, where his uncle Steve was finishing a psychiatric residency. "It was more a ritual reenactment of my mother's murder," he would say later, behavior sometimes seen in children of murder victims. He had a nervous breakdown and hallucinated. He cut his wrists, not deeply, and swung his bloody arms toward a wall to re-create his hellish visions of the murder room.

He was misdiagnosed as having schizophrenia and treated with drugs and counseling. Over the years, living in Boston, he labored to keep his psyche intact. He had few friends and never married. He reached a breakthrough one day in 1988 when he saw some news footage of a small boy waiting in the middle of a large public vigil protesting the impending execution of the boy's father. Sam Reese had waited, just as that boy was waiting, to learn if his father would be executed. Sam began to sob, realizing that he was not the only one ever to carry such a crushing burden. He joined Murder Victim Families for Reconciliation and spoke of his experiences at its meetings. For the first time since he was class president at Culver Military Academy, Sam Reese began to reach outside himself.

On October 27, 1989, a standing-room-only crowd packed the downtown Cleveland City Club auditorium for Sam Reese's noon address. Many in the crowd remembered him as Chip, a forlorn blond-haired boy of seven in a wide-striped T-shirt, sitting on his tricycle, staring into the camera unblinking, his face unbearably sad. At the City Club the audience saw a sturdy, solid man of forty-two. Sam Reese had his father's cleft chin. His brown curly hair receded to his top of his head. He spoke with a tight, nasal voice that sounded somewhat like his father's.

"In this city last month, a career criminal who had associations with my family thirty-five years ago was sentenced to life in prison on an unrelated murder charge. I have reason to believe that this individual conspired with others in the murder of my mother." Sam Reese accused local officials of "dragging their feet" in checking out Eberling's possible complicity and called for Ohio's governor to order a reinvestigation. Though Sam Reese did not mention Eberling by name, he had no more proof to make such an accusation than did coroner Gerber and the detectives in 1954 when they poisoned the city against his father.

That night Sam Reese stayed at Alan Davis's home. At about eight o'clock in the evening he took a telephone call from a retired private eye named James Monroe Sr., who liked to insinuate himself into high-profile cases. Nicknamed "Monsignor" (from Monroe Senior), the old man said that he had been talking to Eberling. "He has something to say to you," Monroe told Sam Reese. "He has information about the murder of your mother, and it might be good." And if you want to meet with Mr. Eberling at the prison, the old man said, it could be easily arranged.

Sam Reese, overwhelmed and surprised by the offer, said he had to think about it.

35

TWISTED STRANDS

SAM REESE SHEPPARD hoped that by speaking to the City Club he would prod authorities into reinvestigating his mother's murder. He had not anticipated being dragged into the case himself. Now he faced a dilemma: either talk to inmate Eberling, or let it drop and cling to the slim hope that authorities would respond to his plea to investigate Eberling. Sam Reese desperately wanted answers, but he didn't think he could pursue them himself because at the time he felt he lacked the emotional tenacity.

At Monroe's urging, Sam Reese found that he could write to Eberling. Inmate 214-343 responded with letters full of chat about prison, praise for Sam's work as an anti-death-penalty activist, and anecdotes about Sam as a seven-year-old boy. Eberling also included tantalizing clues about Marilyn Sheppard's murder. Without naming a killer, Eberling wrote that "her death was not intentional so to speak. The pressure build-up caused temporary insanity." Sam believed that Eberling was describing himself.

What Sam Reese did not know was that Eberling and James Monroe Sr., the self-described "world's greatest detective," were each trying to use him as part of their own far-fetched schemes.

Eberling deluded himself with the notion of writing a book with Sam Reese about their parallel lives and selling it to the movies—two boys who lost their parents and overcame adversity, both connected to the famous unsolved murder. Eberling planned to make himself the hero, saying that he overheard Esther Houk confront and threaten Marilyn Sheppard for sleeping with her husband. He apparently knew that Ohio law barred him, as a criminal, from making money on such a deal because he asked Monroe to get Sam Reese to agree on a fifty-fifty split, with Eberling's share hidden in a trust.[1]

Monroe, who convinced Eberling to pay him ten thousand dollars for his help, wanted to solve the Sheppard murder and "get international fame." Monroe was a wizened chain-smoker with bad teeth and poor health. He worked from an old kitchen table in a stale, dark house in a nice neighborhood. Over the telephone, he gave off a *True Detective* savvy. He had a stack of old court and probate records about the Sheppard case, and mailed them off piece by piece to Sam Reese and to Eberling, persuading each that he had the inside scoop. (They were not aware that these official court records were publicly available on microfilm rolls at the county clerk of courts.) Monroe refused to meet in person, not wanting anyone to see behind the curtain.

In March 1990 Sam Reese traveled from Boston to the rolling farmland of southern Ohio. Among the cornfields and dairy farms was the Lebanon Correctional Institute. His insides were churning because he had finally decided to visit Eberling. Sam Reese had no idea what to expect. Was Eberling simply a manipulator who loved to cause pain to the Sheppards? Would he deny all wrongdoing? What if he confessed?

Eberling came to the meeting dressed in prison blues and holding a packet of court records, props to make his case that he did not murder Ethel Durkin. Sam Reese listened without challenging a word. After a while, Eberling floated a suspiciously convenient story that he hoped Sam Reese would buy: two days before Marilyn's murder, while changing windows at the Sheppards' Bay Village home, he overheard Esther Houk scream at Marilyn Sheppard, "I will kill you if you don't leave my husband alone."

"It was excruciating," Sam Reese Sheppard later would say. "I was exhausted. . . . From my assessment of him, he seemed extremely involved. He had this hypnotic way of talking about the night, describing it. He tried to convince me of the Houk theory. I saw this guy's wheels working in his head. He was ready to burst in a lot of ways."

Sam Reese found himself overwhelmed. He wanted to clear his father's name by finding the real killer of his mother, but he could not even read the documents sent to him without recalling traumatic memories. "I am like a startled deer in the headlights of the moving train," he would write.

By 1991, Sam Reese had hooked up with a defense lawyer from Cleveland, Terry Gilbert, a political progressive who modeled himself after lawyer William Kunstler. As a young lawyer, Gilbert joined the pro bono defense team in Pine Ridge, North Dakota, working on the Wounded Knee case, defending American Indian Movement activists such as Leonard Peltier, who, in a controversial decision, was convicted of killing two FBI agents. Later, in

Cleveland, Gilbert represented accused murderers and flag burners. He used press conferences to put the justice system on trial while defending politically unpopular clients. Many police and prosecutors couldn't stand Gilbert and his grandstanding, but he had good relationships with local news reporters. He told Sam Reese he would help him try to get the Sheppard murder case reopened. He would work on a contingency basis. Another person who joined the growing Sheppard team was a lawyer who wanted to tell the Sheppard family story in a book, Cynthia Cooper. She and Sam Reese agreed to a fifty-fifty collaboration.

On a warm summer evening, many months after my first interview with Richard Eberling, I visited retired police sergeant Vince Kremperger. He hadn't moved to Florida. He still lived in the working-class neighborhood near his alma mater, West Technical High School. With loving pride, he handed me a three-ring binder of the Durkin investigation. It held nearly two hundred single-spaced pages of richly detailed reports. Eberling crossed paths with many people who had died suddenly, not just Ethel Durkin and Marilyn Sheppard, Kremperger had found. But his official duty had been to solve the Lakewood murder, not chase leads in other jurisdictions. He had sent the information about the other deaths to the Cleveland police and other jurisdictions. He said it was up to someone else to check the veracity of the stories.

I was determined to do that but skeptical of claims that Eberling was some sort of multiple killer.

The first name on the list of strange deaths connected to Richard Eberling was that of his foster father, George Eberling. On July 5, 1946, George Eberling, seventy-six years old, was sick with pneumonia and being cared for by Christine Eberling, his sixty-year-old second wife, and Dick Lenardic (he hadn't changed his name to Eberling yet). According to Eberling family lore, the old man, in his confusion, reached for medicine in the middle of the night and drank poison instead. Why a small bottle of poison was left on the bedstand was not explained, but relatives suggested that Richard may have put it there. George Eberling's death certificate shows that he suffered cerebral apoplexy and died four days later. There was nothing to suggest foul play until accusations years later by John Eberling, a grandson, and other relatives. George Eberling had left his farm to his son and two daughters, to be distributed after Christine died. Instead, his offspring ended up with nothing. After his foster father's death, Dick Lenardic changed his name to Richard Eberling and eventually bought the farm, parcel by parcel, from the executor of the estate, Christine Eberling.

Another death over a Fourth of July holiday connected to Richard Eberling took place in 1956. He and a woman he dated, Barbara Kinzel, were returning from southeastern Michigan in her red Ford convertible. Kinzel was twenty-three, a nurse who had worked at Bay View Hospital. In fact, on the day of Marilyn Sheppard's murder, she cared for Sam Sheppard after he was admitted. (She later would say that she believed Dr. Sam was innocent because she could see that morning how badly he had been injured.)

It was night, the road was dry, and Eberling was driving the red car when he crashed into the left rear end of a transport truck parked on the side of a two-lane highway. Eberling said the truck's back end extended into his lane; its driver said he had parked about six feet away. A police report said Eberling had a bump on his head; Kinzel died of a "basal skull fracture." The disparity raises suspicions, as did Eberling's account of the crash decades later. He said that after the collision with the truck, he reached over to his girlfriend and found her crumpled on the floor, unbloodied, her neck broken from smashing her head into the windshield.

Some of these details do not make sense. Kinzel should have been bleeding. Cars in the 1950s did not have seat belts, and she would have been thrown from the convertible, if its top was down. The local coroner, a funeral-home owner, ordered an autopsy, which was unusual in car crashes in Monroe County, Michigan. Kinzel's autopsy report, which was kept at the funeral home, now cannot be found. Michigan State Police performed a perfunctory accident investigation. An accident report shows the truck parked on the roadway, supporting Eberling's story. The trucking company settled with the Kinzel family, paying about five thousand dollars against all claims. Could Eberling have beaten her in the head, then put her body in the car and staged a crash to cover up a killing? Barbara Kinzel's death was puzzling, especially given her ties to Dr. Sheppard, but it is impossible to call it a homicide.

The murder of Ethel Durkin's sister in 1962, however, has disturbing parallels to the Marilyn Sheppard murder. Myrtle Fray was choked and beaten to death at 4:30 A.M. in her apartment in a large courtyard complex at West 110th and Lake Road. Eleven residents heard brief screams. One man said he heard someone gagging, then silence. The building's custodian was called. He talked to a few tenants who were awake, looked outside with a flashlight, then went back to sleep. No one called the Cleveland police. If they had, Cleveland's homicide chief said the next day, there was a 90 percent chance that the killer would have been caught as he tried to get away.

Myrtle Fray had lived alone since her husband had died the year before. She liked to play the ponies, drink whiskey, and meet with friends who used to work with her at the Ohio Bell Telephone company. Eberling didn't like Myrtle Fray. "She had a smart mouth," he said.

Myrtle Fray despised him. Once, while Eberling worked within earshot, Myrtle Fray nagged her sister to get rid of the window washer, who had insinuated himself into Durkin's life. He was "an ex-con," Fray pointed out.

"He's paid for that and he's fine," Durkin replied.

"They don't come that way."

Durkin hushed her sister, "Be quiet."[2]

Years later Eberling displayed a detailed knowledge of the Fray crime scene that had not been made public. For example, he told me that Myrtle Fray's false teeth were in plain view, soaking in a glass. A detective's report noted that Fray's "partial plate" was found on top of a bedroom dresser. Also, Eberling theorized that the killer, spattered with blood, carefully washed off over a sink, put on one of Fray's dresses—she was large, about two hundred pounds—and walked out with the bloody clothes in a shopping bag, undetected.[3] Detectives tested the sink's trap and found evidence that Fray's killer may have washed off blood before fleeing.

There, of course, could be an innocent explanation for Eberling's knowledge. He may have learned these details from Ethel Durkin. It is possible that Cleveland homicide detectives shared inside information with the sixty-nine-year-old woman, though nothing in the thick, detailed homicide files suggests that they did. Further, a bloody fingerprint from a bedroom windowsill was checked against Eberling's 1989 prints, at Kremperger's urging. They did not match.[4]

When I unearthed the crime-scene photos of Fray, much later, I was struck by the stunning similarities between her death and that of Marilyn Sheppard. The victims' nearly nude bodies were in similar positions. Each woman was discovered in bed on her back, her face bloody and repeatedly battered. Each was found with her left arm along her body, her right arm outstretched. In each case, the victim's nightclothes were removed, exposing her breasts. The two slayings looked like sexual homicides, and pathologists made vaginal swabs in each. One key difference was that Fray had been choked, probably to silence her screams. The strangulation started after the first blows landed because Fray's postmortem examination showed blood in her trachea, mouth, nostrils, and stomach. Three decades after Fray's death, without the benefit of seeing photos of the victims or detective reports, Eberling would write, "Myrtle was murdered the same way as Marilyn Sheppard."

—————

Two possible lodes of Sheppard information still needed to be found: any biological evidence that could be tested for a DNA fingerprint, and the official investigative reports. The most probative biological evidence would be the large closet-door bloodstain that Dr. Kirk had collected, tested, and described as "unique." If it could be located and tested, then comparisons could be made to the DNA profiles of Sam Sheppard, Richard Eberling, even the Houks. A grandson of the Houks told me he would provide blood, which might make it possible for DNA scientists to exclude one or the other of his grandparents from the crime scene.

Paul Kirk died in 1970. His daughter, who lived in the San Francisco area, said that she no longer had her father's Sheppard files. She had given them away or they were left at the University of California at Berkeley and probably thrown out. I reached several of Kirk's protégés, who knew nothing of his old files.

I had better fortune locating old police records. In 1977 Cleveland's central police headquarters, county jail, and sheriff's and prosecutor's offices were moved to the new, downtown Justice Center. Before the move, as part of a massive housecleaning, two sheriff's deputies were assigned to dump boxes of old files into a Dumpster. By chance, one of them noticed the word *Sheppard* on thick folders and looked inside. One of the men pocketed an onionskin carbon copy of the top document, a four-page July 4, 1954, police report by Cleveland homicide detectives Robert Schottke and Patrick Gareau. The other deputy had an interest in Cleveland history. He wanted to take the whole file, but he had ridden to work that day on his motorcycle. He grabbed what he thought he could fit into a saddlebag—a thick stack—and abandoned the remainder of the file. Two decades later, I tracked down the two deputies—one in Georgia, a federal agent, the other in suburban Cleveland. The deputy with the large cache told me, "I was kind of disappointed in what was in here." He felt there was no smoking gun, no single startling conclusive piece of evidence. Among the materials was a manila tag with a string tie that read "Marilyn Sheppard." It looked like a toe tag used to identify bodies in a morgue. "This might have some value," I said. He kept the tag and gave me the files.

Either the deputy had not looked through the file closely or he had a Perry Mason misconception of homicide evidence. The documents were a mother lode of valuable information: several hundred pages of detective reports, grand-jury transcripts, and investigative materials. They gave a daily, insider's account of how up to a dozen detectives and lawyers worked this murder investigation, chasing some leads, ignoring others, single-mindedly focusing on Dr. Sam Sheppard as the guilty party and his brothers as possible coconspirators. The reports debunked much of the conventional wisdom I held about the case—that someone wiped away fingerprints at the scene, that Marilyn died hours before Dr. Sam called for help, that the murder

weapon was a surgical instrument. I grew up in Cleveland and had been told
at an early age that Dr. Sam was guilty. At this point, I began to think that
perhaps Dr. Sheppard was innocent.

———

Meanwhile, Richard Eberling, who said he was penniless, was assigned an
appellate lawyer through the Ohio public defender's office. He was David
Doughten, a talented, respected criminal defense attorney. As Doughten
would learn, Eberling felt terrible about dragging Obie Henderson into the
Durkin mess and offered to take a polygraph examination about the Sheppard case if it would help Henderson obtain an earlier release. It was an
offbeat suggestion, but Judge Kenneth Callahan, who was hearing the appeal, said he would think about the offer. Learning of this, I convinced
Eberling to allow me to videotape the polygraph exam, if it took place. I
wanted documentation as to whether he passed or failed, and planned to
use Eberling's results in an article for *The New Yorker,* which had given me
an assignment to write about the case. By this time I felt I could build a circumstantial case that Eberling, not Dr. Sam, was the more likely killer of
Marilyn Sheppard.

The exam took place in a windowless room in the county jail. The polygraph operator, Lee Feathers, was a middle-aged man with an early-Elvis
hairstyle and a chunky pinkie ring. He was retired from the police department in Mentor, a small city east of Cleveland, and ran a detective agency
with his wife. After strapping Eberling into a Stoelting Ultrascribe machine,
Feathers asked innocuous control questions to get Eberling's breathing rate,
pulse, blood pressure, and galvanic skin response.

Then he asked, "Did you cause the death of Marilyn Sheppard during
that July 4 weekend in 1954?"

"No," Eberling said.

"Regarding Marilyn Sheppard, did you cause her death?"

"No."

"Were you present when Marilyn Sheppard was struck on the head during that July 4 weekend?"

"No."

Feathers found "no indications of deception" in Eberling's answers.

Eberling was asked three questions about his claim that two days before
the murder he had overheard Esther Houk threaten to kill Marilyn Sheppard.
The machine said Eberling was being deceptive. The tracings were "terrible," Feathers explained to him.

"I tried," Eberling said. "I'd do anything to help Obie."

"Hey, you gave it a shot," Feathers said. The examiner unhooked Eberling from the machine and had him sent back to his cell. Feathers said later, "It's a simple case of some bum trying to get his buddy out of the slammer."

A week earlier, I was prepared to write that Eberling, rather than Sam, was the more likely killer. I had never expected Eberling to agree to the polygraph test. Likewise, I didn't expect to be allowed to see Eberling's test results, no matter how they turned out. Suddenly, I found myself stung by taking the unusual step, for a journalist, of getting a lawyer and a client to waive privilege and give me access to a new, exclusive piece of forensic information. This stunt made me rethink my story, and I told my *New Yorker* editor I could not deliver the piece I had promised.

Later I learned from one of the nation's top polygraphers that Feathers's results were unreliable. Len Harrelson, who for years ran the Keeler Polygraph Institute in Chicago, analyzed Feathers's report at my request. "I'd say the test is absolutely worthless," Harrelson said. "The best you could say is it's inconclusive. He did not use proper technique and proper procedure."[5] I asked Eberling's lawyer how he came to select Feathers to perform the lie test. "He called me and volunteered he would do it for free," Doughten said.

By early 1995, Sam Reese Sheppard's team had amassed records and interviews that suggested Eberling was a killer and that Dr. Sam was not guilty. Terry Gilbert, the lawyer, had filed an open-records lawsuit against the Bay Village Police Department, which shook loose a slightly redacted copy of its seven binders on the Sheppard case. They had numerous interviews with Eberling and explored some of the strange deaths that surrounded him. A security firm from Virginia, AMSEC, donated its time. Lawyer Cynthia Cooper interviewed Eberling and dug up other records.

In March 1995 Gilbert and the team met with the Cuyahoga County prosecutor, Stephanie Tubbs Jones. She had run the office since John T. Corrigan's retirement in 1990. Her top aide, known as "the first assistant," was an aggressive, experienced trial lawyer named Carmen Marino, a stocky Vietnam veteran, sports enthusiast, and graduate of the University of Notre Dame. Twenty years earlier, Marino had successfully prosecuted a sensational local murder in which a judge, Robert Steele, had hired hit men to assassinate his wife. Marino had read the office's thick Sheppard files back then to see how the paper trail in a high-profile case unfolded. Since then, he'd developed an expertise and a reputation as a "cold case" specialist, the prosecutor who revisited old unsolved murder cases, evaluated them, and oversaw their reinvestigation, if called for. He was fierce but reasonable.

Jones had been a trial judge and assistant prosecutor. She had known Gilbert for years and had even attended his wedding. She had ambitions beyond the county office. (In fact, four years later, she won the U.S. House of Representatives seat vacated by the retirement of Congressman Louis Stokes.)

The meeting would never have taken place under her predecessor. But Jones and Marino were willing to listen to Gilbert's presentation, an hour-long explanation of why Eberling was a likely suspect who needed to be looked at. After the meeting, Marino took the thick binder, read it carefully, then looked for the Sheppard files he had reviewed years earlier. The files, two thick brown folders of materials, had been in the credenza behind the desk of former prosecutor Corrigan, who was retired and suffered from Alzheimer's disease. Marino never was able to find the missing folders.

It didn't take Marino long to conclude that the 1954 investigation had been lousy, that Eberling was a more likely suspect, and that a reinvestigation was in order. Sheppard had no history of violence. The Susan Hayes motive from the first trial was thin. "There was no evidence of a motive," Marino explained. "They have a nice evening together, she is pregnant with a second child, the affair was known to her but over for now. For some reason, Sam got up and bludgeoned his wife to death. That's a hard sell."

Marino found it inexcusable that neither the Scientific Investigation Unit police detectives nor the coroner's office attempted to type the blood trail found in the Sheppard house. If he had been the prosecutor handling the case, he would have insisted on more blood work. Eberling should have been thoroughly investigated. He had access to the home, was already suspected in 1953 of stealing from clients, and had a twisted background.

In July 1995, prosecutor Jones issued a press release that shocked the city's legal establishment. Her office was investigating the unsolved Sheppard murder. "I don't think Sam Sheppard killed his wife," Carmen Marino explained. The investigation had been inadequate. "There was a lot of intervention by politicians who should have backed off and let the police do the work they should have."[6] The blood should have been tested. "If it's not Marilyn's blood, there's no way you can try Sam Sheppard, because Sam wasn't bleeding." All new leads would be pursued. "We'll go back over it and see if there is enough evidence to try Eberling."[7] Marino described him as "a probable serial killer."

Meanwhile, Sam Reese Sheppard shook up his life. He sold all his possessions except for two guitars, and stored boxes of memorabilia and his father's old trial materials in a file room at Northeastern University, where a friend taught in its criminal justice program. While Marino puzzled over the Sheppard murder, Sam Reese began a five-month, sixteen-hundred-mile walk, from Boston to New Orleans, protesting the death penalty. When he finally got the good news out of Cleveland, Sam Reese could not believe what he was hearing—that the State of Ohio was seriously reinvestigating his mother's murder. Amazingly, his efforts to clear his father's name were coming to fruition.

———

Marino assigned an assistant prosecutor, David Zimmerman, and two investigators, both retired detectives, to work the case. Such was the culture of the police department and the prosecutor's office that many thought Marino was crazy to think Dr. Sam was innocent. In October 1995, Marino decided to interrogate Eberling. First he sought advice from Dr. Phillip Resnick, a forensic psychiatrist, about how to approach the interview. Dr. Resnick said to avoid a confrontational interview and appeal perhaps to Eberling's vanity or ego.

Marino traveled with two detectives, both men. They would take turns talking to Eberling, but Marino went first. Eberling came to a private room in a wheelchair and was dressed in prison orange. He had a long, silver beard and had quit wearing toupees. He seemed pleased by the attention.

Do you believe in God? Marino asked him.

Eberling said he did.

You're going to die in here, Marino told him. Before you meet your maker, don't you want to make a clean breast of it?

Marino had misjudged Eberling. For one, the timing of the interview was poor; Eberling still held out hope that he might get a new trial with a successful appeal. Henderson had gotten his murder and forgery counts thrown out on appeal and was left serving five to fifteen years on aggravated grand theft. Eberling was not ready to accept Marino's bleak assessment that he would never leave prison.

He disliked Marino. Marino was a bulldog, a meat-and-potatoes guy, with no flash or trappings of success. Eberling had no reason to warm up to him, and Marino had no patience for Eberling's repeated denials.

Soon thereafter, Eberling wrote: "They felt I should come clean before I met my maker—Hogwash, I said. I said that! They said they would release Obie if I confessed to Marilyn's murder. Bull crap. Told them Obie would lose his respect for me if I told such a lie."[8]

Not long after Marino's frustrating encounter with Eberling, Terry Gilbert filed a lawsuit in common pleas court, on behalf of the estate of Dr.

Sam Sheppard, seeking a declaration of innocence for the late osteopath. In 1989 Ohio lawmakers had made it easier for people who had been wrongfully imprisoned to recover lost wages and damages.

This lawsuit posed novel, untested legal issues. Did Dr. Sheppard's right to sue and collect damages survive his death? Could his estate take advantage of a law written seventeen years after his death?

If the trial court in Cuyahoga County did declare Dr. Sheppard innocent, the next step for his estate, essentially his son, was to petition the Ohio Court of Claims for compensation. The statute capped payment at $25,000 for each year of wrongful imprisonment, plus any lost wages, adjusted for inflation. Using Sam Sheppard's $30,000 income the year before the murder, his son, if successful, could possibly collect $2 million, with one third going to his lawyers.

Gilbert knew the lawsuit would antagonize the prosecutor's office. He now put Marino and prosecutor Jones in a paradoxical position. By carrying on a criminal investigation of the Sheppard murder, the prosecutors would undercut their defense against a costly civil lawsuit.

"I had no choice but to file to be able to get access to evidence," Gilbert said. The Cuyahoga County coroner had delayed or ignored his demands for access to trace evidence of the Sheppard case. "With the lawsuit and media attention, we now had a tool."

The lawsuit was assigned to the docket of Cuyahoga County Common Pleas Court judge Ronald Suster, a former Democratic state lawmaker. Like many of his less hidebound judicial colleagues, Suster was intrigued by the possibility that the more precise DNA testing could be widely used to free the innocent and convict the guilty. In February 1996 the judge ordered Cuyahoga County coroner Elizabeth Balraj to gather up and make available for DNA testing any Sheppard evidence in the coroner's vaults.

It turned out that former coroner Dr. Samuel Gerber had kept the Sheppard materials in an office safe. In 1986, after Gerber's death, some of the more intriguing items were discarded: for instance, the large, battered flashlight that washed up near the Sheppard beach the summer after the murder. Still, more than one hundred pieces of trace evidence were available for testing: hairs collected from Marilyn Sheppard's bedsheets, ten microscopic slides that preserved autopsy fingernail scrapings, slides made from a vaginal swab, a bloodstained splinter of wood cut from steps to the basement, Dr. Sam's cotton pants, hairs plucked from Marilyn's head at the autopsy, and so on.

Coroner Balraj's office could not perform sophisticated DNA tests, especially on old evidence that had been collected and handled under 1950s standards of care. She agreed to send the evidence to a respected DNA scientist in Indianapolis, Dr. Mohammad Tahir, the director of the DNA and serology laboratories at the Indianapolis–Marion County Forensic Services Agency.

Dr. Tahir is a good-natured man prone to overwork. He has a wide black mustache and large wire-rimmed glasses. He grew up in Pakistan's Punjab region on a family farm. Tahir earned a national reputation for being able to extract and type the twisted strands of genetic material in tricky cases. His research and lab protocols on saliva from envelope flaps was used by the FBI to get DNA profiles from letters connected to the terrorists who blew up the World Trade Center. Tahir had published many scholarly articles on DNA techniques and was committed to maintaining high standards in the nation's growing number of police DNA labs.

Tahir agreed to do the work for free. It was an intriguing research problem. His biggest obstacle, at first, was the lack of biological material from Dr. Sam Sheppard and Marilyn Sheppard. He might be able to retrieve some DNA from Marilyn's hair samples. He would have to try to obtain Sam's DNA from the flaps of fifty-four-year-old love letters he had written to Marilyn in college. Also, Tahir said he needed blood or saliva from inmate Eberling.

Suddenly, Gilbert, a defense lawyer, found himself in the position of prosecutor. He asked Judge Suster to compel Eberling to give blood, essentially forcing him to incriminate himself. Without alerting Eberling's lawyer, Suster gave the order, explaining, "This blood sample will go a long way toward answering a lot of questions or actually solving the case."[9]

36

LOCAL POLITICS

TERRY GILBERT USED TO HAVE a full beard and long hair. Now he was clean-shaven and balding. In his late forties, he married Robin Greenwald, who worked at a family antiques business. They moved into the house she grew up in and soon had twin boys. He still was a firebrand, and counted Bobby Seale and Russell Means as friends whom he represented. Gilbert made no secret that he was a leftist lawyer who wanted to change society. He fought by using the courtroom as a theater to present his causes. "There are times when I'm not afraid to push the bounds of propriety in the courtroom, to be outrageous," he would say. "You never know whether it's a stupid or brilliant move until you've done it."

Once, he clamped his hand over the mouth of an assistant county prosecutor because he felt the lawyer was about to reveal damaging, inadmissible information to the jury about his client's previous criminal record. "Your Honor, let the record reflect I was just assaulted by the defense," the prosecutor said. Gilbert apologized. After his client was acquitted, Gilbert defended his actions. The prosecutor, Gilbert later said, "was trying to put an innocent man in jail."[1]

In early 1996 Terry Gilbert enjoyed three developments that pushed the Sheppard case closer to a courtroom conclusion. First, DNA tests of crime-scene evidence were unfolding at Dr. Tahir's laboratory and held out a seemingly magical promise to unlock secrets of the old murder. Next, the county prosecutor's office was being reasonable, saying it would reinvestigate Marilyn Sheppard's murder. And, unexpectedly, Kathy Dyal, formerly Wagner, the former nurse's aide to the late Ethel Durkin, reached the Sheppard team and told them a startling story about Richard Eberling.

Dyal was living in Jacksonville, Florida, and had married and divorced twice since she spent late nights at the Durkin home in 1983, listening to Eberling discuss his favorite topics: the Cleveland Ballet, witchcraft, money, and sex. Dyal learned from a tabloid television show that Eberling had been convicted of murdering Durkin and was a suspect in the Sheppard case. She made a flurry of telephone calls until she reached the Sheppard team.[2]

Terry Gilbert was thrilled with Dyal's new information, and he quickly dispatched a private investigator from AMSEC to Florida to videotape the health aide's account. A month later Kathy Dyal traveled to Cleveland at her own expense and met with assistant county prosecutor David Zimmerman, who was assisting Carmen Marino.

"Describe for me Richard Eberling," Zimmerman told her.[3]

"When I knew Richard Eberling, I thought him to be attractive, cultured, worldly, educated, charming, very, very attractive to women because he knew, he knew the right things to say," Dyal said.

"Did the two of you ever date?"

No, she replied, but we talked about sex quite a bit. "He would brag to me about his conquests with females and talk to me in explicit detail about what he did to these women in a sexual manner. And for a twenty-year-old girl who is just experimenting with sex, that was extremely erotic, for lack of a better word."

Was there ever a sexual relationship between the two of you?

"No, absolutely not," she said. "But there was a lot of innuendo."

"When did he first talk about Marilyn Sheppard?" the prosecutor asked.

Wagner said that discussion unfolded while they were talking about the war movie *Apocalypse Now*. Dyal told Eberling how awful it must have been for farm boys, drafted and sent to Vietnam, to suddenly face killing and death. Eberling asked if she had ever watched anyone die. Wagner replied yes, an old woman she had cared for. The woman died in bed late one night. Dyal told Eberling she brushed the woman's hair, gave her face a touch of blusher and lipstick, then telephoned the woman's family. When the relatives arrived, Dyal said, they all hugged and cried. "It was a very peaceful and positive experience, very touching," she told him.

Eberling mocked her. "Now isn't that just sweet, Katie," he said sarcastically. Abruptly, he switched from her "touching, personal, huggy, kissy" reminiscence into a discussion of "boys from the farm in Vietnam with a bayonet cutting a gook's neck." She recalled him asking her, "Wouldn't it be exciting to cut somebody's throat and watch the life drain out of their eyes?" Eberling seemed to eroticize death.

Dyal stared at him, too surprised to answer.

Eberling asked her if she'd ever killed anyone.

She exclaimed, No! "And he said, 'Well, I did.' And I just looked at him. And he said, 'Did you ever hear of Marilyn Sheppard?' He said, 'I did her and someone else paid the bill.' And I said, 'You mean you killed her?' And he said, 'Yeah. And I knocked her husband out with a pail and . . . the bitch bit the hell out of me, but I got her ring.' "

Dyal said she just looked at Eberling, stunned, and then he told her, "Now, you didn't hear that, Katie."

Okay, she replied.

Zimmerman was taking notes and tape-recording the interview. Did you tell anyone at that time what Eberling said? he asked.

Yes, my mother, Dyal said.

What was her reaction? Zimmerman asked.

"She said, 'Don't listen to him. He's a crazy fag.' "[4]

Dyal's account of Eberling's confession was remarkably similar to Beverly Scheidler's account of how Eberling revealed that he had bludgeoned Ethel Durkin. In both cases, Eberling was flirting with a woman, hoping to cement a relationship that he could later exploit. He had been drinking. His admissions came moments after each had expressed sentimental feelings about another woman's death: Beverly Scheidler said she felt sad that Ethel Durkin died unexpectedly from a fall, then lingered pathetically; Kathy Dyal had described an older woman's death as uplifting and positive. In each case, Eberling slapped down what he seemed to feel was their naïveté about death, and informed them that death was ugly business.

————

After her interview with the prosecutor, Dyal allowed Terry Gilbert to set her up for interviews with friendly reporters. Gilbert usually did this when he secured information helpful to the lawsuit. Favorable stories appeared throughout the country. In California, Sam Reese Sheppard could not believe his good fortune; he allowed himself to hope that he might clear his father's name after all.

Richard Eberling followed these developments from prison, where he had free access to television and newspapers. He sank into depression, realizing the futility of his legal appeals and the inevitability that he would die in prison. "But by the saving grace of God it will all be over soonest," Eberling wrote. "Thank God for the hangman's noose. My so-called life on this planet will cease to be. Peace at long last. Saddest part of all, they should have let me die when I was a baby. Then there would have been no Eberlings nor Durkin and lastly Sheppard. How sad that it was to be."[5]

In the summer of 1996, Dr. Mohammad Tahir started trying to extract DNA from the bits of blood and hair, collected in 1954 at the crime scene, that had been found in a vault at the Cuyahoga County coroner's office. Since Tahir had agreed to work without a fee, he had to squeeze in his lab work before and after office hours and on weekends and holidays. He focused on what he felt might turn out to be key pieces of evidence: a blood drop lifted from a basement step, the large bloodstain on the knee of Dr. Sam's trousers, and a bloodstain from the wood floor of the back porch.

Tahir used a DNA test called polymerase chain reaction, or PCR. This test snips out the same six markers from each twisted DNA chain and amplifies them millions of times, creating a mass of DNA capable of being detected. He used this technique because he was dealing with old, degraded blood that didn't have much DNA to harvest, so he needed to amplify it. The drawback to the PCR method was that it also clipped off and amplified the six markers of any biological material that may have contaminated the evidence.

First, Tahir needed to establish the DNA "fingerprints" of Marilyn Sheppard, Sam Sheppard, and Richard Eberling. With those results in hand, he then could test the biological evidence and, if he got single-source profiles, make comparisons. Tahir told Gilbert that as a lawyer he was taking a gamble; his results might incriminate Dr. Sam Sheppard, and the Sheppard team would have to live with those results. Gilbert said he understood.

Tahir developed a likely DNA profile of Dr. Sheppard by testing envelope flaps and postage stamps from old love letters he sent to Marilyn before they were married. The richest, most promising sources of Marilyn Sheppard's DNA were the organ-tissue slides from her autopsy. Among the slides were two that Dr. Lester Adelson, the pathologist, made from a vaginal swab. Dr. Adelson had stained the slides with a red dye, which darkened the cells and highlighted their outlines, making them easier to view under a microscope. Tahir hoped the slide held enough of Marilyn Sheppard's epithelial cells to determine her DNA profile.

Looking at the vaginal slides, Tahir wondered how Adelson could have seen much of anything there. The stained cell matter was thick and opaque. Under such conditions, spotting tiny sperm cells among the relatively huge epithelial cells would be like seeing an acorn under a thick blanket of fallen leaves.

Tahir dissolved the red gunk from the slides with sterile water and went through a cell extraction, a method of sorting out the cells by size and type, sequestering the female epithelial cells into one "cell fraction" and the male sperm cells, if any could be found, into another fraction. Tahir had been told that no sperm had been seen on the slide back in 1954. He took a quick look at the male fraction under a microscope, as the testing protocol required. Tahir was shocked to see two sperm heads. He asked another scientist in the lab to view the slide, and she confirmed that she, too, saw sperm. Tahir was thrilled with this unexpected discovery. Sperm cells were hard-shelled boxes of DNA that often yielded clean profiles, even after many years.[6]

Each of the two vaginal-swab slides had a tiny bit of sperm. Tahir's test results showed mixtures of DNA for each, overlapping biological finger-prints. This indicated human contamination. Theoretically, the mix of DNA profiles in the sperm samples only excluded 2 to 5 percent of the white male population. However, the sperm on one of the slides did not come from Sam Sheppard, Tahir said.

When testing one sample of the sperm, Tahir found four different markers—1.2, 2, 3, and 4.1—at a location in the DNA chain known as DQ-Alpha. A single individual has at most two markers at this spot. Of the four markers, the 4.1 marker showed up the strongest. This suggested that some-one with a 4.1 marker may be a major DNA contributor to the sperm frac-tion. Richard Eberling had a 4.1 marker. Sam Sheppard and his wife did not. Even so, Tahir said it would be misleading to suggest that these results pointed to any one person as the murder suspect. Ninety percent or more of U.S. men, theoretically, could find their PCR profiles in the results.

Later, respected DNA expert Ed Blake attacked Tahir for overstating test results, which he said didn't make sense in the broader context of the crime. We are to believe that Marilyn Sheppard had sex with two men, neither of them her husband? Blake asked. Tahir defended himself by explaining that somehow the old evidence got contaminated, perhaps from being handled over the years. Even though the test's delicate controls indicated that he was supposed to be getting results only from the DNA of sperm, Tahir felt con-tamination had remained.

Still, finding sperm supported the theory that Marilyn Sheppard's murder was a sexual homicide, not a domestic homicide. How else to explain that sperm from someone other than Sam Sheppard was found in his wife's vagina?

———

Tahir got intriguing results from blood samples from the stairs and from the knee of Dr. Sam's trousers. It was now February 1997, and Terry Gilbert de-cided to release the favorable DNA results at a press conference. His goal was to make national news and pressure the county prosecutor to consider settling the lawsuit. A New York publicist, working pro bono, crafted a confidential, five-page public relations plan that read in part: "The DNA test results release is the moment many media outlets have been waiting for. We will never get a more definitive opportunity to tell the story of the investigation to the media and to declare victory in the long struggle to bring Sam Sheppard's innocence to light."

Gilbert's February 4 press conference was crowded. Dr. Tahir attended and answered questions about his surprising results:

The bloodstain on Dr. Sam's trousers did not contain DNA from Sam or Marilyn Sheppard. Gilbert said the stain was probably put there by the killer when he ripped a ring of keys from Dr. Sheppard's belt loop.

A drop of blood from one of the stairs contained no DNA from Sam or Marilyn Sheppard. This finding destroyed the state's theory that Marilyn's blood dripped from a murder weapon as the killer carried it out of the house.

Tahir's blockbuster finding: a vaginal smear from the victim's autopsy contained sperm from someone other than Dr. Sheppard. Taken together, the DNA results were powerful evidence that a third person had left sperm and blood at the Sheppard crime scene. Sam and Marilyn were excluded as DNA contributors to several of the items. Richard Eberling, Tahir said precisely, "could not be excluded" as a DNA contributor to the blood trail, pants stain, and sperm fraction.

———

Assistant county prosecutor Marino was impressed by Tahir's work. The new information supported Marino's view that Sheppard was the wrong suspect and that Eberling was the likely killer of Marilyn Sheppard. But Marino did not believe the new evidence was sufficient to declare Dr. Sheppard innocent. The case for innocence would be much stronger if Tahir had established Sheppard's DNA profile more conclusively. The only way left to get it, Marino said, was to dig up Sheppard's remains.

As the spring unfolded, Marino was confronted with detectives, senior prosecutors, and judges who thought he was wrongheaded to reopen the Sheppard murder. In Cleveland law enforcement circles, doubting Dr. Sam's guilt was the cultural equivalent of desecrating the United States flag.

Such concerns did not bother Marino. He was secure about his reputation and judgment. He liked the challenge of cold cases and wanted to see if the Sheppard case could be solved. Perhaps more DNA testing would shed light on the mystery. But even though he felt that Sheppard more than likely was innocent, Marino did not make it easy for Sam Reese Sheppard to pursue his lawsuit. Marino and prosecutor Jones decided that Dr. Sheppard's estate should not collect public money for a novel claim from decades earlier. "We have a duty to protect the state funds," Marino said.

A few weeks after his press conference about the DNA results, Gilbert met with Marino to discuss the investigation.

Why aren't you moving forward? Gilbert asked. Are you getting pressure?

Marino said no. His position was based on an analysis of the law. He and the prosecutor felt the statute of limitations for a wrongful-imprisonment case had long expired.

Gilbert felt Marino and Stephanie Tubbs Jones worried about political fallout in the law enforcement community, especially since Jones was aiming for higher elected office. "This case is a no-brainer on the national level," Gilbert told Marino.

"All politics is local," the prosecutor replied.

What is the FBI doing about Eberling? Gilbert asked.

A month earlier Marino had said he might ask the FBI's Behavioral Sciences Unit to analyze the crime scene and assess Eberling and Sam Sheppard as suspects. Now Marino told Gilbert that the FBI was not going to be involved. The case would have to be hashed out at a trial, with all the evidence and testimony put into the record and Judge Suster reaching a verdict.

———

I shared my research with John E. Douglas, a retired FBI supervisor and coauthor of *Crime Classification Manual; Mindhunter; Sexual Homicide: Patterns and Motives;* and other nonfiction works. An expert on criminal personality profiling, Douglas, now in his mid-fifties, had worked the Atlanta child murder case, in which a serial killer was targeting black boys. Douglas helped to steer local police from thinking that the killings were the work of white supremacists to focusing instead on the suspect profile of a single, inadequate-feeling black man in his twenties. Wayne Williams, who fit that profile, later was convicted of two murders.

Douglas had interviewed scores of imprisoned killers, many of them notorious: Charles Manson, Richard Speck, David Berkowitz. As a supervisor in the FBI's Behavioral Sciences Unit, Douglas had helped to fine-tune the inexact methods of criminal profiling and crime-scene analysis. Profiling is an art more than a science, useful as another investigative tool, like interrogation or analysis of trace evidence.

Douglas studied the Marilyn Sheppard autopsy report, the earliest police reports, crime-scene photos, and information about the home, its setting, the socioeconomics of the neighborhood, the occupations and lifestyles of Dr. Sam and Marilyn Sheppard.

Despite the limitations of criminal profiling, Douglas said that there are generally accepted rules about spousal killings. First, there had to be a reason for someone like Dr. Sam to explode into a rage. "You just don't wake up one morning and decide to become a murderer. There is always some predictive behavior," he said.[7] Nearly all men who kill their wives have assaulted them at least once in the year before the murder.[8] In half the cases, police respond to disturbances at the home. No one could find any evidence that Sam had struck his wife.[9]

In his eighteen years at the FBI Behavioral Sciences Unit, Douglas reviewed five thousand felony cases, hundreds of them classified as domestic homicides. It was typical, Douglas said, for a husband to build up rage over a day or two, then explode. His outburst would be triggered by jealousy or by being defied or abandoned through divorce or a breakup. In a domestic slaying, Douglas said, the violence escalates. A husband might grab his wife by the arm, strike her, throw objects, knock things to the floor. An investigator looks for bruised arms, signs of choking, a messy room. The Sheppard bedroom displayed no evidence of argument. In fact, the evening before the murder, Marilyn and Sam seemed affectionate. She made Sam's favorite pie, sat on his lap after dinner in front of the TV, and turned down his bedsheets later that night.

In domestic homicide, Douglas said, a fight escalates until the killer explodes in a thunderclap of rage. He might pick up an object at hand, a so-called weapon of opportunity, and fatally club, choke, or stab his spouse. His rage spent, he suddenly realizes, "Oh, my God, what have I done!" Then he stops his violence.

Most telling to Douglas, the killer left Marilyn Sheppard's body nearly nude, exposing her breasts and crotch. To cover up a domestic murder, a husband might amateurishly stage his wife's body to suggest a sex killing. He might unbutton or drape nightclothes to look suggestive, Douglas said. But a husband would not expose his wife's nipples and pubic hair for strangers to see. Douglas had never seen or heard of such an attempted cover-up. Marilyn was "in a degrading position. He would not leave her spread-eagled. Husbands don't do that."

Despite his favorable publicity and the DNA results, Gilbert felt the momentum slowing. By May 1997, prosecutor Jones was fighting the Sheppard lawsuit at every turn. Staff lawyers argued that the time in which to bring the lawsuit had expired, that the right to sue died along with Dr. Sheppard, and that Judge Suster's court was not the proper jurisdiction. On another front, Marino said a more reliable DNA profile of Dr. Sheppard was necessary to evaluate Tahir's results.

The best way to rule out Sam Sheppard from the crime-scene evidence with scientific certainty was to exhume his remains for genetic material. Sam Reese Sheppard hated the idea of digging up his father's bones. On the other hand, if he didn't give Dr. Tahir a chance to get a second, conclusive DNA profile of his father, he was leaving a weapon in prosecutors' hands as they battled his lawsuit. After an emotional struggle, Sam Reese and Gilbert decided that his father's body should be exhumed. They alerted Tahir that he would be needed for more pro bono work.

On September 17, 1997, Sam Reese, the Reverend Alan Davis, anti-death-penalty activists, and Terry Gilbert traveled to a Columbus, Ohio, cemetery before first light. Forest Lawn Memorial Gardens was ringed by seventeen television satellite trucks, looking like metallic palm trees. Some TV reporters played up the easy irony of the section where the casket lay, the "Good Shepherd" area.

There was nothing delicate about the task. That would come later in the coroner's lab. An operator on a backhoe exposed the casket with jagged scoops. Workers snaked two cables under the casket and cinched it. By 8 A.M., the casket was up and out. Sam Reese wanted to lay twenty-seven lilies—the flower of innocence—on the casket, one for each year since his father's death. He could not afford them and settled for white daisies.

"This seems almost unreal to me," Reverend Alan Davis remarked. "Twenty-seven years ago it never occurred to me that I would be back here someday taking him out of the ground. Funerals are supposed to be the end." Davis led a brief service, and the casket was put in the hearse for a trip to Cleveland. A procession of cars and vans with TV-station logos followed the hearse to the Cuyahoga County coroner's office. The hearse pulled into an underground garage and parked in a separate autopsy bay that was used for decomposed or hazardous bodies. There coroner Elizabeth Balraj collected hair, skin, teeth, parts of a femur, and a collarbone for Tahir to test.

———

At about this time, two criminalists in California made an amazing discovery. Keith Inman, an analyst with the California state crime laboratory, was looking for Sheppard materials to enliven an undergraduate criminalistics class that he cotaught with Dr. Norah Rudin, a DNA scientist and writer. In the small circle of California criminalists, Inman knew many of Paul Kirk's protégés. He had heard that one of them, John Murdock, a firearms expert, might have some old materials.

In 1970, when Kirk had died, Murdock was finishing a graduate degree in criminalistics at the University of California at Berkeley. He had been one of Kirk's teaching assistants. Shortly after Kirk's death, his office on the campus was emptied and boxes of old files were shoved into a hallway, awaiting a trip to the Dumpster. Murdock happened to notice a box marked "Sheppard murder" and rescued it. "I'm a collector," he explained. He didn't know what he would do with the materials, but he thought they were worth saving. He sealed the box with tape and for twenty-five years kept it, unopened, under his desk at the California Bureau of Crime Investigation, where he analyzed trace evidence, before retiring and moving to the federal Bureau of Alcohol, Tobacco and Firearms.

Inside the box Inman and Murdock found a small, well-labeled glass vial of dried blood from the closet door in the Sheppard bedroom. The vial held minuscule, reddish crusts—the untested remainder of the famous "unique blood spot."

"Oh, my God, do you know what this is!" Inman exclaimed. "Have you heard what's been going on with the Sheppard case?"

This brown cardboard box held evidence that I had been hunting for for several years. I had contacted Kirk's daughter, former graduate assistants of Kirk in the San Francisco area such as Chuck Morton and John Thornton, archivists at the University of California at Berkeley, and others. None knew of the existence of what quickly became known as "the Murdock box."

It was an amazing piece of luck that Murdock, on a whim, had saved this evidence from oblivion a third of a century earlier. Even before it dried, this thick, one-inch bloodstain on Marilyn Sheppard's closet door was the most probative piece of evidence in the case. It was unlike any other blood on the scene. Kirk had argued that it did not come from Marilyn Sheppard. Now it showed up at a time when DNA technology could perhaps solve a world-famous murder mystery.

Murdock counted as a friend Dr. Ed Blake, one of the country's top DNA scientists, who also lived and worked in the Bay Area. In the small world of DNA experts, where technique and problem-solving skills are important, Blake was known as one of the best to hire for a tricky job. He felt that he, not Tahir, should be the one to test the closet stain. Terry Gilbert, however, learned of the Murdock box and quickly subpoenaed its materials. Blake, who had a reputation for being arrogant and difficult, previously had clashed with Gilbert on a criminal case. Gilbert trusted Tahir to test the closet stain.

It was uncertain whether a private party in a civil lawsuit could compel

Murdock and Blake to turn over abandoned, historic materials. Rather than wage a legal battle, Blake designed a protocol for testing the old blood and volunteered to work with Tahir. If enough genetic material remained in the closet stain, Blake suggested using short tandem repeat, or STR, a testing method just coming into wider use. An STR profile was millions of times more discriminating than a PCR profile. While a person's DQ-Alpha poly-marker profile might be shared by one person in ten thousand, his STR pro-file was one in billions, a unique biological fingerprint (unless he happened to have an identical twin). Furthermore, even a contaminated sample—a mixture of DNA from two persons—yielded an STR profile that could ex-clude more than 99.9 percent of the population as donors. If, for example, Richard Eberling's profile showed up in the closet-stain mixture, it would be the scientific equivalent of slamming a gavel on a courtroom bench and say-ing, "Case closed."

Blake and Murdock shipped the evidence to Ohio.

Unfortunately, Tahir's lab in Indianapolis was not yet set up to perform the newer STR tests. Instead, he ran the far less discriminating DQ-Alpha polymarker tests.

Even so, the results helped the Sheppard cause immensely. The closet stain, a mixture of two persons' DNA, was unlike all the previous DNA evi-dence. It was possible for all the markers in this stain to be explained by two persons connected with the case: Marilyn Sheppard and Richard Eberling. It was reasonable to assume that Marilyn Sheppard's blood might be under-neath this one-inch blood blot because surrounding it on the door were scores of her blood spatters. If you subtracted her DNA profile from the mix-ture, you were left with a single DNA profile that occurred in one out of forty-two persons. Richard Eberling shared that DNA profile.

————

There was a chance that Gilbert and Sam Reese Sheppard would not be able to present this evidence in trial court. Prosecutor Jones was fighting the case on legal grounds to the Ohio Supreme Court. Her appellate assis-tants filed a writ of prohibition, a little-used legal remedy, asking the Ohio Supreme Court to tell Judge Suster that he was abusing his judicial func-tion by moving forward with the case. The county's appellate lawyers also made the novel "public policy" argument that defending such cases is too costly and difficult for the government, since witnesses have died and evi-dence is lost.

Gilbert felt he needed more public support for his side. On March 5, 1998, he released Tahir's latest DNA findings at a huge press conference in a public auditorium in the Justice Center. His publicist did an effective job. CNN covered the event live. The DNA findings were featured on National Public Radio, the *Today* show, in *The New York Times,* and in hundreds of newspapers. "We now have, in 1998, conclusive evidence that Dr. Sheppard did not kill his wife," Gilbert said to a worldwide audience that afternoon. "In spite of the fact that he was acquitted in a second trial, this community has never owned up to the possibility that a terrible injustice occurred. And even till this day, the fact that we've uncovered all this evidence, which you know about and which we're going to talk about in a minute, there are still people out there who refuse to reconsider their mind-set about this case."

Eight stories above, the county prosecutor was furious. Jones felt disrespected on her own turf. She didn't like being attacked publicly, especially in the middle of a tough Democratic primary race for an open U.S. congressional seat.

At the conference, Gilbert touted the results beyond what Tahir was willing to say. He mentioned Tahir's test of a blood drop on the Sheppards' screened porch. It was a single profile that matched Eberling's. But the PCR test kit's internal control failed, and Tahir had to call this result "inconclusive." As a scientist, Tahir could not state that he had 100 percent confidence in this result. "Dr. Tahir did see the DNA of Richard Eberling's—solely of Richard Eberling's type in the porch stain," Gilbert said, however. "If he were to call that, the frequency would be somewhere in the neighborhood of one out of six or seven thousand people."

Dr. Sam Sheppard is excluded from crime-scene evidence, Gilbert said, but "Richard Eberling cannot be removed from the equation time and time and time again." Eberling's incriminating admissions and his previous murder conviction create "a great deal of suspicion, if not strong evidence, against him. And when you view all that together with the DNA, it presents the kind of compelling case that people are prosecuted for and even put on Death Row every day in American courts." After the press conference, Tahir told me privately that he had seen "people get convicted with this kind of evidence all the time."

———

In late June 1998 Richard Eberling called me from prison. He was sick, unable to walk because of advanced diabetes, and was having allergic reactions to his ever-changing fistful of daily medications. The Sheppard case was killing him, he said. He had to get something out of his mind.

This was a new attitude. Usually, Eberling did not volunteer that the Sheppard murder bothered him. In fact, he avoided bringing up murder altogether. "I've unloaded all the Sheppard material out of my mind," he said. He had told all to another inmate, Robert Parks.

"Why don't you just unload it to me?"

"I don't know. But I had to get the monkey off my back."

I could hear Parks in the background, coaching him. What was going on? Earlier, I made arrangements with Eberling to get on his visitors' list so I could avoid prison red tape and see him more quickly, as an acquaintance rather than as a journalist. The drawback to a speedy visit was that I would not be able to bring a notebook or recorder into the prison hospital at Orient Correctional Institute, ten miles southeast of Columbus.

I met him at the hospital in July. He was in terrible shape, unable to walk, and rolled himself out in a wheelchair. In addition to the diabetes, he had pulmonary disease and kidney and liver problems from lithium and other drugs he took. He had scabs on his forehead. (I later learned from a friend of Eberling's in prison that he had been badly beaten after arranging for sex with another inmate, who brought along several other prisoners, and Eberling ended up getting gang-banged.) He told me he felt like he was going to die soon and had written out answers to everything I wanted to know but those papers had been stolen.

At the time, I was not on a daily deadline, and had the luxury of slowly picking Eberling's brain while trying to understand him. I had not done a final, possibly confrontational, interview. That day he made some tantalizing admissions that supported his guilt. I needed to return soon with a recorder and a notebook, which meant I needed to make arrangements to visit as a journalist. Before I could return to Orient prison later that July, Eberling had a heart attack.

In the early hours of July 25, 1998, Eberling went into cardiac arrest and was taken by ambulance to the Ohio State University Hospital emergency room. He was dead on arrival. The Franklin County coroner performed an autopsy and found that Eberling's blood was loaded with drugs: therapeutic levels of Elavil, Pamelor, Zoloft, and Atarax, and a toxic level of Benadryl. He ruled that Eberling died of natural causes, primarily a myocardial infarction in his left ventricle.

Assistant Cuyahoga County prosecutor Zimmerman, at Marino's direction, obtained a warrant from a Franklin County judge to search Eberling's cell. The affidavit said the prosecutor needed evidence as part of an investigation into the 1954 murder of Marilyn Sheppard. Zimmerman left the prison with several boxes of letters and files from Eberling's cell and locker. Technically, the Sheppard murder had been reopened.

On December 1998, by a 4-to-3 vote, the state supreme court denied the Cuyahoga County prosecutor's request to dismiss the suit. Sam Reese Sheppard had been wrong; a trial would go forward. Gilbert, elated, told reporters he was willing to settle the lawsuit. All he needed was an apology, a declaration of innocence, payments for Sam Reese's suffering, and his legal fees. Called for comment, prosecutor Stephanie Tubbs Jones replied: "Settlement? No, sir. Absolutely not! They have to prove their case."

Jones, however, was a lame duck. A few weeks earlier she had easily won election to Congress. Her successor was to be selected by the local Democratic party. Gilbert hoped the new county prosecutor would be less combative and perhaps willing to settle.

Some of the county's top criminal lawyers clamored to replace Jones, among them Carmen Marino and another senior trial lawyer in the prosecutor's office, Steven Dever. Also politicking for the job was Kevin Spellacy, son of Judge Leo Spellacy, who had prosecuted Dr. Sheppard in the 1966 trial. These skilled lawyers were outworked and outmaneuvered by William D. Mason, a young law director from the large, working-class suburb of Parma. When it was clear that Mason was going to win, Dever threw in with his future boss and Marino dropped his bid. Bill Mason would decide whether or not to settle the Sheppard lawsuit.

Mason was not a Terry Gilbert fan. A couple of years earlier the two men had tangled over a defendant charged with criminal trespass and obstructing the Parma police. Mason, as law director, ended up being called to the stand, and Gilbert put him through a tough cross-examination. "He paints with a broad brush and is very brazen in his approach," Mason later would say. "Everybody is always wrong or lying. He challenges you every step of the way as if you're a villain."[10]

In his first week in office, Mason said he began reading a tall stack of Sheppard materials. He wanted to get up to speed on the high-profile case and make a decision about what to do. After reading the transcript from the first trial and other documents, he concluded that Sam Sheppard more than likely killed his wife. Mason said it was an easy decision to make. Unlike Jones, who argued that Gilbert had not proven his case yet, Mason took a more aggressive stance: Dr. Sam was the likely killer.

Mason ended up making a one-sided evaluation of the case. He did not talk to Carmen Marino, a veteran of cold cases. Nor was he able to read the transcript of the 1966 trial, which had acquitted Sheppard. Mason did not at that time look at the DNA work of Tahir, a police crime-lab director who testified for the prosecution 95 percent of the time. Nor was Mason able to review the hundreds of pages of police reports and witness statements in the Sheppard-trial file of former prosecutor John T. Corrigan because that file could not be found.

Mason admitted there were political and personal reasons for his hard line. He was offended that Gilbert had attacked the prosecutor's office, Judge Spellacy, retired prosecutor Corrigan, coroner Gerber, and others. "Terry has impugned the integrity of a lot of people with their assertions that everything went bad here," Mason said. "He really really attacked the integrity of people, long before I was involved. For me to settle would have put a stain on their careers that they didn't deserve." He based his decision on more than just the merits of the case. "How could I look Kevin Spellacy in the eye?" Mason wondered.

Mason was a confident, ambitious politician who had never been in charge of a murder trial. He had worked for four years as an assistant county prosecutor under John T. Corrigan, then rapidly climbed the ranks of Democratic circles with hard work and social skills that he developed as one of sixteen children, growing up in a less-than-spacious home. Mason, the tenth child, had eight brothers. All of the boys were accomplished scholastic wrestlers. "In wrestling, as in law or politics, it's a one-on-one battle," Mason says. "You win or lose. You need total preparation. Wrestling helps you develop a confidence. Wrestling created an attitude in me that whatever you do, you do to win. You give it all."

Mason decided to try the case himself. On the one hand, trying a high-profile case would give him free, widespread exposure in the local news media and help him build the name recognition necessary to win the popular vote when he ran in the primary election the next spring. But he also faced a risk. He might lose the case and have to shoulder blame.

Mason assigned Steve Dever as his cocounsel on the case, a smart move. Dever possessed trial experience that Mason, as chief executive of a two-hundred-employee law firm, would never be able to develop as county prosecutor. In the past decade Dever had tried more murder cases than any of his colleagues. He was known for his skillful cross-examinations and smooth, compelling closing arguments. It was no secret that he would be designing the state's defense against the Sheppard suit.

Dever and Mason agreed on certain lines of attack. They believed their side would be better served trying the case in front of jurors, not before Judge Suster, who appeared open-minded about Dr. Sheppard's guilt or innocence. Dever knew he had to undercut the other side's strongest evidence: its DNA results. Further, the prosecution had to come up with a motive to explain why Dr. Sheppard would kill his wife. It was not required to have a motive, but jurors liked feeling they knew why a murder occurred. It was lack of a motive that had caused Carmen Marino to doubt that Sam Sheppard was the murderer.

That spring prosecutors contacted Dr. Mitchell Holland, a DNA scientist with the U.S. Department of Defense. Holland was known for his pioneering identification work, such as determining, through elaborate DNA tests, that Anastasia, daughter of Czar Nicholas II, had died with her family, debunking a theory that she had escaped to Europe.

Dever wanted to know if Holland could test Marilyn Sheppard's fetus. If Sam was not the father, then the state could argue that Sam and Marilyn got into a fight over his womanizing, that she reacted by throwing in his face the fact that he wasn't the father of her baby, and then he exploded in murderous fury. It was the same motive that Dr. Gerber and the Cleveland police had pursued hours after the 1954 murder. Now technology might be able to provide an answer.

Holland said he and his lab would certainly be willing to test the DNA of the Sheppard fetus to determine its father. But first the fetus would have to be dug up.

The prosecutor concealed this strategy for as long as possible. In the summer Mason made it known that he wanted to exhume Marilyn Sheppard's remains. Publicly, he said the idea was to take a second look at Marilyn Sheppard's broken teeth and her wounds, hoping to find trace evidence. He didn't say a word about the fetus, which was the true prize.

OPENING

THE BODY OF Marilyn Sheppard was exhumed in late October. Even though Mason and Dever could have done so without Sam Reese's permission, they asked and he gave it, reluctantly. He wanted to avoid being put in the public position of having something to hide. Sam Reese planned to be there and prepared himself for the grisly event by taping up a photo in his studio apartment of the skeletal remains of a mountain climber who succumbed in the Himalayas.

One of the finer ironies of Trial Three, as it would be known, was that Dr. Tahir was training coroner Balraj's staff in the latest DNA techniques and making certain its new DNA laboratory met national accreditation standards. Tahir, the Sheppard expert whom the prosecutors planned on carving up at trial, was training the people poised to damage the Sheppard side if the fetus turned out to be fathered by someone other than Dr. Sam.

The early-morning exhumation at Cleveland's Knollwood Cemetery was tense. Close to the dig, Sam Reese, his lawyer, prosecutors, and coroner's staffers wore paper slippers and masks to contain contamination. When the deteriorated bronze casket was lifted from the mausoleum, its bottom began to fall away and workers quickly slid a pallet under it to keep the remains from tumbling out. Later, forensic experts hired by both sides gathered at the new county coroner's building to examine the disinterred corpse. Parts of its bones were selected for testing.

Both sides held press conferences to spin the day's events to their own purposes. Gilbert had press kits about his trial experts, including Dr. Cyril Wecht, the famous Pittsburgh pathologist and lawyer who worked as an expert on the O. J. Simpson case and the autopsy of Mary Jo Kopechne, the young woman who drowned after Senator Ted Kennedy drove them off a bridge at Chappaquiddick.

Mason jumped out first. He presented Dr. Lowell Levine, a forensic dentist with the New York state crime lab, who looked at the body's teeth and jaw. Marilyn Sheppard's teeth were not broken from biting her killer. "It just didn't happen," he said. Mason trumpeted this as a knockout blow to the Sheppard side's theory that the blood trail came from a flowing wound. Of course, Levine's position did not rule out whether Marilyn Sheppard first bit her killer, who then knocked her teeth out in a rage.

—————

For the past few years Gilbert had used the news media to present his version of the evidence to the public. Mason was just as relentless about trying his case in the newspapers. "We're not going to lie down and let them rewrite history," Mason said. He posted press releases and hosted news conferences, relying on staffers as well as a commercial Web site and a county government site. Mason came across well on camera, cool and controlled.

In the second half of 1999 Mason used his publicity machine to try to convince the public that Sheppard was guilty, releasing piece by piece the building blocks of the state's case. With nothing new to reveal until the start of the trial, set for January 31, 2000, Gilbert could only counterpunch.

In November, for example, Mason touted what he called "a confession" from Dr. Sam Sheppard. Mason said Sam Sheppard had autographed a copy of his book, *Endure and Conquer*, for a woman who worked at a Columbus beauty salon. On one of the first pages, in large type, was the question, "Did Sam Do It?" Underneath, Mason said, Dr. Sheppard wrote the word "Yes."

What Mason did not mention was that the "Yes" was closer to another sentence: "Even the most anti-Sheppard readers will find some doubt." To a neutral observer, it was unclear to which sentiment Dr. Sheppard was saying "Yes." That would be up to the jury to figure out.

—————

Mason was the public face of the state's effort, but Steve Dever put together the elements of a take-no-prisoners defense. He used several assistant county prosecutors, two homicide detectives on loan from the Cleveland Police Department, even a private detective in California to track down Susan Hayes, who had changed her name a couple of times through marriage and was hard to find. It was an impressive sweep of information, building on the files that assistant prosecutor David Zimmerman had assembled.

In late November, to my surprise, the prosecutor subpoenaed all my research. They wanted notes, interviews, drafts of my manuscript, documents, photos, essentially all the Sheppard material I had been collecting for years. It was a fishing expedition, as Dever later admitted to Gilbert. He and Mason hoped to find something in my research that would help the state defeat the Sheppard side. This outrageous request quickly infuriated the news media's First Amendment groups. In effect, a journalist was being conscripted as a private investigator by the government in a civil lawsuit over monetary damages. *Editor & Publisher,* the newspaper industry's weekly trade magazine, called it "legal bullying" and "an outrageous assault" on First Amendment rights.

Even so, Ohio law shielding journalists from government subpoena was weak—it protected only the identities of confidential sources. I was afraid that my years of work so far might become part of the public record through the discovery process. A quick hack with a contract for an instant paperback on the Sheppard murder could exploit my work, destroying my livelihood.

David Marburger, a highly respected First Amendment lawyer at Baker & Hostetler, fought the subpoena, knocking it out on technical grounds. The state sent another subpoena, and Marburger stopped it again on a technicality, all the while trying to jawbone Mason and Dever to our position. They told Marburger they really only wanted missing exhibits or physical evidence from the earlier trials, but I didn't have that material and he told them so.

Instead, I was told by the prosecutor's office that unless I voluntarily accepted a subpoena I would be put on the prosecutors' witness list, thereby keeping me out of the courtroom. In effect, I was being punished for asserting my legal rights. Being closed out of the courtroom would hurt my reporting considerably. In January, on the third attempt, the state hit me with a subpoena that stuck.

Dever and Mason could have gotten almost all of the information they said they needed by talking to the same people I had talked to. They did not care much for the argument that making a journalist their indentured detective threatened the independence of the news media. Would people talk to journalists in confidence if they knew that a lawyer with a subpoena in a civil lawsuit could obtain those notes and tapes?

On the other hand, I did have copies of old police records that had been thrown out a quarter century ago. These records were not the product of my own reporting. I was torn between a strict interpretation of journalistic privilege and the feeling that history might be better served if the old police reports were available to both sides at this historic moment. These homicide-unit files should never have been thrown out in the first place, since the Sheppard murder was an open case.

Now, just before the trial, I was willing to give each side the opportunity to copy the police reports I had. But I refused to give up my reporting and writing. Dever insisted on getting it all and refused to drop the subpoena. Our battle went on.

About this time, I learned that the county coroner's office obtained a DNA profile for the Sheppard fetus, a single-source profile that showed with 99.99 percent certainty that Dr. Sam was the father of the four-month-old fetus. Unfortunately, its organs had been removed in 1954—no records were kept of this unusual procedure—and the fetus was buried in a jar of formalin. The DNA technician did not have enough leftover genetic material to repeat the DNA test and get the same result twice, as Tahir recommended. So coroner Balraj and prosecutor Mason were able to tell reporters that the DNA tests of the fetus were inconclusive, that Sam Sheppard could not be said to be the father. Later, when faced by more informed reporters, Dr. Balraj admitted that Sam was in all probability the father. The state now had to abandon its "unfaithful Marilyn" theory and settle on a replacement.

In the last week of January 2000, jury selection began in *Estate of Samuel H. Sheppard* v. *State of Ohio*. At about this time, I was able to review again the vast piles of discovery materials that had surfaced in this lawsuit. This time I was struck by an entry in the list of more than one hundred items of possible evidence that the Cuyahoga County coroner had turned over to Dr. Mohammad Tahir for testing: the fingernail scrapings of Marilyn Sheppard. In 1954 trace-evidence specialist Mary Cowan had preserved the larger bits of fiber and foreign material from the scrapings and sandwiched them between microscopic slides, one for each finger. There were also slides preserving two hairs that were found wrapped around Marilyn Sheppard's left ring finger, the finger with the torn nail. The popular but still unproved theory was that she scratched her attacker, tearing off a fingernail. If the tangled hairs had roots, they might contain enough DNA to get a result, perhaps even a result that might shed light on the Sheppard mystery.

Separately, I pressed both Terry Gilbert and Steve Dever to test the hair and nail scrapings.

"I've got my case all worked up," Gilbert said, uneasily. He believed he had DNA results that were strong enough to win. It went unsaid that there was the possibility that testing the scrapings, rather than implicating Eberling, might turn up a profile that matched or included Sam Sheppard's DNA.

I made the same request, several times, to Steve Dever.

He dismissed the idea. He had the state's case well prepared, and it relied heavily on attacking Tahir's DNA work. "Why don't you ask Dr. Tahir why he didn't test it?" he said.

I had done that already. Tahir did not recall looking at fingernail scrapings from the coroner's office. That was why it was important to examine this evidence now.

Dever had other things to worry about and didn't want to hear about it. I put in a request in writing to the county prosecutor.

The reactions of Gilbert and Dever to the idea of testing the fingernail scrapings reflected what a prominent law school dean once described as "the indifference to truth that all advocacy entails."[1] The body of Sheppard evidence was nuanced and complex, scattered along a spectrum of reliability. Lawyers from each side selected the sharpest, strongest, most compelling pieces to build their cases. Each insisted that he was on a "search for the truth." Such pronouncements sounded good in the news media but were intellectually dishonest. As courtroom advocates, each presented his best argument. Each wanted to win, to destroy the other side, not to present the most likely scenario of what happened, with nuances and ambiguities in plain sight.

In the midst of preparing for opening statements, Gilbert wrote letters to a couple of A-list actors who had portrayed wrongfully convicted heroes in recent movies: Harrison Ford in *The Fugitive* and Denzel Washington in *Hurricane*. Gilbert told them about the Sheppard lawsuit and offered to pay their way to Cleveland if they would be willing to visit Judge Suster's courtroom "in a show of support for the cause of justice for the wrongfully imprisoned." Gilbert hoped the popular movie stars could generate sympathy for the Sheppard cause among the news media and the jury. Neither actor replied.

Then Judge Suster dealt a blow to the Sheppard side. He ruled that Gilbert, in his opening statement, could not mention Richard Eberling and his connection to the suspicious deaths surrounding his life, such as the murder of Ethel Durkin or her sister Myrtle Fray. There first had to be evidence that showed a connection between Eberling and the murders of Marilyn Sheppard, Durkin, and Myrtle Fray. Gilbert was stunned. The ruling "seems to be taking the whole gut out of our case," he said to Suster.

Outside the courtroom, he backtracked: "I mean it would gut the ability for us to put the case in context." Mason was pleased. He said Suster's ruling certainly simplified his life and the prosecution's case.

The twentieth floor of the Justice Center holds four courtrooms, two on either side of a wide hallway that ends at a foyer, where tall windows offer a sweeping view of Lake Erie and downtown Cleveland. It was here that several television and radio stations set up gear to monitor the remote feeds from the courtroom action, courtesy of Court TV.

Judge Ronald Suster's courtroom was about twenty-five yards away, a quiet, carpeted room with wood paneling, muffling acoustics, and indirect lighting. Today it was about half filled with reporters; Sheppard relatives occupied several more seats; the public took up the remainder.

Suster was a large man with tousled hair and a round, sometimes florid face. Even in suits he looked a bit rumpled. He had built his political career as a moderate Democrat in Euclid, an older blue-collar suburb on Lake Erie. Three months earlier he had lost his race for the Ohio Supreme Court and now found himself focused on this unprecedented case. He wanted the parties to reach a last-minute settlement and had urged each side to negotiate in good faith. He settled nearly all of his civil trials.

Mason said he was not going to bid against himself; the Sheppard side first had to say what it wanted. Gilbert sent him a proposal asking for $3.2 million. Mason had no intention of settling for anything above nuisance value and "some flowery language."[2] He felt his side was going to win.

———

On February 14, the day of opening statements, Terry Gilbert wore a favorite suit. It was a bit roomy. He had lost weight from the high-stress, low-sleep life of almost single-handedly preparing for the trial of his career. He was backed up by George Carr, just a year out of law school, who had volunteered to work for free. Carr had the stamina of youth. Throughout the trial he would keep up his Wednesday-night gigs, playing jazz trombone in a swing band. He worked hard and efficiently but was not an experienced litigator.

Gilbert's partner, Gordon Friedman, was helpful, putting in a half day a week on the Sheppard case. He could spare no more because he had to keep Friedman & Gilbert running and bring in fees while his partner jousted with the state with no guarantee of getting paid.

Mason had a huge staff and had committed vast resources to winning the Sheppard trial, eventually spending more than $100,000 on expert witnesses and travel alone. Mason and Dever were joined by assistant prosecutor Dean Boland and Kathleen Martin, a relentless, single-minded civil litigator who stymied Gilbert with motions about evidence and procedure every step of the way. The Cleveland Police Department also loaned him two top homicide detectives, Bob Matuszny and Tim O'Malley, whose father had worked the original 1954 case as a Cleveland detective.

Gilbert had help from his wife, Robin Greenwald, who took time off from work at her family's antiques store. She backgrounded the state's expert witnesses at the public library and attended the trial each day. She sat in the front row, just behind Sam Reese and her husband. As the trial unfolded, she passed him notes with suggested questions as the witnesses testified.

———

Moments into his opening statement, Gilbert laid out the elements that Bailey had worked so successfully in the 1966 retrial. "Dr. Sheppard was a victim of this crime, too. He was attacked, beaten, unconscious." And Dr. Sheppard was not covered in blood.[3]

He gave the jurors a suspect. "Richard Eberling had motive, opportunity and he confessed. He may be the killer of Marilyn Sheppard."

Tender family pictures of Sam, Marilyn, and Chip were projected on a screen while Gilbert described their marriage. "They had a solid relationship. They were best friends. Their marriage was not perfect, but whose is?"

He moved to Sam Reese, sitting at the trial table, and introduced him. Gilbert had convinced his client to wear a suit and tie throughout the trial, but with his shaved skull, earring, and nervous, birdlike head movements, Sam Reese did not come off as a typical Clevelander. "After he was tucked in by his mother and kissed good night, he awoke to a living nightmare that continues to this day."

Gilbert sounded the themes he planned to prove: "Marilyn was brutally tortured and beaten. Somehow someone got inside the tranquillity of the house. . . . The case was twisted and turned and distorted by forces of power in the community. . . . From day one there was only one suspect in mind." Gilbert mentioned Dr. Sheppard's affair with Susan Hayes, soft-pedaling it before the state could bring it up.

Dr. Sam was convicted, Gilbert went on, and "he did hard, hard time." After he won a new trial and was acquitted, "he was labeled a killer who beat the rap. He literally died a broken man. This is the product of wrongful imprisonment."

He began a smooth, detailed narrative. Sam and Marilyn were happy. They had friends over for dinner that night. Afterward, while watching TV, she sat in his lap. Gilbert gave Sheppard's account of being knocked out twice, waking up on the beach, calling a neighbor. He was in shock, suffering serious injuries, and "police allowed him to be taken to the hospital."

Gilbert brought out a chart listing twenty-three of Sheppard's interviews with authorities. He was not hiding from police. There was a blood trail, but "he had no open wounds, no bleeding wounds that leave a blood trail. . . .

Basically what they did was work backwards, picking and choosing to fit the theory. There was never an investigation of it as a sexually motivated crime." He mentioned the coroner's theory of the bloody imprint of a surgical instrument on Marilyn's pillow. "That false claim was enough to convict him alone.

"This is not about prosecuting anyone," he went on. "We don't profess to have all the answers. It is very difficult to solve a 45-year-old case." He looked to his client. "Sam Reese Sheppard could have walked away from this. He tried that for thirty-five years." Then from prison, a convicted murderer, Richard Eberling, reached out to Sam Reese after learning that he was speaking publicly, protesting the death penalty. Eberling "was obsessed with talking about this murder." The more Eberling talked, the more he raised suspicions, Gilbert said. "The inmate gave conflicting versions of where he was that night. He had a half-inch scar on his left wrist that could have come from the murder. He confessed to a coworker that he killed Marilyn Sheppard. We turned over what we had, a compelling case, to the prosecutor. It was up to the prosecutors to pursue an investigation. It didn't happen, so this case was filed."

The judge ordered old crime-scene evidence to be DNA-tested, Gilbert said. Results clearly show there was the blood and sperm of a third party at the crime scene. The blood of Marilyn and Sam were not part of the trail. Blood tests of a large spot on a bedroom closet door are likely a mixture of the blood of Marilyn and Richard Eberling.

Gilbert named one of his top experts: Dr. Emanuel Tanay, a psychiatrist who would say the crime was not a domestic homicide. The killer sought sexual gratification. "There is nothing in the life of Dr. Sheppard or Mrs. Sheppard that would point to motive," Gilbert said. "To torture his pregnant wife to death while his seven-year-old son was down the hall. It's mind-boggling."

He looked at the jurors, hoping that he had connected. "Sometimes things go very very very wrong. Lives are ruined. Only you can correct this injustice."

38

EXPERTS

BILL MASON TOOK the first half of the state's opening. He did not seem as comfortable as Gilbert. He faced the jurors, then rolled a sheaf of papers into a tube. "What kind of a man would strike her violently twenty-seven times?" he asked. He slowly slapped the tube on the open palm of his other hand, counting, "One . . . two . . . three . . . four . . ." Mason went on until he reached twenty-seven. Several jurors looked away, embarrassed. "Is it a burglar or an enraged husband? That is the question before you."

Mason quickly moved to Sam Sheppard's infidelity. "You will hear evidence that their marriage was a powder keg of emotion. She expected fidelity, security, stability from her spouse. She wanted compatibility. She received rejection, betrayal, uncertainty, disrespect."

Mason gave his version of what police found at the crime scene. The fingerprint man "dusted the obvious places for fingerprints and didn't find them." Dr. Sheppard's thumbprint was found on the headboard of Marilyn's bed. "Maybe they missed it when they wiped it down," Mason said.

He presented a new theory: that Marilyn was motionless during the fatal beating but blood lines on the sheets indicated that her body had been dragged after she died. The medical bag was deliberately displayed. Sam Sheppard staged this crime to make it look like a sexual assault because "there was no injury to her vaginal area and breasts."

And, Mason told the jurors, you will hear about the dog, Koke, that she didn't bark, making it "maybe the silent witness."

Steven Dever, chief trial counsel for the prosecutor's office, took over. He was taller, softer-looking than Mason, at ease in the center of the courtroom.

Within moments, he presented a bold new theory: "There was no evidence of an obvious blood trail." Blood drops from an open, flowing wound had to be larger than a quarter of an inch, he said, and the drops that detectives found were not.

The trail of blood was one of the strongest pieces of evidence for the Sheppard side, especially since DNA tests showed that it was neither Sam nor Marilyn Sheppard's blood. Dever had no choice but to discount it.

Since Sam Sheppard's injuries supported his innocence, Dever attempted to diminish them by borrowing the prosecution's argument in the 1966 trial: Sheppard was injured by Marilyn as she fought for her life.

Dever battered Sheppard's character, asserting that from 1966 to 1970, his life "was occupied by drugs and alcohol." In 1954, both Sam and Marilyn talked about divorce. Sheppard claimed that his wife "couldn't satisfy him," Dever told the jury. "You're going to learn the dynamics of 1954. She had it up to *here* in 1954 with Sam. Then things went wrong that weekend."

It was a replay of the prosecution's successful strategy in 1954.

F. Lee Bailey was Gilbert's first important witness. He was stepping onto the Sheppard stage, again, at a low point in his life. Two weeks earlier, his ninety-year-old mother, a retired teacher, had died. Bailey's wife had died three months before that. He was sixty-six, with his best work behind him. He had tremors in his hands and needed both of them to steady a full cup of coffee before taking a sip on the witness stand. The Florida bar wanted to take away his law license permanently, saying that he had misappropriated $3.5 million from a criminal client. Federal prosecutors said the money belonged to the U.S. government, but Bailey refused to turn it over and spent forty-three days in a federal lockup for contempt of court. Finally, he relinquished any claim to the money and was released.

Under Gilbert's questioning, Bailey outlined evidence he said proved that Sam Sheppard was not guilty, in particular, "This man was so badly injured, somebody else had to be there."

Dever, a skilled cross-examiner, set out to rough up Bailey, but Bailey got the better of it. Dever honed in on Bailey's evaluation and rejection of Eberling as a suspect.

Bailey said that he and his investigator evaluated several suspects. "My view of the murder was not cut in stone," Bailey said. Eberling was rejected because "I thought he passed a good polygraph test."

Dever maneuvered Bailey into providing a perfect sound bite for the prosecution. "I did not form an impression that Richard Eberling killed Marilyn Sheppard," Bailey said.

But Dever had done what lawyers call "opening the door." Bailey had testified about polygraph results. Gilbert could now bring up Eberling's polygraph tests, something he was not allowed, under the rules, to do on direct examination.

Late in the afternoon Gilbert got his chance. He picked up the 1989 Lakewood police report that described expert Len Harrelson's analysis of Eberling's polygraph charts from 1959.

Did you know that an independent polygraph expert had said that "Eberling either murdered Marilyn Sheppard or had knowledge of who did?" Gilbert asked Bailey.

Dever objected, but the judge overruled it.

Bailey answered no.

Gilbert showed him a copy of Harrelson's findings.

Gilbert had not found out whether Len Harrelson was truly an expert or just one of the myriad unqualified polygraph examiners. Lawyers are not supposed to ask a question when they don't know the answer, but Gilbert took a leap.

Have you heard of Len Harrelson, the man who reevaluated the charts?

Yes, Bailey said. Len Harrelson was one of the best, most respected polygraph experts in the country.

"If you knew in 1966 what you know now about Richard Eberling, would that change your opinion about who killed Marilyn Sheppard?" Gilbert asked.

"I would probably have presented Eberling as a suspect, not as a witness," Bailey said.

Afterward, Gilbert practically floated out of the courthouse. In the hallway, he said excitedly, "I got it in! I got in the lie detector test!"

The next morning Gilbert began presenting the fiction that the Sheppards' marriage was untroubled. Mims Adler, the wife of a Bay View doctor, testified by video deposition. "They had shared a life from the time they were teenagers," said Adler, now in her seventies. "He was just very warm, a wonderful athlete. He had a great capacity for pleasure. He was comfortable in his own skin." Adler said they both were thrilled about Marilyn's pregnancy, Sam in particular.

But it was not an ideal marriage. On cross-examination, Adler described a Halloween party at Bay View Hospital where Sam danced at length with Susan Hayes while Marilyn watched. Hayes's fiancé, Dr. Robert Stevenson, was also there and didn't seem to mind, Adler said. "Marilyn didn't seem too upset, either." Instead, Marilyn pointed to Sam and said, "There's the play-boy of the Western world."

———

Gilbert lined up an impressive expert to discuss Sam Sheppard's injuries: Dr. William F. Fallon Jr., director of trauma care at the MetroHealth Medical Center, the city's huge public teaching hospital. He also taught at Case Western Reserve University medical school and was an expert on blunt trauma.

Dr. Fallon testified that Sam Sheppard's injuries were serious and "almost impossible to self-inflict." From reviewing the medical records, Dr. Fallon said it was his opinion that Sam Sheppard had been in shock on July 4, disoriented from blows to his head and from hypothermia caused by his immersion in cold lake waters. Dr. Fallon said he read reports about two sets of X rays of Sam Sheppard—an initial quick screening on July 4 and a more definitive study two days later. The first X rays showed a chip fracture at the second vertebra, and bridging, or "hypertrophic change," between the fifth and sixth vertebrae. Bridging meant that bone spurs had grown from the facing surfaces of the C-5 and C-6 vertebrae and were touching, a condition caused by arthritis or repeated pounding from sports such as football. Overall, Dr. Fallon said, Sheppard had "possibly life-threatening injuries" on early July 4, 1954.

Steve Dever had designed a deviously clever line of attack on the seriousness of Sam Sheppard's injuries.

First, Dever asked Dr. Fallon if he had read the testimony of any of the trial witnesses. He said no; he relied on the primary records: hospital charts, physicians' and nurses' notes. (The original X rays, which prosecutors used as evidence in 1954, could not be found.)

Dr. Fallon's answer told Dever that the trauma expert had not read the 1954 testimony of X ray technician Eileen Huge or that of Dr. Gervase Flick, D.O., the Bay View radiologist who had interpreted and ordered the X rays of Dr. Sam. Under oath in 1954 Dr. Flick said that he felt the first set of X rays had been flawed. The films showed streaking, and he had a difficult time interpreting them. Part of the problem was that the X-ray technician did not take normal views of Dr. Sheppard's skull and neck. Usually at Bay View, Eileen Huge shot such X rays from the back to the front, with the radiation tube set at seventy-two inches from the film. She didn't use this method because she would have had to turn Dr. Sam over onto his stomach. She was afraid to move him because she thought he might have a broken neck. Also complicating her work, Sheppard was unable to lie still. He was moving his head and moaning, she testified. To compensate, Huge took the X rays from thirty-six inches and used a much quicker exposure.

Dr. Flick had thirty years of radiology experience, mostly in Boston. On the July 4 X rays, he saw what he thought was a shadow at the C-2 vertebra, which roughly corresponded with the spot where Dr. Sheppard displayed a swollen, tender neck. But Dr. Flick wasn't sure if he was seeing "an artifact," a defect in the film. On July 6, 1954, after two days of pondering, Flick ordered more X rays of Dr. Sam's injuries. He wrote instructions for the series to be taken under identical conditions—thirty-six inches, the patient prone. However, a different technician did the July 6 work and overlooked these special instructions. Instead he shot the X rays at seventy-two inches, using a different refraction, with Sheppard erect rather than lying down.

This time Dr. Flick did not see a fracture in Sam Sheppard's second cervical vertebra. Nor did he see bridging between Sheppard's fifth and sixth vertebrae. A day later, Flick showed both sets of X rays to Dr. Gerber and Dr. Elkins, and the three doctors puzzled over them closely. At this point, Dr. Flick first learned that the two X-ray sets had been shot from different distances. After this consultation, Dr. Flick decided that the shadow actually was a chip fracture.

Under a tough cross-examination at the 1954 trial, Dr. Flick said that not finding the chip fracture on X rays taken at seventy-two inches did not rule out its presence on an X ray taken at thirty-six inches.

Dr. Fallon was unaware of this information because he had not been given the transcripts of these witnesses' testimony. Gilbert hadn't prepared him for what would come next.

Dever asked the doctor about Sheppard's chip fracture appearing in one X ray and not in a later one. "Can you rule out that the X rays had been substituted or switched?" Dever asked.

"No," Fallon said.

"Never considered a switcheroo?" Dever asked, smiling.

"No," Fallon said.

Dever would go on to suggest that Dr. Steve Sheppard, within hours of the murder, had switched Sam's benign X rays with those of a patient who had a chip fracture, all part of a conspiracy to deceive the police.

Dever's red herring was ingenious, but it defied logic that Gerber and the other doctors, after careful study, would not be able to tell they were looking at X rays of two different patients. Furthermore, on the witness stand in 1954, technician Eileen Huge identified the July 4 X rays as her work. She had coded them for Dr. Sam's patient file with a lead marker. In fact, she picked up the X rays while on the witness stand and identified her mark.

None of this evidence was presented to the jurors at this recent trial. When I talked to a few of them after their verdict, they said they were struck by Dever's "switcheroo" theory and felt it may have taken place.

––––

Over the past five years, Terry Gilbert had been trumpeting the unearthing of a 1954 police report that found fresh pry marks on a basement door at the Sheppard house. Gilbert had used this fact as a double-edged sword: proof of a break-in at the home, which suggested an intruder-killer, and evidence of a police cover-up for hiding the document from Dr. Sheppard's lawyers at two previous trials. He used the report as a foundation in building the case for Dr. Sam's innocence.

Gilbert called Henry Dombrowski, the detective who had made a mold of the pry marks and had written an accompanying report. First Gilbert asked the eighty-year-old retired detective to describe his work at the crime scene, locating and measuring blood drops.

"Was it a blood trail?" Gilbert asked Dombrowski.

"Yes," he replied, undercutting Dever's claim in his opening that there was no trail.

Did you ever testify at the previous two trials about the cast you made of the tool mark in the door? Gilbert asked.

No, Dombrowski said.

For years Gilbert had said that the pry marks were on a door leading into the Sheppard basement from outside the house.

Mason seemed almost gleeful as he questioned Dombrowski. Mason showed him a photograph taken from the inside of the Sheppard basement and asked, Where did you find the tool marks?

Dombrowski pointed to a small, thin wooden door in a foundation wall at the foot of the stairs, about two feet from the basement floor. Dombrowski said the door led into a windowless crawl space.

Dombrowski, Gilbert's own witness, destroyed the break-in theory. Gilbert sheepishly admitted afterward that he and his investigators had been mistaken.

––––

Outside the courtroom, both sides waged a public relations war. Judge Suster had considered, but did not issue, a gag order on the lawyers. Near the end of the first week of testimony, Bill Mason, talking to reporters, said he had always been willing to discuss settling the lawsuit on reasonable terms. Gilbert was asked for a reaction.

They never responded in good faith to our proposal, Gilbert said sharply, even though the judge urged both sides to negotiate. The TV news coverage cast the recently appointed prosecutor in a less-than-flattering light, and Mason decided to fight back.

On February 22, 2000, Sam Reese Sheppard took the witness stand. The courtroom was packed and the jury attentive. Sam's cousins and aunt and two close friends from the anti-death-penalty movement sat in the first row just behind him. The trial had not been as traumatic as he expected. When he finally saw the photos of his mother's battered body, he was relieved. They were not as horrible as his nightmares.

In answering Terry Gilbert's well-rehearsed questions, Sam Reese told a sad, sympathetic story of a young boy who woke up to find that he had lost his mother and his father overnight, then grew up feeling vilified for something beyond his control.

Gilbert brought out all he needed by the lunch break. Dever planned to suggest that afternoon, through cross-examination, that Sam Reese had been manipulated by others wanting to cash in on his mother's death, and that he profited handsomely from a television movie about the case.

Just before lunch, Mason told a local television reporter that Gilbert asked for $3.2 million to settle the case. The noon news program ran the story. Gilbert was enraged. The next morning, newspaper headlines would draw attention away from the story he had hoped to impart, sympathetic accounts of Sam Reese and his quest for justice. Gilbert knew the $3.2 million proposal was going to outrage a lot of people. More infuriating, he felt sandbagged. He had given the other side a weapon to hurt his case. After the lunch break, Judge Suster, his face red, reprimanded Mason on the record. Privately in chambers, he blistered him.

The next morning the *Plain Dealer* ran a page 1 story about Gilbert's $3.2 million proposal. Judge Suster worried about jury contamination. He called in the jurors, one at a time, and asked them if they had read an article in the newspaper about the case. One juror admitted he saw a headline with the $3.2 million figure but did not read the article. What do you think it had to do with? Suster asked him. The juror guessed, wrongly, that the amount had something to do with money paid to Sam Reese Sheppard from books and movies about his life, areas that had come up during Dever's cross-examination. He was mistaken but no one corrected him. To do so would contaminate him further. Judge Suster decided to let the man stay. Gilbert did not ask for his removal but told the judge that Mason should apologize to the jury for making "unfair, tainted accusations." Suster said he would think about it, but later he decided against it.

Later that day the jury heard directly for the first time about a strange and twisted man named Richard Eberling. Kathy Wagner, the former nurse's aide to Ethel Durkin, took the stand as a Sheppard witness. She had remarried and went by the last name of Dyal. She described Eberling as a charming social climber who hired her to care for the ailing ninety-year-old woman. She and Eberling shared secrets about being sexually abused in childhood. One night, after a few drinks, after dark discussions of death, he confessed to killing Marilyn Sheppard. "He told me that he had killed her and that he hit her husband in the head with a pail and that 'the bitch bit the hell out of me.' "

Dyal was an excellent witness for the Sheppard team. She put Eberling onstage and tied him to two murders while appearing sincere and believable. Steve Dever did little to discredit her on cross-examination. He planned to use her first ex-husband later to attack her credibility.

Gilbert was counting heavily on the performance of Dr. Emanuel Tanay, a well-known forensic psychiatrist. It was Dr. Tanay's firm opinion that Marilyn Sheppard's murder was a sexually motivated homicide perpetrated by a sadistic killer. The psychiatrist cited as indicators the prolonged, repeated blows to her face, her spread legs and nearly nude body. Dr. Tanay was also ready to testify that Eberling fit the psychological profile of a sadistic killer and that the murders of Ethel Durkin and her sister Myrtle Fray also fit into his personality. Tanay was the Sheppard side's most important expert. He was going to stitch together the disparate elements of the Sheppard case— Eberling, the crime-scene evidence, Dr. Sam's character—into a beautiful pattern. The prosecutors planned to do the same with their most important expert, retired FBI behavioral profiler Gregg O. McCrary.

Tanay was a Polish Jew and a Holocaust survivor who spoke with an Eastern European accent. He had published widely earlier in his career, including *The Murderers,* a book about what caused ordinary people to kill. A professor emeritus at Wayne State University in Detroit, he was semiretired and made a living mostly by testifying as an expert. He loved the gamesmanship of testifying. He had appeared in court scores of times, often successfully, throughout Michigan. Over the years, local district attorneys were stung by Dr. Tanay's commanding performances. They reacted by creating an informal lending library of his testimony and opinions and advised other prosecutors on tactics to diminish his effectiveness.

The prosecution had no intention of seeing Dr. Tanay testify about the behavioral similarities between the Marilyn Sheppard and Ethel Durkin murders. The judge listened to arguments from both sides about where to draw the line, then listened to Dr. Tanay without the jury. It was a dress rehearsal

for Tanay's testimony, a voir dire, with the judge deciding what would remain in his final performance once the jury was brought back in.

Dr. Tanay took the stand. "That Dr. Sheppard was motivated to kill his
wife and that he proceeded to kill her in this sadistic, brutal manner and then
did a cover-up, that whole thing, psychologically, in my opinion, makes no
sense," he testified. "Dr. Sheppard is a most unlikely perpetrator of this type
of sadistic homicide."

Judge Suster had a few questions. He asked Dr. Tanay if Eberling's
denials and admissions of guilt "are indicative of a person who wants to be
detected."

Dr. Tanay never had the opportunity to examine Richard Eberling. He
died in prison a week before their scheduled interview. Tanay instead based
his opinion on earlier recorded interviews of Eberling and on his voluminous
child-welfare records and prison correspondence.

———

Eberling had admitted that he wanted to call attention to himself, and then
volunteered incriminating information, Tanay told the judge. "I think it
would be a correct inference that at some level, he is sending signals that he
did it."

Suster took a recess to get advice from his law clerk. After the break, he
announced the limits he was placing on Tanay's testimony: the doctor could
testify that Eberling's admissions were a plea to be recognized. He could describe generally the traits of a sexually motivated sadistic killer. He could not
opine that Sam Sheppard, specifically, did *not* fit the profile. Suster's limits
were a sharp blow to the Sheppard side.

After Tanay took the witness stand, Gilbert took him through his impressive résumé: highest awards from the American Academy of Forensic Sciences and from the American Academy for Law and Psychiatry. The
psychiatrist mentioned some of the famous criminals that he had interviewed
over the years, including Jack Ruby and Ted Bundy.

Tanay defined sadism as taking pleasure from causing pain. Sadistic behavior could range from simply humiliating someone to physical torture and
death. He explained spousal homicide. First, a special kind of relationship
had to exist. "It's a kind of relationship where one is dominant. One inflicts
more suffering, humiliation, or pain, and the other one endures it. We call
that sadomasochistic. So you need that kind of relationship. This kind of relationship could have existed for many years. Then you have a sudden
increase in the hostile, aggressive tension. Something happened, some
episode. Maybe the husband discovered that the wife was doing something

wrong or whatever. Some exacerbation of that ongoing hostility." This triggering event happens two or three days before the murder, Dr. Tanay said.

"I call it the 'three-day syndrome.' Under severe pressure, stress, a person can develop what we call an altered state of consciousness. His control is diminished, then he snaps. Call it rage, call it anything, but these are the steps. One item that you need also is a weapon. This stage is very short-lived, this altered state of consciousness. It's quick, the gun is here, there is this rage, you pull the trigger, it's over and the homicide has happened."

Gilbert showed Dr. Tanay the crime-scene photos. "In the forty years of my practice I have never seen anything like that," Dr. Tanay said. "A person who is reasonably morally put together would not engage in such sadistic activity. It takes a certain type of person to engage in such behavior over a prolonged period of time. This administration of one blow after another, one blow after another, that takes a unique type of person to kill in this manner."

Gilbert asked, "Is it consistent with a husband with no history of a psychopathic disorder?"

Tanay said it definitely was not. "We are not talking about humiliation or a little thing, we are talking about an ongoing sadistic activity that will begin as a sexual assault and ends up in a sadistic orgy."

Next, Dever asked Tanay a series of questions. He suggested that the killing, if it were sadistic, must have taken a long time so the murderer could maximize his thrill. Dr. Tanay agreed that a sadistic killing took longer than a spousal killing.

"Did you find any evidence of any type of burns, bite marks, any type of trauma caused to the breast or genital area of Mrs. Sheppard?" Dever asked.

Tanay said he did not see any.

Any torn clothing?

Not that I know about.

"The pleasure that the assailant is seeking is derived from watching the victim suffer?"

"That's true in some situations. What you have here, in my opinion, is a clear-cut sexual type of homicide. You see that you have a young attractive woman with genitalia exposed, and she is badly injured. That's clearly, in my opinion, at least a sexual homicide if there ever was one."

"Did you find evidence of overkill?"

"It would *not* be overkill. Overkill, the term, is used when you have situations where somebody really wanted to commit the homicide—that's the primary objective. And they go beyond what's necessary to accomplish the purpose." In the Sheppard murder, the primary purpose was sexual and sadistic, not immediately taking her life, so her murder was not overkill, Tanay said.

Dever had located a copy of *The Murderers*. He found a passage that fit his theory of the Sheppard marriage and read it to Tanay: "Murder is indeed a family affair because family members both love and hate one another, and the latter, if it becomes excessive, may explode in murder. People invariably kill the ones they love and hate for no one else is important enough to provoke murderous rage. Murder is imported out of the conflict of hate and love. Murder marks the end, the tragic end, of a very ambivalent relationship."

Tanay said yes, he agreed with what he had written.

Dever read another passage about impulsive murder, so typical of spousal killing. The perpetrator in this type of homicide " 'restores himself at the conclusion of the homicide to basically a normal, mild-mannered individual,' is that correct?" Dever asked him.

"Yes," Tanay agreed, "but then the perpetrator becomes aware of what he did and is guilt ridden and horrified. . . . Most commonly they call the police or they call for help."

"There could be a two-, three-day triggering factor for that event?" Dever asked.

"A buildup," Tanay said, "of the aggression within that relationship, a kind of an implosion."

"And the aggression can be on both participants?" Dever asked. He wanted to suggest that Marilyn Sheppard started an argument over Dr. Sam's affairs.

Tanay replied, "The perpetrator is the one who goes in this altered state of consciousness and explodes with aggression, with anger, with rage."

Could domestic homicide include factors other than physical abuse between participants?

"Yes, I agree, sure."

You could include unfaithfulness in this scenario?

Tanay could see where Dever was leading him. He said it depended on who was unfaithful. "If Dr. Sheppard was unfaithful, then Mrs. Sheppard would have good reason to go after him."

Dever asked, "But the triggering mechanism for the event itself can be perpetrated by the victim or the assailant, can it not?"

"No, no, no, no."

"Isn't that the possibility—"

"No, not at all. That's really twisting it totally opposite of what I have described. No, not at all."

You can rule out a domestic homicide?

"Yes, definitely, that is my firm opinion. . . . Particularly if you think that there is a little boy sleeping just next door, this is not a spousal homicide, in

my absolute opinion, no sir." Tanay repeated again: "This is a clear-cut torture. A person who has no conscience who is doing that, someone who
doesn't have an iota of compassion." It was a person who fantasized about
this killing. "They have done this many times before in their mind and now
they do it in reality. . . . This is a unique type of person. It takes a monster to
do something like that."

"And the monster would be inclined to kill everyone in the house, isn't
that so?"

"No, no, not at all."

Dever paused, then, "Nothing further."

Cyril Wecht, M.D., the Allegheny County medical examiner in Pittsburgh, had joined the Sheppard volunteers. He had consulted on the assassinations of President Kennedy and Robert F. Kennedy. Gilbert called Dr.
Wecht as a witness to savage Dr. Samuel Gerber's reputation and to back up
Dr. Tanay's opinion that Marilyn's murder was a sexual homicide.

Dr. Wecht, in his late sixties, a former president of the American Academy of Forensic Sciences, loathed Gerber. Outside the courtroom he referred
to him as "a little Napoleon" and "that little bastard." Wecht belittled Gerber
because he was not a pathologist but still put his name, and no other, on autopsy reports. They clashed in 1967 when Wecht traveled to Cleveland as a
defense expert to review the deaths of three cops and four black nationalists
from Cleveland's poor Glenville neighborhood, the result of a shoot-out during a race riot. As it turned out, two of the policemen had been drunk, the
other borderline. But Gerber's office, at first, did not provide Wecht with
toxicology reports that showed the blood-alcohol levels of the slain policemen, a routine attachment to autopsy reports. Wecht considered this a grave
ethical breach and blamed Gerber. Wecht was present at meetings of the
American Academy of Forensic Sciences when Gerber continued his black-
balling of Dr. Paul Kirk, whose work embarrassed Gerber. "He was a ruth-
less politician," Wecht said.

Wecht had conducted fourteen thousand autopsies and consulted on
thirty thousand others, he told the jury. The killing looked like a sexual assault turned into a homicide. If he had been the pathologist, he would have
included detailed descriptions of her genitalia, flushed her vaginal canal with
saline solution to search for sperm, and swabbed her mouth and anus for
seminal fluid. Gilbert asked about her head wounds. The blows to her skull
were strong but not powerful, Wecht said. An adult with a flashlight could
easily have fractured her skull. Once cracked, the subsequent blows could be
even less forceful and continue the fracturing. None of the pieces of the skull
were indented.

Gilbert did not ask him to address the idea that a strong man deliberately swinging the weapon at half strength could be responsible. Wecht ruled out Sam Sheppard based on the strength of the blows and their number. Wecht had seen the aftermath of hundreds of domestic-rage killings. A spouse's fury exploded and subsided quickly. Marilyn Sheppard's battering was a lengthy affair.

Gerber botched the case, Wecht said. "I believe his actions were quite inappropriate. . . . To go to the hospital, question Dr. Sheppard, to go back to the scene, to not call his experts. I just don't know of this being done. This is not Jack Klugman playing Quincy, where he's all these things tied into one." Above all, Wecht said, "you maintain an unbiased position. You don't make comments affixing guilt. Why have an inquest and a big public production?"

On cross-exam, Dever brought out that Wecht's views on both of the Kennedy assassinations were outside of the mainstream. Wecht believed that more than one gunman was involved in each. Asked about staging, Wecht said he could not rule it out. He said the sperm found inside Marilyn Sheppard's body could have been there for a day before the murder, or longer.

———

Dr. Michael Sobel, a professor of dentistry at the University of Pittsburgh, did his best to tie Eberling to Marilyn Sheppard's murder. Gilbert called him as the next witness. He displayed a color photo of a close-up view of the left wrist of Richard Eberling, taken during an autopsy. The scar was consistent with a gouging of Eberling's skin by a fingernail. Marilyn Sheppard could have done it, he said, while struggling with her attacker. Her third left fingernail was torn off. There were no other wounds on that hand. Sobel said from his experience he guessed that the victim ripped her nail by gouging something. She possibly could have torn it by blocking a blow with her hand, but it was highly unlikely.

———

Steve Dever seemed to enjoy himself more when he could allow sarcasm to drench his questions. "There should be a piece of Richard Eberling under the fingernail, right?" Dever asked.

Not necessarily, Sobel replied. They didn't bag Marilyn Sheppard's hands before they moved the body. It could have fallen out.

Did you see a photograph of the injured hand?

Sobel answered no, a damaging oversight.

Isn't it just speculation, Dever threw at him.

"Everything fits into the scenario. It's one way to explain it."

"You just took four pieces of evidence and concocted this theory—"

Judge Suster sustained Gilbert's heated objection, and Dever sat down.

Dr. Kirk's analysis of the blood-spattered room had led to Dr. Sam's acquittal in 1966. Gilbert and Sam Reese Sheppard had the good fortune of having Bart Epstein, a Kirk protégé, join the team as a volunteer. Epstein was a nationally respected blood-pattern analyst who had just retired from the Minnesota state crime lab. He carefully arrived at interpretations that he believed in 100 percent. He erred on the side of caution, unlike Dr. Tanay or Sobel, and disagreed with Kirk's conclusion that the murderer was left-handed. Since retiring from the crime lab, Epstein worked most often giving blood-pattern-analysis seminars to police departments. Because of his careful reputation, he did not find himself in great demand as an expert for hire, a more lucrative practice.

Epstein built a strong case for Sheppard's innocence. The killer was certain to be spattered with blood from head to knees. Dr. Sam had only a large contact stain on his pants knee. Marilyn was beaten in the same position her body was found, with her head near the center of the mattress, blood sprayed out in straight lines from her head. The large closet bloodstain, a one-inch-wide splotch, got there "from some other mechanism" than flying blood or cast-off from the weapon. Epstein told the jury it likely could have come from the killer touching the door with a bleeding hand.

Gilbert made certain to ask him about the blood pattern on Sam Sheppard's watch. Epstein referred to a county coroner's photo of the watch taken on July 5, 1954, before Mary Cowan swabbed off blood for testing. Those spots were made by contact, probably from a bloody finger, Epstein said firmly. The small tear-shaped stains on the watch bezel were not made by flying blood.

As Dever rose to cross-examine Epstein, his colleagues at the prosecution table were full of anticipation. Dever was going to poleax this witness.

He started out slowly. A blood trail normally has drops a half-inch wide? Yes.

"So, based on size, you cannot say they come from a dripping wound?"

"Yes, I can't say they're all human or from the same wound," Epstein replied.

"All you can say about the trousers is they weren't in the room at the time this woman met her death?"

Yes, that is all he could say with certainty, Epstein replied.

Dever suggested that Sheppard may have changed his clothes or washed them in Lake Erie.

That was possible, Epstein said, but blood clings to leather and should have been detected in Dr. Sheppard's shoes and belt if he were in the bed-room during the killing.

Why wasn't there more blood on Sam's pants if the killer took the wal-let, as Sam Sheppard claimed? Dever asked.

Perhaps the blood had dried before the wallet was taken, Epstein sug-gested.

Dr. Kirk determined the closet stain to be blood group O, correct?

Yes.

"You know that Richard Eberling was blood group A?"

Epstein looked startled. He shot Terry Gilbert a searing look. For Dever it was a rare, glorious "gotcha" moment, dead-solid perfect, one that comes once in a thousand questions.

"I don't know," Epstein said.

"If Kirk's testing is correct, then type O excludes Richard Eberling?"

"Yes."

"We can exclude Richard Eberling even if his DNA shows otherwise?"

If Kirk is right, Epstein said reluctantly.

Dever sat down, and Mason, with a huge smile, whispered excitedly to him, "That was great!"

Gilbert was not able to repair the damage on his redirect examination of Epstein.

For the past two years, Gilbert had believed that his strongest scientific evi-dence came from Dr. Mohammad Tahir's DNA-test results. Tahir was a highly respected DNA scientist with strong academic interests in the field. He had expected to be a research biochemist but landed his first job in a crime laboratory and became hooked. He loved the feeling that came with being a crime solver. "Let us say some innocent person is in custody, and you got him out because of your analysis," he said. "It is a very good feeling. You helped somebody. On the other hand, if somebody is a victim of rape or mur-der and you find the right culprit, it gives you a very good feeling. You are helping the community."[1]

Tahir was eminently qualified. The director of the FBI had appointed him to its DNA Advisory Board, which sets standards and procedures for the na-tion's DNA crime laboratories. The problem was that Tahir's speech was sometimes hard to decipher. Judge Suster said he was allowing Terry Gilbert to ask Tahir leading questions "because this witness is hard to understand."

Terry Gilbert certainly knew how the prosecution was going to challenge the results. For months, Mason and Dever had denigrated the DNA evidence as "contaminated" and "degraded." Both descriptions were true, but such criticism left a false impression. Contamination meant the scientist found more than one person's DNA in an evidence sample, perhaps caused by improper handling. Contamination did not change or destroy the original underlying biological material.

As for being degraded, the Sheppard evidence certainly was. Blood starts to degrade the minute it's spilled; its DNA concentration diminishes over time until theoretically it is too low to be detected and accurately profiled. As evidence degrades, a larger sample is required for testing. Instead of a pinpoint of blood, a scientist might need two or three or a dozen pinpoints to get valid results.

Dr. Tahir gave a brief explanation of how DNA tests worked. Then Gilbert took him through his results. Tahir ran down the "exclusions"—who could be excluded as contributing DNA to the old evidence: the blood on Sam's pants did not come from him or Marilyn Sheppard. Dr. Sheppard could not have left the sperm on one of the vaginal swabs. Tests on the second swab were inconclusive. Neither Sam nor Marilyn left the blood drop that was tested from the stairs. Gilbert was not allowed to tell the jury the most intriguing result: a quarter-inch-diameter blood drop, one in a trail of five that led across the back-porch floor and out the lakeside screen door, matched the genetic profile of Eberling, one shared by about one in seven thousand white males. A control built into the test failed, so Tahir wasn't 100 percent certain of his result, perhaps only 90 percent certain. Under the rules, Gilbert could not tell this information to the jury.

Dever rose to cross-examine Tahir. He tried to undercut Tahir's unexpected discovery of sperm in Marilyn Sheppard's body. Dever suggested that in 1954, before technicians worried about contamination, old or dirty slides were reused. Under Dever's sharp questioning, Dr. Tahir admitted that he expected to see more sperm from the swabs, assuming there had been a full ejaculation. What he saw may have been undegraded sperm left from "prior consensual sex, a day or two before," Tahir said. "Or maybe a person entered her and left pre-ejaculate."

Dever asked him about the ABO blood-grouping results from 1954. Mary Cowan had determined that the blood on Sam's pants was type O but Richard Eberling is type A; therefore he cannot have bled on those pants, correct?

"If the typing is correct, this is an exclusion," Tahir said, but he would need to review her work and notes to make certain. The old methods of grouping blood into four types are not as reliable as his work, Tahir said. "We have airplanes now. We don't want to go back to horses."

For an afternoon, Dever picked away at the scientist's work. He made the point that Tahir was not able to duplicate his results by running certain tests a second time. Tahir said that had been impossible because in most cases he used up all the microscopic bits of blood and sperm in the first round of testing. There was nothing left.

By the time he was finished, Dever created the impression that the DNA results were far less reliable and powerful than Terry Gilbert had proclaimed in his opening statement.

———

Dr. Ranajit Chakraborty, the Allen King Professor of Human Genetics at the University of Texas School of Public Health in Houston, was a world-renowned population geneticist. He built the world's largest database of DNA profiles, which were matched to populations throughout the globe.

He did a statistical study of the closet-door bloodstain, the "unique spot," potentially the most telling piece of evidence in the case. Using statistics from his database, Chakraborty created different scenarios that could explain the different combinations of DNA markers in the closet-door stain. Then he weighed each scenario against the others, and ranked them from the most to the least probable, a scientifically accepted statistical computation called "the likelihood ratio."

The prosecutors pointed out that Tahir's results showed a mixture of DNA on the unique spot that theoretically included up to 83 percent of the adult white population, tens of millions of people.

But not everyone in the country had access to the Sheppard home on July 4, 1954. According to Kirk and Dr. Tahir, some of that closet stain came from somebody other than Marilyn Sheppard.

Dr. Chakraborty started with the sound assumption that Marilyn Sheppard's blood was part of the mixture. Drops of her blood had been spattered into just about every square inch of the door surrounding the large closet stain. When her DNA profile was removed from the "unique spot," all the remaining markers could be explained by a single person whose profile was found in 2.4 percent of the population, or one in forty-two. Richard Eberling happened to fit into that small segment.

If you assume that the killer had been in the house previously or knew the Sheppards, statistics said that the best explanation was that the closet stain was a mix of Marilyn Sheppard and Richard Eberling's DNA. It didn't prove he bled in the bedroom or that he killed Marilyn Sheppard. But it was powerful evidence for the jury to consider.

Unfortunately, this was not communicated to the jury very well during

Gilbert's direct examination. Assistant prosecutor Dean Boland, in his cross-exam, took the geneticist through each of the other DNA results and showed that most of the population could find its DNA profile in each piece of evidence.

However, before excusing the witness, the prosecutor asked Chakraborty, "Can a person who drops type O blood change it to type A?"

Dr. Chakraborty took advantage of the opening. "After 48 hours you cannot reliably type them, before knowing all the details." Type O blood is blood that does not have the A or B elements, the scientist said. "Old samples give false negatives." Therefore, a false negative result on type A blood would give a type O result.

Chakraborty's answer diminished the power of the state's argument that Richard Eberling could not have been the killer because Kirk found type O blood in the closet stain.

After Chakraborty stepped down from the witness stand and the judge called a recess, a *Plain Dealer* reporter covering the trial, Jack Hagan, asked me, "Did you understand any of that with the DNA?"

Not really, I answered, but I hope to eventually.

"Imagine how lost the jury must be," Hagan said.

39

SMOKING GUN

THE PROSECUTION FELT CONFIDENT once it began putting on its witnesses.

Toby Wolson, a key witness, was a tall, tanned man in his early forties who worked at the Miami Dade crime laboratory. He was a blood-pattern expert, mostly. Like many criminalists, he had a sideline, training beginning crime-scene investigators and testifying in court.

With a few exceptions, his blood-pattern analysis pretty much matched Bart Epstein's. Wolson concluded that Marilyn Sheppard was killed in the position where her body was found, her head toward the middle of the bed. Like Epstein, he wondered why the blood trail was made up of mostly drops a quarter-inch in diameter. It was his opinion that it could not be said for certain that the blood trail was from a bleeding perpetrator in the home. He expected such drops to be larger.

However, if the killer flung or snapped a bleeding hand, the drops could be much smaller.

A few years earlier, Wolson had branched out into DNA testing. He was not in the league of Dr. Tahir or the prosecution's DNA expert, Dr. Mitchell Holland, but he was a competent technician.

The prosecution's problem was that Dr. Holland, after reviewing all of Tahir's lab notes and charts, agreed pretty much with his findings. Holland said he would have liked to have color photographs of the nylon strips with Tahir's test results. It was a standard way to double-check such work. The black-and-white photocopies were poor and unreadable. However, judging by Tahir's notes and the notes of a witnessing scientist in the lab, Holland said Tahir's work passed muster.

Wolson instead was asked by the prosecutors to prepare a report on Tahir's DNA work. Wolson said he asked his contact, assistant county prosecutor Dean Boland, several times for Tahir's notes but never received them. Eventually, he was given a computer printout of copies of the color photographs of the strips but not the lab notes. Facing a deadline, Wolson gave a carefully hedged, inadequate report. He could not see the color or intensity of the control dots on the nylon strips, therefore Tahir's results could not be interpreted.

Wolson's great value as a witness for the prosecution was being put in the position, time and again, to say that, based on what he saw, Tahir's results could not be interpreted. This muddied Tahir's results and made his work seem somehow inadequate.

When he stood for cross-examination, Gilbert was angry. Are you trying to tell this jury that Dr. Tahir, a renowned scientist, is presenting faulty science?

I'm not criticizing his results, Wolson said. Based on what I saw, his work cannot be interpreted.

Tahir and his coworker marked in their notes which dots they saw and which ones they did not. Are you saying he made that up?

Wolson said he did not have those notes.

Did you ask the prosecutors for them?

Several times, Wolson said.

Gilbert was able to make it seem that the prosecution was hiding information from its expert in order to make him reach a helpful result. Mason said they didn't get Tahir's notes until March 1. The Sheppard side had been "stonewalling them."

But this was not the case. Tahir said Dean Boland had been to his lab in September and copied them. Mitchell Holland received a set in the fall from Boland and referred to them in his October 1999 expert's report. Boland and Dever had Tahir's notes and referred to them while they took Tahir's deposition in early January.

On a break after Wolson's testimony, reporter Keith McKnight, the *Akron Beacon Journal*'s expert on the Sheppard case, said, "That was the sleaziest thing I've seen in this case so far."

———

The prosecutors came up with a new fact witness to enlighten the jury. Paul Gerhardt, Esther Houk's eighty-year-old brother, worked part-time for the Bay Village police and, on the side, repaired small electrical appliances.

On the stand, he told for the first time about repairing a lamp for Sam and Marilyn Sheppard and leaving it on a table in an upstairs bedroom.

Gilbert could do little with Gerhardt. The man could not remember details about the lamp, its size, color, or material. It had been forty-six years ago. But he was pretty certain that he had plugged it in and left it between the twin beds in the room where the murder took place. The jurors had already seen crime-scene photos of the room. There was no lamp on the tiny table, just a clock and a big black rotary telephone.

Later, outside the courtroom, Mason said of the lamp-as-murder-weapon theory, "This is our smoking gun." It was a theory that Cleveland homicide detectives and coroner Gerber had pursued in the summer of 1954. Dr. Gerber, as part of his coroner's inquest, had privately questioned Chip Sheppard about a possible bedroom lamp.

Chip described a small brass or copper lamp but said it lay on the table in the master bedroom. There was no lamp in the guest room with the twin beds. The room's illumination came from a light fixture.

All the evidence from 1954 supports that the murder room had no lamp. Jean Disbro, a neighbor and occasional baby-sitter, was questioned about a lamp in the room by detective Adelbert O'Hara. She stayed overnight several times in the guest bedroom and did not see a lamp, she told him.[1] Detectives asked Elnora Helms, the Sheppards' weekly cleaning lady, to view the murder room. She said she did not notice anything missing. Authorities had already abandoned the lamp theory by early August 1954 and instead locked into Gerber's notion that the murder weapon was a surgical tool, and began combing medical catalogs.

During Gilbert's cross-examination of Gerhardt, prosecutor Mason held his breath. The lamp theory could come crashing down if Gilbert or his team presented Chip's testimony from the inquest. "We didn't know if Terry would pick up on it," Mason told me later. Gilbert did not.

———

"This witness will make or break our case," Steve Dever said on the way to the courtroom on March 31, 2000.

Gregg O. McCrary, a retired FBI agent who analyzed crime scenes and created criminal profiles, was a dream expert witness for the prosecution. McCrary had studied the Sheppard crime photographs, police reports, and other records, then concluded that the murder "was a staged domestic homicide committed by Dr. Samuel Sheppard." In his opinion, Sam Sheppard had moved and arranged his wife's clothing and body to throw off detectives and make the crime look like a sex murder.

However, McCrary's former FBI supervisor, John E. Douglas, looked at the same materials and arrived at a far different opinion. Douglas said that the Sheppard murder was a sexual homicide, not a domestic homicide. This clash between two experts, both supposedly following the same FBI system, shows how unreliable and subjective the FBI's classifying of crimes can be. The FBI crime-scene analysis was meant to be a tool for detectives when they were stumped. It was far better, Douglas said, to have forensic evidence such as DNA, blood-pattern analysis, and fingerprints. Physical evidence was more reliable. Furthermore, Douglas and another retired FBI agent from the Behavioral Sciences Unit were surprised that McCrary named a guilty party in his report. At the Bureau, agents never accused a suspect by name in such a report. It violated a Bureau practice.

Prosecutor Bill Mason told me later, "We created our case around McCrary." By now, Gilbert realized that McCrary was the witness to knock down. He focused his efforts on knocking out McCrary or, more likely, getting his testimony limited, as the prosecution had convinced the judge to do with Dr. Tanay.

McCrary took the stand wearing a gray suit and dark shirt and tie. The jury was out while Suster decided what he could testify about. McCrary was an intense, aloof man in his mid-fifties. He had worked for fifteen years in different field offices, mostly in New York state. Showing promise as a crime analyst, he was transferred into the Behavioral Sciences Unit for seven years, where his section chief was John E. Douglas. McCrary had spent several dozen hours on the case at three hundred dollars an hour.

Suster asked him how he came up with the domestic-homicide label. McCrary said he based his opinion on four facts: that the Sheppards' marriage was under stress; Dr. Sheppard was not injured; the crime scene was staged; and that Marilyn's murder was an "overkill." Outside the courtroom, crime analysis can be a powerful investigative tool that helps detectives focus investigations. But McCrary based his conclusion on several disputed facts.

McCrary said Marilyn's pajama top had been neatly folded back, proof of staging. McCrary said he had been given both trial transcripts and read parts of them. He either ignored or overlooked the testimony of Esther Houk and Dr. Richard Sheppard, which contradicted his conclusion about Marilyn's top.

Sam's brother, Richard, testified at the August 1954 coroner's inquest that he had rearranged the top of her pajamas. If Gerber had asked follow-up questions, Richard possibly would have explained that he wanted to make Marilyn appear more modest in death, then realized he had tampered with a crime scene and went back and undid his arrangement.

Dr. Richard's account of rearranging Marilyn's top was backed up under oath by Esther Houk. She testified in 1954 that when she first saw Marilyn's body, the pajama top was rolled up under her chin. Photos taken two or three hours later show the top unrolled to the sternum and apparently flipped back. At the 1954 murder trial Dr. Richard Sheppard said that Marilyn "looked as though she had either been pulled or scooted down in bed, because the gown was rolled up tightly in the back and around under the arms. Her chest— breasts—were completely bare, as was the throat."[2]

McCrary had the 1954 trial transcript. Somehow he overlooked or ignored this testimony. Instead, in his report he stated that the killer arranged the body to look like a sex crime.

Also, McCrary said the killer had pulled Marilyn Sheppard's body to the foot of the bed and had positioned her exposed crotch under the crossbar of the four-poster bed, displaying her and protecting her from sexual assault with the same gesture. But the blood-pattern experts from both sides said she had not been moved after death.

At the end of the witness's day, Judge Suster said McCrary could not call it a "staged domestic homicide."

In front of the jury, Dever took him through his methods of analyzing crime scenes and applying one of twenty-eight crime classifications from the *Crime Classification Manual,* a taxonomy of felony arson, rape, and murder. Later, under oath, McCrary would say that he had crafted anywhere from one hundred to a few hundred crime-scene analyses and had never been mistaken. The jurors were impressed. He was the current equivalent of Dr. Gerber and his surgical-instrument theory, damning interpretation offered as fact.

———

Roger Marsters was long retired from University Hospitals as a blood-lab supervisor. In Florida, he lectured occasionally to other retirees about the Sheppard case. A couple of years earlier he sent me a copy of his speech; it did not mention a key fact that Dever now needed him to tell the jury: Dr. Sam's watch face was speckled with tiny impact spatters. This would put the watch on Sam's hand and in the murder room. It had worked in 1966, until F. Lee Bailey saw spots underneath the band and destroyed Cowan's theory about the spots.

Marsters's forty-six-year-old memories were far from the mark, based on evidence photos and documents. Mary Cowan created detailed records of her work. Marsters had not seen Sam Sheppard's watch until after it was photographed and Cowan removed blood spots for testing. Even before her removal, the photo shows blood smears and contact stains, not dozens and dozens of tiny flying blood droplets, as he now told the jury.

The next witness, Dr. Robert White, a retired neurosurgeon, had disliked Sam Sheppard for decades. He had told me years earlier about his embarrassment when Clevelanders referred to Dr. Sam as a brain surgeon. White even wrote a letter to newspaper editors correcting references to Sheppard as a neurosurgeon. The father of ten children, a conservative Catholic, he just didn't like the sort of man Sam Sheppard represented, outside of his feeling that Sheppard had murdered his wife.[3]

White told the jurors that the X-ray films of Dr. Sam from the day of the murder had been "substituted," an unsupported theory that the prosecution had used with great success. Sam Sheppard wasn't injured, White insisted, and it was inappropriate that his own family treated him in the hospital.

Gilbert put him through a brutal cross-examination, almost to the point of creating sympathy. Dr. White held controversial views. He thought that medical science had progressed to the point that a human body could be transplanted to a head, as a host, to keep a brain alive. It would be appropriate to save someone of great value to society, such as the pope or a Gandhi. In fact, White had told me this in 1983, saying it could be accomplished within a year if the medical community poured in resources. Others in his field thought it was ghoulish, a waste of resources, and of questionable medical value. Dr. White had made his reputation as a top brain surgeon at Cleveland's metropolitan teaching hospital, MetroHealth. Like the Sheppards in their early days, he was a relentless publicity seeker, calling gossip columnists about his travels to Russia or to Vatican City to have an audience with the pope. He was a freethinker and unafraid to express politically unpopular views.

Gilbert brought up his philosophical support of using Nazi medical research from Holocaust victims and for body transplants. He neutralized Dr. White's effectiveness by doing what a lawyer never does on cross-examination—asking an open-ended question. Why don't you just tell us about the conspiracy of the Sheppard family? White did, and he diminished himself in the jury's eyes.

After he testified, as the jury was being led out, White was still sitting in the box and started shaking hands and talking to them as they filed out. Gilbert and the prosecutors and the judge had their heads together at a bench conference on the other side. Gilbert asked the judge for an instruction to tell him to stop, and Suster quickly told him not to talk to jurors. So White blew them a kiss instead. He then walked to Sam Reese Sheppard and tried to shake his hand. It was a brief, tense, bizarre moment in the nine-week trial.

Sam Reese jumped back and put his hands behind his back, trying to control himself. The doctor had just attacked his family and now he expected to shake hands.

———

Dr. White was the last prosecution witness. Gilbert brought in rebuttal witnesses and decided that he needed to present evidence about the supposed unreliability of ABO blood typing from old, dried samples. He used Terrence Laber, a criminalist who had worked in the Minnesota state crime laboratory and coauthored blood-analysis training materials with Bart Epstein.

Early in the morning, Steve Dever brought a new table lamp into court and stashed it under the chairs where the judge's bailiff and law clerk sat, out of sight.

Gilbert introduced what he needed through Laber—that Kirk's ABO typing on the closet stain could be wrong.

Dever put a large slide of the bloody pillow stain on the overhead projector and asked Laber some questions about its shape and characteristics. Laber said the symmetrical clawlike stain was produced by the pillow folding over on clotted blood, in his opinion.

With a grin on his face, Dever pulled out the lamp like a rabbit from a hat. This was Dever's Perry Mason moment, a bit of a trick.

Gilbert had not seen this exhibit. He had seconds to decide whether to object. He let it pass.

The lamp had no shade, a small base, and a metal stem about eighteen inches long and a little more than one inch in diameter. If you took off the lamp's socket and harp—the U-shaped bow that surrounded the bulb and supported the shade—the lamp resembled Dr. Kirk's description of the murder weapon being a flashlight.

Don't you see the outline of the harp on that pillow? Dever wanted to know.

Laber did not. It was a contact stain. For a second blood imprint to stand out, the underlying imprint must first be dry.

For this to have happened, Marilyn's beating would have to have taken place in two stages: a first round that stained the pillow, then a second round an hour or more later, in which somehow the lamp's harp got soaked again, then set on the pillow. Also, the killer would then have to have turned the pillow upside down, for some reason, because Gerber testified in the first trial that the U-shaped imprint was on the underside of the pillow.[4]

You don't see the outline of harp in there? Dever asked again.

Laber said no, it was a contact stain.

No matter. The smoking gun was before the jury.

Gilbert complained to Suster that Dever had not shown him the lamp, an exhibit, before presenting it in court, as rules require. It was end of the trial, and everyone was worn down. Suster asked why he hadn't objected.

If Gilbert had more time with the lamp, he might have noticed that its harp was four inches across at its widest point, easily surrounding a standard lightbulb's 2.5-inch diameter. If he compared the dimensions of the harp to the U-shaped impression on the pillowcase, he would have noticed that they do not fit. There was a ruler at the bottom of the pillow photograph. The clawlike impression was 2.75 inches at its widest, barely able to fit around a standard lightbulb. The stain simply did not match the lamp. The impression needed to be about 50 percent larger.

40

FINALE

TERRY GILBERT SPENT the first part of his two-hour closing argument trying to place the murder in the context of its time. "People were living the American Dream. The suburbs were blossoming. The idea that, in 1954, in Bay Village, that some sick individual, some pathological mind, could come into our homes, our sanctified homes, was unthinkable." So the community wanted to seize on the husband as the killer because it was more comforting.

He listed the evidence that showed Sam couldn't have been the killer. He did not have blood on his pants or belt. He could not have left some of the blood and sperm found at the crime scene. He did not have the personality needed to murder Marilyn, let alone kill her in a brutal, sexual way. He told a consistent account. "He never wavered from his story. If he was concocting this thing, he'd have come up with a better story."

Mason handled the first half of the state's closing argument. He gave a criminal prosecutor's close, beatifying the victim and debasing a suspect. He showed a photograph of Marilyn Sheppard. "She was pure and clean, pure innocence." Her husband, on the other hand, "spent his time with other women. He told people his wife can't sexually satisfy him. This is a guy who drives around in a Jaguar. Marilyn buys a dishwasher and he gives her grief. He's a name dropper—always talking about Otto Graham. She was a trophy to him. What's most important to him? His reputation."

Sheppard humiliated his wife as well as his mistress, Mason argued. "While he was shacking up with Susan Hayes, his doctor friends were there. He didn't even have enough respect to get a hotel room, this tightwad."

Dever presented a compelling, tightly crafted argument. He dismissed the scientific evidence and argued about matters not in evidence. Why didn't

Steve Sheppard come into this courtroom and defend his brother? Because he shielded his brother and was involved in a "switcheroo." The jury had no way of knowing Steve Sheppard had twice set appointments to be deposed by one of Mason's assistants, but the prosecutor's office canceled each time.

What happened to the lamp? Dever said. "It's reasonable for a lamp to be in that room."

Dever backed off his sharp treatment of Sam Reese Sheppard. Dever said he understood why, in his desperation, a son couldn't believe that his father was a murderer. Dever said he never intended to "suggest that he is motivated by money or wealth. But people close to him were."

The DNA tests meant little. "You can't say the material tested was blood," Dever argued. He mentioned for the first time that two California scientists, Dr. Ed Blake and Keith Inman, tested some of the blood found in Kirk's files. "We never got those results," Dever said. With not a shred of support, he suggested such results were hidden by the plaintiff because they might contradict Dr. Tahir's work and show that someone "tampered with that stain."

Dever made a new assertion: that the blood drop on the basement step was not connected to the homicide. "Yet they come in and say DNA is the answer." Tahir tested "a little thread" from Sam's pants, Dever said sarcastically. The DNA was unreliable. "It was just a crap shoot. They are all contaminated. That is science used by these experts to confuse you. You can't understand their answers. . . . That is the danger when science takes the witness stand. Science is not perfect. That is why the Shuttle blows up and we have not cured AIDS. These scientists come in and say they've solved it. Use your common sense.

"This case breaks down to human behavior, common sense, what should be in that room and what isn't." Why was there no blood on the wallet? Dever asked. Why didn't he stay and guard his son? Where is the lamp? His T-shirt? "Why doesn't he have blood all over his trousers if he fought the killer? Did he clean himself up? The assailant had time."

What about his watch? "If you find spatter on the watch, Dr. Sam's got a problem," Dever said. "The dog didn't bark that night. It doesn't make sense."

He passed along McCrary's prejudicial misinformation that 50 percent of domestic killings do not have previous violence. And no "fingerprints of value" were found, only wiping, Dever said.

At this point, Gilbert was overwhelmed. The prosecutors had gone way beyond what he felt were "the rules of engagement." He could not answer all the new accusations. He decided to take his remaining thirty minutes to restate his best evidence and then sway the jurors emotionally.

"They asked you to use common sense," he started out. "Does it really make sense for Sam Sheppard to kill his wife in this monstrous fashion, fill his four pockets with sand, put a five-inch tear in his pants, somehow lay in the lake to get hypothermia, punch his neck, and break his teeth?" These facts are objective evidence that is inconsistent with domestic homicide. The state's antiscience position was nonsense. "Day after day they rely on science. Why did they exhume the body? Why did they hire all these experts if science wasn't relevant?"

Gilbert became impassioned. Dr. Sam Sheppard "for 16 years gave every ounce to endure this tragedy. . . . For once and for all, bring peace to this family." The lawyer seemed overcome himself. "Never forget one thing— it's a story of pain and trauma for forty-five years. End this fight in this community. Bring some end to this horror story. . . . Give us justice, please."

Sam Reese's cousin Melissa was sobbing as the judge sent the jury home. It was late. He would instruct them the next morning on the law.

The next morning, after hearing the law from Suster, the jury went to a deliberation room at 11:15, elected a foreman, and went to lunch. By 4:30 P.M., they had reached their verdict.

——

Terry Gilbert's wife, Robin, thought her husband was having a heart attack. When the lawyer heard that they lost, he dropped his head to the trial table, his face ashen, his mouth agape. Sam Reese Sheppard was surprisingly stoic as the jurors were individually polled and found against him 8–0. Two of the women in the jury box had been crying. Sam Reese comforted his lawyer, rubbing his shoulders.

Later, outside the court, prosecutor Bill Mason stood flanked by his staff of lawyers and aides at a press conference. They were elated. "This case was overstated from the beginning," Mason said. "We had a duty to give an accounting. At the end of the day, justice was done." Days later, as the verdict sank in, it seemed less persuasive. Mason would say that his team had presented enough evidence that if Dr. Sam were still alive, they could have gotten him convicted of murder.

The next day Gilbert intruded on the state's victory. In news articles, he criticized the verdict and talked about an appeal, saying the result was another "mockery of justice."

He could still provoke Mason. "His 15 minutes of fame on the Sheppard case are over," Mason shot back. "It's time for him to move on."[1]

Sam Reese handled defeat with less rancor than many expected. He had prepared himself by following some prison advice from his father: hope for the best but prepare for the worst.

Shortly after the verdict, he and two good friends in the anti-death-penalty movement went to a Cleveland Indians home game. Many people cheered him, told him they supported his cause, and stopped to shake his hand. He was buoyed. Perhaps the court battle had changed people's minds after all.

People asked him what was he going to do next. Keep fighting? Drop it?

Sam Reese Sheppard said he had no plans. But he did. He was going home to Oakland, to his room at a boardinghouse near Berkeley. He was going to roll his bike out into the spring air and take a long, long ride.

EPILOGUE

Frantic orthodoxy is never rooted in faith but in doubt. It is when we are not sure that we are doubly sure.

— REINHOLD NIEBUHR

THE JURY'S QUICK DECISION was not surprising. The jurors I interviewed said they simply had not reached the tipping point where they could eliminate Sam as the killer of his wife.

Some of the most compelling evidence in the Sheppard case—DNA test results on blood and semen from the crime scene—had not registered with the jury. Dr. Tahir's lab work showed that sperm from a man other than Dr. Sheppard was in his wife's vagina when she died. But Tahir's heavily accented testimony was "hard to follow," as Judge Suster put it. Furthermore, Terry Gilbert's direct examination of Tahir failed to give the jurors a solid understanding of how DNA worked, said assistant prosecutor Steve Dever, who was grateful. As a result, Dever found it easier to broadly dismiss Tahir's results as "mumbo jumbo" and junk science. (Dever's position posed great irony since he, as a criminal prosecutor, routinely used DNA test results, produced by coroner's office technicians trained by Dr. Tahir, to get convictions.) As in the O. J. Simpson trial, this jury simply dismissed the DNA evidence. "It was all tainted," one juror told me. Another, who had a science doctorate, put it bluntly: "The DNA was all crap."

While the Sheppard side's best evidence was ignored, the State of Ohio made the most of its with crime profiler Gregg McCrary. Cocksure, overreaching, he classified Marilyn Sheppard's murder as a domestic homicide; several jurors said they had been tremendously impressed by his presentation, especially his assertion that Marilyn Sheppard's pajama top had been folded back, proof of staging.

But McCrary constructed his expert opinion on a shaky foundation. He assumed, inaccurately in the view of two blood-spatter experts, Epstein and

Wolson, that Marilyn's corpse had been pulled down the bed after her death. McCrary said the killer wanted to suggest a sex crime, an attempt to divert suspicion. Also, in coming up with his theory that the murder was a staged domestic homicide, McCrary relied on a photo of Dr. Sam's upended black leather medical bag with only its middle compartment open. In fact, this police photo depicted an inaccurate *reassembly* of the crime scene, taken two weeks after the murder. Photos of the black leather bag taken several hours after the murder show that its three compartments were unclasped and its contents widely scattered in the hall. Unfortunately for the Sheppard team, McCrary "was really the one who put it all together," a juror said.

The jury foreman, Doug McQuigg, was swayed not only by McCrary but by unrebutted allegations by the prosecutors, including how Dr. Sheppard's neck injuries supposedly disappeared from the first set of X rays to the next, and why the Sheppard dog didn't alert the household to the presence of an intruder.

In the wake of the quick verdict, county prosecutor William Mason brashly insisted that the jurors as a group believed that Dr. Sheppard killed his wife with a lamp. That, however, is not the case. One of the jurors told me he did not believe a bedroom lamp was the murder weapon. Another juror said the state's assertion that a lamp had left a bloody imprint on a pillow was simply an interesting theory.

Since the 1954 trial, the image of this pillow has served as a metaphor for the Sheppard mystery: people can gaze at its huge bloodstain and see whatever they want—a surgical tool, the harp of a table lamp, a rivulet of clotting blood folded into a symmetrical shape. But knowing what we do now, the Sheppard murder can no longer remain a national Rorschach test, open to free interpretation. For decades Cleveland took comfort in being doubly sure that Dr. Sam was guilty, despite his 1966 acquittal. To consider otherwise, to believe that he indeed was the wrong man, you had to embrace a disturbing notion: that an enormous mistake had been made against a family, one that was impossible to undo.

If you analyze the once-discarded Cleveland police reports and grand-jury transcripts, after testing new evidence and consulting independent forensic experts, hard facts will stand out: Dr. Sam Sheppard did not kill his wife.

The supporting physical evidence is straightforward. In all likelihood someone else's blood, not Dr. Sam's, was found mixed with Marilyn's on the murder room wall. Furthermore, there was no blood spatter on his pants, belt, or shoes. Someone injured Sam Sheppard that morning with a powerful blow to his neck. His teeth were chipped. He was in near shock. He suffered what is now called "a mild traumatic brain injury," and displayed typical symptoms: sensitivity to light, difficulty finding words, memory problems, missing reflexes, and weakness on one side of his body.

The crime did not display the usual elements of an unplanned domestic homicide. Missing were signs of escalating violence: bruised upper arms where he might have grabbed her, signs of choking, nearby disarray. Typically, in the course of a fight, a husband might erupt, pick up an object at hand, and attack his wife, then quickly stop as his fury is spent. Marilyn Sheppard was struck repeatedly, about twenty-five times. The blow that fractured her upper jawbone had to be powerful and may have snapped two front teeth as her jaws crashed together. Other blows fractured her skull, which cracked more easily once the first fracture was made. Coroner's X rays showed that some of the skull fragments were separated but none was depressed. Was someone toying with her, intent on marking her face, not trying to kill her outright? The prolonged battering better matches the behavior of an obsessive killer rather than the conduct of an enraged spouse.

"Let me state unequivocally that there is no such thing as the person who at age thirty-five suddenly changes from being perfectly normal and erupts into totally evil, disruptive, murderous behavior," says Robert K. Ressler, John Douglas's mentor at the FBI and the man who coined the term "serial killer." "The behaviors that are precursors to murder have been present and developing in that person's life for a long, long time—since childhood."[1] In 90 percent of cases where women are killed by their partner, a history of physical violence can be determined. I could find none for Sam Sheppard. Further, this murder has been called a "crime of passion." But that description posits a lovers' battle. By all evidence, their marriage was one-sided. Sam lacked passion for Marilyn; he loved her as a sister. He was not jealous and controlling, the mark of spouses who kill.

———

Unlike Sam Sheppard, Richard Eberling, from infancy, was deeply disturbed. He was abandoned, left in a crib, bereft of the maternal bonding that is essential to normal neurological development. Before he could walk he had seizures and held his breath until he passed out. As a boy he wet his bed, set fires, and fondled other children. A foster father may have raped him as a child. He displayed all the warning signs of someone who could turn into a killer. It is clear he held enormous rage for being abandoned, time and again, by a series of foster parents who had gotten close to him, then disappeared. To cope with trauma, he developed obsessions. He compulsively rearranged furniture in an orphanage, an attempt perhaps to feel he had some control of his life. He was driven to rise above being a throwaway child, trying to become someone who mattered. Anyone who challenged his goal faced Eberling's barely controlled temper.[2] He created fantasies that comforted him—that he could be a doctor someday, that any woman who wronged him would be punished (especially mother figures who abandoned him).

Eberling revealed his transgressions. When arrested in 1959 for burglary, he told police he bled in the Sheppard home. He had stolen rings and keepsakes from dozens of other women, but of all these larcenies, he emphasized one crime to police: his theft of Marilyn's rings. It alone weighed on him. He had kept her ring as a fetish. He had the "stones" of "a dead girl."

Eberling's various accounts of cutting his finger and bleeding at the house are incriminating. He told me that he bled only in the kitchen and immediately cleaned it up. Other times, he told police he shed drops throughout the house, even after wrapping his hand. Why would Eberling ever leave blood on the floors of an important client if he had the chance to clean it up?

The five quarter-inch blood drops across the back porch floor were telling. DNA tests on one of the drops came up with a profile found in one of six thousand people, including Richard Eberling, but with a large caveat: the test's internal control, which indicates when the test is 100 percent reliable, did not register. By protocol, Dr. Tahir described this result in his report as "inconclusive," meaning it could not be used in court. The reliability of this DNA result was closer to 80 percent, insufficient to convict a suspect or release a prisoner. Even so, this DNA result is more reliable than hair comparisons, criminal profiling, and eyewitness testimony. This blood from the porch is simply another piece of evidence that leads toward Eberling's guilt.

In our conversations Eberling described Marilyn Sheppard both as a sex object and as the perfect mother he never had. He told of her sitting him down next to Chip one summer day, feeding him brownies and milk, inviting him to bring his swim trunks and use their beach, making sure that he, a twenty-four-year-old man, had a chance to play. He always referred to her as "a lady," pure, dressed in white. But in the next breath, he said that her white shorts were tight, cut high on her thighs, and that her voice was sexy, with a "dirty little laugh."

Eberling envied and resented Dr. Sam Sheppard. "I think he just was a prick," Eberling said. He was particularly offended that Sam sat on the bench of the Bay Village High School football team during games, "thinking he was so special." This remark is revealing.[3] Eberling was not allowed to play sports—his foster mother forbade him—and he dreamed of being a doctor. Dr. Sam embodied both of those unfulfilled longings.

A possible scenario of what happened the morning of July 4, 1954, can be developed from the physical evidence, interviews with Eberling, analysis by forensic experts, and by extrapolation from the much-studied behavior of those who commit sexual murders.

Two days before Marilyn's death, Eberling cleaned the Sheppard's windows. He felt angry or betrayed when he found out that she was pregnant. Very early on July 4, he drove and parked across from Huntington Park on Lake Erie, where, according to police reports, a car was seen parked. Eberling wondered why the Sheppards bought a home in Bay Village, "especially on the fringe of Huntington Park."[4] Why would owning a home near a scenic lakeside park be undesirable unless Eberling was perhaps thinking that the park made the house vulnerable to someone who could slip into the park at night, climb down to the beach, and proceed undetected one hundred yards along the shore to the Sheppards' backyard?

Eberling walked to the Sheppard home. It was dark except for a light upstairs in the small entryway to the master bedroom. Locked in fantasy, he crept into the first floor through the den door, probably unsure about what he was going to do next. In the den, he quietly pulled out desk drawers in an orderly fashion, looking for the intensely personal items he liked to steal. Perhaps he left the drawers out as a message to Dr. Sam, his imagined nemesis, that his suburban home could be defiled at will. The trophies on a shelf in the den infuriated Eberling. He snapped the figures from a track trophy and from a bowling trophy of Marilyn's. The two athletic figures, a man and woman, ended up on the floor, a broken couple.

Eberling took Sheppard's medical valise and spread it wide, opening all three compartments, spilling its contents, and faced the bag to the Lake Road door, in a perfect line of sight for whoever came in from outside or down the stairs through the kitchen. He worked silently in the dark, knowing that the family was sleeping, not seeing or disturbing Sam, who could sleep through anything, on the daybed. Upstairs, Eberling was surprised to find that Marilyn, an object of his fantasy, was alone. It was time to teach her and Sam a lesson. He climbed on her and covered her mouth with his hand, telling her to be quiet and she wouldn't get hurt. He shoved up her top and pushed down the leg of her pajamas and started to rape her. She finally fought back, biting his hand. In a rage, he swung his fist or a forearm and broke her jaw. He pulled her legs under the bed's crossbar, pinning her. Picking up a weapon, a flashlight he brought with him, he hit her in the face, marking it with medium-impact blows, again and again, toying with her while he was sprayed with blood from his head to his knees.

For Eberling, locked in fantasy, a manic state, time seemed suspended. He was not acting rationally or planning his moves.

Marilyn Sheppard probably was not dead when Sam interrupted Eberling. But Eberling's rage had already been spent. He did not have enough left to kill again. As his life would show, his victims of choice were women, not men. He hit Sheppard, knocking him out, then tore the doctor's key ring from his belt loop. It had a fraternity charm and a class ring, the totemic, hard-to-replace items that Eberling liked to steal and look at later to relive the crime.

Chased by Sam, Eberling ran outside and down the underbrush to the lake, making a path noticed by detectives.

At the beach, he got the best of Dr. Sam, who was shaky from having been knocked out. Eberling stripped off Sam's shirt to wipe himself or tore it off while dragging the doctor into the lake. The person who killed Marilyn "was mentally not that person that night," he once said.[5]

In July 1998, in a final interview, I spoke with Eberling in the hospital ward of an Ohio prison south of Columbus. Looking back, I believe he knew he was dying. Sweating and agitated, he sat in his prison wheelchair. At one point, he excused himself and rolled away to his nearby cell. I heard him retching.

As was often the case, his conversation that morning wandered, like a radio signal scanning the dial, coming in and out of reception. Suddenly, Eberling took himself back to 1954. He described himself as snapping to alertness and finding himself in the Sheppard's blood-splashed bedroom. He saw a crimson mess everywhere. He was horrified. "My God, I had never seen anything like it," he said. "I got out of there."

I asked a follow-up question but Eberling wouldn't answer. Catching himself, he wouldn't talk about it anymore.

It turned out to be as close to a confession as I would get. Richard Eberling died before I could return.

NOTES

CHAPTER 1: EVE OF DESTRUCTION

1 Esther Houk, interview by Jan Duval, undated 1973.
2 Lester Hoversten, letter to Sam Sheppard, 18 May 1954.
3 Ibid.
4 Nancy Ahern, grand-jury testimony, 16 August 1954.

CHAPTER 2: INDEPENDENCE DAY

1 Time of this call is crucial. The report of the morning by Fred Drenkhan, first police-man on the scene, said the Houks told him the call came around 5:40 A.M. Spencer Houk later moved it about ten minutes later.
2 Spencer Houk grand-jury testimony, 16 August 1954.
3 Ibid.
4 Esther Houk, interview by Jan Duval, undated 1973: "Chip was a very sound sleeper. He . . . slept like a little log."
5 Betty Sheppard, statement.
6 Otto Graham, Beverly Graham, interview by author, 13 November 1997.
7 Michael Grabowski, trial testimony.
8 In fact, H. Max Don, a Bay View doctor who came to the Sheppard house to help that morning, later testified that he heard Gerber tell the detectives, "It looks like Sheppard did it. Go get his confession."
9 H. Max Don, trial testimony.
10 Dr. Sam Sheppard, *Endure and Conquer* (Cleveland: World, 1966), p. 16.
11 Samuel R. Gerber and Oliver Schroeder Jr., eds., *Criminal Investigation and Interrogation* (Cincinnati W. H. Anderson, 1962).
12 Robert Schottke, Patrick Gareau, trial testimony, 1954.
13 Cuyahoga County Coroner, Marilyn Sheppard file, Case M 7280, two-page time-of-death report, undated 1954.
14 Lester Adelson's notes and lengthy autopsy report, Case 76629.

15 Det. Patrick Gareau, report to Capt. David E. Kerr, Cleveland Police Department, 4 July 1954. "We questioned Dr. Sheppard with reference to the rumor of Hoversten's infatuation and he stated that he was aware of the rumor and said that perhaps it was true and he further stated that several men liked his wife but that he was thoroughly convinced of her faithfulness."
16 Samuel Sheppard, trial testimony; Robert Schottke, trial testimony,
17 Det. Patrick Gareau, report to Capt. David E. Kerr, Cleveland Police Department, 28 July 1954.

CHAPTER 3: GATHERING STORM

1 Cleveland reporters were not as unscrupulous as those during the Front Page Era, when picture chasers, usually teenage boys, routinely carried a jimmy to break into homes to steal photos of murder or rape victims.
2 *Cleveland Press,* 5 July 1954.
3 The medical branch was founded in the 1870s by a farmer and businessman named Andrew T. Still, who turned against doctors after he lost three children to spinal meningitis.
4 First-grade report card, Coventry Elementary School.
5 Det. Robert F. Schottke, report to Capt. David E. Kerr, Cleveland Police Department, 28 July 1954.
6 G. H. Deutschlander, Bay Village Police Department report, 7 July 1954.
7 *Cleveland* magazine, July 1974.
8 *Cleveland Press,* 6 July 1954, p. A-1.
9 Charles Elkins, trial testimony, *State* v. *Sheppard,* 1954.
10 Ibid.
11 Ibid.
12 *Cleveland News,* 7 July 1954.
13 F. Lee Bailey, interview by author.
14 Stephen Sheppard, *My Brother's Keeper* (New York: McKay, 1964), p. 5.
15 Stephen Sheppard, unpublished manuscript, November 1985.
16 Ibid.

CHAPTER 4: DOC

1 Det. Robert Schottke, report to Capt. David E. Kerr, Cleveland Police Department, 8 July 1954.
2 *Cleveland News,* 8 July 1954.
3 Norman Gevitz, *The D.O.s: Osteopathic Medicine in America,* (Baltimore: Johns Hopkins University Press, 1991), p. 85.
4 IRS tax return, 1953, for Samuel and Marilyn Sheppard.
5 Samuel Sheppard, letter to Dr. Edward Abbott, 12 April 1952.
6 Fred Drenkhan, interview by author.
7 Stephen Sheppard, "Pattern for Progress," *Forum of Osteopathy,* February 1953.
8 *Forum of Osteopathy,* December 1953; J. Fitzgerald, assistant editor of *Forum,* letter to Sam Sheppard, 19 December 1953.
9 Alfred Kinsey, *Sexual Behavior of the Human Female,* 1953.
10 Mary Cowan, interview by author,
11 Stephen Sheppard, interview by author,
12 *Cleveland Press,* 9 July 1954.

13 Carl Rossbach told reporters that Dr. Sam gave these answers.
14 *Cleveland Press,* 9 July 1954.
15 Dorothy Sheppard, letter to Marilyn Sheppard, 28 August 1950.
16 Stephen Sheppard, letter to Marilyn Sheppard, 31 August 1950.
17 *Cleveland Press,* 9 July 1954.

CHAPTER 5: MARILYN AND SAM

Unless otherwise noted, quotes of Sam Sheppard's in this chapter are from a handwritten autobiography that Sheppard wrote in fall 1954 to help William Corrigan prepare his defense.

1 Sam Sheppard, letter to William Corrigan, undated, fall 1954.
2 *Cleveland News,* 10 July 1954.
3 Sam Sheppard, letter to William Corrigan, undated, fall 1954.
4 Marilyn Reese, letter to Sam Sheppard, fall 1941.
5 Ibid., 16 December 1941.
6 Marilyn Reese, Skidmore report card, May 1942.
7 Sam Sheppard Papers.
8 Sam Sheppard, letter to Marilyn Reese, 28 August 1942.
9 Ibid., 5 October 1942.
10 Ibid., 15 March 1943.
11 Ibid., 22 October 1942.
12 Ibid., 15 March 1943.
13 Sam Sheppard, letter to William Corrigan, undated, fall 1954.
14 Ibid., 15 March 1943.
15 Quoted by Thomas S. Reese, letter to Marilyn Reese, 21 February 1946.
16 Keith Weigle, statement to Det. Pagel, 29 July 1954.
17 John Costello, *Virtue Under Fire: How World War Two Changed Our Social and Sexual Attitudes* (Boston: Little, Brown, 1985).
18 Sam Sheppard, interview by William Levy, Tape 1, Side A, 1966.
19 Ibid.
20 Ibid.
21 Weigle to Pagel.
22 Ibid.
23 Ibid.
24 Levy interview.
25 Ibid.
26 Ibid.
27 Ibid.
28 Lester Hoversten, grand-jury testimony, 16 August 1954.

CHAPTER 6: NOISY NEWSBOY

1 Hawkins report to James McArthur, Cleveland Police Department, 9 July 1954.
2 *Cleveland News,* 10 July 1954.
3 *Cleveland Press,* 9 July 1954.
4 *Cleveland News,* 9 July 1954.
5 *Saturday Evening Post,* 10 July 1954.

6 Ibid.
7 Based on author's review of hundreds of pages of daily investigative reports filed by Bay Village police and the Cleveland police homicide unit.
8 Cleveland Police Department report, 24 July 1954.

CHAPTER 7: THE OTHER WOMAN

1 John E. Reid and Fred. E. Inbau with the Chicago Police Scientific Detection Laboratories, *Criminal Interrogation and Confession.*
2 Cleveland Police Department report, 10 July 1954.
3 Stephen Sheppard, interview by author.
4 *Cleveland News,* 3 August 1954.
5 Susan Hayes, grand-jury testimony, 17 August 1954.
6 Ibid.
7 .Ibid.
8 Sam Sheppard, letter to William Corrigan, undated, fall 1954.
9 Stephen Sheppard, interview by author.
10 Hugh Hefner began publishing *Playboy* in fall 1953.
11 Susan Hayes, statement to George W. Kemp, chief deputy district attorney, Los Angeles County, 13 July 1954.
12 Ibid.
13 Sam Sheppard, interview by Bill Levy, 1966.
14 Donna Bailey, interview by Det. Robert Schottke, Cleveland Police Department report, 30 July 1954.
15 Sam Sheppard, note to William Corrigan, undated, fall 1954.

CHAPTER 8: MARY COWAN

1 Mary Cowan diaries, 24 May 1931.
2 Ibid., 13 June 1933.
3 Charles Cowan and George Cowan, Mary Cowan's nephews, interviews by author.
4 This section on Cowan's lab work is based on her extensive notes and reports, and her trial testimony.
5 Roger Marsters, University Hospitals, letter to Mary Cowan, Cuyahoga County coroner's office, 8 July 1954.
6 Dorothy Lewis, letter to Mary Cowan, 11 July 1954.

CHAPTER 9: MEDDLING

1 Cleveland *Plain Dealer,* 16 July 1954.
2 Esther Houk, interview by Jan Duval.
3 *Cleveland Press,* 14 July 1954.
4 *Cleveland Press,* 22 July 1954.
5 *Cleveland Press,* 12 July 1954.
6 Sgt. Jay Hubach, Bay Village Police Department report, 21 July 1954.
7 The three tests for blood were bendizine, phenophthalein, and leucomalachite green tests. See "In Re: Marilyn Sheppard, Case 76629, Autopsy M7280," a report of the Cuyahoga County coroner's laboratories.
8 *Cleveland Press,* 15 July 1954.
9 Transcript of Los Angeles District Attorney's Office interview of Susan Hayes.
10 Louis Seltzer, *The Years Were Good* (Cleveland: World, 1956).

11 *Cleveland Press,* 17 July 1954.
12 *Cleveland Press,* 19 July 1954.

CHAPTER 10: DO IT NOW

1 Cleveland *Plain Dealer,* 25 July 1954.
2 *Cleveland Press,* 12 July 1954.
3 *Cleveland Press,* 30 July 1954.
4 Spencer Houk's contemporaneous, handwritten notes, William Corrigan Papers.
5 Stephen Sheppard, interview by author.
6 Det. Adelbert O'Hara, report to Capt. David E. Kerr, Cleveland Police Department, 24 July 1954.
7 Deputy Sheriff Carl Rossbach, report to Cuyahoga County Sheriff Sweeney, 1 October 1954, summary of interview with Jack Krakan Jr.
8 Esther Houk, interview, Jan Duval Papers, 1981.
9 Leah Jacoby, interview by author.
10 Ibid.
11 *Cleveland Press,* 20 July 1954.
12 Jessie Dill, statement to John Mahon, 26 July 1954.
13 Sgt. Fred O'Malley, report to Capt. David E. Kerr, 16 August 1954.
14 John Reese, interview by author.
15 *Cleveland Press,* 21 July 1954.

CHAPTER 11: INQUEST

1 Dr. Sam Sheppard, *Endure and Conquer* (Cleveland: World, 1966).
2 Ibid.
3 Transcript, Cuyahoga County Coroner's Inquest, Marilyn Sheppard, July 1954.
4 *Cleveland Press,* 24 July 1954.
5 Excerpts from "Cross over the Bridge," sermon by Rev. Alfred C. Kreke, from the William Rhys Papers, University of Rochester, New York.
6 Ibid.

CHAPTER 12: FOLLOWING A TRAIL

1 *Cleveland Press,* 5 August 1954.
2 It became widespread after Senator Gary Hart, running for president in 1988, invited reporters to follow him, then got caught with Donna Rice.
3 Sgt. Harold Lockwood, report to Lt. Thomas P. White, Cleveland Police Department, 23 July 1954.
4 *Cleveland Press,* 26 July 1954.
5 Det. Harold E. Boyett, report to Dep. Inspector James McArthur, Cleveland Police Department, 25 July 1954.
6 Ibid.
7 Cleveland Police Department letter re Graham.
8 Det. Adelbert O'Hara, memo to Capt. David E. Kerr, Cleveland Police Department, 24 July 1954.

CHAPTER 13: ARREST

1 *Cleveland Press,* 24 July 1954.
2 Susan Hayes, eight-page statement to Story, Schottke, Parrino, and McArthur, Cleveland Police Headquarters, 27 July 1954.

3 *Cleveland News,* 27 July 1954.
4 Jack Howard, letter to Roy Howard, 27 July 1954, Roy Howard Papers, Box 277, Library of Congress.

CHAPTER 14: THIRD DEGREE

1 The account of Sheppard's interrogation and police thinking is detailed in a series of lengthy reports from each detective team on 31 July and 1 August 1954.
2 *Cleveland Press,* 31 July 1954.
3 Sam Sheppard, interview by Gene Lowall, August 1964.
4 Det. L. Doran, report to Capt. David E. Kerr, Cleveland Police Department, 28 July 1954.
5 Det. Pete Becker, report to Capt. David E. Kerr, Cleveland Police Department, 31 July 1954.
6 Sam Sheppard, notes to Bill Corrigan.
7 Ibid.
8 Dr. Sam Sheppard, *Endure and Conquer* (Cleveland: World, 1966), p. 50.
9 Ibid., p. 47.
10 Sgt. Harold Lockwood report to Capt. David E. Kerr, Cleveland Homicide Bureau, 3 August 1954.

CHAPTER 15: GRAND JURY

1 Dorothy Lewis, letter to Mary Cowan, 9 August 1954.
2 *Cleveland Press,* 5 August 1954.
3 Henry Dombrowski, report to Supt. David Cowles, Cleveland Police Department, 31 July 1954.
4 Elmer Roubal, report to Supt. David Cowles, Cleveland Police Department, 3 August 1954.
5 Henry Dombrowski, report to Supt. David Cowles, Cleveland Police Department, 5 August 1954.
6 Henry Dombrowski, interview by author.
7 Transcripts of the grand-jury testimony obtained by the author.
8 Nancy Ahern, grand-jury testimony, 16 August 1954.
9 Ibid.
10 Ibid.
11 Esther Houk, interview by Jan Duval.
12 *Cleveland Press,* 14 August 1954.
13 Spencer Houk, grand-jury testimony, 16 August 1954.
14 Lester Hoversten, grand-jury testimony, 1954.
15 Ibid.
16 Cleveland *Plain Dealer,* 23 November 1954.
17 Elnora Helms, grand-jury testimony, 16 August 1954.
18 Samuel A. Gerber, grand-jury testimony, 17 August 1954.
19 James McArthur, grand-jury testimony, 17 August 1954.
20 *Cleveland Press,* 18 August 1954.
21 Stephen Sheppard, *My Brother's Keeper* (New York: McKay, 1964).
22 *Cleveland Press,* 8 August 1954.
23 Sam Sheppard, jail diaries, 31 August 1954. One of Corrigan's tactics was having a client like Sam write a detailed autobiography. Corrigan needed to figure out his client and make Sam come alive as a sympathetic courtroom presence as well as learn about

and prepare for his weaknesses. Using pencil on a yellow legal pads, Sam wrote long, detailed letters in jail and handed them to his lawyer during visits.

24 Ibid., 23 August 1954.
25 Ibid.
26 Ibid., 21 August 1954.

CHAPTER 16: PRETRIAL

1 *Cleveland Press,* 18 October 1954.
2 Sidney Anhorn, a local columnist, 22 October 1954. Quoted in Paul L. Kirk and Alys McColl, *The Doctor Sam Sheppard Case,* unpublished manuscript, p. 270.
3 New York *Daily News,* 25 October 1954.
4 *Cleveland Press,* 9 October 1954.
5 J. F. Saunders, letter to reader, 2 September 1954.
6 New York *Daily News,* 17 October 1954.
7 Radio script, Winchell Collection, Reel 9, New York Public Library.
8 Lee Israel, *Kilgallen* (New York: Delacorte Press, 1979).
9 *New York Journal-American,* 17 October 1954.
10 New York *Daily News,* 18 October 1954.
11 Ibid.
12 *Cleveland News,* 20 July 1954.
13 Dorothy Kilgallen sworn statement in *Sheppard* v. *Maxwell.*
14 Less accurate were the true-detective magazines, the supermarket tabloids of the day, which made up details that a "good murder" demanded. *Inside Detective* wrote that Marilyn was slain in her "luxuriously furnished home" with blows so ferocious "that blood spurted to the ceiling." In fact, the furnishings were secondhand and no blood was found on the ceiling.
15 Esther Houk, interview by Jan Duval.
16 Corrigan and Mahon wrangled over jury selection for several days. Jurors were dismissed if they said they did not support the death penalty or if they had made up their minds about the case and couldn't be changed. Corrigan tried to ask jurors for their views about extramarital sex, but the prosecution objected and Judge Blythin agreed, saying, "We are trying no one here for a sex offense." Corrigan shot back, "You are here, and you are going to. You are blocking me from a most important point." Susan Hayes has already been announced as a star witness, Corrigan argued, so "why do I have to be faced with a juror who is prejudiced against the defendant. You know when you go into the subject of sex that some people have very strong opinions about it. Some consider a sex crime or sex deviation worse than murder."
17 *New York Journal-American,* 28 October 1954.
18 What Sam's sisters-in-law wore was constantly reported, usually by a woman reporter assigned to the feature side of the news. *Cleveland News* reporter Doris Millavec wrote, "The trial's fashion leader, Mrs. Stephen Sheppard, today left her silver blue mink cape at home and appeared in a beige cashmere coat over a patterned brown and white tweed topped by a small brown hat. Mrs. Richard N. Sheppard wore multiple ropes of pearls and costume gems to brighten her beige attire and a small striped wool hat in various shades of brown and adorned with two pompoms."
19 *Cleveland Press* headlines that hammered the jury pool and public include: QUIT STALLING AND BRING HIM IN; SAM DECLINED JULY 4 LIE TEST; SAYS DR. SAM TALKED DIVORCE; TESTIFIES SAM CHANGED STORIES; CHARGES SAM FAKED INJURIES; SAYS MARILYN CALLED SAM A "JEKYLL-HYDE."
20 Sam Sheppard, jail diaries, undated.

21 Israel, *Kilgallen.*
22 Oliver Schroeder, interview by author.

CHAPTER 17: PROSECUTION

1 William Joseph Corrigan, interview by author, 21 June 2000.
2 Cleveland *Plain Dealer,* 8 November 1954.
3 *Cleveland Press,* 25 August 1954.
4 F. Lee Bailey, interview by author,
5 Cleveland *Plain Dealer,* 8 November 1954.
6 Sam Sheppard, jail diaries, 5 August 1954.
7 Sam Sheppard, notes to William Corrigan, 5 November 1954, William Corrigan Papers.
8 Ibid.
9 *Cleveland Press,* 3 November 1954.
10 Transcript, *State of Ohio* v. *Samuel H. Sheppard* (1954), p. 1667.
11 Ibid., p. 1666.
12 Ibid., p. 59.
13 *New York Journal-American,* 4 November 1954.
14 Ibid.
15 Cited in Theo Wilson, *Headline Justice,* (New York: Thunder's Mouth, 1996), p. 105.
16 Transcript, *State* v. *Sheppard,* p. 1866.
17 Lee Israel, Kilgallen (New York: Delacorte Press), p. 257.
18 *Editor & Publisher,* 23 October 1954.
19 Transcript, Cuyahoga County Coroner's Inquest, Marilyn Sheppard, July 1954.
20 The *Cleveland News* overstated Houk's testimony with the headline TESTIFIES CARS AND FURNITURE CAUSED ROWS. Reporters like Kilgallen were struck by how everyday the disagreements were. "The state cannot make much capital of that. If every husband who opposed his wife in the area of house furnishings and choice of automobile resorted to murder, there would be few married women left alive in the United States."
21 Sam Sheppard, interview by Gene Lowall, August 1964.
22 Patrick Gareau, report to Capt. David E. Kerr, Cleveland Police Department, 18 November 1954.
23 Harold Lockwood, report to Capt. David E. Kerr, Cleveland Police Department, 20 November 1954.
24 Transcript, *State* v. *Sheppard,* p. 1752.
25 Corrigan based his questions on blood washing on Paul Kirk's reference book, *Crime Investigation: Physical Evidence and the Police Laboratory* (New York: Interscience, 1953), which Cowan said she used on occasions. He had performed experiments with bloody fabrics, testing different methods of washing, even boiling.
26 Robert Schottke, report to Capt. David E. Kerr, Cleveland Police Department, 9 December 1954.
27 *Cleveland Press,* 24 November 1954.
28 Transcript, *State* v. *Sheppard,* p. 3224.

CHAPTER 18: THE DEFENSE

1 Untitled 23-page manuscript, Margaret Parton Collection, Box 45, Folder 2, University of Oregon Special Collections. Alfred Kinsey's groundbreaking study showed that extramarital and premarital sex were more prevalent in society than people had assumed.
2 Lee Israel, *Kilgallen* (New York: Delacorte Press, 1979), p. 273.

3 Transcript, *State of Ohio* v. *Samuel H. Sheppard* (1954), p. 3822.
4 Ibid., p. 4096.
5 Ibid., p. 4780.
6 Ibid., p. 5021.
7 Paul Holmes, *The Sheppard Murder Case* (New York: Bantam, 1962), p. 175.
8 Israel, *Kilgallen.*
9 Ex-reporter Corrigan of course knew reporters had nothing to do with writing the bold headlines appearing above their stories; that was the task of the copy editors back in the office.
10 Holmes, *Sheppard Murder Case,* p. 206.
11 Anne Foote, interview by author, 6 May 1998. Interviews were conducted in spring 1998 with all five of the surviving jurors: Foote, William Lamb, Howard Barrish, Beatrice Orenstein, and Lois Mancini.
12 William Lamb, interview by author.
13 Foote interview.
14 Asheville *Citizen,* 23 December 1954.
15 Dorothy Kilgallen, King Features Syndicate, 28 December 1954.
16 *Newsweek,* 3 January 1955.

CHAPTER 19: THE SCIENCE OF MURDER

1 Paul L. Kirk and Alys McColl, *The Doctor Sam Sheppard Case,* unpublished manuscript, ch. 2, p. 1.
2 *Cleveland Press,* 23 December 1954.
3 Ibid.
4 Jan Sheppard Duval, unpublished manuscript.
5 Sam Sheppard, interview by Gene Lowall, August 1964.
6 Stephen Sheppard, *My Brother's Keeper* (New York: McKay, 1964).
7 Ibid., p. 191.
8 Ibid., p. 198.
9 Kirk explained them and taught them to law enforcement groups. Cleveland Scientific Investigation Unit detective Henry Dombrowski, for one, was familiar with them.
10 Kirk and McColl, *The Doctor Sam Sheppard Case,* p. 286.
11 Ibid., p. 494.
12 Cleveland *Plain Dealer,* 7 July 1954.
13 Kirk and McColl, *The Doctor Sam Sheppard Case,* p. 104.
14 Ibid., p. 364.
15 Paul Kirk affidavit was part of a defense appeals motion for a new trial in *Ohio* v. *Sheppard.*
16 Kirk and McColl, *The Doctor Sam Sheppard Case.*
17 Sam Sheppard, prison journal, 8 June 1955.
18 Ibid., 14 June 1955.

CHAPTER 20: THE WALLS

1 Sam Sheppard, letter to Stephen Sheppard, 21 July 1955.
2 Parole Authority files, Sam H. Sheppard.
3 Stephen Sheppard, letter to Sam Sheppard, 5 April 1955.
4 Sam Sheppard, letter to Bud and Mary Brown, undated, fall 1955.
5 Sam Sheppard interview with William Levy, 1966.

6 Erle Stanley Gardner, *The Court of Last Resort* (New York: William Sloane Associates, 1952).
7 Allen M. Hornblum, *Acres of Skin: Human Experiments at Holmesburg Prison* (London: Routledge, 1998).
8 Chester M. Southam, interview by author, 10 July 1998.

CHAPTER 21: DEAD GIRL'S STONES

1 *Cleveland Press,* 12 November 1959.
2 Richard Eberling, interview by author.
3 George Jindra, interview by author.
4 Eberling interview.
5 Ibid.
6 Ronald B. DuPerow, Bay Village Police Department report, 12 November 1959.
7 Ibid.
8 Eberling interview.

CHAPTER 22: UNLOADING

1 This section is based on nearly one hundred pages of extraordinarily detailed case-file reports on Richard Lenardic. He provided the author with a waiver to obtain these records in 1993.
2 Cuyahoga County Child Welfare Board Family Record 729, Lenardic, 23 August 1933.
3 Ibid., 3 March 1932.
4 Louise Lenardic, Family Record, Case 729. This is an extraordinarily detailed account of each contact she had with the Children's Aid Society and the CCCWB.
5 Richard Eberling interview by author.
6 CCCWB 729, 15 September 1936, summary.
7 Eberling interview.
8 Dr. Emanuel Tanay, a forensic psychiatrist who had evaluated Eberling, made this observation to me in February 2000.
9 Psychological Report, CCCWB, Lenardic file, 19 January 1939.
10 CCCWB, Lenardic file, Treatment Conference memo, 15 May 1939.
11 Ibid., 21 December 1939.
12 Eberling interview.
13 This account is built from numerous entries and verbatim notes in Richard Lenardic's CCCWB file.
14 Eberling interview.

CHAPTER 23: POLYGRAPH

1 William J. Yankee, director, Polygraph Institute, Department of Defense, report to Lt. James R. Tompkins, Bay Village Police Department, 28 April 1989. Yankee reexamined the polygraph charts, questions, and technical data of the 1959 test.
2 Leonard Harrelson, interview by author.
3 Assistant county prosecutor Merle McCurdy asked Rocky River detective George Jindra if he minded if Eberling's charges were reduced to petty larceny, a misdemeanor. The ninety-dollar theft was just below the grand-larceny threshold. Jindra said he replied, "Hell no! This is just the tip of the iceberg!" He wanted burglary added on. "Eberling, he had some suck," Jindra explained. It was a quality Eberling would display more dazzlingly years later.

CHAPTER 24: F. LEE BAILEY

1 Stephen Sheppard, *My Brother's Keeper* (New York: McKay, 1964).
2 Ibid.
3 F. Lee Bailey, interview by author, 20 October 1996.
4 F. Lee Bailey, *The Defense Never Rests* (New York: Stein and Day, 1971), p. 62.
5 Bailey interview.
6 F. Lee Bailey, transcript of deposition, *Estate of Samuel H. Sheppard* v. *State of Ohio,* 15 November 1999.
7 John T. Corrigan, letter to Parole Commission, 5 December 1962.

CHAPTER 25: ARIANE

1 Supt. Lamoyne Green, letter to Ariane Tebbenjohanns, 8 January 1963.
2 Ibid.
3 Pat Roberts, interview by author,
4 William Levy, interview by author.
5 Paul Holmes, letter to Steve Sheppard, 13 February 1963.
6 Decades later, serial killers Ted Bundy and Richard "Night Stalker" Ramirez found mates and got married while in prison. Sheila Isenberg explored this phenomenon in her book *Women Who Love Men Who Kill* (New York: Simon and Schuster, 1991).
7 Ariane Tebbenjohanns, letter, 21 April 1963.

CHAPTER 26: MOCKERY OF JUSTICE

1 Sam Sheppard, interview by Gene Lovall, Sheppard archives, undated, probably 1965.
2 Columbus *Evening Dispatch,* 13 March 1964.
3 Lee Israel, *Kilgallen* (New York: Delacorte, 1979), pp. 377–78.
4 Paul Holmes, *Retrial* (New York: Bantam, 1966).
5 Kay Bailey, *Behind the News,* Chicago Newspaper Reporter's Association yearbook.

CHAPTER 27: SHANGRI-LA

1 Anthony Whobrey, director of Psychological Services, memo to Joseph Doneghy, Ohio Pardon and Parole Commission, 12 December 1962.
2 Sam Sheppard diary, 10 October 1964.
3 Jack Harrison Pollack, *Dr. Sam: An American Tragedy* (Chicago: Regnery, 1972), p. 155.
4 Roy Huggins, interview by author.
5 Sam Sheppard, interview by Gene Lovall, Sheppard archives, undated, probably 1965.
6 F. Lee Bailey, letter to Russell Sherman, 11 October 1962.
7 F. Lee Bailey, letter to Sam Sheppard, 19 August 1964.
8 Ibid., 18 September 1964.
9 Ibid., 8 October 1964.
10 Sheppard, Lowall interview.

CHAPTER 28: A DECISION

1 Janice Schuetz and Kathryn Holmes Snedaker, *Communication and Litigation: Case Studies of Famous Trials* (Carbondale: Southern Illinois University Press, 1988).
2 Brief for Petitioner, at 14.
3 U.S. Supreme Court papers, National Archives. In addition, I listened to a recording of the oral arguments.

4 Jack Harrison Pollack, *Dr. Sam: An American Tragedy* (Chicago: Regnery, 1972), p. 164. Pollack attended the hearing.

5 Stephen Sheppard, interview by author.

6 William Lamb, interview by author, 18 April 1998.

7 Letter, 17 October 1966, *Sheppard* v. *Maxwell,* U.S. Supreme Court files, National Archives.

8 As months passed, the *Sheppard* decision was misread as a call for a gagging of the press. The American Bar Association even proposed a plan in which media would not publish or broadcast information about a suspect's criminal background before trial. The *Estes* and *Sheppard* decisions kept cameras out of the courtrooms for decades, and to this day in federal courts. Beneath overreaction of some in the press and the bar, solutions were obvious. The Court carefully put the burden of preventing "trial by newspaper" on the shoulders of public officials—not the news media. For instance, the trial judge could issue a gag order, telling the prosecutors and defense lawyers not to discuss the case until after a verdict. High-profile trials in inflamed communities could be moved to calmer jurisdictions. During jury selection, prospective jurors should be more easily removed for cause if they admitted to reading or hearing negative articles about the defendant. Judges could sequester jurors during trial to protect them from outside influences. With effort, the judge in a celebrated case could protect the legal process, reporters could report, and a fair trial would unfold.

9 *The New York Times,* 11 June 1966.

CHAPTER 29: RETRIAL OF THE CENTURY

1 Sgt. Harold Lockwood, report to Lt. Louis Kulis, Intelligence Unit, cc: Prosecutor John T. Corrigan, Cleveland Police Department, 14 June 1966.

2 *Southern California Law Review,* July 1990.

3 Stephen Sheppard, *Impact,* unpublished manuscript.

4 Surveillance logs from Bay Village Police Department's Marilyn Sheppard homicide file.

5 Jack Harrison Pollack, *Dr. Sam: An American Tragedy* (Chicago: Regnery, 1972), p. 176.

6 Sam Sheppard, letter to F. Lee Bailey, 1 September 1966.

7 Jack Harrison Pollack, unpublished profile of Bailey, August 1967, Pollack Papers, Box Office Barrister.

8 *Cleveland Press,* 13 October 1966.

9 There is some dispute over this amount. Bailey told me in December 2000 that Ariane brought him $10,000. But in 1968, under oath at a divorce hearing and decades closer to the event, Ariane said the amount was $25,000. I decided to use her more contemporaneous recollection of what was, for her, more of a singular event—paying a large legal fee—rather than Bailey's much older recall of, for him, a more routine event.

10 Direct quotes in this section are from the trial transcript.

11 F. Lee Bailey, interview by author.

12 Leo Spellacy, interview by author.

13 Ibid.

14 Transcript, *State of Ohio* v. *Samuel H. Sheppard* (1966), p. 931.

CHAPTER 30: THE VERDICT

1 Transcript, *State of Ohio* v. *Samuel H. Sheppard* (1954), p. 3056.

2 Transcript, *State of Ohio* v. *Samuel H. Sheppard* (1966), p. 1019.

3 One typewritten page of Cowan's observations from fall 1966, part of discovery materials provided by the Cuyahoga County Coroner's Office in the Sheppard estate's civil lawsuit.
4 Leo Spellacy, interview by author.
5 Paul Kirk, letter to William Corrigan, 9 June 1956. William Corrigan Papers, Western Reserve Historical Society.
6 Transcript, *State* v. *Sheppard,* p. 1144.
7 Sam Sheppard, *Endure and Conquer* (Cleveland: World, 1966), p. 326.
8 William Levy, interview by author.
9 Sam R. Sheppard, interview by author.
10 Cleveland *Plain Dealer,* 17 November 1966.
11 Paul Holmes, *Retrial* (New York: Bantam Books, 1966), p. 240.

CHAPTER 31: DEMISE

1 William R. Pringle, foreman, to presiding Common Pleas Court Judge Roy F. McMahon, Cuyahoga County Grand Jury Report, 15 December 1966.
2 Cleveland *Plain Dealer,* 16 December 1966.
3 Sam R. Sheppard, letter to Ariane and Sam H. Sheppard, 13 June 1967.
4 *Samuel H. Sheppard* v. *E. W. Scripps Company, et al.,* C 67-838, U.S. District Court, Northern District of Ohio.
5 Stephen Sheppard, *Impact,* unpublished manuscript.
6 *Martin L. Duffy* v. *Samuel H. Sheppard,* Mahoning County Common Pleas Court, State of Ohio.
7 *Marcia Lopez* v. *Samuel H. Sheppard,* Mahoning County Common Pleas Court, State of Ohio; Jean Disbro Anderson, interview by author, 10 March 1994.
8 Columbus *Citizen-Journal,* 10 December 1968.
9 Jerry Dempsey, letter to Russell H. Volkema, 11 March 1969.
10 Columbus *Citizen-Journal,* 1 November 1969.
11 *Cleveland* magazine, July 1974.
12 Cleveland *Plain Dealer,* 3 July 1994.

CHAPTER 32: DICK AND OBIE

1 City Hall and the courthouse, library, public auditorium, and school-board building were all part of a design grouping that brought Cleveland a national reputation for progressive municipal vision.
2 *Cleveland Press,* 3 April 1973.
3 Based on Linda Newton's observations, her testimony in *Ohio* v. *Eberling,* and written statements to Lakewood police.
4 Kucinich had survived a tumultuous first term, during which the business establishment tried to destroy him by getting Cleveland banks to refuse to roll over short-term notes the city held, throwing Cleveland into a technical default, making it the first big city to default since the Depression. Bogar backed Voinovich not for political reasons but out of revenge. Kucinich tried to shut down her business, Pat's Go Kart Speedway, a hangout for teenagers and troublemakers on Brookpark Road, a honky-tonk strip near the Chevrolet plant and other industries. She built the track and on its opening night suffered a small race riot. She'd hired only one off-duty cop for security, and a patron was badly disfigured in the mêlée. The constant revving of engines annoyed neighbors at night.
5 Patricia Bogar, interview by author.

6 Patricia Bogar, handwritten letter, undated, Lakewood Police Department, Durkin homicide file.
7 Ibid.
8 Interview by author.
9 Her father had abandoned and beaten her mother, and Kathy got wild in eighth grade. At fourteen, hating her mother because her father was not around, she moved to Columbus to live with him. He was working in the hard-core porn industry, booming at the time with Larry Flynt, who brought hard-core porn out of the underground and onto newsstands. One of her father's friends raped Kathy. Kathy says she told her father, but he did nothing. Ever since, she says, she has had confused notions about sex and love. She had been so rejected and unloved that she had to be reassured that men desired her. If she could see that in their faces, then she felt more in control.
10 Interview with AMSEC International, 23 March 1996.
11 Kathy Wagner, interview by author, January 1998.
12 Virginia Haskett, interview by author.
13 AMSEC interview.
14 Al Davis, statement to Det. Kurt Fensel, 30 August 1988, Lakewood Police Department File 88-032287.

CHAPTER 33: REVENGE

1 Dale Scheidler, interview and polygraph exam by Det. E. Favre, Lakewood Police Department, Durkin homicide file.
2 The account of the Durkin investigation was based on the *Ohio* v. *Eberling,* voluminous and detailed Lakewood police reports, interviews with Bogar, Henderson, Eberling, Dan Gaul, Vince Kremperger, Kurt Fensel, and other parties.

CHAPTER 34: THE PURSUIT

1 Cleveland *Plain Dealer,* 4 August 1989.
2 Richard Eberling, interview by James Monroe, 3 August 1989; interview by author.
3 Richard Eberling, interview by author, 19 October 1989.
4 Steve Sheppard, interview by author; Stephen Sheppard, *Impact,* unpublished manuscript.

CHAPTER 35: TWISTED STRANDS

1 Richard Eberling, letter to James Monroe, 30 October 1989.
2 Arlene Campbell, a niece, said she was party to this conversation. Plaintiff discovery, *Estate* v. *Ohio,* Exh. 78, affidavit of interview.
3 Eberling kept copies of his letters to Cooper, Monroe, Sheppard, and others, which were made available to me by prosecutor Marino before the trial and surfaced in discovery in *Estate* v. *Ohio.*
4 Det. James Svekric, report to Lt. John James, Cleveland Police Department, 9 August 1989.
5 Leonard Harrelson, interview by author.
6 *Newsday,* 14 March 1996.
7 Cleveland *Plain Dealer,* 13 February 1996.

8 Richard Eberling, letter to Cynthia Cooper, 15 October 1995; Trial 3 discovery materials.
9 Cleveland *Plain Dealer,* 24 February 1996.

CHAPTER 36: LOCAL POLITICS

1 Cleveland *Plain Dealer,* 26 April 1998.
2 Kathy Wagner, interviews by the author. Wagner, whose married name was Collins, also said in 1989 she read an article about Eberling's connection to Durkin's murder and, shocked, called Cleveland detectives to tell them about his admission that he had killed Marilyn Sheppard. She said she was brushed off.
3 Kathy Collins, interview by David Zimmerman, James Riley, and Joseph Wegas, 26 April 1996.
4 Wagner's mother, Virginia Haskett, in an interview, said her daughter told her about Eberling's Sheppard-murder remarks in 1983.
5 Richard Eberling, letter to Cynthia Cooper.
6 Mohammad Tahir, deposition, *Estate* v. *Ohio,* 3 January 2000.
7 Mark Olshaker, *The Cases That Haunt Us* (New York: Scribner, 2000).
8 *The New York Times,* 15 January 1995.
9 Doris O'Donnell, a *Cleveland News* reporter at the first trial, wrote four decades later that Sheppard pushed his wife down a flight of stairs in 1950, causing her to miscarry. They were living in a first-floor apartment in Los Angeles at the time, and despite all my efforts, I was unable to find any evidence that Sam Sheppard was violent. A Bay Village policeman testified at the 1954 trial that he had checked the department's files since the couple moved to the village and found no record of police making a call to the Sheppards' house.
10 Cleveland *Plain Dealer,* 26 April 1998.

CHAPTER 37: OPENING

1 Anthony Kronman, Yale Law School dean, as quoted in Jeffrey Toobin, *The Run of His Life: The People v. O. J. Simpson* (New York: Random House, 1996).
2 William Mason, interview by author.
3 I attended the trial in Judge Suster's courtroom. Direct quotes come from transcripts, audio recordings, and my daily notes. Testimony without direct quotes was paraphrased from what I heard.

CHAPTER 38: EXPERTS

1 Terry Gilbert, interview by author.

CHAPTER 39: SMOKING GUN

1 Cleveland Police Department report, 24 July 1954.
2 Transcript, *State of Ohio* v. *Samuel H. Sheppard* (1954), p. 4103.
3 Robert White, interview by author.
4 Transcript, *State* v. *Sheppard,* p. 3010.

CHAPTER 40: FINALE

1 On May 1, 2000, Gilbert appealed the jury verdict, calling it the latest "mockery of justice," and asked the judge to set it aside, citing various legal grounds. As of fall 2001,
the appeal was working its way through an Ohio appeals court.

EPILOGUE

1 Robert Ressler and Tom Schachtman, *Whoever Fights Monsters* (New York: St. Martin's Press, 1993).
2 Dick Moore, interview by author, 12 February 2000.
3 Richard Eberling, interview by James Monroe, 3 August 1989.
4 Richard Eberling, letter to Sam Reese Sheppard, 29 July 1990.
5 Richard Eberling, interview by James Monroe, circa 1990.

INDEX

ABOUT THE AUTHOR

JAMES NEFF, a prizewinning journalist and editor, grew up in Cleveland. He was a reporter and columnist at the *Plain Dealer* for a decade. He has written four books, one of which, *Mobbed Up,* was adapted as the HBO movie *Teamster Boss*. He serves as chairman of Investigative Reporters and Editors, a 4,500-member nonprofit organization that trains journalists worldwide. He lives with his wife and two sons in Seattle, where he is investigations editor at the *Seattle Times*.

ABOUT THE TYPE

This book was set in Times Roman, designed by Stanley Morison specifically for *The Times* of London. The typeface was introduced in the newspaper in 1932. Times Roman has had its greatest success in the United States as a book and commercial typeface, rather than one used in newspapers.